I0224522

Coming soon from Connaissance Sankofa Press:

Words of Flame: An Anthology of Devotional Fiction

Dr. Danger's Big Cryptid Activity Book: North America

Walking With The Gods

Modern People Talk About Deities, Faith, and Recreating Ancient Traditions

W. D. Wilkerson

Connaissance Sankofa Media: Tulsa, OK

Connaissance Sankofa Media, Inc.

219 W 31st Street

Sand Springs, OK 74063

www.connaissancesankofamedia.com

Published by Connaissance Sankofa Media
Copyright 2014 by Wendi D. Wilkerson
ISBN: 978-0-9915300-1-4

All rights reserved. This edition has been published under the following Creative Commons Copyright license: Attribution-NonCommercial-NoDerivatives-4.0 International. Readers are free to copy and redistribute the material in any medium or format. In instances where material is being presented, user must provide the author's name, copyrights, license notice, disclaimer, notice and link to original material. User must indicate if modification to the material were made and retain an indication of all prior modifications. User may not redistribute or alter this work for commercial advantage or monetary compensation. A user's changing the format of the work does not create a derivative work. If user remixes, transforms, builds upon, or otherwise alters this work, the modified material may not be distributed. User may not apply legal terms or technological measures that legally restrict others from doing anything that this Creative Commons Copyright license permits.

Printed in the United States of America

Table of Contents

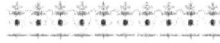

Dedication

This book is dedicated to the polytheist community, especially to those who by choice or circumstance find themselves without a religious community of like-hearted people, yet remain steadfast in their religious practice. I am especially grateful to the polytheists who participated in this study. I remain humbled by your trust in me and your willingness to share your stories and your experiences as candidly and completely as you did.

This book is also dedicated to Dr. Marcia Gaudet and Dr. Barry Ancelet, my professors in the Folklore Studies program at UL-Lafayette. Of all the things you taught me, the two most important are that ethnographers are always as accountable to the communities they study as they are to the Academy they work from, and that ethnographers should be able to give something of value back to the communities who shared so much valuable knowledge with them. Duly noted and steadfastly enacted—thank you.

i

Preface

Writing does not occur in a vacuum. Many different forces have converged over the last few years which pulled this research together and ensured that it would take the form that it now has. As this book makes its way out into the world, I imagine that it will in turn exert at least some small degree of those forces which brought it into being. Perhaps the most important thing to keep in mind is that this book is not meant to be taken as a singular instance of communication. It is, in the best sense possible, an ice-breaker, a conversation starter, a proposal to look at an old topic in different ways. The old topic being, of course, humanity's relationship with the Divine. While this relationship can take myriad forms, the religious sensibility under discussion here is polytheism. As it turns out, there are a good many theological and spiritual implications that come from reifying and venerating multiple Divine Beings which differ significantly from those found in monotheist religions.

To be honest, it was never my ambition to contribute to the burgeoning field of polytheist theology. In fact, <u>Walking With The Gods</u> began as part of another author's project. In February of 2011, I attended a Chinese New Year party at a colleague's house. At this party, I met a man I shall refer to as R. R is a well-known polytheist, activist, and spirit-worker. I'd long been fascinated by his work and felt very fortunate to be able to make his acquaintance. R is gracious, witty, and wise. He gifted me with one of the most important conversations I have ever had. Talking with R helped me crystallize a thought which had nagged me for years: mainstream Western culture more or less assumes that people who worship the old Gods are imbeciles, lunatics or cult victims who are imagining things and in dire need of psychiatric help. Yet history shows that until the monotheist Abrahamic faiths of the near-East came to dominance, humans everywhere widely and actively worshipped multiple Deities, ancestors, nature spirits, and other spiritual entities. These are the same ancient humans whose architectural prowess gave us the Coliseum, the ziggurats, the pyramids, the city of Petra, and the Great Wall of China. Their intellectual acuity gave us democracy, philosophy, geometry, astronomy, and the beginnings of chemistry—just to give a handful of examples. How could they have accomplished those things if they were insane or intellectually deficient? Why must contemporary polytheistrs be regarded the same way?

As R and I talked, we were reminded that even a cursory review of the planet's ecological state should be enough to convince reasonable people that modern Western, first-world culture has been highly toxic to our lives and our world. Yet, we bury our heads in our iPads and sip our fancy Starbucks coffees while pointedly ignoring the growing continent of plastic, floating garbage that drifts around the Pacific Ocean. Indigenous people, who are typically polytheistic and animist, strive to maintain a right relationship with the land, their God(s), their ancestors, and each other. Their struggles ensure that the local environment is kept clean and healthy so that the tribe and the plants and animals can live on it in perpetuity. But because of their spirituality, and the fact that it permeates each aspect of their culture, these indigenous people are often viewed as primitives—possibly even as savages—who have a simplistic, superstitious religion, and view the universe with a naïve and childlike wonder. It never occurs to contemporary Westerners that these indigenous people's way of life would never, ever, not in a million years, perpetrate the kind of savage ecological violence that we do casually and thoughtlessly, simply by purchasing gas and driving a hundred miles back and forth to work each week. These "primitives" have a better understanding of man's impact upon the planetary scheme of things than "modern" people, and yet they are considered to be the ignorant ones who would benefit from Western-style modernization. It seemed to R and I that if Westerners adopted some of the polytheist spirituality of indigenous people, we might finally understand that however marvelous, miraculous, magical, and just plain nifty our gadgets may be, the planet is not impressed by our Ipads, our Starbucks, our internet, our Large Hadron Colliders, or our Escalades. Especially since all of these just distract us from taking responsibility for the damage we have been doing to this planet and to the future of humanity.

Our conversation pointed out how people often forget that it wasn't until Christianity had established a foothold in Europe that Western intellectual development fell to its nadir. From the 17th century onward, the near- and middle-East have been struggling intellectually to reconcile Islam with modernity, and this struggle has obstructed the educational and economic development of the Islamic world. It wasn't until the Renaissance that the West began to recover intellectually, and this was largely due to the fact that Christianity was reined in by new humanist attitudes and Imperial ambitions. Modern, rational understandings of humanity's place in the universe and the origin thereof finally began to emerge during the Enlightenment. This is the very same Enlightenment that is characterized by the rejection of Christianity and a subsequent embracing of civil secularity—a secularity inspired by the polytheist, democratic culture of Greece and a civil sensibility drawn from the equally polytheist culture of ancient Imperial Rome. The Gods were tossed out, but the ideas fostered in Their cultures were adopted and have become enduring Western values. Yet, there remains this belief that polytheism is a backward, retrograde, and ridiculous religious practice.

R shared my frustrations with the way that Western society chooses to view polytheism, or indeed any sort of religious experience that is counter to that found in contemporary Christianity. In an effort to present polytheism as being at least as reasonable, rational, socially valuable, and culturally evolved as the near-Eastern monotheist[*] religions, R had decided to publish a book on contemporary polytheism. Because he is a pluralist and values the experiences of others, R wanted to publish a collection of essays from several writers. The subject would be "polytheism and faith" and the discussion would be meant to reify the Goddesses and Gods, and give people the opportunity to share the personal theologies they've developed that interpret and solidify their religious practices. The problem was, R hadn't gotten many essay submissions, and wasn't sure what to do to encourage more people to submit their stories.

Having spent almost a decade teaching freshman composition at the college level by day, and conducting ethnographic fieldwork in the drag queen/king communities in my spare time, I knew perfectly well why there had been so few submissions. First and foremost, I know that writing can be a really daunting and frightening thing. Nobody likes criticism, but we are especially sensitive to criticism of work we that we feel insecure about. People who are inexperienced

---

[*] In his landmark study <u>God is Red</u>, indigenous American author and scholar Vine Deloria, Jr. first coined the term "near-Eastern monotheism" to identify the religious tendencies of Islam, Christianity, and Judaism. Having done so underscores the fact that these three religious share fundamental assumptions about human relationships with the Divine, nature, and each other, as well as the personality, character, and priorities of their single male supreme being. Their shared assumptions ensure that for all their differences, these three religions have more in common with each other than with any other religion on the planet.

with writing are terrified of putting their work out there for anyone to see and judge. There is also the fact that writing is a time-consuming business, taking multiple drafts to get a piece in shape for audiences to read. A lot of people don't have that kind of time, and many aren't willing to make the time if they don't feel that their writing will be good.

The second reason that people weren't submitting essays is that they were being asked to write about their encounters with the Numinous, and experiences like that really aren't that easy to put into words. How do you express your experiences with the Divine in a way that actually communicates what you experienced yet allows another person to understand? That, too, is a daunting task. Complicating matters further is the fact that we live in a rationalist, monotheist over-culture that has very definite expectations about God, faith, and religious experience. The experiences these polytheists have had with their Gods defy and explode those expectations. They know full well that any attempt to explain the powerful personal gnosis that comes with such experiences would, at best, find them ostracized as moronic lunatics, most likely denounced as devil-worshippers, and at worst committed to a mental institution—as it turns out, one of my respondents has had a particular experience with the latter circumstance. When one realizes that writing is a formidable task, and that it is very difficult to explain personal experience of the Numinous, and that many fear the hostile and harmful reception to their accounts, is very easy to understand why people weren't thronging to submit their stories to R.

Because of my background in ethnographic fieldwork, I also knew how to work around R's dilemma. The best way to get personal narratives about people's religious experiences with the Gods was to carefully, respectfully, and thoroughly conduct ethnographic interviews with them. The interviews could be formatted and published in his book. The difficulty would come in building trust with the potential respondents, but with time and care this could be done. R was interested in seeing what I could come up with, and agreed to collaborate. He gave me his original CFP to transform into a call for interviews. Within a few months, I had posted the revised call for interviews online in every Pagan website, forum, or blog that I could find, I had emailed every Pagan I knew, and I had sent fliers to friends of mine who run occult shops. My call for interviews was reposted in other countries and on other types of forums. The response was far greater than I had ever imagined it would be. Originally, I had expected to have maybe 20 interviews. At the time of writing, I had done over 120 ethnographic interviews with polytheists from the U.S., the U.K., Portugal, Canada, Lebanon, and Chile. I have reserved the extended discussion of my methods for another section of this book. What I will admit here is that the interview process was painstaking, laborious…and richly rewarding beyond my wildest expectations.

The interviews and transcription process began on April 7, 2011, and continued through June 30, 2013. During that time, I was also struggling to live and work as an adjunct professor/guest lecturer/migrant academic in New York City while trying to balance a deepening of my own devotional practices and my other research commitments. The biggest trouble was getting everything transcribed and into print. Unfortunately, while the questionnaires, interview notes, chart data, and analysis were spared, 2012's Superstorm Sandy wiped out 30 of the interview MP3 files when a power surge ate my computer. I left New York in December of 2012 and, after a long visit with another colleague, I relocated to Tulsa, Oklahoma, to look after my parents, and get this book written.

Beyond making contributions to R's project, I was not certain what sort of scholarly or academic work might also come of this ethnography. I figured that research directions would appear to me as I continued to work. A few things became clear to me during the interview process. The first thing I realized is that the material I gathered would be enough to fill several volumes. 20 of the interviews would go into R's book. The rest of the interviews would be transcribed for inclusion in at least one volume about contemporary polytheist practices in Western culture. As it turns out, R has published a book on polytheist theology, and will publish his volume—including those interviews—at a later time. In the meantime, this book will be published.

The next thing I realized is that the biggest priority for this work wasn't academic; it was social. Most of the polytheists I interviewed mentioned experiencing some degree of friction with others because of their emphasis on a religious practice which reifies and venerates multiple Divine Beings. Sometimes this friction occurred with non-Pagans who, out of monotheist mental habit, demonize or ridicule the polytheists' practices and beliefs. Then there were several cases of conflict between respondents and their non-Pagan families over their choice of religion. I was a bit surprised to find that some of the polytheists I spoke to felt marginalized not only by the monotheist overculture, but also very often by other Pagans. For these polytheists, devotion and connection to the Gods, the ancestors, and the land, and the spirits is more important than goals of self-development, personal empowerment, or magickal practice which are often the priorities of mainstream Paganism. In fact, many of my respondents' practices don't really match up very well with the esbat/sabbat magickal ritual practices that have helped define Paganism. Some of the people I interviewed feel so alienated from Paganism that they don't really consider themselves to be Pagan at all. The overwhelming desire of these folks was to be heard and respected, and to connect with others who share their experiences and their attitudes toward the spirits which they consider to be most holy.

Another thing that became clear to me was that my initial impulse to collect as many definitions of "polytheism" and "faith" as possible was the correct one. Both of these terms can pose problems because people's understanding of them is varied, and the philosophical approaches that arise from those understandings can conflict. The reason I asked for definitions of both terms from each person is that I was aware of the scholarly tendency to define terms from other cultures, and then construct arguments using those terms in ways that may not reflect the culture's interpretations of those terms. The resulting research is quite reflective of the researcher's interpretation of the findings, but not necessarily an accurate reflection of the culture's attitudes and beliefs. I thus thought it best to begin with a simple dictionary definition, and then reconstruct it from the bottom up, by asking each interviewee what they thought it meant, and then drawing conclusions based on their definitions.

I soon discovered that I could juxtapose two polytheists who worship the same Gods, have similar religious practices, and have similar conclusions about the metaphysical makeup of our world and the role of humanity within it, yet whose definitions of "faith" are so completely opposite such that substantial arguments could arise between them. Getting 120 definitions of "faith" allowed me to draw some conclusions about whether the term might have a substantially different meaning in a polytheist context than in a monotheist one.

Never in my life have I encountered a more problematic term

than "polytheism." I have informally studied Queer theory for fifteen years. And anyone familiar with that field knows how fraught the concept "Queer" is in terms of language, definitions, and politics.. This should have prepared me for what I encountered in exploring the concept of "polytheism." It didn't. In retrospect, I'm not sure anything would have. Never in my wildest nightmares did I expect to encounter the level of hostility and argumentativeness that I did as a result of attempting to define this single term.

The mistake that I made was in believing that one would think, upon reading the dictionary, that the meaning of this term is self-evident. The Merriam-Webster dictionary—silly thing—lead me to believe that polytheism both denotes the reification of multiple distinct, independent, Divine Beings, and connotes veneration and worship of, or ritualized interaction with, those Divine Beings. "The Call For Interviews" I sent out specified my interest in interviewing polytheists who identify as such according to that definition of the term. 110 of my interviews were concurrent with the common dictionary definitions. Yet, when I broached the topic of my findings on Pagan message boards, blog comments, or web sites, it ended in a heated controversy every single time. Paganism has a time-honored tradition of adopting terms, interpreting them differently than what may be encountered in the over-culture, and then using these newly re-envisioned terms to define one's self. "Polytheism" is one of these terms.

Many, many Pagans who self-define as polytheist see the old Gods and Goddesses not as beings, but as archetypal images or metaphors. For them, the "belief in many Gods" translates to "belief that the one great God, or one great totalized Godhead comprised of a polarized gendered pair, has many archetypal or metaphoric facets." Many Pagans seemed to vehemently reject the possibility that their definitions might come closer to mon., and, instead, focus on deepening their relationships with their Holy Powers, and serving their Gods and communities. Their decision to stop fighting ended the heated discussion, but the questions and emotions raised in the fracas still linger.

In the end, I suppose that this controversy should not have come as a surprise to anyone. It is in the nature of religious movements to evolve, divide, and even to schism. The history of near-Eastern monotheism is rife with schism, sectarianism, and rebellion, not to mention bloody holy war. Paganism is old enough and large enough to start experiencing the growing pains of a rapidly expanding religious movement. The conception of polytheism and where such conception fits into larger Pagan practice is only one issue of many that is likely to emerge and shake up the Pagan community. That the controversy has emerged is a sign that Paganism is evolving into a rich, complex, multifaceted, nuanced religious practice. More to the point, Paganism is in a position to learn from the disastrous instances of religious conflict that near-Eastern monotheism has given to history: the Malachite genocide, the Crusades, the Inquisition, and Jihadism…to name a few. Religions should not be concerned with warfare, violence, and compelling people to accept only one view of the world. Ideally, religions are about connection with the Divine, the land, our highest good, and each other, which leaves plenty of room for fostering an appreciation of diverse worldviews. All of these are held as highest values in Paganism, and will hopefully help guide the movement through the conflicts that will continue to arise.

Based on the ethnographic research I have done and my related scholarly research on ancient polytheist cultures and contemporary indigenous religions, I have developed a pretty strong conception of the term "polytheism", and have solid ideas about how it should be defined. After listening to these interviews numerous times, reviewing my interview notes, chart data, and respondents' questionnaires, and going through the transcription process, a pretty consistent picture of contemporary Western polytheism emerges. If I so desire, I can argue that regardless of whether polytheism continues to be considered part of Paganism or gets accorded its own separate status, there are commonalities among "hard" polytheists that hold their religious practices apart from the larger Pagan movement. However, this work is, to my knowledge, the first instance of ethnography being used to trace the contours of theology as it appears in a living, contemporary, Western polytheist practice. It is also, to my knowledge, the first time that ethnography has been used as tool of serious theological inquiry. Therefore, the drawing of those social scientific conclusions might be less useful at this point than exploring the theological implications of the differences between the patterns of polytheist practice among contemporary Westerners and what is found in the dominant monotheist culture.

Regardless of the controversy about conceptions of the term

"polytheism," the fact remains that polytheistic religions are not respected in mainstream overculture. The specter of near-Eastern monotheism has continued to dominate our perceptions of what religion, faith, and the Divine should be. The issue that really needs to be tackled at this time is this near-Eastern, monotheism-saturated culture's reflex reaction of dismissing and ridiculing polytheistic religions. While it is clear to me that Paganism should not be conflated, wholesale, with polytheism, it is likewise clear that Paganism is a polytheistic religious movement. As such, "hard" polytheists do have a place within it, should they themselves wish to continue participating in the movement. Regardless of whether the Gods are seen as archetypes or as individual beings, Paganism brings much-needed challenges to the monotheist mindset that underpins contemporary Western culture. Even from their place within Paganism, "hard" polytheists uniquely and effectively pose a very specific, unexpected set of challenges to the monotheist perspective. Their polytheism poses uncomfortable questions about the relationship between humanity, Divinity, religion, and the planet that deserve to be respected and addressed.

Nonetheless, the story's the thing. Rather, the stories are the thing. Regardless of theoretical or theological contributions I might make on the subject of contemporary Westerners who worship the ancient Deities, the most important part of this book is the collection of stories that people have shared with me. That they allowed me to glimpse the numinous through their eyes moves me deeply. Their bravery in proudly and clearly stating their spiritual truth and sharing their personal experiences without qualification or reservation was humbling to experience. I admire and respect each and every one of the people who I interviewed. Even when the interview process went roughly (I'm looking at you, Skype; you, too, T-Mobile) the experience was rewarding. For the purposes of time and expense, I have limited myself to publishing only a fraction of the interviews I originally performed. It is my hope to publish at least one other collection of these interviews. Until then, I am honored and pleased to present the stories and experiences of these remarkable polytheists. And to them, I humbly say, "Thank you. May the Deities, ancestors, and spirits of place bless and keep you."

W. D. Wilkerson, August 23, 2013

Methods

As has been mentioned previously, modern Western thought cannot conceive of reifying the Gods and Goddesses of old. In fact, the reason I wanted to speak specifically with people who view the Gods and Goddesses as real, existing, individual, distinct Divine Beings is because this viewpoint didn't seem to be very well-represented in the existing Pagan literature. It is virtually nonexistent in Western culture outside of a Pagan context. The closest that serious theological inquiry gets to discussing polytheism is the study of Hinduism, which nonetheless seems always to proceed from a monist or pantheist perspective. The underlying assumption that all Hindus see the Deities as simply avatars, emanations, or manifestations of a single immense, transcendent Being rather than Deities in their own right throbs beneath that discourse, like a security blanket for the monotheist perspective. With that lone exception, the cultural assumptions engendered by a near-Eastern monotheist perspective have taken polytheism as a religious practice completely out of the realm of reasonable thought, and consigned it to the dustbin of fantasy and folly. The guiding drive behind this ethnography was to redeem polytheism from the clutches of marginalization by sharing the experiences and points of view of contemporary, Western, modern people who happen to also reify and venerate the Gods and Goddesses.

Because this was not originally designed to be a probability-based statistical survey, I was not concerned with the randomness or size of my data pool. Rather than craft a web-based survey for large numbers of people to anonymously fill out, and then post a link to the survey on every forum I could find, I created a "Call for Interviews" information sheet, and posted it to every message board, web site, blog, forum, Facebook page, or other site frequented by polytheists that I could find. I also made a point of reaching out to the Ár nDraíocht Féin Druid Fellowship, Hellenion, Religio Romana, the Kemetic Orthodox Temple, and the Troth, all of which are polytheist groups dedicated to reconstructing the religions of the ancient Celts, Greeks, Romans, Egyptians, and Teutonic/Anglo-Saxon/Scandinavian peoples. The CFI provided information about the kind of respondent being sought, the project and its purpose, what the project outcomes might be, my relationship to the subject and credentials for conducting research about it, and contact information for those who were interested in participating. The wonders of the internet age provided me with a more random sample than I had expected to get, with thirty respondents inquiring from places outside the United States. I had over 150 inquiries, of which 120 interviews actually took place.

This project combined survey questionnaire responses and ethnographic research. The original intent of the work was to gather qualitative data to be published in a collection of essays discussing faith in a polytheist context. The surveys were designed to help me become more familiar with each potential respondent's religious practice so that I could tailor portions of the interview to fit the individual respondent. However, the analytical and scholarly possibilities for this research increased dramatically when the number of participants in the project grew from the projected 20 to a whopping 120. There are certainly more than 120 polytheists floating around in contemporary Western society, and it would be inappropriate to generate hard, final generalizations about the beliefs, views, experiences, and practices of contemporary Western polytheism based on this research. However, the sample size is large enough to credibly warrant a discussion of recurrent themes, patterns, and features as possibly being characteristic of polytheism in contemporary Western culture. Due to the increased amount of data, the survey questionnaires helped provide quantitative data regarding occupations, ages, genders, geographic concentrations, lists of Deities worshipped, education levels, family and partnership status, etc.

The interview situations varied, with about 50% taking place over the phone, 10% taking place on Skype, and the remaining 40% taking place in person in New York, Louisiana, Oklahoma, Texas, and Massachusetts. I did not formally conduct field observation of polytheist religious practices in addition to the interviews, but I did participate in a number of rituals with a mixed-tradition polytheist group, a Northern tradition group, and a Pagan coven during the two-year research period. Each interview was recorded with permission having been granted to do so at the beginning of each session. Each respondent was asked the same list of questions, but follow-up and clarification questions were tailored to each polytheist. As a result, each interview features a quantitative data set to be compared with other respondents to locate common themes, ideas, practices, or other significant features, and a qualitative data set that allowed for each polytheist to elaborate on their personal experiences and theology.

Because I personally have experienced misrepresentation of my theological views and persecution for my religious practices, I was acutely aware that many polytheists have a level of mistrust and apprehension regarding people who wish to interview them about their beliefs. Therefore, the most important concern I had going into this study was to conduct this research with integrity and respect, and to craft narratives that render my respondents' experiences as honestly, fairly, and accurately as possible. Their willingness to share their stories and my willingness to explore unfamiliar territory from their point of view is a touchstone of this work.

The interview process was designed according to the principles of reciprocal ethnography introduced by folklorist Elaine Lawless, and the methods of collaborative ethnography developed by Luke Eric Lassiter. In describing her work with reciprocal ethnography, folklorist Elaine Lawless describes it as "a check on the writer's tendency to confiscate the material and run away with it" (Lawless: 1991).[1] Lawless explains that this sort of ethnography is reciprocal because the ethnographer and interviewees "have established a working dialogue about the material, a reciprocal give and take" characterized by "sharing and building knowledge based on dialogue and shared/examined/re-examined knowledge." Ethnographer Luke Eric Lassiter defines the methodology of collaborative ethnography as an approach that "deliberately and explicitly [emphasis his] emphasizes collaboration at every point in the ethnographic process."[2] Collaborative ethnography "invites commentary from our consultants and seeks to make that commentary overtly part of the ethnographic text as it develops," resulting in "texts that are co-conceived or cowritten with local communities of collaborators and consider multiple audiences outside the confines of academic discourse, including local constituencies" (Lassiter: 2005).[3]

In order to accomplish my reciprocal and collaborative goals, I carefully crafted some guidelines to follow over the course of publication. I decided that I would not include any questionnaire responses or interview transcriptions until the respondent had been given a chance to review the transcripts and questionnaires, and had confirmed that they had done so. The respondents were invited to clarify, edit, revise, or add to the material in their interview transcripts, and the resulting document would the raw material for subsequent publication. I felt it was important to make a good-faith effort to incorporate any additional research sources, suggestions, criticisms, or other ideas that my respondents gave me. I also decided not to publish any interview material from respondents who changed their minds about participating in the project. In order to respect their privacy, I allowed my respondents to use a pseudonym, craft name, or simply their initials in order to protect their privacy. Perhaps my most stylistically challenging decision was to edit the interviews as little as possible, building a spare interpretive context by providing only the most basic connective and transitional material between narrative passages. Essentially, my goal was to be the presenter who stands far left of center and out of the way while the interviewees and their stories take center stage. Given my collaborative and reciprocal goals, it would have been inappropriate to attempt to erase myself from the proceedings altogether. Still, there was no need for me to be the lively emcee inserting myself and my opinions into the front of the narratives where I simply didn't belong.

It is very important to me for readers to recognize that these ethnographies are, as are Lawless', co-created narratives, born from an intense dialogue between my interviewees and myself. As such, it is my intent, one shared by Lassiter, that these narratives reflect the perspectives and concerns of my interviewees rather than those of myself, and retain their relevance to the larger community of contemporary Western polytheists outside of the scholarly realm. One consequence of this approach is my choice to severely limit the amount of theorizing I present in this work. After reviewing each interview, and completing the transcription process several times, the most blatantly obvious fact is that my theories about contemporary Western polytheism are not as important as these polytheists' own theories about the Deities, religion, faith, and practice. Another concern was that presenting my theoretical interpretations at this juncture might limit how these narratives are received and understood by readers. Presenting my theories might guide them toward reaching my conclusions rather than leaving them more free to learn how the interviewees' theorize their own experiences, and draw conclusions from those. This isn't to say that there is no interpretation or contextualization of these narratives. The introduction raises the theological benefits to be had through an ethnographic approach to Paganism and polytheism. The overview presents and interprets trends in my data set, and then contrasts those findings with corollary concepts in near-Eastern monotheism. From that point on, readers are left to learn about the interviewees experiences and then build their own theories about what they've found in those narratives. So far as this volume is concerned, nobody has pulled their interview from this project. I have received pointed criticism about assumptions and terminology from a number of respondents, whose candor I am truly grateful for. The majority of the transcripts have been so heavily revised by the respondents that these published narratives truly are collaborative documents co-written by myself and the respondents.

When I decided to conduct ethnographic research into contemporary polytheism, I had a very specific definition of the term in mind. My intent was to interview people who reify the old Deities—people who believe in the existence of multiple, distinct, individual, Gods and Goddesses and have built their religious practice around this belief. The project was designed to account for respondents' personal definitions of the term "polytheism" with the intent of developing a more group-representative definition of the term as the project progressed. Of those interviewed, 110 shared a view of the Deities as being individual, distinct Beings who exist outside of and independently from the human imagination. There was a wide variation in the particular conceptions of the Goddesses and Gods beyond that shared foundational view with several discussing a pantheistic or monistic framework in addition to their polytheism. Those who are pantheistic as well as polytheist tend to view each individual Deity as the distinct, individual Divine embodiment of a particular set of natural forces; however the practices of the respondents who hold this view are more consistent with those held by the other 110 respondents who view the Gods and Goddesses as distinct, individual Beings. The remaining respondents did not have a uniform view of the Deities or practices that resembled those of the otther 110. Some viewed the Deities as archetypes or metaphors which are dependent upon the human imagination or "collective unconscious" for their existence. Some viewed the Deities as emanations of a single Divine Source. The practices, approaches, and attitudes of these respondents tended to differ significantly from those of the other 110.

Prior to my research, I already knew, from my experience with contemporary Paganism, that there are myriad definitions of the term that are being used, some of which are very much at odds with one another. Standard dictionary definitions indicate that polytheism is the belief in, and very often the worship of, multiple Divine Beings. This definition denotes reification and connotes veneration. However, many Pagans, especially those inspired by Jung and Campbell, think of the old Gods and Goddesses as being human-generated archetypal images. When they define "polytheism," a metonymic substitution takes place within the definition which morphs it from meaning "the belief in multiple Divine Beings" into "the belief in many archetypes," or occasionally, for those who interpret archetypal images as metaphors, "the belief in many metaphors." There are any number of good reasons that someone might take this view, which might range from an atheistic unwillingness to continence the existence of Diety, all the way to a theistic acknowledgement that Deity, or the totalized

Godhead, is so immense, ineffable, and pervasive that one can only comprehend it through contemplation of archetypal or metaphoric images. If one's reason for embracing Paganism is to spur spiritual growth and personal empowerment, then there is no pressing need to reify Deity in any form, archetypal or not, and this definition is perfectly appropriate.

However, problems arise with any attempt to apply this Jung-inspired archetypal understanding of polytheism outside the bounds of a contemporary Western Pagan context because this definition utterly fails to accurately describe the beliefs and practices of ancient polytheists or contemporary Western and indigenous peoples who reify and venerate multiple Divine Beings. Although the term "archetype" dates back to the time of Plato, the understanding of "archetype" which many Pagans use in relation to the term "polytheism" is very modern. Jung's concept of the archetype, drawn from Plato, Kant and Schopenhauer,[4] debuted in 1919, and Jung continued to develop and refine it until his death in 1961 (Samules: 1986). In his work Religion and Psychology, Jung described the term as "forms or images of a collective nature which occur practically all over the earth as constituents of myths and, at the same time, as autochthonous, individual products of unconscious origin."[5] The image of Deity is "a very important and influential archetype"[6] (Jung: 1966). The single most important aspect of the Jungian archetypal view is that archetypes are dependent upon human imagination and psychology to exist, and have no independent existence outside of the minds of humanity. This quasi-Platonic conception of archetype is only one part of Jung's philosophy, not the whole of it. Furthermore, despite assertions to the contrary from contemporary classicists (who unconsciously work from the near-Eastern monotheist perspective), Platonic idealism is not, de facto, a form of monotheism[7] (Faguet & Gordon: 2010). But even if it were, this view was certainly not the prevailing attitude towards the Gods and Goddesses who were worshipped by ancient Greeks.

In actuality, the concept of the archetype being used in this definition of polytheism is thoroughly modern and thoroughly Western. To survey the religious practices of ancient peoples, and assume that they really only believed in archetypes and not actual Divine Beings is to project upon them a modern understanding that did not exist then, and does not actually apply to the historically and culturally specific situation in which human experience with the Deities arose. The same principle holds true for contemporary Westerners who gaze upon some groups of contemporary indigenous people, and claim that they believe in archetypes rather than multiple

Divine Beings. It is inappropriate to assume that the concept of the archetype is shared cross-culturally, and that all people see Divine Beings as simply archetypes or metaphors. There are contemporary people from indigenous cultures and increasingly from modern, Western cultures who believe in and venerate multiple Divine Beings. These Beings are not seen as manifestations or emanations of one source, manifestations or psychological constructs of the human unconscious, archetypes, metaphors, or fictional characters. They are considered to be real—real Deities, manitou, ancestors, angels, and spirits. Polytheism in practice is reification writ large.

Perhaps the biggest obstacle posed by the pervasiveness of this "archetypal/metaphoric" polytheism is that it helps to efface and erase evidence of non-monotheist perspectives. An insistence that polytheists now don't, and historically didn't, actually reify and venerate real Gods and Goddesses creates the illusion that polytheism is actually monism or pantheism, and never really existed as a religious practice rooted in reification. It allows the near-Eastern monotheist perspective to maintain the illusion that multiple Gods do not exist, and have never been thought to have existed by anyone, anywhere, ever. Whether or not one's interest in interpreting the Gods as archetypes is attached to belief in Deity of any sort, the willingness to dismiss the existence of Gods and Goddesses is a remnant of the near-Eastern monotheist perspective, and only serves to further entrench it. It is precisely this entrenchment that my ethnographic enquiry was meant to alleviate.

For the purpose of avoiding confusion between the two types of polytheists, the term "archetypal polytheist" will be used in the author's interpretive text to describe those who see the Deities as archetypes/metaphors, and the term "polytheist" will be used to describe those who see the Gods and Goddesses as individual, distinct, Divine Beings that exist independently of and well outside of the conscious or unconscious human imagination. However, the terms "soft polytheist" and "hard polytheist" will still appear in the narratives as given by the respondents. "Hard polytheist" refers to one who reifies mulitple Divine beings, especially Deities, and whose belief is often accompanied by a votary practice, and "soft polytheist" refers to one who sees the Deities as metaphors, archeptyes, or other quasi-entities which are facets of either a larger Godhead or projections from humanity's collective unconscious.

Chapter Notes:

1. Elaine J Lawless, <u>Holy Women, Wholly Women: Sharing Ministries of Wholeness Through Life Stories and Reciprocal Ethnography</u> (Philadelphia; University of Pennsylvania Press, 1991), pg. 61.

2. Lawless, <u>Holy Women, Wholly Women</u>..., 83.

3. Luke Eric Lassiter, <u>The Chicago Guide to Collaborative Ethnography</u> (Chicago: University of Chicago Press, 2005), 15-24.

4. Andrew Samuels, <u>Jung and the Post-Jungians</u> (London: Routledge, 1986), 18-20.

5. Carl G. Jung, <u>Terry Lectures, Psychology and Religion</u> (New Haven, CT: Yale University Press, 1966), 63.

6. Jung, <u>Terry Lectures: Psychology and Religion</u>, 73.

7. Emile Faguet and Homer Gordon, <u>Initiation into Philosophy</u> (London Indo-European Publishing, 2010), 19.

Introduction
From Monotheist Perspective to Polytheist Theology

Ancient poets and mystics from places as diverse as Sumeria, China, Egypt, India, Rome, and Greece wrote copiously about their Deities. Other cultures in Africa, North America, Scandinavia, and Australia maintained a rich oral tradition about their Gods that lasted until the incursion of Christianity and Islam in the first millenium of the Common Era. With the rise of Islam in the Near and Middle East and Christianity in the West and the Americas, the monotheist perspective became the only one that could safely be discussed. To do otherwise was to court excommunication, exile, or execution. After those religions were established, this perspective became the only one at all because the non-monotheist religions had been decimated by Christian and Islamic empire builders.

Such has been the situation for the last 2,000+ years. Because of this situation, it has been nigh on impossible to even discuss the possible existence of, much less reify, the old Gods and Goddesses. Discussions habitually limit Them to being archetypes, epic figures, fairy-tale characters, emanations or manifestations of a single source, projections of the unconscious, psychological constructs, metaphors, or comic book superheroes. To broach the topic of one's personal experiences with these Deities as actual Beings might get one sent to the psychiatric ward. Perhaps even more difficult to discuss is the possibility that ancient polytheist religious traditions of worshipping the old Gods and Goddesses weren't simply convoluted systems of primitive superstition, but rather valid, complex, and evolved religions that were vital to the health of their communities. To the modern, Western mind, those religions are foolishness or madness or both. It is simply inconceivable to most people that polytheism's reification of the ancient Deities might provide an invaluable counterpoint to current assumptions about humanity, nature, religion, and Divinity which are generally found in contemporary discussions about religion.

Over the last two millennia, monotheism created a habit of thought which has ossified into a disdain and outright dismissal of the validity of polytheist spirituality. This habit is particularly distressing in relation to the disciplines of theology and religious studies. Polytheist religions have very different conceptions of divinity, ontology, Deity, the sacred, the purpose of religion, and the place of man in the larger scheme of things than are found in near-Eastern monotheism. Taking them seriously and including them in the discussion will almost certainly yield new insight about the fundamental operating assumptions underpinning monotheism, which in turn could yield, within the monotheist perspective, radically new and different conceptions of Deity, religion, and humanity. These are the very conversations that students of theology and religious studies should be having if they wish to better understand human religiosity as it exists all over the world, rather than as it exists in the minds of learned monotheist religious leaders. This sort of inclusive, wide-ranging, and challenging discussion is important to developing interdisciplinary research, and creating new knowledge and understanding about humanity, spirituality, and religion. Yet until polytheism is seriously and respectfully included in the curriculum, these much-needed discussions will not occur.

For the last two thousand years, the vast majority of writing and teaching in the Near East and the West concerning man's relationship with the Divine has been from some sort of monotheist perspective, even when discussing the beliefs of non-monotheist peoples. In descriptions of the Chinese religion that were sent back to Rome, 16th century Jesuit missionaries insisted that the Chinese were monotheists who believed in and worshipped a single "Master of Heaven" (Sangkeun: 2004).[1] The Chinese who learned about Jesuits' impressions of their religion strongly objected to what the Jesuits claimed, and insisted that they worshipped many Gods and Goddesses and also venerated their ancestors, but these objections were discredited by the Jesuits (Paper: 2005, Dan: 196).[2] Prior to the missionary incursion, indigenous North American tribes who honored the "Great Spirit" were honoring a large, benevolent, cosmic-scaled natural Force that had no distinct gender or personality, nor was it anthropomorphized in veneration (Murray: 2007).[3] Christian missionaries and colonists in the New World insisted that this "Great Spirit" was actually a single male "Creator" God, identical to Jehovah, and used this interpretation of indigenous religion to advance their aims of Christian colonialism. The prevalence of this version of the Great Spirit in the writings and orations taken from Native Americans in the 18th and 19th centuries is a testament to the efficacy with which Christianity shaped indigenous polytheism into a pattern that favored monotheist Christian belief (Paper: 2005 & Deloria: 2003).[4]

Missionaries are not the only ones to interpret the religions of polytheist others according to their monotheist perspective. As European empire-builders traveled east and began to encounter strange-seeming people with even stranger-seeming religions, Western scholarly institutions responded to the need for studying the world's diversity of religious expression by constructing a curriculum that would eventually become the "Big Five" approach to world religions: a focus on Christianity, Judaism, Islam, Buddhism, and Hinduism. Early academic studies of Hinduism and Buddhism were heavily influenced by European colonialism (Lopez: 1995, King: 1999)[5] which was an inherently monotheist enterprise (Miller: 2012 & Tinker 1993)[*] The academy institutionalized the notion that each of the five is a "world religion:" a unified religion with a root orthodoxy, rather than a cultural philosophy, that includes a dazzling array of diverse practices and beliefs. For both Hinduism and Buddhism, Western scholars ascribed a set of core texts that defined the essence of each religion, conferred theological legitimacy upon the ideas presented by politically powerful clerics, dismissed the practices of common people and rural clerics as "local variations" of the established religion, and deemphasized the aspects of the religion that did not mesh well with monotheist assumptions (Lopez: 1995, King: 1999).[6] In short, Orientalist scholars of both Hinduism and Buddhism academically constructed both religions to be as close to Christian monotheism as possible, and only those aspects which are most easily intelligible from a monotheist perspective were taken seriously as essential to these religions.

It seems that prior to the 20th century, the fields of theology and religious studies almost went out of their way to avoid taking even the idea of polytheism seriously as a religious perspective. Instead, they created an opportunity to interpret even the most obviously polytheistic of subjects through a filter that is, at the very least, amenable to monotheism. This state of affairs exists because the primary cultural effect of the monotheist perspective is a selective blindness wherein vast swaths of experience and viewpoint are rendered invisible because they do not conform to monotheist expectations regarding religious experience.

---

[*] The intimate relationship between monotheism and empire began with the emergence of missionaries and the rise of monotheists into positions of political power. The scope of this relationship in Christianity exploded during the reign of Charlemagne, whose conquest of continental Europe utterly decimated the indigenous polytheist religions there. This relationship reached new heights in the sixteenth century with the issuance of the Papal Bulls that built the theological foundation for the conquest and exploitation of the New World. This foundation is referred to by postcolonial theorists and decolonization advocates as the "discovery doctrine." Strains of the discovery doctrine can be found in the Marshall Plan and in contemporary Western economic expansion into developing nations around the world. For more information, please refer to Robert J. Miller, et al. <u>Discovering Indigenous Lands: The Doctrine of Discovery in the English Colonies</u> (Oxford: Oxford University Press, 2012); and George E. Tinker's <u>Missionary Conquest: The Gospel and Native American Cultural Genocide</u>, (Minneapolis, MN: Fortress Press, 1993).

Understand that when I use the term "monotheist perspective," it is not a claim that all near-Easterners and Westerners are religiously monotheist Christians, Muslims, or Jews, or that they have any religious beliefs at all. If the experiences of my colleagues at Fordham and NYU are any indication, a growing number of agnostics and atheists have taken up the discipline of religious studies, as have a growing number of contemporary Pagans. Rather, I use the term "monotheist perspective" to describe underlying habits of mind that are deeply ingrained in anyone who grows up in a monotheist-dominated culture regardless of their religious convictions or lack thereof. These mental habits are deeply ingrained in the subconscious, and many people are not aware that they have them. This perspective, which necessarily underpins any and all research on the topic of religion in the West, is comprised of assumptions about the nature of Divine Beings; the nature of religion and its role in society; the ontological necessity of a given Divine Being, and the proper religious worship of that Being; the eschatological consequences of belief or disbelief in that religion and its Divine Being; and most important of all, the relative superiority of monotheism—for whatever reason—to other religions. The monotheist perspective undoubtedly shapes one's view of the world, regardless of whether or not that view acknowledges an unseen spiritual realm.

I had two experiences during the course of researching this book which amply demonstrate the monotheist perspective in action. The first involves a retired philosophy professor whom I cat-sat for one summer. I had only just begun the interview process which would result in this book. My data set was somewhat sparse after only 20 interviews, and my observations were too preliminary to be worth seriously discussing with another academic. I wasn't really interested in discussing it at length just yet, so I kept quiet. During our first dinner meeting, the discussion touched on art, travel, and the complications that come with teaching college students. Prof. O eventually got around to asking me about my field. I had barely completed the word "folklore" when he cut me off to ask if I studied religion. When I answered that I did study aspects of religion, he immediately demanded to know my professional opinion on why people continued to cling to such "superstitious nonsense" as belief in God. Prof. O explained that he was raised in Chassidic Judaism but abandoned that burden to become proudly and irascibly atheist. He spent the next thirty minutes dissecting and dismissing every nuance of religion. Monotheist religion, that is. After he finished, I looked at him and explained that his philosophical objections to religion really only apply to the monotheist religions of the near East, and that my current research on polytheism suggests that those objections don't really apply to all religions, or justify dismissing the social value of those religions on the grounds of their being harmful superstition. He looked at me blankly, possibly because he was in shock. He quickly changed the topic to the "virtue of tolerance." Eventually the dinner concluded. I did end up cat-sitting in his squalid nightmare of an apartment that summer, but I made myself so busy with work that I didn't have time to ponder my surroundings. I made a point never to discuss my progress with him. He never asked about it, anyway.

The second instance came about in the fall, nearly five months after my dinner with Prof. O. I received a brusque email from a Professor Madya R, ("Madya" is equal to the rank of associate professor in Malaysian universities). He had seen my call for interviews, which had apparently been reposted on an academic website in Asia. The message was two lines long, and it demanded that I turn over my sources about polytheism to him: no explanation, no introduction, no respect. I was shocked at the rudeness and presumptuousness of the man, so I declined to do so unless he formally introduced himself and his research project. Prof. Madya R tersely explained that he was an associate professor studying Islam, and he was writing an article on what he saw as the polytheist nature of Christianity and Judaism. He wanted my sources so that he could use them to show how both of these religions are actually "primitive" and "polytheist" as opposed to Islam, which is "advanced" and "monotheist." What really bothered me was this professor's belief that polytheism is so backward that it could be used to severely discredit two other major world religions. I was stunned, to say the least. It took me two days to construct my reply. In it, I disclosed how offensive it was to be treated in that manner by another academic, and that his view of polytheism as a possible critique of Judaism and Christianity was inherently disrespectful to polytheists. Then I explained that my concept of polytheism was not being taken from existing theological or anthropological literature but rather being built though a painstaking process of interviewing contemporary polytheists about their experiences, and that I was nowhere near ready to present my findings. I did not turn over any part of my research to this professor. I did send him a copy of the questionnaires and interview questions that I used to gather my data, and invited him to attempt to locate and interview any polytheists currently living in Malaysia so that they could share their experiences with him. He never responded to tell me how his interviews went. Then again, I didn't follow up with him about it.

These two experiences exemplify well the "monotheist perspective" as it manifests in cultures dominated by near-Eastern monotheism. In the case of Prof. O, the possibility that polytheism could differ so substantially from monotheism as to seriously problematize his objections to religion had never even occurred to him. It had never crossed his mind because polytheism as a religious philosophy is thought not to exist outside of "primitive" cultures or ancient history. It is literally unthinkable, from the monotheist perspective, that people would ever honor Gods who they didn't believe were omnipotent, omniscient, omnibenevolent, and omnipresent, or that they would have any reason to do so. As regards Prof. Madya R, polytheism is assumed to be a "backward" and "primitive" religious philosophy that is nowhere near as evolved as monotheism (the only version of which he seems to appreciate being Islam). The possibility that polytheism is a rich, nuanced, complex religion capable of sustaining powerful, valid, and valuable spiritual experiences, rather than a simple "primitive" stepping-stone to a more highly evolved consciousness, is apparently also unthinkable from a monotheist perspective.

This begs the question, what exactly IS thinkable under the terms of a monotheist perspective? To determine this, it is helpful here to do a quick, general run-down of what seem to be the major points of religious near-Eastern monotheism, followed by a similar rundown of what seem to be the major points of atheism that were presented to me through those experiences, years of informal study, and observance of these ideologies at work in the larger world around me. There are those who will argue that not all religious believers or unbelievers agree with each of the following statements. Yet, if one looks honestly and closely at the theological foundations of near-Eastern monotheist religions, as well as the recent athiest discourse, it is fairly obvious that all of these assumptions play a foundational role in the various theologies and philosophies currently in play, regardless of whether particular individuals or small groups might dispense with one or several of them.

It is assumed that monotheist, religious believers generally agree that their God is male, single, all-powerful, all-knowing, all-loving, all-good, and always present. They see God as immortal and unchanging, even if human perceptions of Him do change. Monotheists tend to believe that this God has given man dominion over all of nature, and that mankind was created to be superior to all other creatures. These believers see their religions more or less as the rules of life by which this God wants humanity to live. The precepts of the religion are written down in holy scripture which was, at the very least, written under the express guidance and inspiration of their God. Monotheist believers' religions teach that this God responds negatively when His rules aren't kept and may take punitive action, or that He may encourage His followers to take punitive action against transgressors on His behalf.

Believers see their God as mysterious and ineffable. Many think He intercedes in the course of human events if He deems fit to do so, and they hold a trust and faith in their God which are not necessarily reflective of their lived experience or the quantifiable evidence in a given situation. When terrible events happen that defy man's ability to reason them out as the actions of a good and loving God, monotheist believers remember that their God is mysterious and ineffable, and they have faith that His reasons are ultimately always good. These believers think that humans, in their limited capacity to gauge the infinite mind of their God, can't always expect to understand His reasons. They often believe that their God has a plan for the life of each human being. This plan culminates with a joyous afterlife in a distant and perfect paradise far from earthly cares. They tend to believe that this afterlife can only be reached if they have spent their life observing God's rules.

Near-Eastern monotheism is predicated on the notion mankind is fallen and degenerate, and believers tend to see man's primary life purpose as the progression from sinful, fallen wretch to purified, obedient child of God. For most of the last two millennia, many monotheists have amply demonstrated their opinion that anyone who does not share their particular belief in God and their particular religious practices is a barbaric, sinful, degenerate "Other" who is probably "less than" themselves. Religious monotheists have also demonstrated discomfiture with living in close geographic proximity to unbelievers or those with a different religion than theirs. The Jewish people have tended to deal with the discomfort of proximity by separating into self-sustaining, isolated communities within a larger culture and striking a balance between their community identity and general civic responsibilities. Christian and Muslim believers have tended to see it as the duty of missionaries and clerics to rescue people—by force, if necessary—from wallowing in turpitude by converting them to whichever Christian or Muslim denomination that the missionaries or clerics belong to, thus affecting personal greater comfort through religious conversion of those neighbors.

The near-Eastern monotheist theology underpinning Western perspective on religion has manifested across a vast theological spectrum. At one end lies the heavily orthporaxic Judaism, which tends to privilege practice and de-emphasize faith. At the other lies the heavily orthodoxic Christianity which tends to privilege faith and de-emphasize religious practice. Because it strongly incorporates both faith and practice, Islam tends to fall in the middle of the spectrum. However, when one looks at Judaism's 600+ behavioral, sartorial, dietary, and ritual proscriptions and taboos, Islam's five pillars, and Christianity's faith in Jesus, it becomes clear that all of the near-Eastern monotheist religious practices are undertaken as acts of faith predicated on belief in the supreme power of their creator-destroyer Deity and fear of the consequences that their Deity's displeasure and condemnation might bring. Regardless of the relative levels of orthodoxy or orthopraxy, the main concern is to maintain spiritual uprightness so that believers may forestall their Deity's displeasure at the iniquity and sinfulness of man and any consequences that this displeasure might bring, rather than to foster devotional engagement with the Divine for its own sake, or to foster community cohesion among believers.

Not all doubters and disbelievers will argue the following points with the piquant vehemence and biting sarcasm of Professor O, but if you look closely at the arguments which have been made historically, and are continuing to be made in the public sphere today, it is clear that all of these assumptions underpin religious doubt and disbelief in cultures dominated by near-Eastern monotheism. Those living in monotheist cultures who either doubt or outright reject the existence of a Divine spiritual realm typically begin by problematizing the validity of claims a religion makes about its Divine Being. Occasionally these arguments begin by asking, "if God is so real and powerful, why doesn't He do..." this thing or that thing, as if magical wish-granting capacity conferred in response to ill-considered human whim should be the baseline for determining a Deity's significance or power. Fortunately, most disbelievers will eschew that line of inquiry, and opt instead for citing both secular historical record and religious text to make their claims. They use these sources to argue how unreasonable it is to believe that a being who commits, or allows to be committed, gross atrocities, famine, disease, disaster, or war could be considered ever-present, all-loving and all-good. Disbelievers explain that if He is all-good, then such things could only reasonably happen if He isn't omniscient, omnipresent, or omnipotent, because only a fiend could be omniscient and omnipotent, and yet allow for the horrors of the world which happen to occur.

After discrediting the omniscience, omnipotence, omnibenevolence and omnipresence of the Deity, the unbelievers progress to condemning religion. Unbelievers think religion is ridiculous and foolish at best, or destructive and oppressive at worst, and see it as a force that acts to suppress intellect, reason, and individual liberty. Next, the disbelievers move on to discrediting the religion's conviction that a particular set of scriptures is the word of their God rather than the philosophizing of fallible human beings with political agendas. Particular scorn is reserved for the mechanism of faith, which is understood to be an imbecilic belief based upon blind hope that the scriptures are factual and true, rather than upon material, quantifiable evidence. The unbelievers then move into an eloquent discussion of the myriad well-evidenced, scientific principles which satisfactorily explain the nature of the cosmos and the origin of life on Earth. They are certain to demonstrate how these theories explain the origin of everything without resorting to some superstitious belief in Divine intervention. If and when the pre-monotheist religions of the ancient world, or the animist, polytheist religions of contemporary indigenous peoples are brought into consideration at all, the fairly immediate conclusion is unflattering to say the least. The idea seems to be that humanity has progressed from "primitive" polytheist "nonsense" to a more civilized monotheist superstition but has finally reached the point of being able to embrace enlightened, non-theist rationalism. At last, the disbelievers argue, this abandonment of God and religion will lead to the realization of man's immense intellectual potential and the ultimate uplifting of society. Disbelievers seem to have grown increasingly uncomfortable sharing geographic proximity with the religious, and are beginning to adopt some of the methods of religious proselytizing such as advertisements, commercials, billboards, and activism to represent and promote their pro-humanist convictions within their communities.

Between these two polarized viewpoints, some common features can be extrapolated. These features are the core assumptions of the monotheist perspective that underpins near-Eastern-monotheism-dominated cultures. The monotheist perspective expects that man should be set above nature, by virtue of either his rational capacity or Divine election to such a state. It assumes nature is significant insofar as it can be used for human gain and enjoyment, or function as a canvas upon which humankind's intellectual and technological genius, if not a Deity's creative prowess, may be painted. The monotheist perspective privileges individualism and free will. Although significant material factors (or Divine intervention, if you are religious) may alter one's life course and choices, the achievement of the individual's potential (for religious redemption or personal excellence) should be a constant preoccupation for all of humanity. Progress is a paramount virtue in the monotheist perspective; it is believed that humanity has evolved past a primitive, ignorant, superstitious past, and is perpetually moving towards moral, intellectual, physical, and technological improvement.

Insofar as the idea of Deity is countenanced, it is thought that there should be only one such entity, which is expected to be omnipotent, omniscient, omnipresent, ineffable, infallible, immortal, perfect, unchanging, male, and utterly, singularly solitary. Religion, in the monotheist perspective, is expected to be based on a core set of written scriptures, espouse a particular ontology and accompanying eschatology, and promote particular precepts as the Divine commands of their Deity which must be adhered to if one is to garner His grace and avoid His wrath. Within those scriptures, one expects to find an accounting of the universe from its origins through to the end of time, and a portrayal of the creator/destroyer role their Deity plays in that process. The monotheist perspective expects religions to believe that their Deity has a plan for each person's life, death, and afterlife, and that this afterlife takes place in a distant paradise far from earthly attachments or mundane cares. The monotheist perspective assumes that the purpose of religion is to worship this Deity and vigilantly follow His commands. The monotheist perspective assumes that the primary practice of religion is to "have faith," which specifically means to engage in the mental action of belief. It also assumes that faith demands humans to suspend those instances of intelligence and lived experience that might conflict with such insights as have been revealed through faith and religious precepts. The monotheist perspective further recognizes that this faith is expressed through observing the preferred conduct, taboos, and behavioral proscriptions handed to humanity from the Deity via their religion.

Those who doubt or reject even the notion of Deity tend to maintain the first four secular assumptions, and pattern their rejection according to the latter religious assumptions. As a result, any religion or spiritual practice that does not correspond with or adhere to both the secular and the religious assumptions of the monotheist perspective is all but invisible to the monotheist gaze. If noticed at all, those practices will meet with amusement, debunking, and/or derision rather than honest respect or fair regard. The only context in which these religious practices might be engaged with critically and analytically rather than amusedly or derisively is an academic one.

While the monotheist perspective has impacted Western civilization's understanding and respect of ancient cultures and other peoples, it is only fair to recognize that the academic realm has a rich tradition of curiosity regarding the mythologies and rituals of both groups. The discipline of psychology owes much to Jung's work with archetypes, which was pioneered through his analysis of Germanic mythology and its impact on German psychology between the World Wars. Concerned as they are with theorizing human behavior and social interactions, the fields of Anthropology and Sociology have always taken very seriously the respectful analysis of other cultures and their religions. Since its inception, the discipline of Folklore has taken tremendous care in gathering and interpreting the meaning of the myths and rituals from other cultures and championing the relative cultural value of these traditions. Visual Arts, Theater, and Literary Studies departments have always had a love affair with studying the ancient Gods and Goddesses who were so often invoked in the great classical works of art, drama, and literature. Classics departments frequently juxtapose texts from Pagan Romans and Greeks alongside texts from Christians to illuminate precisely what happened, linguistically, when the latter came to dominate the former.

Yet with all of this interest in the myths and rituals of polytheist peoples, it is highly unlikely that one would find anybody discussing the polytheism of ancient and indigenous peoples, in its own right, as a valid religious philosophy that has serious theological merit. Myths and rituals are discussed from many different perspectives, but the religions that they come from, and their reification of the multiple Divine Beings, have often been shut out of serious theological inquiry. Classics scholar and Pagan theologian Edward Butler elucidates the issue quite succinctly. "According to convention," he says, "the category of 'theology' is reserved for exegetical works on the Abrahamic faiths, with other religious traditions expected to be treated in a historicist or anthropological fashion" (Butler: 2012).[7] Non-monotheist religions do not seem terribly welcome in theology curriculums.

One of the most revealing arguments ever to express the ideology of the monotheist perspective comes from religious historian Brent Nongbri. In Before Religion, (2013)[8] Nongbri argues that rather than being a natural, universal, human experience, "religion" is a modern concept developed by Western monotheists. Nongbri further argues that the concept of religion has been projected backward in time onto the practices of polytheist peoples, and subsequently naturalized as a fundamental component of human experience. For those reasons, he thinks it is inappropriate to recognize the spiritual and metaphysical practices of ancient peoples as constituting a religion. Essentially, Nongbri thinks that monotheists (Christians) invented religion, and if a spiritual tradition isn't monotheist (Christian), then we shouldn't call it a religion or study it as if it were. The most that can be said here is that at least Nongbri admits how deeply monotheism (in the form of Christianity) has colored scholarly inquiry into and interpretation of polytheist and ancient cultures. It's a pity that he doesn't recognize how his own fundamental assumptions of what religion is, what distinguishes the secular from the religious, the role religion should play in society, and the nature of the practices that comprise it are also dictated by this monotheist perspective. His assumptions about religion are so dictated by the monotheist perspective, in fact, that he honestly thinks it fair and appropriate to dismiss the rich and varied forms of polytheist religious expression that have existed across millennia rather than countenance them as being valid religions. Nongbri's work creates quite a problem for polytheism because his argument puts the study of polytheism squarely and fairly outside the realm of theological inquiry. He perpetuates the situation that Edward Butler has long lamented, wherein "to write on these [polytheist] religions is to be denied even the recourse to phenomenological insight, much less to classical metaphysics whose connection to the Paganism of its founders had been deemed accidental or denied outright" (2012).[9] Indeed, one wonders if Nongbri recognizes the inherent neo-Platonism underpinning his ideas about religion and religiosity, though there is no doubt he would deny Plato's polytheism as being part of a valid religion (Faguet and Gordon: 2010).[10]

Fortunately, the purpose of academic inquiry is to study and interpret religion, not create it. The monotheist perspective which has pervaded scholarly approaches to religion has shifted somewhat in the greater Western society since the mid-twentieth century. Recovering from the massive psychological trauma of two world wars and coming to terms with powerful communist enemies who did not cotton to the notion of Deity or religion of any kind destabilized the monotheist perspective. The movements toward social justice, economic parity, and racial and sexual equality served to further secularize attitudes toward education, government, and civil society. This cultural milieu was the fertile ground from which New Age spirituality (drawing heavily from Eastern religious philosophies and indigenous tribal mysticisms), and Paganism (drawing heavily from pre-Christian Indo-European polytheism and Western occultism) sprang forth. Of the two, Paganism steps closest to embracing the polytheism of ancient civilizations and indigenous peoples which has been denied legitimacy vis-à-vis the monotheist perspective. Therefore, Paganism is one of the best places to look to find a viewpoint that challenges the monotheist perspective.

These challenges first became established in the 1940s and 50s with the debut of contemporary Paganism. On the West coast of the United States, Victor Anderson and his wife Cora were assembling Anderson's research and experiences with non-Western cultures into a uniquely American Pagan theology that would eventually become Feri.

Feri, which until recently was rarely spoken publicly about by its adherents, is a witchcraft and mystery tradition rooted in the celebration of ecstasy and personal empowerment (Mogliocco: 2004).[11] In 1950's Britain, Gerald Gardner celebrated the British government's repeal of anti-Witchcraft laws by publishing <u>Witchcraft Today</u> and <u>The Meaning of Witchcraft</u> (Adler: 2006).[12] Gardnerian witchcraft, which emphasizes fertility and connection to nature, became well-established in Britain and had crossed over to the U.S. by the mid-1960's. Increasing feminist consciousness and the demands for gender equality within Paganism spurred the development of Goddess Spirituality, of which Starhawk's Reclaiming tradition of witchcraft is perhaps the most famous example. LGBT issues, environmentalism and multiculturalism have influenced Paganism since it first began, a fact reflected in the continued growth and evolution of the religious movement.

From its inception, Paganism has employed both large-scale and small-scale methods to disseminate its spiritual practices and techniques. At this point, thousands of books have been written by Pagan elders for the benefit of the wider community. Some books focus on specific Pagan traditions such as Reclaiming, Feri, Wicca, British Traditional Witchcraft, and Dianic Witchcraft, to name a few. Others are written specifically to aid those who want to experience Pagan religious practice on an individual, solitary level. Some books are concerned with discussing ritual techniques associated with magic, meditation, or consciousness development. While some choose to remain solitary in their religious practice, there are hundreds of Pagans who practice together in covens, teaching circles, or other types of groups. The rise of the internet has made information about Paganism much more widely available, and has made it much easier for isolated Pagans to connect and share their knowledge and experiences.

One conclusion that will doubtlessly be reached by anyone who studies all of this Pagan literature is that it has become such a large, diverse, complex movement that it is very difficult to identify exactly what Pagans believe. Paganism isn't a creedal religion and does not demand that Pagans adhere to any particular set of beliefs. If anything, Pagans tend to oppose any attempted imposition of theological concepts or doctrine onto themselves or the religious groups they belong to. The result, as Pagan scholar John Michael Greer pointed out, is that Paganism lacks dogma, or any other sort of unifying theology (Greer: 2005).[13] This is entirely appropriate because, as Pagan scholar Sabina Mogliocco explains, Paganism is orthopraxic, not orthodoxic (2004).[14] Paganism is rooted in common practices rather than prescribed belief. This isn't to say that all Pagans have the exact same practices, or that each person who identifies as a Pagan maintains each and every one of the practices that are found across the spectrum of Paganism. Such is not the case. But it is true that there are a core group of ritual practices that the majority of Pagans share, and there is a shared set of assumptions about Deity, magic, nature, and individual empowerment that underpin these practices.

Pagans tend to assume that ritual is an important part of religious experience. They embrace the power of ritual to foster connections with each other, with the earth and its natural cycles, and to the Divine in whatever form It may take. They tend to celebrate calendrical and personal rites. The eight major sabbats of Yule, Imbolc, Ostara, Beltane, Midsummer, Lugnasadh, Mabon, and Samhain follow a solar timetable in accordance with the solstices and equinoxes; taken as a whole they trace out the planet's seasonal fertility cycles in terms of birth, growth, harvest, death, and rebirth. Of special importance is the place of humanity within that larger context. Each lunar month finds Pagans celebrating the full moon with esbats, which tend to focus on the business of the group, the spiritual development of the individuals within the group, and magical workings for ends determined by the group. Paganism also emphasizes rituals as a means to celebrate the individual's life stages and relationships within the community; these relationships are featured in rites of passage such as pregnancy rites, baby namings/Wiccanings, puberty rites, handfastings and marriages, cronings/sagings, and death rites. Rites of initiation are also major parts of Pagan practice, be it initiation as admittance into a coven or magical group, initiation as a marker of progress within a given tradition, initiation into a particular mystery tradition, or self-initiation into a Pagan spiritual path. Another significant feature of Paganism is that the group will create ad-hoc rituals for itself or at an individual's request in the instance that such ritual observance is deemed necessary and beneficial by those who would conduct and participate in it.

Pagans tend to assume that magic is integral to religious practice. Magic can here be understood to mean the ritual practice of concentrating the will and manipulating spiritual energies in order to facilitate specific ends (Adler: 2006).[15] While it is true that some Pagans abstain from magical practice, the fact of magic is implicit within the ritual structure that is commonly featured in Pagan religious practice. Most, if not all, Pagan rituals involve the creation of liminal spiritual space by "casting a circle" that prevents mundane and negative energies from intruding upon and diminishing the spiritual potency of a particular ritual (Mogliocco: 2004).[16] This circle is usually oriented according to the cardinal compass points and the correspondence of particular elemental energies to those points, which actions anchor the magic circle as a liminal space within the mundane world yet allow for the unimpeded flow of spiritual energies during the ritual. Some rituals may only be performed when certain astrological correspondences are in effect or during specific moon phases, as it is believed that such correspondences will impact the efficacy of the ritual. Regardless of whether the Pagan in question believes in a particular Deity, in general, most rituals will invoke a particular Deity or set of Deities whose symbolic correspondences, mythological features, and/or archetypal aspects are considered to be potentially beneficial for the outcome of the ritual.

Often, ritual tools such as candles, incense, chalices, knives, robes, and masks are used because it is believed that they impact the spiritual energies that are being called upon, or created, through the ritual. Regardless of which tools, Deities, astrological ephemera or elemental correspondences are in play during a given ritual, nearly all Pagan rituals will have most of these general features. Beneath these features lies the assumption that there exist any number of unseen spiritual energies which can impact human beings, and that a properly performed ritual must not only account for these energies but also adeptly direct their flow in order for the ritual to go well.

Pagans embrace connection to the earth, spirit, and each other in ways that indicate a clear rejection of the near-Eastern monotheist perspective (Adler: 2006).[17] Pagans have rejected the notion that humanity wallows in a sinful, fallen state punctuated by acutely damnable carnal desires. They instead view humanity as inherently spiritual, human sexuality as sacred, and the ambitions and desires of humanity as those things which motivate us to be better, stronger people. Near-Eastern monotheism's separation of humanity, nature, and the Divine has been replaced in the Pagan mind with a view of humanity as being a part of nature, which is Divine and possessed of a profound wisdom which can only be discovered through living in contemplative harmony with nature. Although Paganism rejects the proscription of belief in or about Deity, it commonly accepts the sanctity and Divinity of the feminine. For most Pagans, the purpose of religion is to engender personal empowerment, connect to nature, and commune with like-minded people. Paganism embraces collective religious expression but rejects organized religion as it is practiced in near-Eastern monotheism (Berger: 1999).[18]

While it is true that Paganism does not hold a given stance regarding the existence or nature of Deity, my review of the books that Pagans have been writing about their practices and traditions over the last fifty years reveals that certain understandings about the Divine seem to be more common than others. Generally speaking, there seem to be two basic models of Deity that one will encounter in these works: the first is an all-encompassing single Deity who is characterized more often than not as female; the second is a Divine heterosexual Pair consisting of a great Goddess and a great God who are the manifested polarities of a single totalized Godhead. Many of those who view the Godhead as a Divine Pair see the Goddess as the primary Deity and the God as Her consort. Although emphasis on the Divine feminine is a very strong counterpoint to near-Eastern monotheist expectations of a male God, the recognition of a single totalized Godhead divided into a gendered Divine pairing is certainly a departure from near-Eastern monotheism's single Deity.

One of the most innovative attributes of Paganism is the tendency to blend religious philosophies, and the resulting interpretations of Deity have typically syncretized attributes of monism, pantheism, and polytheism into a coherent understanding that challenges the conventional monotheist perspective. The monistic view comes into play insofar as Deity is regarded to be the sole origin and source of all things and beings that exist, and that all things and beings emanate from this source. These models of Deity are often also pantheistic in that Deity is seen as all-encompassing, imminent, and inseparable from the natural world. Both the monist and the pantheist aspects of Pagan conceptions of Deity can be traced to Pagans rejecting the separation of the spiritual and the material and the subjugation of nature by humanity which is characteristic of the monotheist perspective.

Paganism has an interesting relationship with polytheism that has resulted in a spectrum of attitudes towards the myriad Gods and Goddesses of antiquity. The single Deity and unified duotheistic Godhead models both tend to view the ancient Deities as facets or masks of an essential Divinity. The "Cunningham diamond" theory—so named in Pagan folklore because this theory is thought to have originated somehow with the work of Pagan author Scott Cunningham—is the belief in a single, great, many-faceted Deity who is ineffable, immense, and therefore incomprehensible to the human mind. The only way that humanity can relate to this is Deity is to filter the experience through relationships with the smaller and more comprehensible old Gods and Goddesses of antiquity. Metaphorically, the single immense Deity is likened to a diamond, and each of the ancient Deities is but one shining facet of that diamond. The Deity you choose to interact with is but one mask worn by the larger and more incomprehensible Deity.

The duotheistic, totalized Godhead model also assumes the

ineffability, immensity, and incomprehensibility of the Godhead, except that gender is regarded as such an essential phenomenon that a sharp distinction is maintained between the Deities. The Gods and Goddesses are emanations of the source Godhead, and are interacted with accordingly. All of the Goddesses worshipped by ancient peoples are masks worn by the one Great Goddess, and all of the Gods worshipped are masks worn by the Great God. In both models, to honor one Goddess of one culture is, in effect, to honor all Goddesses of all cultures because all Goddesses are the same singular Great Goddess. The same is thought to be true of the God when He is worshipped.

It is important to acknowledge that both of these models are polytheistic because they make a point of acknowledging and accommodating the old Gods and Goddesses in religious practice. As such, these models powerfully challenge the monotheist perspective which pervades mainstream culture. However, because both of these views emphasize an underlying unity and emanation from a single or totalized ultimate source, they have enough in common with certain basic assumptions underpinning monotheism that their challenge to the monotheist perspective is not too alarming, confusing, or alienating.

Yet it is inaccurate to equate this view of a multi-faceted Deity or a Godhead comprised of two multi-faceted Deities with the polytheism traditionally practiced by ancient peoples and contemporary non-Western, indigenous groups. It is true that the idea of Divine unity was a concern for the Egyptians, Greeks, Indians, and Babylonians to name a few, but as Egyptologist Jan Assmann explains, "[u]nity in this case does not mean the exclusive worship of one God, but the structure and coherence of the Divine world, which is not just an accumulation of Deities, but a structured whole, a pantheon" (Assmann: 2004)[19] While some ancient philosophers—notably the Neo-Platonists and Stoics of Greece to name only a few—have tended toward a monist view of Diety, their views were not shared by their polytheist predecessors, or even by the common people who were their contemporaries (Polymnia: 2001).[20] Therefore, it is useful here to identify the aforementioned beliefs that the Deities are simply archetypal or metaphoric masks of a larger Deity or totalized Godhead as comprising an "archetypal polytheism," rather than as polytheism per se.†

It would be likewise inaccurate to leave the impression that these two models of Deity, however prominent and pervasive they

† As a more detailed discussion of archetypal polytheism was given in the "Methods" section, the concept will not be further elaborated upon here.

may be, are the only ones present in contemporary Paganism. Truthfully, there are myriad views of Deity to be found within Paganism. According to Pagan theologian Christine Hoff Kramer, "[w]ithin Paganism are practitioners who reject even the vaguely indicated oneness of saying 'the Divine,' and others who are uncomfortable with the separateness and distinction implied by 'the Gods.'" She further explains that, "these two incompatible perspectives are linked by a theological middle ground where the majority of contemporary Pagans find themselves on a day-to-day basis" (Kraemer: 2012).[21] The middle ground, of course, is provided by the aforementioned orthopraxic nature of Paganism.

Recently, both Christians and atheists have joined this middle ground to partake in aspects of Pagan religious practice. The Christian contingent, usually called "Christo-Pagans" are those who still largely accept the monotheist Christian perspective regarding Deity, sin, and redemption, but who wish to explore mystery and ecstasy as forms of direct spiritual knowledge; connect to nature and the Divine feminine; and have a richer, more meaningful ritual practice than is presently available in conventional, patriarchal, protestant Christianity. Many of them do considerable research on the Gnostic traditions of early Christianity, and frame their discoveries within a Pagan ritual structure (Townsend: 2012)[22] Atheists who have adopted Pagan practices and concepts refer to themselves as "humanist Pagans." They remain firmly rooted in a scientific, rationalist epistemology which rejects the possible existence of an invisible spiritual world or Divine Beings. As such, they tend to parallel the atheist contours of the monotheist perspective in mainstream Western culture. However, they also recognize that religious ritual, appreciation of nature, and meditating upon mythic archetypes can be powerful aids to the development of one's psyche and the empowerment of one's "self."

As will be made clear through the narratives contained in this book, within Paganism there are also those who have founded their religious practice upon polytheism as they understand it to have been practiced in the ancient world. These people reify and venerate the Deities of antiquity. They acknowledge the existence of multiple, individual, Divine Beings, and their religious practice is geared towards building relationships with those Beings. Their practice comes closest to academic and social scientific conceptions of the term "polytheism." Gods, ancestors, nature spirits, angels, elementals, and other spiritual entities are among the "Holy Powers" that these polytheists venerate. It is believed that being in positive balance, or, "right relationship" with these Beings will bring spiritual wisdom, balance, fulfillment, good fortune, and deep purpose to one's life, family, community, and the whole planet. For these polytheists, the purpose of religion is about engaging in relationships with their "Holy Powers," and applying the benefits of those relationships to their daily, mundane lives. Some of these individuals strongly identify as Pagan, but others do not recognize themselves to be Pagan at all, preferring to simply call themselves "polytheist". Many of them belong to religious groups like the Ár nDraíocht Féin, The Troth, Hellenion, Religio Romana, The Kemetic Orthodox Temple, or Natib Qadish which are dedicated to reconstructing the religious practices of ancient peoples, beginning with the adoption of the ancients' indigenous, ancestral polytheism. There has been tremendous debate in the Pagan world as to whether these polytheists truly belong within the Pagan movement or whether their practices constitute unique religions that are separate from Paganism.‡ Given that the social and political biases created by the monotheist perspective affect all non-monotheists equally, many polytheists realize that they have much to gain socio-politically from a continued identification with Paganism as a social movement, and are willing to set their theological differences aside in the name of social parity and progress.

Despite the reluctance of academic Religious Studies and Theology departments to engage with a serious study of polytheistic religiosity, a small but devoted group of scholars has been working to bring contemporary Paganism into the realm of academic inquiry. These academics have challenged the scholarly environment, which has been inhospitable to the serious theological study of polytheistic religions. Pagan scholars Ronald Hutton, Helen Berger, Sabina Mogliocco, Charles Clifton, Jr., Margot Adler, and David Strmiska—to name only a few—have been invaluable in bringing Paganism to the attention of the academy. These scholars have been steadfast in their demand that Paganism be taken seriously as a religion. They have made it quite clear that Paganism has emerged in spite of the monotheist perspective, and that the rise of Paganism parallels important social developments that find unique expression in Pagan religions. Though they stop well short of reifying the old Goddesses and Gods, they reify and validate the religions that are reintroducing modern Westerners to those Deities. Especially important is the fact that beyond relying on previous scholarship and presenting their own academic theories about Paganism, several

---

‡ It is beyond the scope of this volume to recount the debate here. For more information about the controversy, consult the PaganSquare website, the Wild Hunt blog, and the Patheos Pagan forums. The individuals included in this ethnography represent a spectrum of opinion about the matter with some polytheists embracing a Pagan identity, others rejecting it because it does not really describe what they do, and many others whose views fall between these polar perspectives. Several of the respondents included in this book have personal blogs where they discuss the matter extensively, and readers are encouraged to seek them out.

scholars—particularly Mogliocco, Berger, and Adler—have made a point of foregrounding ethnographic research on the perspectives of everyday, ordinary, contemporary Westerners who practice these religions.

The last decade has also seen the rise of Pagan theology. This material differs significantly from the majority of books about Paganism that have been published. Prior to these theological endeavors, books about Paganism focused on practical knowledge. This is to say that all of the material was presented in such a way that the individual reading it could immediately put it to use in their own practice. While many of these books contain some discussion of the nature of Deity, the value of religious experience, and the purpose of religion, the Pagan reluctance to proscribe a particular belief system tends to keep those discussions short. The works of Pagan theology which have been published recently tend to be much more scholarly in nature, and the monotheist perspective of contemporary Western culture is much more directly challenged in these works. Given that Pagans themselves tend to view the philosophizing and theorizing about humanity's relationship with the Divine as an individual responsibility, and that they are disinclined to countenance theological orthodoxy, the emergence of Pagan theological works is a bit curious. If there can be no expectation that Pagans will feel it necessary to read these works, then who have these theological treatises been written for?

The "Introduction" to Pagan theologian Michael York's seminal work Pagan Theology, written in 2003, gives a very clear answer to this question. He explains that the purpose of his book "is to situate Paganism as a world religion, that is, as a legitimate spiritual perspective that already exists globally." He goes on to say that while "the numbers of those who adhere to Pagan religion may not be as numerically significant" as Christians, Muslims, and Jews, "their numbers are still impressive." [23] In his 2005 work on contemporary polytheism, World Full of Gods, Druid theologian John Michael Greer asserts that monotheism is not "the only view with something to contribute to conversations about religion and spirituality" because the idea of polytheism "has much more to offer today's discussions of religion, religious diversity, and the nature of sacred realities."[24] Christine Hoff Kraemer echoes similar sentiments in her 2013 book, Seeking the Mystery: An Introduction to Pagan Theologies. Kraemer's primary goal is to show that "despite a great diversity in beliefs and practices, there are recurring attitudes and behaviors that meaningfully unite contemporary Pagan traditions into a single religious movement (rather than a single religion)." She also hopes "to give non-Pagans a starting point from which to approach a religious movement that might otherwise look dizzyingly varied."[25] Having noted a distinct paucity of theological works in historically and traditionally polytheist, non-Western cultures, polytheist theologian Jordan Paper explains in his 2005 work, The Deities Are Many: A Polytheistic Theology, that:

> *There is no need of [theology] in polytheistic cultures, but there is a great misunderstanding of these cultures in Western monotheistic ones, for Western religions are based on the premise that polytheists are either inferior human beings or the most despicable of enemies. Monotheists historically have not defined themselves positively, but negatively, as not being polytheists. Hence, a sympatic rendering of the hermeneutics of polytheism may be of more value to a hopefully more tolerant contemporary Western civilization in gaining a non-pejorative understanding of non-Western traditions.*

These statements strongly suggest that much of the contemporary polytheistic theology to date has been written as much for the non-Pagan theology and religious studies scholars working from the near-Eastern monotheist perspective as for theologically-inclined Pagans. While York's statements might lead one to think that the purpose of this theology is to argue the legitimacy of this polytheistic Paganism, this is not actually the case. What York, Greer, Hoff, Paper, and the many, many other Pagan theologians have begun to realize is that when religious studies and theology scholars begin to seriously study polytheistic, Pagan religiosity, they will undoubtedly do so from the monotheist perspective that underpins their disciplines. Equally undoubtedly, they will misinterpret what they find by constructing a model of Paganism that is easily comprehensible from the monotheist perspective.

In other words, what the Jesuit missionaries did to Chinese and Native American religion, and what Victorian academics did to Buddhism and Hinduism, will undoubtedly be what modern theology and religious studies scholars do to Paganism unless Pagans themselves set the criteria for the discourse. Otherwise, the aspects of Paganism which most challenge the monotheist perspective will be effaced by scholars, and the religion thus constructed will bear little resemblance to anything Pagans actually practice. In writing their works, these contemporary Pagan theologians are creating an opportunity to define themselves before academics writing from a monotheist perspective do it for them. They are setting up the vocabulary, theoretical framework, and philosophical perspectives that they believe should provide the foundation for scholarly study of their religious traditions and, hopefully, avoiding the distortion that comes from the monotheist perspective.

It is quite clear that the serious study of Paganism has much to offer the disciplines of theology and religious studies. Christian theologian David Miller recognized this three decades ago with his seminal work <u>The New Polytheism</u>, an exploration of the psychological benefits of using old Gods and Goddesses as archetypes to inspire contemporary Christians (Miller: 1981).[26] A monistic, archetypal view of Deity is quite comprehensible from a monotheist perspective, and indeed has been explored in research on Hinduism and Buddhism that would compare interestingly with the multi-faceted Deity of Paganism. The totalized Godhead comprised of a polarized, gendered Pair which has been explored in scholarship on early Judaism and Gnostic Christianity would also provide an interesting comparative study with the Pagan God and Goddess. However, there is a concern that the biases present in the monotheist perspective could lead researchers to primarily study those Pagan traditions that focus on the multifaceted single Deity or duotheistic, totalized Godhead approaches to religion. The danger is that it is very easy for monotheists to interpret these forms of Paganism in ways that aren't accurately reflective of the religious perspectives held by actual Pagans. Enquiry into Paganism should include all the varieties that are found within it. This requires stepping out of the scholarly comfort zones created by the monotheist perspective. Studying the perspectives of Pagan polytheists who reify their Holy powers through devotion and ritual veneration would certainly accomplish that goal.

Studying those Pagans whose religious practice is profoundly polytheist, often to the point of being patterned on models from ancient polytheist cultures, will be particularly useful in deepening the interdisciplinarianism that needs to be taking place in theology and religious studies departments. As will be seen throughout this work, contemporary Western polytheists have developed a strikingly different understanding of the Divine nature of "Godhood," and as a result they have developed strikingly different expectations of their Gods and Goddesses. Their conceptions of belief and their expectations of faith are also very different than what is found in near-Eastern monotheism. Their ability to incorporate multiple Deities, ancestors, nature spirits, and other Divinities into a meaningful and coherent religious practice imparts an interesting lesson in how disparate religious philosophies such as monism, animism, pantheism, and polytheism can coherently coexist within one religious practice, a situation that is unheard of, and frankly impossible, within the confines of monotheism. The role of ritual and ceremony in the religious practices of these polytheists contrasts interestingly with the religious expression found in near-Eastern monotheism. This polytheism, practiced by modern Westerners, offers a radically different conception of the relationship between humanity and the Divine, and the role that religion plays in this relationship. Perhaps the most important contribution to be made by the study of contemporary Western Pagan polytheism is that an understanding of this religious sensibility will better prepare scholars in the disciplines of theology and religious studies to properly respect the polytheism of indigenous and non-Western, non-monotheistic peoples. Without this respect, there can be no real understanding, and without understanding, there can be no fruitful, mutually-enriching inter-cultural dialogue.

The Pagan and polytheist theologians soundly argue that it is almost impossible to understand polytheistic religions without understanding the religious practices that comprise them. Because of this insistence, theological scholarship focusing on polytheistic religions offers a unique opportunity to connect anthropological, sociological, and folkloric research with theological and comparative religious studies research. Given that the monotheist perspective has led to tremendous difficulty in creating interdisciplinary research that connects Theology and Religious Studies with the Social Sciences and other Humanities, these emerging polytheistic theologies can offer new methods and new theories that will bridge this divide. Especially important to this endeavor is the use of ethically-conducted, ethnographic fieldwork and personal interviews with practicing Pagans and polytheists. Ethnography also offers an opportunity to see how people with more than one theological perspective on a given aspect of religion nonetheless forge common practices and build religious community. Perhaps the most significant aspect of including ethnography in theological inquiry is that it affords normal, average people, who adhere to a particular religious tradition the opportunity to have their voices heard and their practices acknowledged as being equally legitimate to the views and practices of scholarly "official" theologians. It is through this work that one can see how a religion is truly "lived" by those who practice it, instead of only knowing how the religion is "preached."

One does wonder what Catholic theology might look like if the practices of Cajun traiteurs from Breaux Bridge, mestiza curanderas from Guadalajara, or crucifixion re-enactors from San Pedro Cutud were included alongside the works of St. Augustine of Hippo or St. Thomas Aquinas in the Roman Catholic canon. It would be less Eurocentric, but it would be more inclusive of the Catholic faith as it is actually lived by people around the world. At this point in time, polytheistic religions offer the only perspectives that demand the participation of ethnographers alongside scholars in developing complex theological understanding that well-reflect the religion of entire groups of people. In fact, the development of polytheist theology will increasingly depend on theologians' willingness to engage with both clergy and average, every day, "regular-Joe" polytheists when drawing parallels of experience and constructing intricate understandings of Divinity, humanity, and religion.

The collected narratives in this volume are meant to present examples of how contemporary Westerners are reclaiming polytheism as a religious practice. The narratives may indicate potential directions for further research; in no way should this volume be considered the final, comprehensive, discussion of contemporary Western polytheism. While the commonalities of practice, perspective, and experience are present across a large percentage of the respondents' accounts, there are those whose perspectives are decidedly different about a given issue. Some of these narratives have been included in this volume so as to be more representative of the entire range of respondents. The following overview will introduce statistical data about the respondents, trace the common philosophical threads that were found across the 120-respondent data pool, and then contrast those ideas with the corollaries found in the near-Eastern monotheism. The purpose of the overview is to familiarize readers coming from a monotheist perspective with the alternative philosophies they will be encountering. It is hoped that being familiar with the underlying theology will encourage readers not to dismiss the experiences and practices of the respondents out of hand on the basis of those practices seeming strange or threatening.

The following narratives chart the experiences of 24 very distinct contemporary Western polytheists. Even those who share practices and pantheons have unique perspectives on their Deities, their communities, and the way they live their lives. Quite often, these accounts are thought-provoking. Some accounts are short; others are very, very long. Some are very moving. A few are quite humorous. However, all of these narratives have been offered with love, integrity, and the respondents' sincere desire to honor their Holy Powers. Whether or not one accepts the invitation to reconsider their own convictions in light of these very different religious philosophies and practices, it will be difficult to avoid the conclusion that polytheism, as it is being practiced by contemporary Westerners, challenges many of the fundamental assumptions underpinning the monotheist perspective.

Chapter Notes

1. Sangkeun Kim, "Ricci's Translation Of the Divine Name Shangti and the Western Missionaries' Responses" in Strange Names Of God: The Missionary Translation Of The Divine Name And The Chinese Responses To Matteo Ricci's "Shangti" In Late Ming China, 1583-1644 (New York: P. Lang, 2004), 159. Hebert Allen Giles, Religions Of Ancient China (Cambridge: Cambridge University Press, 1905), 16-17.

2. Jordan D. Paper, The Deities Are Many: A Polytheistic Theology (Albany: State University Of New York Press, 2005), 111-12. Dan Jen Li, trans, China in Transition, 1517-1911, (New York: Van Nostrand Reinhold Company, 1969), 2. Kim, Strange Names of God, 247-257. Edward Butler, Essays on a Polytheistic Philosophy of Religion (New York: Phaidra Editions, 2012), 82.

3. Thomas, R. Murray, Manitou and God: North-American Indian Religions and Christian Culture (Westport, CT: Praeger, 2007), 35-36.

4. Paper, The Deities are Many, 108-109; Jordan D. Paper, Native North American Religious Traditions: Dancing For Life (Westport, CT: Praeger, 2007), 64-65. Vine Deloria, God is Red: A Native View of Religion, 3rd ed. (Golden, CO: Fulcrum Publishing, 2003), 77-96.

5. Donald S Lopez, Curators of the Buddha: The Study of Buddhism Under Colonialism (Chicago: University of Chicago Press, 1995), 8-20. Richard King, Orientalism and Religion: Post-Colonial Theory, India and "The Mystic East" (London: Routledge, 1999), 102-104.

6. Lopez, Curators of the Buddha, 19-20. King, Orientalism and Religion, 102-104.

7. Edward Butler, Essays on a Polytheistic Philosophy of Religion (New York: Phaidra Editions, 2012), x.

8. Brent Nongbri, Before Religion (Yale University Press, 2013).

9. Butler, Essays..., x.

10. Emile Faguet and Homer Gordon, Initiation into Philosophy (London Indo-European Publishing, 2010), 19.

11. Sabina Magliocco, Witching Culture: Folklore and Paganism in America (Philadelphia: University of Pennsylvania Press, 2004), 70.

12. Margot Adler, Drawing Down The Moon: Witches, Druids, Goddess-Worshippers, And Other Pagans In America (New York: Penguin Books, 2006), 64.

13. John Michael Greer, A World Full of Gods: An Inquiry into Polytheism (Tucson, AZ: ADF, 2005), 70-71.

14. Mogliocco, Witching Culture, 69-70.

26   Introduction

15. Adler, Drawing Down the Moon, 7-9.

16. Mogliocco, Witching Culture, 190.

17. Adler, Drawing Down The Moon, 24-39.

18. Helen A. Berger, A Community Of Witches Contemporary Paganism and Witchcraft in The United States (Columbia, SC: University Of South Carolina Press, 1999), 10-12.

19. Jan Assmann. "Monotheism and Polytheism" in Religions of the Ancient World: A Guide, ed. Sarah Iles Johnston (Cambridge, MA: Belknap/Harvard University Press, 2004), 17-32.

20. Athanassiadi, Polymnia, "Monotheism And Pagan Philosophy In Late Antiquity" in Pagan Monotheism In Late Antiquity (Oxford: Clarendon Press, 2001), 41-68. Edward Butler takes issue with the contemporary understanding of "Pagan monotheism" as it has been traced to the Stoics and Neo-Platonists. However, current scholarly thought seems to embrace the idea as pervasive and omni-present in Neo-Platonic monotheism.

21. Christine Hoff Kraemer, "Deity, Deities, and the Divine," Seeking the Mystery: An Introduction to Pagan Theologies (Englewood, CO: Patheos Press, 2012).

22. Mark Townsend, Jesus Through Pagan Eyes: Bridging NeoPagan Perspectives with a Progressive Vision of Christ (Woodbury, MN: Llewellyn Publications, 2012), 2-3.

23. Michael York, Pagan Theology: Paganism as World Religion (New York: NYU Press, 2005), 7.

24. Greer, A World Full of Gods, 1-2.

25. Kraemer, Seeking the Mystery, Chapter 1.

26. David Miller, The New Polytheism (Silver Spring, MD: Spring Publications, 1981).

Polytheism, Practice, Perspective:

Tracing the Contours of Polytheist Experience

Polytheism is more than useful, it is enjoyable. That is, polytheism has not just made my life more meaningful…it has made my life exhilarating. —*Jordan D. Paper, The Deities Are Many*

The following narratives demonstrate that there is a wide variety in practice and belief among contemporary Western polytheists. The attitudes and ideas these polytheists have about religion, Deity, faith, and the role of humanity in the proceedings are strikingly different from what are generally accepted and expected within our larger, monotheist-dominated culture. What is most striking about these accounts is that each of the respondents is very self-aware and self-reflexive about their beliefs and their practices. They make valid points. They raise uncomfortable questions. They offer alternative views of what religion should be. Only the most obtuse and egotistical of casual observers could possibly accuse them of being superstitious or ignorant.

It might be helpful to have a demographic snapshot of my project data to get an idea of the kind of people who participated. The Call for Interviews yielded 150 inquiries which resulted in 120 actual interviews. The average age of my respondents is 41. The gender breakdown is 70 women, 49 men, and one person who identifies as gender neutral/third gender, with seven of my respondents indicating that they are transgendered. The most common areas of employment are technology, healthcare, and the creative industries, and several are self-employed or business owners. 15% of my respondents either have attained or are in the process of completing postgraduate degrees. 9% of my respondents were from countries other than the United States.

Questions about political orientation, marital status, ethnic background, and sexual preference were not directly addressed in the questionnaires or the interview question lists; therefore solid statistical data about those things cannot be drawn from the existing 120-respondent data pool. However, many of the respondents did discuss the ways that their religious practices are related to and impacted by gender, politics, ethnic background, and family structure. LGBTQI experiences are discussed in about 12 of the 120 interviews. Four of the 120 respondents identified as politically conservative while discussing friction they have experienced in the larger Pagan community. Seven of my interviewees discussed how their ethnic backgrounds have impacted their personal religious practices and their experiences in the Pagan community. Three of the 120 respondents mentioned living in a polygamous, polyamorous, or other non-monogamous family grouping. It would be inappropriate to extrapolate statistical generalizations linking alternative lifestyles to polytheism based on these instances, due to the possibility that there may be other respondents who share these experiences or lifestyle features but did not mention them because no questions were directly asked about them. While it is not unheard of for contemporary Western polytheists to live alternative lifestyles, what can be surmised from the data pool is that these lifestyle choices are not necessarily linked to, nor do they necessarily tend to be a significant feature of, the respondents' polytheist religious practice. Of cases where respondents do live an alternative lifestyle but did not discuss it in the interview, it has been assumed that those choices are tangential rather than intrinsic to the respondent's religious practices as discussed in the interview. In other words, while there is every indication that polytheism affirms and supports alternative lifestyles, polytheism does not, in and of itself, constitute an "alternative" lifestyle choice.

Loss and Recovery Amidst the Disconnect

The religious practices of my respondents have much in common with the polytheism of ancient and indigenous peoples. However, it is not the finding of this study that the polytheism emerging in contemporary Western culture is identical with the polytheism of ancient and contemporary indigenous peoples. There are significant factors which differentiate it from those religious traditions. The first major difference is that this polytheism is emerging as a minority practice in contemporary Western culture, which is dominated by the monotheist perspective. Polytheism has historically formed the bedrock of a city's or tribe's well-being, but this emergent polytheism arises in opposition to the practices and beliefs of a larger, philosophically inhospitable culture. Whereas ancient and indigenous polytheism was a civil and state affair as well as a family and cultus one, contemporary polytheists often practice as solitary individuals, families, or small groups that convene periodically for the purpose for worship and religious ritual. The natural connections between civic welfare, community cohesion, and polytheist religiosity are not present in the larger society, nor are the shared beliefs about Deity, ancestral spirits, and the land which are foundational for large-scale civic celebrations.

Many of my respondents expressed a sense of sorrow and frustration because the traditions and techniques for connecting with the Deities, ancestors, and land spirits—collectively referred to by some as "the Holy Powers"—were destroyed by near-Eastern monotheism. Every single one of my respondents has done at least some degree of research into the religious practices of their Indo-European, African, and Indigenous American ancestors. Many have made headway in their attempts to piece together ancient rituals and esoteric practices. Groups such as Religio Romana, the Greek-based Hellenion, the Norse Troth organization, the Canaanite revivalist Natib Qadish group, the Egyptian-based Kemetic Orthodox Temple, and the Celtic-based Ár nDraíocht Féin Druid fellowship are committed to reconstructing as much of the ancient religions as they possibly can. In so doing, they are providing opportunity for people to worship the old Deities and venerate the spirits in a manner similar to that of ancient cultures. There is a willingness among several of my study's respondents to syncretize ritual practices from Asian, Indigenous American, and Afro-Caribbean religions. This syncretism is not driven by a desire to appropriate ethnic identity, but rather by the need to develop effective practices for certain kinds of rituals—especially shamanic and ancestor veneration rituals—because similar practices that were indigenous to a particular ancient Indo-European culture have been irreparably lost. What cannot be reconstructed must be recreated from whatever materials are available. Those who forge such syncretism are keenly aware that their need to syncretize is the result of their ancestors' ancient polytheist religions having been destroyed, and often experience at least some degree of philosophical unease at needing to borrow from other cultures.

Cultural appropriation is a significant issue for these emerging polytheisms. But practicing polytheists, such as the participants in this study who wish to connect deeply with their Holy Powers, are left with little choice but to borrow spiritual technology from the living traditions of others in order to do so. A significant difference between these polytheists and those who appropriate from living traditions, especially those in the New Age community, is that they generally do not claim to have the cultural authority, ritual expertise, or group membership that belongs to legitimate tradition-bearers within that living tradition. Rather, these polytheists recognize that they are borrowing methods and techniques to engender knowledge and connection which must be adapted to fit within the polytheists' own religious framework. A good analogy would be the difference between stealing a bicycle and pretending you own it, or borrowing a bicycle to learn how it's put together and then finding the parts and building your own. These contemporary Western polytheists aren't bicycle thieves; they just need help building bicycles to get them where they want to go.

The polytheists of my study highly value "personal gnosis," or personal interpretation and understanding of religious experience. Personal gnosis is highly valued as a valid means to gain spiritual knowledge. Yet because religious experience is distrusted, diminished, and dismissed by contemporary Western culture, these respondents are aware of the need to remain silent on the matter when dealing with anyone who isn't also polytheist. Those who engage in spirit possession or shamanic and ecstatic religious practices are fully aware that if they discussed these things openly, they might find themselves institutionalized. They know that when faced with these spiritual techniques, the reigning rationalist paradigm might prefer to electroshock or medicate these practitioners back into secular sanity rather than grant them any degree of legitimacy. These respondents' willingness to rely on personal gnosis without seeking external validation is just as related to Western culture's marginalization of their experiences as it is to their own privileging of individual interpretation of those experiences.

As a result of occupying a marginal space in the larger culture, the polytheists of my study have had to develop a sort of subtle double-consciousness. They acknowledge that the Gods, ancestors, and land spirits exist and are Holy Powers. Yet they are fully aware that when dealing with mainstream culture, they are up against the presumptions of near-Eastern monotheist religion on the one hand, and the hyper-rationalist, mechanistic, scientific assumptions of secularism on the other. My respondents boldly and faithfully practice their polytheist traditions. However, they are always aware that they may be called upon to explain, justify, or defend their position, and they have developed sophisticated philosophical arguments for that purpose.

Polytheists of the ancient world had no need to subject themselves and their practices to this constant self-analysis, or to cultivate a constant awareness of how they were seen in order to safely practice their religions. The current double-consciousness affects how contemporary polytheists network, the location and performance of their rituals, and the strategies they adopt for living an inconspicuously polytheist life. None of these concerns were an issue for ancient polytheists, and they only became issues for contemporary indigenous peoples because of colonization and near-Eastern monotheism's religious conquest. The polytheists of my study might look forward to the day when such double-consciousness isn't necessary, but until that time they maintain awareness that they are living in a Western contemporary society which is defined by the monotheist perspective, and they outwardly behave accordingly.

Perspectives on Divine Beings

The number of Deities worshipped is not the only difference between contemporary Westerners' polytheism and the monotheist perspective of mainstream culture. The nature of Deities, and the divinity of ancestors, nature spirits, and other entities are key considerations as well. These polytheists have a very different relationship to ontology and eschatology as theological concerns. Their relationship to sacred texts is quite different as well since, in the context of contemporary Western polytheism, mythology regains its power as sacred narrative; the interpretations of a given narrative rely on how much spiritual truth it has rather than whether it reports literal fact. In addition to the mythology, these polytheists invest significant amounts of time and energy into historical research to learn more about the cultural context from which those myths emerged. The role and character of religion in humanity's relationships with the Goddesses and Gods is also significantly different for these polytheists. Perhaps the most significant difference between these polytheists and the monotheist culture around them is their conception of faith and how it relates to their religious practice. What becomes obvious as contemporary Western polytheism is further explored is that its religious practices raise questions about the way that mainstream Western culture has naturalized its conception of God, nature, religion, scripture, and faith.

The fact that the polytheists in this study do not believe in or worship a singular, male God is perhaps the least important difference between them and monotheists. Some of the most important distinctions involve scale and scope. The monotheist idea of God is that He is a perfect, Universe-sized Creator, an ineffable, all-powerful, all-knowing, omnipresent and paternal Figure who has mapped out the fates of each person and can be prevailed upon to render Divine intervention into human affairs from time to time. Some polytheists think of their Gods as Universe-sized, but the majority of those in my study, around 87%, do not. They see the Gods as being large, mysterious, powerful, and simultaneously immediate and transcendent, but also somewhat human-scaled and possessed of very human-like personalities. They believe that the Deities are concerned about the well-being of humanity, and work actively to see that the planet and humanity return to a proper balance. However, they also believe that the Gods and Goddesses are busy, and aren't necessarily always present and constantly watching over their devotees as if they were toddlers incapable of taking care of themselves. These Deities are recognized as having character flaws, a fact that much of humanity's collected mythos attests to. Even so, the polytheists of my study acknowledge that the Gods and Goddesses are completely Divine despite their seeming flaws and limitations.

The disconnect between "perfection" and "divinity" is significant because much of the monotheist perspective is heavily invested in the sinful iniquity of man in relation to a perfect, judging God. He is also a wrathful and jealous God who seems to need humanity's love and obedience so much that He would destroy them for disobeying Him. Polytheists tend to think that the Deities don't actually need anything from humanity or depend upon humanity in any way. Further, the old Gods and Goddesses worshipped by these polytheists have definite—and differing—ideas about which behaviors are right or wrong. In the experience of my respondents, these Deities can and do evaluate the worth of a given human being according to that person's attitudes and deeds. But such judgment never begins with the notion that human beings are born debased and lacking. According to many in my study, the Gods can and do punish wrongdoing. They will also bring into a devotee's life whatever strife is necessary to bring the spiritual understanding and development that the devotee has been seeking. But the old Deities do not consider humanity to be profane and tainted by nature, and They do not hold humanity to an impossible standard of perfection. As a result, the drama of sin, sacrifice, and redemption do not have any place in the theology of these polytheists. The Divine grace of these Deities seems to be not in the mercy shown to the unworthy, but in Their willingness to care for humanity, and share their love and Divine knowledge to help humanity grow spiritually, despite that fact that They, being powerful Divinities, probably have better things to do, and can exist perfectly well without our love, worship, or even acknowledgment. A relationship with the Deities benefits humanity far more than it does the Goddesses and Gods.

While the Goddesses and Gods are immeasurably wise, They aren't necessarily omniscient. Most of the polytheists of my study do not believe that their Deities have the fate of the universe and each individual human being mapped out, or that They have absolute control over the events of material reality. Natural disasters, economic meltdowns, awful vehicle accidents, epidemics, and terminal illnesses are a handful of the many things that theGoddesses and Gods cannot control outright. However, even where They lack control, the Deities can still wield tremendous influence. To the minds of contemporary Western polytheists, the unseen worlds where the Gods reside are as real as the visible, material human world. From Their elevated vantage point in the unseen world, the Gods and Goddesses can see problems before they arise, and can give fair warning to Their devotees in the visible world. While the Gods cannot control the visible, material world to the point of stopping disasters altogether, They can move in the unseen world to mitigate disaster. The Deities help Their devotees escape the path of danger, minimize the damage suffered, and gather the resources to rebuild and regain strength.

Respondents consider the Deities' ability to influence material events rather than control them to be one of the most positive features of polytheism. The burning question of why bad things happen to good people, which causes tremendous strife in a monotheist context, does not exist for the people of my study. They do not have any expectation that an omnipotent, good God is willing to allow bad things to happen to them for mysterious reasons. For them, the Goddesses and Gods in all likelihood have no control whatsoever over some things, but They will wield Their influence to help Their devotees get through those disasters or other of life's vicissitudes. This is perhaps even more important than the fact that the Deities can also be called upon to wield this influence to positively influence one's personal relationships, career, and good fortune.

A significant feature of contemporary Western polytheism is that the sacred mysteries maintained by the Gods are accessible, if ineffable. The study was evenly divided between those who see the Gods as being primarily mysterious and ineffable, and those who see the Gods as understandable and easily relatable. In general, however, it was acknowledged that even the seemingly most accessible, down-to-earth Deity is the care-taker of tremendous sacred mystery regarding Their fields of specialty. It has been the respondents' experience that the Deities tend to specialize in limited areas of human experience, and accrue an enormous depth of specialist knowledge about those areas. Among the polytheists in this study, there is a sense that each realm of knowledge over which a Deity presides has spiritual as well as psychological and material aspects. The spiritual aspects of a particular knowledge field constitute a sacred mystery.

If there is a skill, a life experience, or a field of endeavor that a devotee wishes to learn more about, he or she will initiate a relationship with one or two Deities who hold that expertise. This is similar to what might happen when a Catholic begins a devotional practice for the patron saint of their profession or hobby. The difference is that whereas the Christian monotheist is simply looking for protection, guidance, and opportunity, the polytheist devotee is also seeking the mystery. The farmer who prays to Ceres isn't just asking for a healthy growth cycle and bountiful harvest. She is seeking to become skilled in understanding how to grow better crops and keep the land healthy. But she is also seeking to learn the Divine mystery of blood and soil—the relationship between human beings and the land which they farm that begins at birth, and ends with planting the dead corpse in the ground. In the experience of my respondents, the Deities who care-take these mysteries are happy to share this knowledge with devotees who demonstrate discipline, interest, reverence, and respect for the knowledge being sought. However, many polytheists maintain devotional relationships with Deities out of love and affinity that are not necessarily based on a deeper desire to seek the mystery.

The polytheists of my study experience very different relationship dynamics with their Deities than monotheists do with their God. Relationships with the Goddesses and Gods are fluid in contemporary Western polytheism, and personal agency plays a major role in building relationships with Them. According to many of my respondents, The Gods and Goddesses might approach human beings, but the humans can refuse the relationship without fear of wrathful reprisal. Or, someone may approach a Deity whose mystery they feel particularly drawn to, only to be held at a distance because the Deity does not, for whatever reason, have the same level of interest, at which point the person would seek out a Deity who seems more responsive and more interested in a relationship with him or her. My research has found that, much like the Chinese polytheists Jordan D. Paper studied, contemporary Western polytheists hold no assumption of a prima facie relationship with the Deities.[1] By and large, there is no belief that you must worship the Deities whenever They ask simply because you are a mere mortal, and They will destroy you if you reject Them. Moreover, in the experience of many respondents, every single Deity does not love the entirety of humanity. They are drawn to some people but not to others, and may possibly reject a potential devotee. Some of Them, for instance the Canaanite sea God Yamm, are reportedly pretty disinterested in humanity as a whole, but have been known to take interest in relationships with specific devotees.

This is radically different from the monotheist perspective, which believes that God loves each and every human being on the planet, and wishes nothing but the best for them, which He will gladly bring about if only they believe in Him. To reject that God is to court His vengeful wrath, and to remove one's self from the possibility of receiving that God's gracious blessings. Most of the polytheists of my study do not experience that difficulty. A few respondents view the Gods and Goddesses with such a significant degree of fear, awe, and wonder that they emphasize worship, praise, and obeying the Gods and Goddesses above all things. But this attitude is due less to the wrathfulness of the Deities than to the respondents' sense that the Deities are numinous, powerful, holy, and mysterious.

However, the majority of the polytheists in my study respect the power and seek the mystery, but are also likely to see the Deities are friends, allies, mentors, and protectors with whom devotional relationships can be built if one so desires. Yet, even among the latter respondents there is a tendency to engage their Deities with tremendous reverence and respect that goes beyond the degree expected of such relationships between two human beings. For example, one's attitude toward the Deity mentoring their poetry is very different than would be shown to a human poetry mentor.

Another interesting feature of the polytheism practiced by my study's respondents is their expectation of reciprocity in their relationship with the Gods. Within the monotheist perspective, believers reject all other spiritual allegiances, adhere to behavioral constrictions, and maintain philosophical orthodoxy. In exchange, their God bestows His favor upon the people, smiles upon their earthly lives, possibly spares them from disaster, and hopefully rewards them with a paradisiacal afterlife. To violate any of those things is to court His wrath, and absent one's self from His beneficence. The polytheists of my study have a very different sort of reciprocity with their Deities. This reciprocity is predicated upon the integrity and honest-dealing of both sides. They love their Deities, and understand that that their Deities love them also. They give devotion, and make offerings out of love and respect, and know that their Gods and Goddesses will offer blessings, guidance, and protection in return for this devotion. The love and devotion are not given with the demand that the Gods will do specific things in return. They are offered because the person sincerely wants to better know that Goddess or God, and feels that their life will be enriched through knowing that Deity beyond whatever material benefits might be accrued through the relationship.

What makes these relationships special is that personal agency and sincerity are the core; nobody HAS to do anything, but everybody WANTS to contribute to each others' well-being. This is what is meant by characterizing polytheists' relationships with the Goddesses and Gods as "reciprocal." For my respondents, the lack of a prima facie relationship with the Deities makes these elective devotional relationships that much more important because they are entered into of a devotee's free will, and depend on the good character, integrity, and honorableness of both sides. The same cannot always be said of near-Eastern monotheists' relationships with their God.

According to my research, there have occurred instances where a person may begin a more practical relationship with a particular Deity for the purposes of gaining help and intercession on a particular matter. A person may make certain offerings at the time of the petition, and then promise to make another offering, or complete an act of ritual service for that Deity after the petition has been granted. If that Deity accepts the offerings and devotion yet does not, for whatever reason, deliver what was petitioned for, the devotee is not required to deliver the ritual service or special offerings. Moreover, they are free to seek help elsewhere without facing the wrath of the Deity who was originally petitioned. On the other hand, if a devotee makes a promise of offerings or services to be given upon the granting of a petition, the promise must be kept, or the devotee rightly faces the wrath of the Deity who granted the petition. These instances are certainly more quid-pro-quo than the devotional relationships because exact boons have been asked, and exact payment has been specified. However, it was rare among the respondents of my study to petition a completely new God or Goddess with whom they'd had no prior experience. Usually petitions are made with Deities with whom the respondent has a prior existing relationship. Quid-pro-quo petitioning of a Deity is often practiced alongside, and in addition to an existing devotional relationship with that Deity, but does not necessarily constitute a religious practice in and of itself.

After the first few interviews, it became clear that I needed to ask future respondents whether or not they had active devotions to their ancestors and/or nature spirits. The necessity was revealed to me because all seven of the first interviewees I spoke with had talked about their ancestors and land spirits/nature spirits/spirits of place as being important to their religious practice, without having even been asked to do so. I became curious as to whether veneration of ancestors and land spirits might be a significant aspect of religious practice for contemporary polytheists, and included a question to address that. As it turns out, 107 of 120 respondents include veneration of their ancestors in their religious practice. 87 of 120 honor spirits of place or land and nature spirits. While the vast majority of the polytheists in my study acknowledge the existence of the Gods, several of them have chosen to rely on building relationships with their ancestors or land spirits rather than with the Deities.

The practice of ancestor veneration in contemporary Western polytheism is multi-layered. The primary explanation given for initiating ancestor and land veneration in one's religious practice is that they were worshipped by the ancients, who believed they had specific roles to play in the Divine order of things; if we wish to be in a correct, productive, relationship with the Divine order, and we wish for our ancient polytheist religious practices to be efficacious in creating these relationships, then we must include the land and the ancestors. This is not to say that they are an afterthought for contemporary polytheists—far from it. The general consensus seems to be that the Gods have Their knowledge and perspectives to share, but so do the land spirits and ancestors, and their wisdom is just as vital to the well-being of humanity and the preservation of this planet as that of the Deities.

The current popular interest in all things paranormal necessitates that a differentiation between "the dead" and "ancestors" be made now. Cultures that have practiced ancestor veneration*—and whose theologies and practices are being revived or adapted by the polytheists of my study—distinguish very sharply between "the dead" as being all those who have died in general, and "the ancestors," who are specific persons of merit (DeGruyter: 2011; Hsu: 1948; Ephrim-Donkor: 2010; Lau 2008). They recognize ancestors as being those individuals whose value to their descendants and communities was so strong in life that a continued relationship with these worthy individuals after they have died would be beneficial and advantageous to all. Ancestors are also those who one recognizes as having has a significant impact on their personal, individual growth as a human being.

It is important to note that cultures which venerate ancestors

---

*Ancestor veneration is common in Asia and Africa, and there are remnants of it in Latin America. Ancestors play an important role in Indigenous North American and Australian cultures, but not necessarily to a venerative extent. For more information, please consult the following works: Ancestors, ed. George Newell (Berlin: De Gruyter, 2011); Francis L. K. Hsu's Under the Ancestors' Shadow: Chinese Culture and Personality (New York: Columbia University Press, 1948); Anthony Ephrim-Donkor's African Religion Defined: A Systematic Study of Ancestor Worship among the Akan (Lanham, MD: University Press of America, 2010) 1-29, 111-133; and George F. Lau's "Ancestor Images in the Andes," in Handbook of South American Archaeology, eds. Helaine Silverman & William H. Isbell (New York: Springer, 2008), 1027-1047.

don't see the afterlife as some sort of paradisiacal, lock-down, gated community where your loved ones go to forget all about you, never to return. It's understood to be more like a paradisiacal village just over the mountain where your ancestors reside, and from which they may, of their own will, return occasionally to visit or in answer to requests by their descendents for aid or advice. It's also important to understand that such cultures do not relegate ancestors to the dustbin of history, finding them relevant only because they existed in "the past", and thus helped to create the present moment. Rather, the ancestors are recognized as being a very vital part of "the present" because they are capable of participating in community life even after having passed on. Their experiences of "the past," still have bearing and relevance to "the present." It is understood that when the wisdom and experience of the ancestors is combined with the actions and ideals of the present, a bountiful future is created for the descendants and the community.

In ancestor-venerating cultures, ancestors are sharply differentiated from "ghosts," "shades," or "earth-bound spirits," etc. who are trapped on this shore of the metaphysical divide, and have yet to cross beyond the veil. In fact, ancestor-venerating cultures often have very specific ritual practices performed before, during, and after death to ensure that the deceased does complete their crossing over from this life. They also have rituals designed to deal with those spirits who have not, for whatever reason, completed their crossing (Ephrim-Donkor: 2010; Rinpoche: 2002).[2] The troubled spirits of the deceased are either avoided by the living altogether, or aided in their difficult crossing by community members trained for this work. They are not petitioned for aid, advice, or intervention in the way that ancestors are. There are strains of Western esoteric practice, specifically the practice of necromancy, which may approach the spirits of the dead in this fashion (Williams: 2003). Those strains have little to no connection with the resurgence of ancestor veneration as practiced by the polytheists of my study.[†] The handful of respondents documented here who do have involvement with troubled spirits of the dead are engaged in helping them complete their crossings, and not venerating or petitioning them in a devotional fashion.

According to my respondents, there are many reasons to include ancestors in one's religious practice over and beyond the fact that the ancient peoples honored their ancestors. One common reason people give for honoring their ancestors is that doing so acknowledges that one belongs to a long line of people whose love, work, and sacrifice made their life possible. It is a way of maintaining a connection to the traditions, customs, and worldviews of those who came before. Venerating the ancestors is an acknowledgement that each individual human is born into a vast web of relationships that stretches across time as well as space, and it is a reminder that everything one does touches everyone else in that web.

Metaphysically speaking, the ancestors are seen as being energetically and psychologically "closer" to living humans than the Deities, and their concerns about the well-being of humanity are likewise "closer." Whereas the Deities are concerned with the well-being of the planet and humanity's continued existence upon it, the ancestors are recognized as being concerned specifically with their descendants' well-being. The Goddesses and Gods are concerned with the larger spheres of life and Divine mystery which concern all of humanity—balance, fertility, craft, medicine, magic, communication, agriculture, etc. Their perspectives and Their actions on humanity's behalf will reflect these concerns. On the other hand, one's ancestors are first and foremost concerned with the health and well-being of the family line and community, and are interested in making sure that the descendants are healthy, happy, and materially stable. It is believed that whereas the Gods and Goddesses are pretty busy attending Their spheres of influence and may not be constantly watching out for individual humans, the ancestors are always present, and always looking to protect the descendents and communities they left behind. Because the ancestors exist in the unseen world, it is also thought they are privy to information that humans are not. They can see impending danger or difficulty—from sources both seen and unseen—before it strikes, and can act much more quickly than the Gods to warn about, avert, or stop those dangers. The belief in the ancestors' ability to protect the living from danger and misfortune is consistent with similar beliefs found in the polytheistic cultures of Asia, Africa, and the Caribbean (Tan: 2011; Ephrim-Donkor: 2010; Murrell: 2009).[3]

Another reason that contemporary Western polytheists honor their ancestors is because they have perspective that we living people don't. It is easy to think, given the light-year leaps human technology has made, that the life experiences of even our grandparents no longer apply to the modern world. Yet the terrible economy, the rabid

[3] It is difficult to find contemporary scholarship on necromancy and the modern Western esoteric tradition, but there are several non-academic reference guides and encyclopedic works on the subject. Necromancy was first brought to prominence in the modern Western esoteric tradition by French occultist Alphonse Louis Constant, more popularly known as Eliphas Levi. In 1910, Levi's "Dogme de la Haute Magie" and "Ritual de la Haute Magie" were translated into English and published as Transcendental Magic, its Doctrine and Ritual in 1910 by Arthur Edward Waite. Levi's influence upon the Hermetic Order of the Golden Dawn was tremendous, and as a result, many of the esoteric organizations that broke off from the Golden Dawn were influenced by Levi's works about magic and necromancy. Thomas A. Williams, Eliphas Levi, Master of the Cabala, the Tarot and the Secret Doctrines (New York: Venture Press, 2003).

consumption of natural resources, a dwindling affordable food supply, and the alienation people feel when attempting to interact with their material, real-world communities may become serious issues within the next fifty years. Who better to guide us back toward bustling financial opportunity, thriftiness and craftiness, living off the land, and connecting to our local communities than the generations that survived the Great Depression? Wikipedia does not know what they know, and it has considerably less concern about whether or not you have food, clothing, or shelter. Even beyond that, the knowledge base of our ancestors goes back farther than a few generations, a fact that several of my respondents are counting on as they work to reconstruct and recreate ancient religious practices. According to them, if one can connect to the polytheist generations that thrived prior to the incursion of Christianity, those ancestors will be helpful in reinventing the rituals, techniques, and metaphysical knowledge that was destroyed by the conquerors. One of the frustrations that many of my respondents have is the need to adapt and improvise specific practices because the knowledge about those practices has been lost. This sense of the ancestors' ability to provide social and cultural knowledge is quite consistent with ancestral veneration as it has been practiced by cultures in Africa and Asia. In those oftentimes polytheistic cultures, the ancestors provide the cultural continuity, and enforce the social mores that hold the community or tribe together.

The polytheists of my study who engage in ancestor veneration do not limit themselves to blood relatives. It is felt that those who have profoundly influenced your life are your spiritual ancestors, and they also deserve to be honored. Adopted family members are honored, as are dear family friends, mentors, and teachers who played a significant role in one's life. Personal heroes are another group who are commonly venerated. One respondent has an ancestral veneration to famed New Orleans mambo Marie Laveau, whose magical power is less important to this devotee than Laveau's love of the city and generosity to its people in times of need and plague, despite their open distrust of her. Historical figures and notable people whose lives and deeds embody one's personal values or ideals are also often venerated. For example, another respondent honors as his spiritual ancestor the Emperor Julian, the last Pagan emperor of Rome. Members of a certain profession might venerate the founder of that profession, and have a group altar dedicated to others who belong to that profession. An actor I know has a shrine to Thespis, Shakespeare, and Edmund Keane. A professional soldier I've spoken with has a shrine to honor the military dead and war veterans. Some whose practice emphasizes ancestor veneration might adopt a marginalized group, and honor them as ancestors. One of my transgendered colleagues has an altar for the transgendered dead, with special emphasis on those who were victims of hate crimes.

This isn't to say that ancestor veneration is without problems for contemporary Western polytheists. Some of those I interviewed were unfortunate enough to have come from abusive homes. According to them, their more recent ancestors are emotionally toxic, and either unable or unwilling to help. Those respondents who braved this stuation to begin a practice of ancestor veneration have had to undertake rituals of containment or even banishment to protect themselves from those ancestors, and then go further back in the family tree to build relationships with ancestors who aren't so terribly damaged.

Respondents from multi-ethnic bloodlines reported a different kind of difficulty: choosing sides. How does one who is descended from both African slaves and Caucasian masters undertake ancestor veneration when a significant portion of the line thrived off of the exploitation, dehumanization, and abuse of the others in their line? Those of mixed Caucasian and Indigenous American descent are faced with a similar difficulty: how does one venerate a group of ancestors whose colonization and expansion caused mass atrocity and genocide for another group of their ancestors? Can these groups become reconciled, and the massive spiritual wounds be healed? If so, how can it be done, and what is the descendant's role in the process? If not, how does one choose whom to honor? These are questions that indigenous peoples and the ancients did not have to ask, but which the historical and social forces that forged contemporary Western culture have demanded be answered. It will be interesting to see what strategies contemporary ancestor venerators come up with to address these issues, and also to see if those strategies can be adapted to address the ethnic and cultural strife that still affects every human being living in Western society.

The practice of ancestor veneration points to a key difference between contemporary Western polytheists and the monotheist perspective generally held by Western society. near-Eastern monotheism is very clear in its assertion that that the human soul, once it has passed away from material existence, completely abandons the material world for an afterlife that takes place elsewhere as eternal torment or reward. Love, concern, and family allegiance end upon death when the weary soul departs this world, never to look back. That popular culture embraces this sentiment is shown by personal experience narratives about departed relatives who appear to family and friends immediately after they die but before they pass into the next life, never to be heard from again.

The polytheists of my study indicated a wide range of beliefs about the afterlife, with belief in some sort of delayed reincarnation taking place after one's immediate descendants have passed away being the most commonly held. However, it is what takes place during that interim delay between death and rebirth that is particularly significant for ancestor-venerators. According to them, the dead merely cross into another phase of existence, moving from the visible world into the invisible world, which exists concurrently with the material reality humanity lives in. Most of my respondents believe that there are realms in the invisible world where the dead might go to rest which are ordinarily inaccessible to living humans, but also that the dead may freely cross to and from these death realms and do so frequently to watch over and aid their descendants. It is these respondents' view that love and family relationships continue to be powerful ties even after death. They feel that ancestors, when engaged regularly through ritual veneration, can and should continue to be a vital part of a family's and community's well-being. For some respondents, there is a sene that a given ancestor may forestall or even forego reincarnation or peaceful retirement in the afterlife to serve as a sort of guide or guardian for future generations of the family line.

In addition to Deities and ancestors, the polytheists interviewed in this study venerate a third category of beings who are tied to the places in which we live. Nature spirits, kami, tulu bhuta, elementals, land spirits, genii locii…the names for these spirits of place are as varied as the polytheists who honor them. Truthfully, the conception of these spirits is somewhat vague and indeterminate. One of my respondents has a mental image of them as androgynous, 30-foot tall, half-human, half-dog beings. For a few of my respondents, this category is comprised of the four classic Pagan elements of Earth, Air, Fire, and Water, which are in turn symbolized by the mythical beings traditionally associated with those elements: gnomes, sylphs, salamanders, and undines (Ellis: 2004).[4] Many of my respondents recognize these beings as the plant and animal spirits referred to as manitou by several Indigenous American tribes. Others see them as being similar to the Roman lares, or the fairies of European legend. The majority of respondents, however, identify them simply as spirits of place, and leave it at that. Regardless of what is thought to be the specific origin or nature of these spirits, the consensus is that these are the spirits who belong to a specific location. They have come to reside, through whatever means, in a given place, and they have significant influence over the well-being of others who share that place. These places can be cellars, kitchens, attics, urban neighborhoods, wooded hollows, vast beaches, desert valleys, and Iowa cornfields.

Unlike the abstract and immense "Gaia" being honored in other contemporary Pagan religions, these spirits are decidedly local. They are regarded as having a strong connection to the abstract planetary "Gaia" being, but are important in and of themselves because they care-take the material well-being of a particular place. Sick and unhappy spirits of place, it is believed, might bring sickness and strife to your garden, your family home, your workplace, and your neighborhood. Happy, healthy spirits bring those things and prosperity to your family, workplace and community.

Offerings made to the spirits of place seem to be less acts of veneration, and more acts of neighborly hospitality and gratitude. The respondents of my study tended to see these spirits as beings who should be acknowledged because we, as humans, share their space, and depend indirectly upon them for our survival. There is nothing humans eat, utilize, or otherwise consume that does not originate from the ground. Electricity is generated primarily through the mechanical exploitation of radioactive elements, churning rivers, and burned petroleum. Without servers built of raw materials taken from the earth to host it, and devices made from those same raw materials to access it, the internet would not exist. The material bounty that provides for humanity is yielded forth from the ground but we rarely, if ever, stop to consider this fact. For the polytheists of my study, honoring the spirits of place is an acknowledgement of how much humanity really depends upon the land on which they live and the ecological health of their immediate environment. It is a way to recognize the continued generosity of the spirits of place in caring for the land that sustains our material well-being. Venerating the spirits of place is acknowledgement that humanity is but one part of a vast spiritual ecosystem, and that on every single acre of this earth, we humans share space with other beings, both seen and unseen, who impact the way that we live in that place.

For polytheists who embrace an animist understanding of nature, venerating spirits of place blends into taking care of the wild animals that live in the area. Bird feeders, salt licks, fruit and vegetables, and repurposed pet food are all some of the things that might be put forth as offerings for the wild animals of an area to enjoy. This is done in acknowledgement that human beings are not the only important species on the earth, and that other living creatures have as much right to thrive on this planet as we do. These respondents make offerings in remembrance of the fact that the living creatures we share space with are not necessarily lesser or lower than human beings simply because they are animals. They, like the other spirits of place, are our neighbors and have their own contributions to make to the well-being of our homes and neighborhoods, as well as to the earth itself.

Whereas the veneration of multiple Deities challenges near-Eastern monotheism's view of "God," and veneration of the ancestors challenges its view of death and the afterlife, the veneration of land and its spirits challenges the presumption of man's "God-given" dominion over all of nature. The polytheists who venerate spirits of place readily recognize the relationship between the pollution of the physical landscape and degradation of the spirits who exist on that land. They reject the monotheist presumption that man is inherently superior to other forms of life, and entitled to do as he wishes with the land and its resources. They reject the belief that man has the right to destroy animals' natural habitats, thus bringing them to extinction, simply because those beings and their homes are in the way of commercial progress and economic gain.

In the view of polytheists who honor spirits of place, all beings have both a physical and spiritual nature, and all life is sacred: clover, cobras and cockroaches are but three of the more than 8 million plant and animal species on this planet that have legitimate reasons for existence which are totally unrelated to the uses humanity might have for them. From that perspective, it is pretty easy to recognize that the only species impressed with cars, I-pads, Prada, the internet, and Blu-ray technology is the same species which is ruining the planet for everyone else. Venerating spirits of place is acknowledging that the planet and its beings could continue to function perfectly well without the presence of humanity, and that it is the collective graciousness of the land and its beings that gives humanity life's necessities. Deities such as Demeter and Azacca have much to teach and give, but even They could not coax grain from demoralized, polluted land.

Perspectives on Theology

The religious practices of these polytheists have a very complex and multi-faceted relationship with mythology. Mythology is simultaneously viewed as sacred narrative, allegory, and historical document. They do not see it as gospel fact. The polytheists I interviewed almost never undertake the study of the myths without also studying the history and the culture of the people who first worshipped those Deities. It is thought that to properly understand the power of a given sacred narrative, one should understand the context from which it comes. The myths are historical documents insofar as they record culturally specific attitudes toward the Gods and Goddesses and the spheres of life They govern. Respondents were uniformly clear in their explanations that myths can convey spiritual truth even while they defy literal fact. None of the respondents claims that the myths are literally true, but most of them believe that these sacred narratives have tremendous value for spiritual growth. Several feel that myths can be very helpful with engaging the Deities and Their mysteries. For example, many of the respondents tend to regard origin myths as metaphoric and symbolic narratives that demonstrate fundamental principles and values, rather than as literal accounts of the universe coming into being.

These polytheists do not experience the same level of cognitive dissonance suffered by near-Eastern monotheists when contemplating recent scientific discoveries in the context of accounts given in their sacred texts. Explanations about the explosive origin of the universe, the gradual development of the Earth from mere space rocks and gravity, and the millions-of-years-long evolution of amoebas into human beings don't conflict with these polytheists' ontologies because their understanding is not rooted in a literal understanding of a sacred text, but rather in their personal experiences. In the view of many respondents, the material world seems to have an invisible, spiritual component. Therefore, it is entirely possible that that the unseen world of spirits developed alongside the visible material world as it was pulled together from star stuff and dark matter. Regardless, the polytheists of my study are not preoccupied with ontology because they are focused on connecting to their Holy Powers in the here-and-now; myth is simply a means to help build that connection.

On a basic level, the myths contain information about the preferences, personalities, attributions, and areas of influence related to the Goddesses and Gods. This information is very useful if one seeks to build a relationship with a particular Deity by extending offerings and hospitality to Him or Her. The high value placed on personal gnosis creates an environment where personal interpretation of the myths is a significant part of one's spiritual development. Respondents recognize that the myths have symbolic, metaphoric, and mystic levels, the pondering of which engenders spiritual growth and understanding of the Deities and Their mysteries. Several of the polytheists I interviewed recognize that many myths contain the seed of sacred mystery, and celebrate those myths in a ritual setting approximate to what might have been found in the sacred cults of antiquity. It was not uncommon for respondents to indicate that their experience of particular Deities did not match up well with the mythology attributed to Them. In such cases, the respondents rely upon their personal gnosis to guide their interactions' with that Deity. In fact, it is very common among the respondents of my study to privilege their personal gnosis over recorded mythology when building a relationship with their Deities. For example, one respondent said that upon encountering a Deity for the first time, she regularly receives an alternate perspective on, or retelling of, that Deity's most prominent myth, and that she uses that retelling to guide her engagement with that Deity.

Not everyone has recourse to myth, however. Historically, the Goddesses and Gods of ancient Rome weren't really known for Their myths, but rather for the role They played in human affairs. The myths which came to be attributed to the Roman pantheon were translated from Their Hellenic counterparts and superimposed upon Them (Harris & Platzner: 1997).[5] With few exceptions, the syncretic Deities celebrated in Roman Britain and Hellenic Egypt do not have myths associated with Them, either. Those who venerate "minor" Deities of more well-known pantheons rarely have mythology to draw from. In cases where mythology is scarce, the devotee will undertake even more historical research to see where and how the Deity was worshipped and identify epithets associated with that Deity. This research is then combined with the personal gnosis gained through engagement with the Deity or Deities in question. Generally speaking, the less extant the mythology, the more the devotee will have to research and work to build the relationship.

The flexibility with which these polytheists view and interpret myth is radically different from the way that near-Eastern monotheism views its sacred texts. The level of personal involvement with the interpretation of these myths and the lack of orthodoxy regarding the understanding of them has no corollary in near-Eastern monotheistic religions. There is good reason that those religions are referred to as "religions of the book" (Clark: 2011.)[6] It is true that the spread of liberalism has created small pockets of tolerance in near-Eastern monotheism. However, the debate still rages over exactly how much should be regarded as historical fact, and how much should be regarded as metaphoric religious narrative. While it has become untenable to believe that their God created the world in one week's time, they have yet held onto the conviction that their God is still somehow directly responsible for creating the universe, this planet, and our species. Although myriad alternative interpretations of those events have cropped up, the downfall of mankind into sinfulness in the Garden of Eden is still largely believed to have occurred as written. Some have begun to wonder if perhaps Mosaic law might best regarded as a handbook for surviving the Bronze age, but many still believe it is God's direct proscriptions to His chosen people. Jesus of Nazareth's historical existence is hotly contested, but the events of His life, sin-cleansing self-sacrifice, and resurrection are still believed by Christians to have taken place. Even moderate, modern, Westernized Muslims still regard the Koran to be the holy words of Allah as delivered unto to his prophet, Mohammad. The scriptures are inextricably linked to historical fact in the minds of near-Eastern monotheists. The relationship between belief and history is fundamental in these religions. In essence, they are utterly dependent upon a particular ontology in order to function. Although these three religions differ on the plot particulars, the near-Eastern monotheism underpinning all of them relies on a carefully crafted understanding of history as their God's unfolding plan, which has been recorded for posterity in the religion's sacred texts.

The reason that near-Eastern monotheism insists upon an ontology proceeding from the actions of a singular, male creator-God who has specific demands of His worshippers is because of the terrifying eschatology they also embrace. According to near-Eastern monotheist eschatology, the loving, paternal creator-God has decreed that at some future point, He will turn Destroyer. He will finally eliminate the sinfulness of mankind by destroying the earth and everyone in it save for those who faithfully follow His decrees, or in the case of Christianity, Christ's decrees. Terror of the wrath of their God is what motivates near-Eastern monotheism to embrace a particular version of history. The fervent recourse to the texts which record that history is made to ensure that every action and attitude called for by their God—or in the case of Christians by their Jesus—is wholeheartedly performed to the best of the believers' ability.

As a result, these religions are very concerned with certifying their ontological and eschatological claims: hence the birth of monotheist theology. The process of certifying these claims involves theological exegesis of the texts held sacred by the respective religions. This demand for written authority is quite pronounced in near-Eastern monotheism because it is much easier to assert certainty about an issue when one can appeal to written evidence concerning it. (This is also the reason that oral tradition, a mainstay of indigenous and polytheist religions, is so under-valued in theological exegesis.) The flexibility of interpreting such sacred texts, however, is limited by the content of those texts. Interpretations which rely on too much outside input, and stray too far beyond the accepted understanding of the content and ideas presented in those core texts will often be rejected and dismissed at best, or demonized as heresy at worst. This process of interpretation and certification has as its end result the creation of orthodoxy. Orthodox belief in the truth of a particular historical narrative is the cornerstone of near-Eastern monotheism. Because modern monotheists were not present for the portentous events of sin and grace which are thought to have shaped the course of history thousands of years before they were born, they have no choice but to believe without evidence that the sacred texts are truth if they are to avoid the dreadful wrath of their God. Near-Eastern monotheism's concept of faith is defined by this belief in past events (without direct experience or hard evidence) which in turn guides present behavior which should be undertaken to avoid the fallout from a prophesied future cataclysm.

The monotheist perspective governing Western culture, which proceeds from near-Eastern monotheism, is also rooted in a demand for orthodoxy as based on written authority. Those in monotheist cultures who reject Deity altogether often rely on well-documented scientific discoveries and the philosophical writings of figures such as Nietzsche, Darwin, and Dawkins, et al. to articulate their position. (In a monotheist culture, it would seem, even atheism is a religion of the book.) They, too, are intensely preoccupied with ontology. For these unbelievers, it is vitally important that they experiment, explore, and scour scientific data to decipher the origin of humanity, the planet, and the cosmos. Only in so doing can an alternative history of the universe be written: one that demonstrates how unnecessary the figure of the Supreme Being really is. It is believed that when one dispenses with the Supreme Being, humanity can finally be free of His dreadful eschatology, and religion becomes utterly unnecessary. Humanity will finally be free to fulfill its intellectual potential, thereby reaching the pinnacle of human development, one where science and technology are embraced as the greatest of human achievements.

Yet there doesn't seem to be much thought about the decline that necessarily follows a pinnacle achievement. Little consideration has been given to the resources that must be consumed to fuel that innovation. The possibly disastrous consequences of humanity's exporting their wastefulness, disrespect for life, and feverish consumption of natural resources while colonizing other planets just aren't worth pondering. The absurdity (and near-perversity) of proclaiming a pro-human agenda and siphoning billions into projects like the Large Hardon Collider and free internet access while at least 50% of the world has no electricity infrastructure, sanitation, or plentiful food does not occur to them. Honestly, the ordinary events of secular society don't exactly justify the optimism and faith that non-believers have in humanity's capacity for developing moral and intellectual excellence unassisted by religion. In the end, there is no more proof that a Godless society will be a better, brighter one than there is that a Supreme Being created the cosmos, the earth, and humanity. The unbelievers of a monotheist culture seem to exhibit utopian tendencies regarding their Godless society; perhaps they rely as much on this optimistic futurist narrative as near-Eastern monotheism relies on its tragic historical one. And they do so in a decidedly monotheist fashion: through recourse to textual authority instead of direct personal experience. Ironically, direct experience likely played a role in unbelievers' rejection of Deity, and if honestly appealed to, that same direct experience would at the very least disabuse them of any unwarranted optimism.

Near-Eastern monotheism and its commensurate atheism share a lack of recourse to the kind of immediate, lived experience which underscores the religious practices of the polytheists in my study. The monotheists see religion as a means whereby God is appeased, and faith is affirmed. Personal relationships with God are undertaken in the interest of a spiritual growth and personal purification that will ultimately serve to shield them from His dreadful eschatology. Unbelievers in this monotheist culture seem to view religion as a pernicious form of social control which serves to impede intellectual development and human achievement.

Ontology and eschatology[$$] do not play a significant role in the religious beliefs and practices of this study's respondents. More than anything, however, it is their direct personal experiences of the Holy Powers that guide their religious endeavors. The polytheists I interviewed do not engage in religious practice in order to affirm their faith in historical narratives or to avoid apocalyptic consequences. For most of them, the point of religious practice is to connect with the Deities, ancestors, and land because these relationships enrich their lives, and help them make the world a better place. The polytheism of my respondents strikes a healthy balance between devotion and self-interest.

For these respondents, connection with the Holy Powers is a potent aid to engendering their spiritual growth and personal development. The rituals of veneration and connection provide an opportunity for devotees to extend hospitality to their Goddesses and Gods, who in turn grace the devotee with Their presence and blessings. Many respondents report feeling a sense of joy and pride, and strongly sense that their offerings and other acts of devotion are

[$$] This observation that contemporary Western polytheism does not rely on dynamic ontological and eschatological tensions which underpin near-Eastern monotheism echoes a similar conclusion reached about indigenous American religion Vine DeLoria, Jr. in chapters 5-8 of God is Red.

sincerely appreciated. They also indicate feeling a sense of security in knowing that they are deeply connected to the powerful forces of both the visible and invisible worlds. The myths of their Deities, and the historical records describing the worship of those Deities, are not approached as sacrosanct ontological testaments proving the existence of those Deities, but as points of departure for journeys of discovery to better know and understand those Deities...and through those relationships, to better understand themselves and the world around them.

Perspectives on Religious Practice

The orthopraxic nature of polytheist religions has been discussed throughout this work, but a general description of the range of polytheist practice has only been touched upon. Each of my study's respondents gave a description of the practices they keep in observance of their religion, and these descriptions are included in the narratives. Some of the practices are group-oriented social affairs, but most of the practices they described are kept individually, or within a small family context. Some of the rituals are quite elaborate, but the majority of the rituals are smaller and more intimate. Generally speaking, group rituals fall into two categories: seasonal celebrations and veneration of the Holy Powers. Some groups combine these two types of rituals for the eight major holidays of contemporary Paganism (Mogliocco: 2004).[7] The seasonal celebration rituals observed by the respondents tended to involve a Deity or set of Deities, but the purpose of the rituals seems primarily to be the bonding of the group members to each other and their Goddesses and Gods through shared ritual celebration.

The Deity veneration rituals are celebratory events wherein a Deity or set of Deities is ritually honored by a group of devotees. An altar will be built and decorated with items and images associated with that Deity. The Deity will be formally invited and welcomed to the gathering as a guest of honor. Food, drink, gifts, songs, dances, music, poetry, and praise are among the most common offerings that will be made to the Deity.[‡] Devotees will formally give gratitude for blessings which the Deity has bestowed. During these rituals, some groups will petition the Deity for healing, knowledge, aid, or other blessings. Occasionally, vows of service and requests for patronage will be made.

[‡]Two of my respondents, both of whom honor Heathen and Afro-Caribbean traditions, practice ritual animal sacrifice during Deity veneration rituals. Animal sacrifice might also be given during an ancestor veneration ritual. The practice of animal sacrifice is well-documented historically in ancient Norse and contemporary Caribbean cultures, and it is only fair to recognize that sacrifice has always been an important part of veneration in those cultures. However, the majority of my respondents do not perform animal sacrifice, nor would they feel comfortable participating in a ritual with those who do.

If the group has trained practitioners of spirit possession, or incorporates African Traditional Religions such as Vodou, Candomble, or Lukumi[§] (Lopez, 2004)[8] into their practice, a priest or priestess might "horse," or, become possessed by, the Deity who is being honored. The Deity will then interact with Their devotees. The purpose of such rituals is undoubtedly to venerate the Deity, and strengthen the devotees' bonds to that Goddess or God, rather than create group cohesion. Yet these rituals generate a secondary effect of bonding the devotees together through the sharing of profound spiritual experience. Imagine being present for a ritual dedicated to the Goddess Asherah…how could anyone else who was not present truly appreciate the depth of your experience, especially if that experience involved Deity possession so that everyone could interact with Her? Those who have attended Deity veneration rituals report having profoundly moving experiences with powerful emotion and deep spiritual connection, regardless of whether or not spirit possession occurs. Many also report the difficulty they have in explaining the experience of a veneration ritual and the feelings engendered thereby to anyone who has not experienced one.

Veneration of the ancestors and land spirits seems to be a definite shared feature of the polytheist practice of my respondents, but collective ritual veneration of these two groups is less well-defined. Veneration rituals held for the ancestors are very similar to those held for the Goddesses and Gods. Food, drink, music, dance, and song are given to the ancestors, and gratitude is given. Ancestors are given gratitude because of the work they do in the invisible world to take care of their descendants and the community. Descendants also give gratitude for the personal sacrifices ancestors have made in their lives, and for the love and service they gave while they were alive which helped their loved ones to flourish. Ancestors who were the victims of injustice in life are mourned, and their help and guidance may be sought to help devotees currently working to correct social injustice. Because ancestor veneration rituals are honoring literally thousands of people, it is less likely that spirit possession will be sought by those facilitating the ritual, but it has occurred on occasion. Large group veneration rituals for the land/nature/elemental spirits are considerably less defined; in fact, I have yet to attend any of them. The specifics of such rituals are open to speculation, but it is likely that such rituals will emerge as distinct practices at some point in the future.

Some of my respondents also maintain an esoteric magical

[§] "Lukumi," is another name for "Santeria.' The term comes from Ulkama, which is the name of a Yoruban kingdom from which the first practitioners' ancestors came.

practice in addition to their devotional religious practice. The majority of respondents do not seem to consider their magic to be a part of their religious devotion, but those respondents who belong to esoteric groups and Craft-based traditions very much consider their magic to be integral to their religion. Because esoteric magical practices are veiled in reverent secrecy and each group is very particular as to its traditional practices, it would be inappropriate to recount details of those practices here. Therefore, no attempt will be made here to describe the esoteric magical rituals and practices of those participants in this study who keep them.

The bulk of the ritual practices described by my study's respondents are smaller and more personal, and they tend to be devotional in nature. Shrines to the Deities, ancestors, and land spirits are built and maintained in the devotee's home and yard areas, and occasionally in their workplaces. Offerings of food, drink, or incense will be given, usually on a daily or weekly timetable. It is common for the respondents to undertake acts of service in honor of their Holy Powers, or in recognition for blessings received. For example, one of my respondents dedicated his undergraduate studies to the Goddess Athena. Another offers her professional writing as a devotion to Bragi, the Norse God of poetry. One respondent maintains a small cairn for the Goddess Diana in gratitude for her help with his ailing dog. He has built similar cairns for other Deities and spirits he honors in the places he travels to, and then geotags them so that others who wish to give honor at those shrines may do so. By far the most frequent acts of ritual are prayer and devotional meditation. Prayer for these polytheists seems to be similar to prayer offered in a monotheist context. Help, understanding, and opportunity are sought through prayers to the Deities, ancestors, and land spirits, but very often, devotees will also offer elaborate, poetic prayers of thanksgiving and praise. Many respondents feel that the most important thing they can do is devote time to meditating in front of the shrines, thus connecting to their Holy Powers. The rituals discussed here and in the narratives are only a small sample of the most common practices maintained by the polytheists of my study. By no means should these examples be considered as wholly representative of the vast array of sophisticated religious practices to be found among contemporary Western polytheists.

Faith turned out to be a hotly contested concept among the polytheists of my study. Many respondents equated faith with unsubstantiated belief. Some feel that without their faith that the Gods exist, they would be unwilling to engage the Gods, and thus not have a functional polytheist practice. Others feel that their religious practice has given them certainty that the Deities exist, thereby erasing the lack of substantiation that characterizes faith-as-belief; because of this, they feel that faith plays no role in their religious lives. Still others denied the relevance of faith altogether because they believe that it is practice, rather than belief, that builds a relationship with their Holy Powers.

In looking over these viewpoints, about the only thing that can be said for certain is that polytheist religiosity does not depend upon faith in the way that near-Eastern monotheism does. As has been discussed, "faith," in that monotheist context, is the unsubstantiated belief that: God exists, that history occurred as written, that the future will also occur as written, and that by following the ancient decrees of God—or in the case of Christians, Christ—one can avoid the terrible fate that their Creator/Destroyer God will bring to the planet in the future. The mental action required by near-Eastern monotheist faith is enormous and laborious. One cannot simply believe that God exists; one must also accept an unproven chain of causality and destiny, and then conform to a set of proscriptions to mitigate the dangers posed by that unsubstantiated chain. In comparison, the mental action of belief among the contemporary Western polytheists of my study is much simpler and clearer. One simply suspends their disbelief and undertakes ritual practices to engage with The Deities and build reciprocal relationships with Them. In the process of engagement, one experiences sufficient enjoyment, enlightenment, support, and love that they continue to engage. Or one experiences nothing, and then tries again with other Beings until they finally experience the response they have been seeking. These experiences themselves justify any belief that the polytheists come to hold about the existence of the Deities, ancestors, and land spirits.

The basis of faith, in a polytheist context, is not necessarily the mental action of belief, but instead is the practical action of reverent devotional engagement. Faith is not felt; rather, it is kept. Whether or not the respondents agreed upon a definition of faith or the relevance of faith to their religious practice, 104 of my respondents indicated through their interviews that belief alone is insufficient without practical engagement, even if the only engagement one makes is regular prayers of petition, gratitude, and praise to the Holy Powers. These contemporary Westerners do not simply believe in the Gods, ancestors, and nature spirits; they actively honor Them through practices of ritual engagement which are understood to be reciprocal in nature.

Although there are many other interesting aspects of

polytheist religious practice which are featured in these narratives, perhaps the most enigmatic is the revival of an Indo-European shamanic tradition, which some of these respondents practice. Shamanism seems to have historically been a part of ancient European cultures from Scandinavia to Thrace, but the techniques of shamanism were destroyed by Christian conquest. With the return of polytheism to Western culture, the need for those who specialize in spiritual techniques has also returned. To that end, some of those I spoke with have undertaken the study of shamanic techniques from the Asian, African, and Indigenous American cultures. Their studies were not done to appropriate ethnic identity, but rather in order recreate the spiritual techniques of shamanism within an Indo-European context (Wallis: 2003).[9] They do not recognize themselves as representatives of, or speakers for, the Asian, African, and Indigenous American people whose techniques they have adapted.   Rather, these contemporary polytheist shamans have necessarily adopted the techniques of others as a starting point to recreate these otherwise lost Indo-European traditions.

These individuals understand themselves to be acting as mediators between the visible and invisible worlds. From these shamans' perspective, the community is actually comprised of both the living humans around them, and the Spirits who intervene in mundane affairs. They have taken as their spiritual avocation the task of interceding between the human beings in their communities and the Deities, ancestors, and nature spirits who affect the land and the people living on it. Through their dedication and determination, they have forged new methods for serving the spirits, the Gods, the dead, and their human communities, methods they believe will help bring balance and spiritual health back to the planet.

There are a handful of other practices that are mentioned in these narratives, ranging from God-spousery to oracular trance to sacred poetry and beyond. Whenever appropriate, the respondents were asked to elaborate on the terms they used and the practices thus described. When necessary, explanatory footnotes have been added. These practices undoubtedly warrant an entire volume to themselves. Unfortunately, I did not encounter enough polytheists who engage in these practices to be able to authoritatively draw conclusions about them at present. Rather, it seems best to acknowledge that the features of polytheist practice that have been discussed to this point are those most widely shared by the respondents of this study, and that other practices also exist which might be explored more fully at a later time.

Now that the contours of their common experiences have

been broadly outlined, it is possible to go beyond the monotheist perspective while reading these accounts. Personal experiences of a religious and mystical nature are often difficult to recount, even to friends and loved ones. Given their experience of Western culture's derisive responses to polytheist practices of any sort, it is quite remarkable that the women and men of this study chose to share their stories with a total stranger. Those who participated in this study have done so out of love for their Gods, ancestors, and land. Their bravery in speaking about their religious practices is born from a deep desire to see their Holy Powers and religious practices given respect, if nothing else. It is the respondents' hope that their willingness to share their stories and theologies is met with the readers' willingness to respect those religious experiences and the practices that engendered them.

Going further, readers will no doubt note a distinct lack of academic theorizing. There are several reasons for this. The available Pagan and polytheist theological texts tend to elevate personal experience above religious philosophy because they affirm the orthopraxic nature of polytheism. The vast mountains of academic theology and religious studies are concerned with either near-Eastern monotheism proper, or a near-Eastern monotheist rendering of Hinduism, Buddhism, and occasionally indigenous or alternative faiths. As was established in the introduction, the assumptions, perspectives, and concerns of near-Eastern monotheism so little address polytheist religiosity that its theology is certainly irrelevant and all but useless to elucidating anything about polytheism. The folklorists, anthropologists, and sociologists responsible for bringing the serious study of Paganism into the academy are exacting in their inquiry into contemporary polytheistic and Pagan religions. But their works inevitably grow out of a rationalist, social-scientific, academic discourse relying on psychological interpretations, anthropological analysis, and cultural criticism. They can interpret what a group believes, what its rituals are, what the rituals and material accoutrements mean to group members, how the group compares to (or reacts against) the mainstream, what psychological processes are at work during ritual, and what impact those beliefs have on group members. What those researchers can't do is step beyond the bounds of rationalist, social-scientific academic discourse to reify the Gods, ancestors, spirits, and other Holy Powers, which is the first requisite step in developing a meaningful and relevant polytheist theology. As such, their theories are of limited use in theorizing polytheism as a valid theological perspective.

But the biggest reason of all to de-emphasize theory in the

present work is that doing so allows the perspectives and theories of my interviewees to take precedence over my own interpretation of their stories. It also leaves readers more free to raise their own questions, develop their own theories, and draw their own conclusions about these narratives.

Deciding to leave my theoretical chapters on the hard drive freed me to include narratives of interviewees whose perspectives, beliefs, and/or practices differ from the contours of experience shared by the majority of respondents. Theories are drawn from interpreting a preponderance of data, and information falling outside that preponderance often goes unreckoned. Such was not my desire or intent. There are some polytheists here whose conceptions of Deity and of the relationship between humanity and the Divinities differ significantly from those held by the majority of respondents. But the fact that their views are less common does not make their views less important or relevant to polytheist practice and polytheist theology. It is only right and proper that their voices be heard and accounted for here.

The introduction raised the possibilities and contributions of polytheist theology, and this overview challenged pervasive theological assumptions. Within each interview, I have provided context where appropriate, and created transitional commentary at key points. Beyond that, these narratives have been edited and processed as little as possible so as to allow the respondents to speak for themselves with as little obstruction from me as possible. It is hoped that readers will engage as deeply as possible with the experiences of these respondents, and that greater respect and understanding about contemporary Western polytheism prevails.

Chapter Notes

1. Paper, The Deities Are Many, 14.

2. Ancestors, ed. George Newell (Berlin: De Gruyter, 2011). Francis L. K. Hsu's Under the Ancestors' Shadow: Chinese Culture and Personality (New York: Columbia University Press, 1948. Anthony Ephrim-Donkor's African Religion Defined: A Systematic Study of Ancestor Worship among the Akan (Lanham, MD: University Press of America, 2010) 1-29, 111-133. George F. Lau's "Ancestor Images in the Andes," in Handbook of South American Archaeology, eds. Helaine Silverman & William H. Isbell (New York: Springer, 2008), 1027-1047. Sogyal Rinpoche's The Tibetan Book of Living and Dying: Revised and Updated (New York: Harper Collins, 2002).

3. Wing Lu Tan, "Communal worship and Festivals in Chinese Villages" in Chinese Religious Life ed. David A Palmer, et al. (New York: Oxford University Press USA, 2011), 30-50. Anthony Ephrim-Donkor, African Religion Defined...: 1-29, 111-133. Nathaniel Samuel Murrell's Afro-Caribbean Religions: An Introduction to Their Historical, Cultural, and Sacred Traditions (Philadelphia; Temple University Press, 2009).

4. Gina Ellis, "Elements and Elementals," in The Encyclopedia of Witchcraft and Neo-Paganism, ed. Shelley Rabinovitch and James Lewis (New York: Citadel Press, 2004), 87-88.

5. Stephen L. Harris and Gloria Platzner, Classical Mythology: Images and Insights (Houston, TX: Mayfield Publishing Co., 1997), 855-859.

6. Gillian Clark, Late Antiquity: A Very Short Introduction (Oxford; Oxford University Press, 2011), 43-44.

7. Mogliocco, Witching Culture, 71-73.

8. Christian Lopez, Lukumi: Santeria's Beliefs, Principles, and Direction in the Twenty-First Century (Lincoln, NE: iUniverse, 2004), 2-4.

9. Robert J. Wallis, Shamans/Neo-Shamans: Ecstasies, Alternative Archaeologies and Contemporary Pagans (London: Routledge, 2003), 24-35.

Helio

Helio, a Portugese academic and historian, has been a polytheist for over a decade. His is a solitary practice. Helio observes traditions from pre-Christian Rome, and he has also syncretized "some Egyptian and Norse-inspired ritual practices" into his religion. He honors the Roman pantheon, but has personal devotional relationships with Egyptian and Norse Deities as well. In addition to the Gods, Helio honors his ancestors, the house and land wights, the spirits of place, and a group of heroes consisting of the Emperor Julian* and two Portuguese kings. His religious practice includes daily prayers and offerings as well as a highly structured monthly, seasonal, and annual festivals and holidays.

Helio characterizes faith as "a personal and not scientifically proven belief which doesn't imply religious practice. Faith is different than worship. That is a very important distinction when it comes to polytheism." Polytheism, according to Helio is the "belief in and worship of several Gods." When asked what role faith plays in his relationships with the Gods, Helio asserts, "a huge role! There's a lot of faith in praying, offering, reading omens or divination, making devotional work or dedicating daily activities to Gods." Helio feels driven to do these things because of his "belief that They are real: They can listen, receive or reject what I offer, act and take part in my life, laugh or take pity, guide and teach me, be curious about human affairs or enjoy a good prank." Yet Helio is very clear about his understanding of polytheism as an orthopraxic religion. "As someone who understands orthopraxy," he explains, "I also believe that there can be religious practice without any particular faith, even if personally my practices are often very faith-embedded." Even though he does not see religious practice as being reliant upon faith, Helio finds that faith is one of the things that inspires one to worship the Gods.

*The last non-Christian emperor of Rome, Julian ruled from 361-363. He was a noted philosopher and writer, and a devout polytheist. During his reign, he worked to extricate Christianity from the Roman government and restore the ritual practice of the ancient Roman religion in the belief that doing so would save the Roman empire from dissolution. He also attempted to rebuild the Jewish Temple of Galilee in an effort to foster other religions besides Christianity. Julian was killed by a Sassanid spear in the Battle of Samarra during the Persian campaign, although Christian historians perpetuated the story that he was assassinated by St. Mercurius. Christian historians renamed him Julian the Apostate. In the view of many contemporary Western polytheists, Julian is a hero.

There is a drive that makes you worship the Gods one way or another. One may, of course, perform religious ceremonies without faith. That's pure orthopraxy. But personally, it plays a huge role because it's the drive. If I believe that Mercury is actually out there and can give me a wink, I will try and develop a pattern of religious practices that appeals to Him (and to me), that is pleasing to Him. If I read the myths as sort of a guidebook to a God's personality, I'm taking a leap of faith that these myths actually tell me something about Him, because even if it's not literally true, it's telling me something in the sense of "What's His personality?"

The road of polytheism is not easy for anyone. But for those like Helio who are professional academics, or invested in an intellectual approach, it can be even more challenging. Helio finally managed to reconcile reason and faith by understanding that one demands very different kinds of consideration than the other and that both are equally valid.

Initially, when I was 18 years old and actually started my religious quest, I started reading everything I could find on religions so that I could pick up one of my own. I knew I wanted one, I just didn't know which one. The first few years I felt extremely conflicted about it, because I was extremely rational. So I couldn't believe in something that wasn't somehow at least scientifically plausible e.g. Divine entities who can speak, feel, etc. It was only possible two or three years later when I decided to separate faith. One thing is reason and another is faith. When I made that division, I kind of felt like, "Jump! Jump! Make as big a leap of faith as you want to, and give yourself the freedom to believe. I don't care if it's irrational and meaningless to others. If I want to believe, if it makes me feel good, if I can find some sort of logic to it, I'll go for it." So long as I keep telling myself that though reason and faith are not the same thing, there should be some sort of checks and balance. Otherwise faith can become an exaggerated feeling that overpowers reason and leads to fundamentalism.

There's one example I usually give people who see faith as inimical to reason: every single human emotion is caused by some sort of chemical process — every time you laugh, cry, feel happy, sad or angered, that's chemistry working in your body. But if you ask someone, "Do you love me?" That person isn't going to answer, "Well, look at my blood test. Chemical process A and B are occurring, so yes, I love you." No, it's a romantic question and you have to answer with a romantic gesture. That is one example of how faith – i.e. a feeling or emotional experience, which is how I often see faith - can co-exist with a scientific experience: the fact that chemical processes are scientifically known to be the mechanism behind feelings doesn't mean you can't live them emotionally, artistically or religiously. So long as you keep faith or emotion in check, so that it doesn't become homicidal, suicidal, radical.

Helio, hadn't been raised in a particularly religious home. Like many before him, came first to Wicca before arriving at his present polytheist path. Eventually, Helio found himself growing distant from Wicca. "It was like drifting away from Christianity," he explains, "I never really was a part of it."

My parents never gave me a specifically religious education. They just wanted me to choose my path on my own. Back when I was 18 years old, I found a book on Wicca. About two years later I was moving to the full-fledged polytheistic path. There were two things that made me move away from Wicca. The first was an increasing concern over historical accuracy. I am, after all, a historian, so both a fascination and a concern for how accurate my practices were slowly moved me away from Wicca. The second reason was an increasing interest in the Norse God Freyr. As a result, I became a reconstructionist and a polytheist through Asatru. The thing that made me drawn to polytheism was a sense of freedom. I don't have to stick to one God and then make a whole lot of pressure not to believe in or worship other Gods. Feeling free to worship whatever God I wanted to. That, and greater acceptance of being gay.

After Wicca, Helio's first major polytheist religious practice was Asatru. Ironically, it was "the experience of living in Sweden" that helped Helio realize that Asatru wasn't the right religion for him.

Sometimes you only find out your own identity when you've been in contact with other identities. Before I went to Sweden, I was fully a Heathen. But after I came back from Sweden with an awareness of Swedish folklore traditions and Swedish Heathens, I sort of came back knowing that I really didn't feel at home there. So, when I came back, that's when Janus sort of started knocking on the door. I started looking for Roman things. Nothing negative happened in the least, it was just a matter of not identifying with it entirely.

Upon embracing a hard polytheist spirituality, Helio felt "the sense of freedom when you are no longer constrained by the forced belief in just one God and you can have as many as you want." He also felt liberated at "having the chance to believe without worrying if it's scientifically reasonable." Polytheism also helped him make the "eye-opening discovery of orthopraxy as opposed to orthodoxy." Helio explains that "overall," he felt "a general sense of connectedness with the world in its diversity, cycles and multiple life forms: no longer the absolute rule of one God, but the presence of many [beings] with different takes on things."

Helio acknowledges that he has had experiences that confirmed for him that the Gods exist. In Helio's view, the fact that these experiences are subjective and personal in nature does not make them any less viable as proof that the Gods not only exist, but that They also interact with us.

> There was one several years ago where I decided to make a special offering to the Norse God Freyr. Shortly I made the offering, as I walked away from the place, there was this very short, soft, rain for, like, ten seconds. Then it stopped. Which I took a sign of, "offering accepted." Then, more recently...the one to Freyr was like 10 years ago. More recently, I began worshipping Mercury, and when I bought my Caduceus, you know the winged serpent staff, I bought it on eBay. The same week that the caduceus arrived, I also found a 5 euro bill on the floor. Nobody was immediately around the 5 Euros, but they were on the floor of a college canteen during lunch time, which made the whole thing weirder, since no one seemed to notice a bank note on the floor...so I took it. I bought a lottery ticket and won 25 Euros off of it. Considering the Mercury is a God of luck, I'm pretty sure He does exist somewhere.

When asked to describe his relationship with the Gods, Helio indicates that those relationships are not always clear-cut. What is clear is that Helio does not have the identical relationships with each of his Gods; his relationships are as varied as the Gods Themselves.

> It depends on which God, and sometimes it's a mixed relationship. Sometimes it can be a parent-like relationship. Ancient Romans gave their Gods tiles like "Father"—Father and even the Virgin Goddesses like Vesta and Diana were called "Mother". Basically that is a filial relationship. Friendship, too. And sometimes, co-workers. Sometimes I like to worship Gods that relate specifically to areas in which I work. And I can have all types of relationships simultaneously. It's not just co-worker or friend or family—it can be all three.

Janus was the first Roman God that Helio knew. Many years have passed since then, and Helio's relationship with Janus remains as strong and vital as ever. Particularly important for Helio, is that Janus' unique viewpoint gives Him special insight into situations.

Ironically, He was the God who brought me to Roman polytheism. He started the whole thing. I fell in love with Him at that point. Really fascinating. A two-faced God who presides over every single beginning. That is a really fascinating thing. He's incredibly useful. One of those Gods who somehow is everywhere—[in life] you're always starting something new. A very fascinating character. Ever since I had a first passion for Him, I kind of have been keeping Him in my practice. Even if it sometimes looks as if it is only for ritual purposes. Because you know I also make Him offerings at the beginning of every month, and the beginning of every year, at the beginning of every new enterprise or activity, I tend to make Him offerings. Personally, I find Him incredibly fascinating because He's that kind of God that, not only is He a very good protector because He watches over the entries and the doorways, but He also has a unique perspective on things in being able to see from both ends of the question.

Helio's fascination with thunder prompted him to honor Jupiter. Over time, that relationship has gained emotional gravity.

I brought [Jupiter] into my religious practices for ritual reasons. The 13th or 15th day of every month is dedicated to Him. The Ides. But recently I have been developing a more emotional relationship with Him. For several years, whenever I thought about thunderstorms, I thought about Thor. Only recently have I shifted that emotional sense and moved it towards Jupiter. I guess it's been part of the process of moving from Heathenry to Roman polytheism.

Juno is a significant part of Helio's ritual practice. While many see Her as the Roman version of the Greek Hera, Helio sees Her as a great mother who gives birth to each new month.

[P]eople tend to think of Her as the Roman version of Hera: "She's really jealous. I don't like jealous women so I don't think so." Honestly, I tend to worship Juno in two ways, or two senses. One is a very ritualistic one. Every first day of every month is consecrated to Juno because ancient Romans tended to see Her in some way as a moon Goddess and since the original Roman calendar was lunar, well…She sort of gave birth to every new

month, so the first day of the month is dedicated to Her. That is the ritual role She plays in my practice. I also tend to call on Her to help my mother sometimes. I don't at this time have a personal relationship with Her. It may happen, it may not happen.

Diana is an important part of Helio's ritual practice, even though he does not have any personal relationship with Her whatsoever. His veneration of Her has come about in gratitude for blessings She has bestowed.

A few years ago, I would not have included Diana on the list. I was not particularly drawn to Her, especially since She is a Goddess of the hunt, and I'm certainly not a hunter, and part of me is very vegan. So while I acknowledged Her existence and had no desire to offend Her, we didn't actually get along and I sort of kept a respectable distance. You can say our worlds were different. Around a year ago, one of my dogs fell sick. She had a lot of lumps in her uterus and it needed to be completely removed. And since She could have died during surgery, I decided to make a vow to Diana, hoping the Goddess would protect my pet and help it during the surgery. Which is what happened, so I fulfilled my vow and erected a small altar of stones to Diana, which I occasionally visit to make sure it's still there and rebuild it when necessary. That brought Diana to my personal practice. Her inclusion in my pantheon is derived from a vow for very specific and practical reason, not by a particular attachment to the Goddess or a professional interest.

Although Helio's religious practice is Roman-based, he honors Gods from many pantheons. Helio's relationship with Freyr is the longest of any that he has had with the Gods. What has become a rich and deep relationship began quite unassumingly with an encyclopedia entry that he pulled from his parent's bookshelf.

It's been a very long one. It's like 12 years now. It actually started accidentally. I opened up an encyclopedia my parents had on myths and religion, where I found an entry on Freyr. Eventually I felt the curiosity to look more into it, and it just grew from there. I think the first time I saw a picture of Freyr was when I was, like, 17. Four years later I was already actively searching for things in Asatru. And that's when Freyr kicked in as an actual God I worship. He's been around ever since, even though I moved along from one religious group to another trying to find one where I felt at home. And He's always been there. I've always brought Him along with me. I've switched to many religious groups; From Wicca to Druidry, from Druidry to Heathenry, from Heathenry to the Roman religion. I always brought Them with me. I kept worshipping Them all throughout that period. No matter how much I changed from religious groups. It's been a very consistent, stable point in my religious life. A recent development in this has been my Latinization of my cult to Freyr, with the translation of titles – e.g. Dominus Ingui, Deo Mundi – and the creation of symbols and rituals that follow a basic Roman structure while keeping Norse elements. It's still very much a work in progress, but it's developed enough for me to go public with it in my blog.

Over the years, Helio has also developed relationships with Egyptian Gods. Anubis has long been honored by Helio, who feels particularly close to Him. The Egyptian potter-God Khnum has also played an interesting role in Helio's devotional practice.

In a way, [Anubis] is an old timer. I'm a dog person, I love dogs, I have two dogs. So, a dog-God tends to somehow enter my soft point, something like that, so to speak. So I naturally felt drawn. And once I started paying my respects to Khnum, I thought, Why not pay them to Anubis, too. I eventually found a small image of Him in canine form for sale in Lisbon, and I made Him a little shrine. It's still a very fluid relationship. I'm organizing my religious calendar and settled for an annual feast to Anubis in early February, just a few days before the Roman festival of Parentalia, which honours the family dead.

I started with Khnum like a year and a half ago, probably. I made a clay statue of Saturn. Several weeks later I started having memories of some Egyptian God I'd seen online, on Wikipedia or something, years ago. Then, when I started searching for it, I came across the image again. It turned out to be a potter-God, which I found significant. I'd started having those memories after I'd made a clay statue of Saturn. So I thought to myself, maybe Khnum wants a statue, too. So I made Him one. After I finished Khnum's statue, He seemed to have stepped back, as if I had done what He wanted. Incidentally, I got the sense of "Khnumness" again later in 2011 and, after some research on ancient Egyptian practices and calendar, I marked October 29 as my annual feast day to Khnum. And again He seemed to step back as if I'd done what He wanted.

Helio's mention of the God Saturn is noteworthy, because many Pagans are somewhat reluctant to engage Him. Saturn has been seen as the God of boundaries and constraint, yet Helio's experience with Saturn is largely informed by his celebration of Saturn's raucous and gift-giving holiday, the Saturnalia.

Academically speaking, Saturn is actually a bit of a question mark. Ancient Romans probably revered Him as an agriculture God, an old king and God of agriculture, but at some point He may have had something to do with purification before New Year. In any case, agriculture, the seed and sowing are connection points with Freyr. Saturn also had a big midwinter feast: Saturnalia. I mean, a huge feast. Which resonated with me, since I've always loved Christmas. Even when I started moving away from Christianity I kept several mid-winter traditions and, at one point, started adding more every year because I love the season. So a popular Roman festival around the winter solstice naturally caught my attention and I thought, why not add it to my practices? Which meant adding Saturn to my pantheon. He came in the flow of adding whole new practices and traditions and actually gave a new meaning to several. For instance, for five years now, I've been making a crazy amount of small cakes that I give to my friends, [going] door to door and with a candle lantern in my hand. Now Saturn is a very gift-giving God, the God of Saturnalia. Since I give my friends gifts during midwinter, I thought, why not start with the God who presides over the festival of gift-giving? So the first cake I bake is given to Him, thereby adding a religious layer to one of my midwinter traditions. The whole scary part about Him-I don't know. Ancient Romans started to adopt a lot of myths from the Greeks, with some stories that are not necessarily "true." Sometimes it was something about the Gods, sometimes it was the identification of one God with another. So I tend to skip a lot of origin myths. Originally the Romans didn't have much of a story for their Gods, anyway. At least not that we know of.

Myth, for Helio, often serves as a sort of etiquette manual for dealing with the Gods. The myths may not be literally true, but they do give an indication of a particular God's preferences and personality.

Well, for me myths tell me a bit about Their personality, that's how I see it. Myths are tales. They are things you tell about the Gods and it doesn't mean they are necessarily true in the sense of telling real events, especially now that scientific knowledge has replaced myths in the historic account of reality. But, it does convey something about how They tend to act, what's Their objective, how They tend to react to things, what's Their personality, so to speak? In that sense, myths are useful, as sort of a guidebook on how to deal with the do's and don't s of a particular God.

The ancient Romans are well-known for their annual festival calendar, so seasonal, annual celebrations are a major part of Helio's practice. However, the specific holidays he has adopted, the Holy Powers he honors, the traditions he observes, and his general manner of celebrating these holidays is highly syncretic of many cultures.

Three times a month - the Calends (1st day), Nones (5th or 7th day) and Ides (13th or 15th) - I make offerings of incense to most of Them and once a month to Freyr, Freya and Njord. If there's an annual festival, such as Saturnalia, Quinquatria or Midsummer, I also perform a more formal ritual. I visit graves of my deceased family members (including family pets), usually along with my parents, who have taken the habit of aiding me in some practices, namely the New Year ritual, taking care of the graves of our loved ones and maintaining an altar of heaped stones to Diana. My parents, however, are not polytheists (at least not actively so, though they are very open minded)…

Making cakes to offer several friends of mine, that's one of my traditions. Watching the sun set and the sun rise at both midwinter and midsummer isn't so much an invention. It was done in the past. But I manage to do it in a very personal way. I always travel to my homeland to do it. I have specific spots in which I watch the sun set and the sun rise. I blow a blowing horn nine times and make a toast to the sun as it rises. If it's in midwinter it's a toast of milk, because the newborn sun is like a child and you want to breastfeed it in a sort of way so to speak. Then at midsummer it's a grownup sun, so you give it a wine offering. I also started doing something recently. I took inspiration from the midsummer poles in Sweden. To celebrate Freyr at midsummer, I got a huge staff and ribbons and strips of cloth of several colors, namely yellow, blue and green. At sunrise on midsummer I placed the staff with the ribbons and a flower sunwheel on a hilltop and leave it there for the rest of the day, then I pick it up…

I sometimes erect simple shrines in public spaces (parks, beaches, etc), usually heaped stones, and list them online so other polytheists can use or upkeep them. Also, offerings to landwights or specific Gods can be made at any given time in my daily routine or while on a journey somewhere: leaving small coins in walls or by statues, pouring water on plants, pilling rocks on crossroads, etc.

In addition to celebrating major festivals, Helio has built a personal daily practice to honor his Holy Powers. He devotes a portion of each day to honoring his Gods, heroes, ancestors, and land spirits. The lares, or ancestral spirits, and the wights, or spirits of place, are very important in Helio's practice.

I honor my ancestors, my heroes, the housewights, Janus, and Vesta, and I also pray to Freyr, Freya, Njord, Gerd and the Elves of Alfheim at the start of each day. It depends a lot on what I have on hand. If I don't have anything to make an actual offering, I will burn incense, and I will salute them. This saluting also includes Mercury, Diana, Jupiter, Minerva, and Juno. If I don't have the means to make an offering, I'll usually burn incense. It's the easiest thing to do. Even if I'm out of my house on a journey, I tend to go to a corner and light up some incense if possible. On a daily basis—that's pretty much it.

I believe that every family has a protective spirit, a lare, and that when my family members die, and when I say family members, I say family pets, too, I believe that they join that spirit and become themselves lares, sort of family protective spirits if you will. Housewights are different. Housewights can be spirits that already lived in the place where the house was built. They can be spirits of animals or people who died in the house. A housewight may have moved in from elsewhere with a living person, say when someone moved in to a house and brought along wights from someplace else. As for offerings, I give them incense, sometimes food, though that depends on whether I have a fireplace at my disposal). There is a small practice I picked up in Galicia, when I was in Spain about a year ago. It's pretty amazing. If you go to any old coffee shop in a historic area, you will notice small coins—hundreds of them—in the walls. And the owners of the coffee shops actually leave them there so long that the coins actually turn green. I picked up that practice of leaving small coins in small cracks in the house or in the furniture as an offering to the house wights.

Of late, there has been controversy in the Pagan world over the concept of polytheism. Whether the conflict has to do with the meaning of the term or deep-seated assumptions about group identity is difficult to say. Helio had valuable insight to offer regarding the situation.

There has been a discussion on the Pagan and polytheist blogosphere recently about it. Someone wrote a post about "why

I'm not a Pagan, why I'm a polytheist"…A lot of people have been giving their takes on that. Personally, I have found that to say I am a polytheist is a lot more enlightening in terms of a first impression. If I say I'm a Pagan, usually people assume that I have an eightfold calendar or year, that I'm some sort of Wiccan or Wiccan-ish. But if I say I'm a polytheist, it immediately puts people in a very different mindset. It breaks immediately with the modern assumption that everyone is either a monotheist or some sort of monist. It breaks off immediately. If I add that I'm a Roman polytheist, it's like a direct reference. Immediately you think of ancient Romans. Even if they do consider it in a very prejudicial way, like a friend of mine who thought that ancient Romans had a religious command to kill Christians. Even if saying I'm a Roman polytheist brings to mind people's prejudices about it, that's okay because first, I'm breaking them of the monotheist pattern, and secondly, their prejudices are about a historical period from which I actually draw my practices, so I can work with that. I can talk to them about ancient Roman practices, authors and beliefs, going directly to the heart of what I do instead of them assuming I'm some sort of Wiccan, in which case I have to correct them in every single sentence without ever really getting the chance to explain what I am because I keep having to discuss what I'm not. After a few years, that can be very, very frustrating.

A few months ago, a friend of mine who's an atheist, came to me and said, "I never met a polytheist before. Which Gods do you believe in?" A very good question, but not the best one to ask to someone who is a polytheist. Believing doesn't necessarily imply that you worship any Gods, at least not in my case. I tend to, by default, believe in every single God people claim to exist. I don't as a rule, make a judgment of "eh, I'm not sure about it." People who worship Gods other than my own believe in Them and I usually see no reason to deny Their existence. A different question is "which ones do I worship and how?" That is a significant thing to your identity as a polytheist. I turned to him and I said, "well, you should have asked me which Gods I worship, because that will tell you which kind of polytheist I am—it identifies my ritual praxis and hence my religious identity. If you ask me, "which Gods to you believe in?" I will say "All of Them. That will tell you nothing about me." He didn't really say a thing." Of course, the problem with that question is that when people think of religion, they still think in terms of monotheism. Polytheists are different. You should specify by asking "which Gods do you worship?" because that

*will tell you a lot more about a person. That is pretty much it.
The question tends to come around once in a while when people
ask me about it. There's always a tendency to take the mindset
of default monotheism, which also links with the whole "faiths
of the world," and "what's your faith?" thing. In terms of
polytheism it works best when you discuss your practice. It
describes me better than "what's your faith?"*

*A lot of the arguments that atheists have are tailor-made for
monotheistic religions. They're not structured to all the religions
of the world, especially because atheism is a very Western
phenomenon. It's very commercial this atheism, it's very Western,
and let's face it, the best known religions in the Western part of
the world are Christianity, Islam, and Judaism. It's all the same
bag and naturally they must make the arguments toward the
particular group that is best-known or most popular in the areas
where atheists are living.*

Of all the things that Helio wishes people understood about
polytheism, he most sincerely wants them to understand that it's a
legitimate religion. Polytheism isn't about wearing togas and playing
with plastic swords: it's a real religion.

*[I]t's for real. It's actually for real. It's not like "you're too young
to know what you want," or "you're just being playful," or
"you're saying that but you actually believe in one God who has
many faces." No it's actually real. Strict polytheism, lots of
Gods and Goddesses and unknown gender entities. It's for real.
It's serious. It's not a game or a playful moment. It's not a stage
in your childhood or a teenage rebellion sort of thing. It's for
real. It's serious. People actually worship, people actually believe
in these Gods, and they want to be taken seriously. That is one
thing I would love. Because I have actually had the experience of
Catholic priests, or Hindus, or just plain atheists, after being
told I'm a polytheist, say, "could you explain that again? You're
actually kidding, right? Is this some sort of stage in your life?"
It's annoying. It's very common. Recently, a Portuguese Catholic
priest who does a lot of interfaith work wrote a book on
interfaith dialog. It was intended to make a short analysis or
presentation of all the different religious philosophies of the
world, for the sole purpose of bringing about world peace. But
when it came to polytheism, he had like half a page that said
something like, "There really isn't any polytheistic religion.
Because polytheists are actually monists." This, from a guy who's
been doing interfaith work for years and years and actually*

should know better. So one thing I want people to know about polytheism is that it's real, it's serious, and it's actually polytheism, not something else.

72

Aleksa

Aleksa, a 39-year old legal assistant, recognizes that she has been a polytheist her "entire life," although it wasn't until she turned seventeen that she "formalized" her religious commitments. She observes the pre-Christian animism of her Native American Wampanoag ancestors, and has blended some of the ancient Slavic traditions from her father's ancestors into her practice. While polytheism and animism are defining features of Aleksa's religious expression, she does, generally speaking, consider herself to be Pagan. Aleksa primarily works with her ancestors, especially the woman she calls Grandmother. Whale, Raven, and Beaver are the three Manitou that she honors specifically. She has worked extensively with the mother Goddess Mokosh[*], the blacksmith God Svarog[**], Hecate, and the Morrighan "in Her 'washer-at-the-ford' form." She also briefly worked with Odin and Hella. Through working with "the Washer and my ancestors," Aleksa eventually recognized that she has also worked with Squannit,[***] an ancestral wise woman of the Wampanoag tribe. While she does on occasion interact with the larger Pagan community, Aleksa says her "animist beliefs don't really fit in the general 'box'," and that her practice tends to be a solitary one.

When asked to describe her personal understanding of polytheism, Aleksa says that polytheism is "the belief in the existence of separate individual Deities that have free will and agendas, and the power and will to use them." When asked to comment upon how she first came to know the Gods as individual and distinct entities, Aleksa replies that "I met Them individually and was introduced to Them individually so I have never known Them to *not* be separate and distinct. They also...feel distinct." Each Deity, she believes, is a unique Divine being; an individual with Their own characteristics. "You may find a Deity described in some cultures who is claimed to be the same as a similar Deity in another one," Aleksa explains, "[but] I find that that's not true. They are in fact separate beings." While many people, polytheist and not, readily speculate on the origin and

---

[*] Mike Dixon-Kennedy, Encyclopedia of Russian and Slavic Myth and Legend (Santa Barbara, CA; ABC-CLIO publishers, 1998), 194.

[**] Ibid, 171-172.

[***] She is also known as "Granny Squannit," and has played a major role as culture hero in the Mashpee and Wampanoag tribes. William Scranton Simmons, Spirit of the New England Tribes: Indian History and Folklore, 1620-1984 (Hanover, VT: University of New England Press, 1986), 246-247.

nature of the Gods, Aleksa says that such discussion "is not relevant to me or my practice." The key point is that "They are separate. They feel different, They look different, They interact with me differently, and as such They are different beings." It is inappropriate, in Aleksa's view, to take beings who are "described in different ways across different cultures, and then project the same [single] Deity across [those] cultures as if 'it's all the same one…' that's not the same Deity." She feels that it is important to recognize that the Deities "live in different places and are in different localities, and have different cultures as such."

In discussing Aleksa's religious practice, we also discussed the concept of "faith" and what role it plays in her religion. If faith is "merely a religious belief," then it doesn't play much of a role in her practice. But, if faith "includes the trust that things which cannot be proven to those who do not believe" are real, then Aleksa acknowledges that "its role is far greater." Aleksa defines faith as "quite simply…the trust and belief that something that I can't see, touch, taste, or feel exists even though I can't prove it…I know it's there." She knows the ancestors and Gods are real "because I have evidence that I have interacted with Them." Aleksa recalls talking with another person who has interacted with Grandmother, and that person "described her in precisely the same terms as I described her to my grandfather and my mother. This is a person who had not only never met me in person but [who] has never met my family members person, either."

Experiences like this confirm for Aleksa that "Grandmother's out there. I know she's there guiding me. There's an element of truth to me that's facile to everyone else, but I'm just having faith, a belief, that I'm right." At first "it would be faith," Aleksa explains, "and later it becomes knowing." In other words, faith goes beyond simply believing that something exists, toward trusting this something to guide your actions; it is the "willingness to do what They ask whether I [understand] it or not—that's the faith part. And then after the fact, when the evidence comes in, then [faith] becomes knowing." Ultimately, faith is "an every day, normal part of my existence that the Gods and spirits are there, offering guidance. Like breathing, or the sun rising."

While she does in fact identify as polytheist, Aleksa wishes to make clear that her practice is founded with her ancestors at the center, and the belief in the divinity of all things. She also has a unique perspective of Deity's relationship to human ancestors.

Because I believe that all things have a spirit, all things are

Divine, and animists see the Divine in everything. My ancestors have an aspect of the Divine, of a lesser level than what Deity has. They also have taught me that those Deities would not be Deities without having been ancestors first. And it's an interesting perspective. So I have a practice that I do every day, where I get up each day and I give thanks to my ancestors. I ask for guidance from the spirits of my land, and my home, and the plants and animals that live around us, and they give me their guidance. I believe I have faith that they're there and would be when I need them.

When I was a small child, and I mean very small, I had my first encounter with Grandmother, the woman ancestor who is Grandmother. And She is in fact, my mother's great-grandmother, but I had never met her in person; She died before I was born. What was interesting about it was that when I described her later to my mother and her father, they both recognized the woman that I was referring to. They both said it was impossible for me to know who she was because she was dead. In various conversations after that, I confirmed that it was her that I was interacting with. She has a very strong bond with my family, the family members who are living today. She keeps a very close eye on them. And that's how she works with us, I guess. For the most part, she is a teacher and a guide.

Prior to formalizing her polytheist practice, Aleksa was raised Catholic. She struggled spiritually through much of her young life, because while the Christian God seemed to be utterly absent and non-communicative, Grandmother and her ancestors were very present and forthcoming. Explaining this to her family or other people was a very frustrating experience.

I left the church when I was a teenager/young adult—my college years. I'd ask for guidance from the church and from God—the monotheist Christian God—but I never got an answer. He never responded to me and I never got an answer. And when I asked Grandmother and my ancestors for guidance they were always there and always answered. That was something that touched me very strongly, and it's always been that way with me. I later learned that she was always there, even though I may not have remembered her being there at the time, she was always there, in the shadows....

I did not like growing up in the Catholic church. I was referred to as a troublemaker, because I asked all the questions that they didn't want asked. I was there a lot, and my mom would pick me up and she would ask me, "why can't you just shut up?" But that's not me. I just didn't like it. It was interesting because I ended up being my brother's sponsor for confirmation; he is now an atheist. I went away to school and my experiences with spirits and ancestors increased exponentially when I was at school.

A number of factors converged when Aleksa turned 17 which encouraged her for formalize her polytheism. Incredibly powerful things happened to her during a trip abroad, things which left her both spiritually and physically changed.

Because I deal with ancestors, I deal with the dead a lot. I did a trip abroad and found myself in Piskaryovskoye Cemetery outside of Saint Petersburg, Russia which is where they buried the siege victims. I had a very significant issue while I was there. I had people try to give me messages to deliver to their descendants and the people who survived the siege; they would not leave me alone. Thousands and thousands of dead unsettled spirits would not leave me alone for anything. I found myself trying to flee. I could not. Because of where I was, and the things going on in my life, I could not stop them or block them out. I hadn't yet learned how. Eventually I found myself in a subset of the cemetery, and there were names on all the tombstones, and they were all sailors. I told them that I come from a long line of sailors and people who are associated with the sea. The first thing they asked me was, "why are you here?" and I told them. They said, "well that's not right. You're not here for that right now." The Russian sailors actually escorted me through the cemetery and helped me get out and kept those siege victims at bay.

During that trip I had other flashes of "this is my ancestry;" part of my family's past and different bloodlines coming together that were broken and separated and it was just really chaotic. When I went to Moscow I had brown eyes, and when I came back they were grey. I've been told that your eyes don't spontaneously change color, that they always stay the same. But my eyes did change color; in the pictures from before my trip my eyes were brown. When I came back, they were gray. They're still gray.

It was at that point that I said I am done with the Catholic Church. I am not doing this anymore. I will continue with what my ancestors have for me to do, because clearly they have something for me to be doing. And I've been doing it ever since…

I can't do mass deaths sites. I don't do battlefield sites unless I have to. As much as I love civil war history, I will not go civil war battle sites if I can avoid them. I cannot do it. I know that I no longer have the problem that I had when I was there in the cemetery in Saint Petersburg; I know that I now have sufficient wards and guards that I can keep them out and they'll back away, but I will still not do it. As much as I would like to honor some of the ancestors I have and go into those places, I will not do it. It's a bad idea.

When asked about her experiences with the Gods, Aleksa explained that in an animistic, shamanistic practice such as hers, one will have intermediaries with Deity. Very often, she says, those intermediaries will be your ancestors.

Grandmother is very much an intermediary for me. She teaches me what I need to know and how to interact with Deity, how to ask the right questions and make sure I don't ask the wrong ones. You must be very specific, or you can get yourself into some serious trouble when interacting with Deity. Her guidance in that regard has been very useful. I have been able to negotiate…Spirit workers tend to have very stringent ties with Deity. I have been able to negotiate out of that, because of Grandmother: She and her ancestral bloodline laid claim to me. It's resulted in some very interesting experiences.

One thing that Aleksa stresses is the importance of understanding that the Gods do in fact have agendas: opinions, desires, and needs of their own that They wish to have met. She explains that there are times when these agendas can create thorny situations for someone whom the Gods wish to press into service to meet a particular goal. Her ancestors, Grandmother in particular, have been very helpful to Aleksa in negotiating these thorny debacles.

I was at a conference once where we were doing seithwork. The entire group was stopped at the bridge on the way to Helheim, the Norse land of the dead, and had to wait because there was a woman in the group whose ancestor said she should go no further until certain contractual obligations were made clear. And as it turns out, the woman was me. It was really wild because the person who was the seithkona in the session actually had to stop the group and ask permission from the native spirits of the area for me to be able to continue to certain point. And they said "yes, but that she's only going to be allowed to do X, Y and Z, and she's not allowed to go any further." All of that seems kind of strange, but that's how all of my interactions with Deity are: very carefully negotiated via my ancestral relations. And they keep a very close eye on me, to make sure all of those Deities, who all have an agenda of Their own, don't get me wrapped up in Their agendas...

The Gods call who They will for reasons of Their own choosing. They call whoever They need to get that agenda met, which is one of the reasons that my ancestors carefully negotiate my actions with Them. Because I am not a servant of a specific Deity or a pantheon of the Deities, my duty is to work with a variety of cultures and people and be a bridge. I am a bridge between my ancestors and my family, I am a bridge between the living and dead, I am the bridge between cultures. I actually do a lot of cross cultural work. I've done a lot of various eclectic rituals that I studied in school. I studied everything from Latin America to Russia and I have weird interests. The reason [for that] is that I am a bridge.

Many times Aleksa's role as a bridge has brought her into contact with different Gods and Goddesses. Often, she is called upon to be a messenger, as her work with Odin, Hella, Skadi, and Lilith attests.

I've worked with individuals who need that connection, need an intermediary—an intermediary by nature is a bridge—between themselves and another and I've acted as a messenger. I've even acted as a messenger between Deities. I had an experience when I was delivering a message between Odin, who sent me to Hella, who had me forward it to Skadi. It was very bizarre. I don't know what the message was. All I know is that I found myself in Odin's hall and we were talking. He said "go do this." The next thing I knew, I was going down the steps and the gates of Helheim opened to me on the very strict subject that I go from the gate over to Hella and deliver the message. Hella then said, "No, no, no. I need you to deliver this message to Skadi." There is a stairway behind Her throne that I went up and I found myself in the woods. I met up with Skadi, and then She said, "okay, now go off." Then I found myself skiing home. I don't know what the message was, I did walk through some interesting places to deliver it. But I did it. And that was the purpose of my trip: "you will be a messenger." Helheim isn't really that scary, you just have to know what to expect and not expect much. I'd been dealing with the dead since an early age; the dead don't bother me.

But I've also done other things. I have a friend, actually she was a friend of a friend, who had a really, really bad relationship with a man who was abusing her. And I got a really angry message from Lilith. I said "OK, I will deliver this message." And then She asked me to do some work to help Her help this woman. And now the woman is doing very well and the person who was abusing her is not doing so any longer, and has developed an interesting amount of respect for her. I know his message was really hard, because Lilith is like that.

Knowing the way forward depends knowing which direction you are coming from. In her work with the Gods, Aleksa has found it necessary to do her homework and research as much about the Gods she is working with as she possibly can. She was once surprised to discover that, despite the volumes of historical research she had been doing, she had forgotten to take the original sacred narratives into account. Doing so is what eventually led her in the right direction.

I've worked with Hecate, who I actually happen to really like. I've worked with Her in all of Her aspects at various times for various reasons. I was trying to figure out some work, I was getting these messages from the Norse pantheon, and They kept asking me to do things for Them, and I could not figure out why, so I decided to do some research on the pantheon. I'm somewhat academic; I like history, so I like to do this research. My father's an engineer, my brother's an engineer, so I tend to approach things the same way. I wasn't getting anywhere. I remember asking Hecate about this during a ritual, and She (proverbially) smacked me and said: "you're reading the wrong damn book." What I was reading was a very academic study of the pantheon. What Hecate wanted me to do was go back to the origin stories, you know, the stories of how things came to be. I've actually stopped going for the academic sources until after I've read the origin stories as a result. I find that when I go the other way and read academic sources first I wind up getting in my own way and not being able to figure it out.

Like many Native American tribes, the Wampanoags have a deep reverence for the manitou, or Deity spirits. However, their relationship with the manitou is rooted in animism, thus this understanding of what Deity is differs significantly from the polytheist perspectives of Deity held by the peoples of ancient Europe, Asia, and the Middle East. Aleksa blends both into her practice as a way to meet her goal of bridging cultures.

My great-great-grandmother of whom I speak was a

Wampanoag Indian. What I have learned in my interactions with her is that when native peoples see the Manitou—the Manitou are the Deity spirits of the native peoples—what they see are simultaneously the existence of the Divine and a creature of nature: a stone, or a tree, or a hawk, or a deer, or the stars, or the moon, or the sky (the Great Spirit- the universal spark that makes everybody want to live life). You will get lower case "manitou" to reference the spirits of nature, and upper case "Manitou" to reference the Great Spirit.

Unfortunately in white speak the concept of the Great Spirit is the Christian God, but it just doesn't translate well. I use "white speak" because that's how it's come to us. We have no frame of reference for the native concept of Manitou. There used to be. But it's long since faded from memory. It might be in the genetic memory, which is how I think we get polytheists today.

Native people have practices that are very nature-oriented. Even their embrasure of Christianity still reflects those practices. Christianity among Wampanoags today still contains the Manitou that gives life and fertility to the earth. It still contains the bad spirits that cause problems, and strife, and ill health. It still contains all of those manitou which are a part of pre-Christian native culture. And I was taught that nature talks to us and that I have to interact with it in a harmonious way. I need to make sure that my home is reflecting of the nature around me, so I have to honor manitou and Manitou. I do go home every year if I can manage it. Sometimes I can't. It's actually very painful when I can't but I do try to go back every year and I do feel better when I'm home. I know how close I'm getting to be ancestral land because I can actually feel it. I'm from Cape Cod and we have a strong attachment to the water. Even here, I can feel the tidal current of my hometown. I know when it's high tide there. Which is weird because I don't spend that much time near the water. I can always tell when the land changes, and how we're getting a sea breeze and its coming up the Potomac. I can smell the seasons change. I can pay attention and listen to those sorts of things and those are what my ancestors want me to be paying attention to. They want me to be closer to the earth so that I can remember that. They want me to live there [in my hometown] if I can. They want me to do things that bring me into that connection. And those are very native aspects.

In Wampanoag culture, the health of the community depends on everyone contributing in any way they can to the well-being of the tribe. Outsiders tend to misinterpret the Pauau as some sort of massive weekend party event. What they don't understand is that the Pauau is essential to healing the strain that time and distance place on the tribal community. It also affords an opportunity for a powerful healing rite to take place which benefits the entire tribe.

"Pow-wow" is actually a Wampanoag word that means "healing ceremony." But the Wampanoag spelling is more like "P-a-u-a-u." Wampanoag is practically a dead language. It is being restored from the memory of the very old who remember certain words, but the dialect doesn't make much sense. That's one of the reasons that native people often won't talk about this work to outsiders. Because every time they've done so more and more of their culture was stolen and taken from them and treated wrongly and interpreted wrongly. I act in accord with how well Grandmother taught me and that's what she thought. Acting according to her teachings is a healing rite.

Pauau is a healing rite because it brings you home. But it incorporated many rites. In one case we have a healing ceremony that's a fireball game. I love me some fireball. It's a male-only game and only men of the tribe are allowed to play it. Basically what they do is they take the ball—nowadays they use chicken wire that is stuffed with rags that have been soaked in kerosene for about a year. And they light it on fire and they play rugby with it. And they do it shirtless. They coat themselves in bear grease but they play it shirtless. And they will hold the ball as long as they possibly can. There is a reason they're doing this, and this is lost on most outsiders. The first thing outsiders say is, "why can't women play?" Well, it is because women are nurturers by nature. But a warrior who undergoes a ritual of suffering is nurturing his tribe in another way by taking on their pain. Each player plays for specific person, or family, who is suffering. The more the more they suffer during the game, the more they alleviate the suffering of others. This is a whole different kind of nurturing. It's a whole different kind of healing. The players aren't saying that women aren't able to do this. What they're saying is that as a warrior, it is to my duty to do this. And that happens every year at Pauau.

Pauau is a healing ritual overall when the tribe comes home. In coming home, we talk to family, we get together, we come back to the land, we refresh ourselves, and we have regeneration. We talk to people we haven't seen in a long time and that homecoming is itself healing. Which is another part of Pauau that is lost on outsiders. Most people think that Pauau is just a reason to get together to eat fry bread and dance in a circle and play the drum. But that's not at all what it's about. It's about healing the rips and tears that happen in the community over time and long distance. So I do try to make a practice of going home for Pauau specifically.

The Wampanoags convene Pauau once per year to renew tribal ties to the land, the Manitou great and small, and to each other. But the small daily ritual she does each day is what helps Aleksa remain rooted and connected to the land and her ancestors.

Every morning I get up and restore my connection the land and the ancestors. It's a very small thing. You wouldn't necessarily look at me and say that I was doing a ritual. But I get up every morning and go around my yard when I take my dogs out to go to the bathroom. I greet the Sun, I greet the sky, they say goodbye to the Moon. I greet the earth and I say hello to the animals who live in my yard and around the property. I ask each of them for guidance that day for whatever I might encounter during the day, hardships, confusion, frustration and things like that. I remind myself that I am connected to my ancestors and to my descendants. Ancestors are not limited to those who came before—they include those who will come after.

When asked if she had ever experienced any conflict with others regarding her religious beliefs and practices, Aleksa relates that she has. Some of her conflicts have been with her family, and the conflict often comes as a response to Aleksa's intense work with her ancestors.

Because I have such a connection to the ancestry, when other members of our family died, or when close friends have died, I don't react to death in a very negative way. That it's this sudden end, and all of a sudden there's nothing there, and no way to remember and everything ends. I never react that way, because I see them all the time. I don't see death as an end, I see it as yet another step on our soul's journey. I can still interact with those who have gone before. In all honesty so can the members of family, they just don't because they have a blockage. So I've not gone to a few funerals and I'm sure this created rifts in my family. Like when my grandfather died. I didn't go to his funeral because I helped him cross over—I just didn't need to go.

I brought Grandmother and his mother with me when I saw him the last time. They sat with him and when it was time for him to go, I helped him cross and they crossed with him. I see him periodically even now. The rest of my family goes all, "It's a horrible. I miss them. I will never to talk to them again. When will I get to see them again?" I just look at them and say, "Your grandmother is sitting there in the chair, why don't you go talk to her?" They look at me like I've got four heads. I would happily explain that to the children, but nobody wants me to. They say, "Oh, the kids aren't ready for that," and I say, "Really 'cause I think they're more ready for it than you." So there's the rift where the family just looks at me and says, "yup you're a little weird but you come from a weird part of the family," like I'm insensitive.

Aleksa has also experienced conflict with other Pagans due to her indigenous perspective on cultural revival. Wampanoag traditions come from a living culture, but Paganism largely comes from attempts to revive, recreate, or reconstruct dead cultures. She sees that there are things that Paganism could learn about how to foster a living tradition from the Wampanoags, if Pagans are interested in those things. Aleksa has discovered, unfortunately, that many aren't interested in her perspective.

And then I've had rifts with other Pagans because even though Wampanoag language is dead, the culture is still alive, even though we have incorporated things in that may not be originally ours. Native peoples do that all the time. It's still rather consistent. There are still Wampanoag in the United States who live on Wampanoag land, eat Wampanoag food, and live in Wampanoag houses. They practice their tribal laws that have been given to them over the centuries. And like any other culture, it is organic.

Most of the Pagans that I know practice a dead culture. They have no living reference to what they are attempting to practice. They're trying to restore something [that] they based on the historical attributions of foreign writers who really didn't understand what they were looking at. Those cultures are not alive today. I've had moments where I've said, "Look, this is how we manage to keep this going. We've tried to do this; it might help you to bring these things back." I'd get pooh-poohed.

Aleksa says that there are many things Pagans can do every day if they want to help revive and recreated the traditions of their ancient cultures. Some of them are incredibly simple.

> *I had an interaction with Hecate one day in Her maiden aspect...The question I had was, "How can I give the most honor to my ancestors, and practice the most honestly in my daily life?" Her answer was, "Live. Stop looking at elsewhere. Stop trying to do something you 'think' is right. Just live every day. Be aware and be honest in your approach." It sounds trite, and I have to admit I said, "huh?" And She said, "you know what I said, now go away." I thought about it for a while and I was like, "OK." So I do that. When I get up and go to work, I take care of my dogs, I weed my garden, I eat right, I exercise; in all of those things I try to live most honestly with myself and with my family while I am living in the moment, today, always. And I have found, over time, when I stopped thinking about "how would the ancestors do it"...well, duh. They'd make soup. They'd take care of the animals. They'd go fishing. They'd get up in the morning. They'd go to work. They do what they do. And that is how I should live: with the presence of spirituality in every moment.*

Aleksa's unique perspective about polytheism has also caused a stir in her local and online Pagan circles. Certain concepts that Grandmother taught her differ significantly from the beliefs of many Pagans that she had met.

> *[One of] these concepts that Grandmother gave me [was] that the Deities would not be Deities if They hadn't been ancestors first. THAT caused quite an interesting scuffle on a list one day. To some Pagans and polytheists, the idea that the Deities have ever been anything BUT Deity is just sort of strange and something that they can't grasp or cope with. That's a very post-Christian view of things: that there is nothing there but Deity. When you explain that that's a Christian attitude, it just causes rifts. Because any time you try to tell a Pagan what they're practicing is actually monotheism, they don't want to go there...You get the whole "all Goddesses are one Goddess and all the Gods are one God who is a manifestation of the Goddess," that's just more monotheism.*

The trouble with a Christian monotheist view, Aleksa explains, is that in gets ingrained into your way of thinking about all sorts of things. Christianity, she notes, is very ethnocentric. Even when you reject the Christianity, the habit of ethnocentrism remains; it underpins any interpretation of history and culture well beyond the concerns of religion and spirituality.

In many ways that manifests everywhere in issues of all sorts. Issues like communications, and how you interpret what cultural material you find. I don't say that I practice an unbroken tradition because certainly it's not. But my culture is still alive so far as it can be. The Wampanoags were Christianized. Our numbers were wiped out quite significantly: there was genocide but we don't need to get into the politics right now. But we are here today. I don't think I know any modern Vikings, or actual ancient Greek oracles living in a niche in the hills. Most Pagans I know are in fact trying to restore or practice a faith, the existence of which they don't actually have any evidence of. They are kind of creating it out of what they think they know. At least when you have a long-living tradition there's a lot less interpreting what you're doing through the archival eyes of the Other. I try not to take it personally. It's a lack of understanding. There's a basis of "it's all the same anyway" and it's not. I try to give people the benefit of the doubt.

When asked if there was anything she wished other people understood about polytheism, Aleksa said that she wishes people would understand that the Gods are real and that there are actually very sensible reasons to believe in more than one God.

The biggest thing is that polytheists believe in God, they just happen to have more of Them. They have Gods for specific purposes. That makes perfect sense. In our lives you take a car, a train, a bus, or a plane to your destination depending on where you're going and how fast you need to get there. They are all equally good but they aren't equally as useful for every kind of trip. Imagine taking a jet plane to the corner store down the block. But it doesn't occur to people that Deity works the same way. To say the one God can do everything equally is absurd. However, I want people to know that polytheists and pantheists still respect, in many ways, the Gods of others more than you would think.

This is certainly not to put the golden age of Paganism or pre-Christian era on it—or the noble savage or whatever. I'm not saying that. It's true that my ancestors didn't have a name for starvation. We didn't have a word for starvation or that kind of suffering because nobody did it. Everyone helped everyone else. Interacting with everyone else in that way healed everyone. But, they also fought over resources, that happened a lot—but nobody starved. And even when Native people would take slaves—and it did happen—the slaves were housed and clothed and eventually became members of the tribe and the family. And in many cases they wouldn't even consider going back to their original land. So, I think that looking at polytheism and pantheism in a simplistic way like that, or even that "golden age/noble savage" thing does great injustice to polytheism... They are very complicated subjects; really, really nuanced. But they can exist harmoniously with the other religions.

Laura

Laura, 43, is a medical professional living in New England and a Northern Tradition Pagan who had been raised in Santeria by her Cuban grandmother. She also had Christian and Jewish influences from her parents and extended family. She belongs to a kindred in the New England area, but works with Deities from both Santeria and the Northern traditions. Her strongest relationships are with Loki, Ellegua, Chango, Oshun, and Yemaya. Ancestors are a very important part of Laura's religious life, as are the spirits of the land and sea.

Laura says that while she has been practically a polytheist her entire life, she has only been conscious of it for the last 14 years. Her mother had converted to Judaism upon marrying her stepfather. Laura's husband was Greek Orthodox. She has several Catholic relatives. Laura says that she is "comfortable with a multiplicity of belief," and that "for years I'd go to synagogue with my parents and go to church with my husband...and do what I wanted to do at home and with my friends." She says that she "stopped doing that and even pretending to try to fit in when I realized the tolerance I was extending to monotheism was not in any way reciprocated in turn." She wouldn't describe what she did as converting to a new religion, "so much as finally dropping any attempt to placate my monotheist relatives and becoming more open about my personal spiritual beliefs and practices."

Having been raised in Santeria and only later in life coming into a relationship with northern European Deities has given Laura an interesting take on the concept of polytheism. While Laura admits that many Santerians would not consider themselves to be polytheist, Laura sees that the idea of polytheism does seem to fit the religion.

> That's an interesting one for me because I was raised with Santeria, and Santeria doesn't necessarily think of itself that way. Just like Vodou it has its feeling like there is an overarching creator, but it is an energy that is disconnected to the everyday running of the world, so that there is a pantheon in place to help with that. It took me a while to even come to the realization that "oh, yeah, it's pretty much polytheism." I define it as a belief in numerous Deities. Numerous Holy Powers that are much bigger, more powerful, stronger, and older than

humanity, have a lot more wisdom than humanity and can be petitioned and engaged with and [who] engage in personal relationships with people and the land. I guess I would define it as believing in more than just one Deity- multiple Deities.

According to Laura, "Faith, in a more generic way, is belief in something that is not scientifically proveable." She tends to view it "in a religious context as a belief where you know there is something out there that is much bigger than you. That you are a part of something larger." Faith is an awareness "that you are a part of, for lack of a better term, a spiritual ecosystem, as opposed to just alone, individual, and dealing with mundane things." Laura says that faith has played a very important role in her relationships with the Gods. "Faith is key," she explains, because "you need faith in order to have the sort of devotional life that is necessary to build strong reciprocal relationships and to really trust where you are being taken."

Looking back on her upbringing in Santeria, Laura has come to realize that she was raised in a very polytheistic way. At the time, though, it wasn't something that she or her grandmother had ever really considered while she was growing up. Part of this is because Laura and her family were too busy being engaged with the rewarding and fulfilling relationships they were building with the Orisha to worry about the theological particulars.

I was raised around Santeria and it took me a while to be conscious that it was actually, no matter how it was defined, it was polytheistic. I consider the Orishas to be Gods. It kind of was organic. I grew up hearing the stories of different Orishas and different Deities and how They interact with people in a very real, very personal level. They have very distinct personalities. They were never presented to me as archetypes in any way, but as distinct beings with Their own personalities, Their own agendas, Their own likes, that are very powerful and very present. That was how I came to it, just in interacting and knowing these beings and Their stories and feeling Their energy around and watching. My grandmother [who] had a very strong devotion to, and was owned by, Chango—watching my grandmother go to Chango for problems. Different members of my family belonging to different Orishas and their different relationships.

When as an adult, Laura finally recognized that she had come to a path of polytheism, it was both a happy and a sad realization. She had a new understanding of her spirituality, but the person she most wanted to share it with, her Grandmother who had taught her everything she know about serving the Orishas, had already died.

It was bittersweet, in a way. Because by the time—the person who was most influential in my life in terms of my spirituality and my practices and my path was my grandmother. She died when I was 10. So, after She died, I grew closer to her and tried to maintain that connection and keep that connection vibrant so I got more interested in the things that sustained her. I got more interested in Santeria, more involved. It was bittersweet because when I was then, a younger kid, I wasn't at an age to maybe ask her all the things I wanted to ask her that later I really wanted to ask. I could still communicate with her but I still wished that I could have sat there at the kitchen table and had talks with her and had the kind of access that my mom had with her by being able to know her for a longer period of time. I was lucky that I was close with a lot of my grandmother's friends, so I had them as a resource as well. The bitter part came because my mother who was raising me went in a very different direction...When she got remarried to my dad who adopted me—he's Jewish—and my mom converted to Judaism. So my mom was going very much in a monotheistic route, and so were a lot of my family that I was around. It was kind of isolating in a way. My grandfather was still alive and he was a good resource, but it did make it a kind of a charged thing with mom. I think I did have an easier time of it because I was a Cuban in Miami and working with Orishas. What could be more natural than that? I was lucky, I guess.

In Santeria, the Orisha with whom you have the most intense devotional relationship is said to "own your head." That is to say that the Orisha has taken a deep personal interest in guiding your physical health and well-being, as well as your spiritual growth and development as a person, ever since the day you were born. The understanding is that this Orisha owns you because They helped form who you are and how you see the world. In return, you offer service to this Orisha who "owns your head."[*] Laura had a very interesting experience because when the time came for her to divine who owned her head, she discovered that one who owned her head…was actually the Norse God Loki.

Even before I was aware, there was sort of a "reserved for" sign on me. Actually, it wasn't a strange concept to me because I grew up knowing that everybody had a ruling Orisha, a ruling

---

[*] Mary Ann Clark: Santeria: Correcting the Mysteries and Uncovering the Realities of a Growing Religion (Westport, CT: Praeger), 125-127.

Deity, and it means that They have a very close connection to you. You belong to Them, for whatever reason. I very much believe that They pick you rather than you pick Them. They are your patron. They are with you throughout your life and They sort of guide you from behind the scenes. Sometimes openly and sometimes not so openly. You can choose to embrace it or you can choose to resist it. I was raised in a culture where you embraced it. So I did. Which made it a lot easier, I think. Part of it is that part of your wyrd or your destiny is to be a work partner for that Deity and do Their work, be Their hands and eyes and mouth in the world. And take orders.

For years I grew up with Santeria. I always figured that that would just be it for me. It's an ancestral tradition for me as well. I still do practice it as much of what I do. But I got swooped down upon by and owned by a Norse Deity. I found that very hard to say no to. I always thought I was going to end up staying with Santeria. Then, it was made known to me who that was, who owned me. It was Loki. That was great, but it did take me into this whole other arena.

Laura grew up honoring Elegua, Chango, Yemaya, and Oshun. She explains that although she is owned by Loki, she has still strong, close, relationships with these four Orishas. Laura tends to see her Orishas as Gods, and uses the terms "God" and "Orisha" interchangeably.

My relationship with Them continues. They are like family. That didn't stop. There is an ancestral tie there as well. I have different family members and different ancestors who are owned by each of Them. Those relationships remain strong and close and connected. That continues. So I believe in many Gods, some of whom I'm close to, others that I'm not as close to, but I respect Them all.

According to Laura, she has had several experiences that confirmed for her that Deities are real and interested in interacting with us. She also says that Santeria prepared her for these experiences because in the culture of Santeria, these sorts of experiences are expected and affirmed.

I think that is one of the things that made all of this easier for me. I was raised in a culture where I expected that and that was the default position. They interact with us. They interact very actively and guide us, sometimes rescue us in tough situations. I grew up hearing about stories that each of the Orishas had actively done. I remember a story that my grandmother told once. She accidentally offended one of Them and They appeared to her to let her know. Yeah, so. She had done something—I don't know what it was, she wouldn't discuss it. But she had Yemaya appear to her in chains, very upset. You best be believin' it was a bad day to be a chicken in Havana when that happened. Because she went to fix it very quickly.

Even my mother, who ran away from Santeria because it overwhelmed her and she was kind of scared of it. She told me a story when I was growing up that she had done something and had said something about not needing Chango. Chango is syncretized with Saint Barbara My mother had this beautiful color picture of Saint Barbara in a frame in her room and she walked into her room after making that comment and there was this flash because the picture inside the frame had caught on fire. Yes. It had burned up to ash. All that was left was this image in ash of Saint Barbara burned into the back of the frame. Which freaked her to no end. That day was also a bad day to be a chicken in Miami, because my grandmother got busy. There's a lot of, well, chickens don't do well with Cubans. I think we've established that. So, yeah, I grew up with that.

Always, even in my dreams as a kid, if I ran into trouble, even in my dreams if I was having a nightmare, in my dream I would start screaming out for Chango and Chango would show up in my dream to protect me. In life, whenever there would be a problem or something would go awry, I would call out to one of Them. Interestingly enough, things would be resolved in a certain way, usually a way characteristic of the Orisha I had asked for help. So, I very much grew up believing that there are powers and forces greater than us and They definitely interact. Loki was very active and arranged things a certain way that when everything clicked, doors began to open and things began to go a certain way. So yeah, definitely. A lot of experiences with having Them be very present and very personal.

When They show up, that to me confirms that They are real. When They pop in on you and very loudly let you know what They want or don't want. Also, things that will happen, like when They come in to tell you that something is going to happen or somebody is going to help you out unexpectedly and you're like, yeah, that's not going to happen. And then all of a sudden the person They said is going to help you out helps you out. That, to me, is a big confirmation. When you go to Them and you are up against the wall and because you are up against the wall, you ask for a favor—something very specific—and that specific thing then happens. That is another confirmation.

Loki was really, really clear with me and gave me specific names of people who were going to be very important touchstones on my journey. At the time, I didn't know them. He gave me a couple names, like "Person A" and "Person B" are going to help you out a lot, and you're like, "yeah right, because I have never met Person A or Person B, and I don't see how that's going to happen." And then within the space of a couple weeks, someone you know says randomly to you, "you should contact Person A or Person B. I know them. Let me ask them if it's okay if I give you their contact information." And so you contact them and then they say, "you need to come out and meet with me because Loki said that I'm supposed to help you out with something." All of a sudden you are like, "Wow! I didn't even know Person A and it's 3 weeks later and I'm on my way to go visit Person A and hang out with them because Loki told them the same thing that He told me, and Loki told them to invite me to hang out." Yeah, so that kind of stuff, absolutely kind of confirms it and seals it for me.

Because her introduction to Loki came from her experiences with and personal gnosis of Him, Laura did not have any of the preconceptions about His character or personality that would have come from reading the Norse mythology and folklore. As a result, she looks upon the lore as a starting point to understand certain things about Him, but not as a definitive reference source.

The thing that's interesting with a lot of the Norse mythology that is written down is that while the religion was actually being practiced pre-Christianization, it was primarily an oral tradition. You had a lot of people recording things a hundred, two hundred, three hundred years after it was already fading as the dominant religious path. So, my relationship to the lore is: I read it, I look at it, there are parts of it that I connect with more than others. I always, in the back of my mind, kind of take it as a jumping-off place because I know it may have been influenced by the agenda of the Christians who were writing it down, who were not practitioners of the religion. So, I look at it as a jumping-off place as a way to connect.

But it's not the only way to connect, because the Gods are real and not archetypes. I don't think that They have been static and not doing anything. I don't think that They're ossified like a fly in amber, trapped in the lore and what the lore has to say. They've been doing Their thing for the past millennia, whether people have been consciously aware of it or interacted with Them or not. So, it is a jumping-off place. I try to bear that in mind and I'm open to the final decision, which is "what do They have to say about Themselves?" And what do They want? There are things that the lore doesn't address at all, because it's very modern.

I find that Loki is very conversant with modern technology. And is able to understand and deal with things like, and sometimes in pleasant and unpleasant ways, with things like computers. He can crash a hard drive, I'm sure. So, it's just kind of interesting. I also think that not only are They active, I think that even Gods from different pantheons have cross-pantheon alliances and relationships. I can tell you, I swear, that Loki and Eleggua hang out. I know. I'm just like, He and Eleggua hang out. That's just my take on it.

Laura characterizes her relationships with the Goddesses and Gods as being very familial. In her experience, the Gods want to connect with the people who love and serve Them. Laura feels this connection very strongly.

They are closer than close, They are like family. When you work with Them for a long time over time...especially growing up and hearing about the Orishas and the patakis—Their stories and legends—hearing about how They have done things and helped different members of the family. Just knowing that even if no human being likes you or cares about you, even if the world is pissed off at you, you still have someone to go to and even if your own mother is upset with you, do you need a mother? Go to the ocean, talk to Yemaya about it and walk in Her water. Talk to Her and take it there. Shed your tears. Let Her know. It's just an overwhelming feeling of connection to Them. They know what we're about and They can really read our thoughts and our hearts and They're able to connect. They want to connect, I think They're hungry for that. That's no different in any pantheon. One of the things I would like to see more of within the Norse pantheon is people engaging with Them in that level. There are a lot of people who follow Norse traditions but are hesitant, wanting to keep the Holy Powers at sort of an arm's distance and that's not where They want to be. They want to weave Themselves into our lives and our stories and our fabric. The want to become a part of that. They want us to wake up in the morning and talk to Them and to say goodnight when We go to sleep. They want that connection just like the Orishas have with Their followers and Their devotees. They are craving it. Possibly even more so because They've been ignored for so many centuries.

Laura has experienced conflicts between herself and others because of her personal emphasis on a very hard polytheism. She takes issue with those who insist that the Gods are facets or archetypes, and is willing to speak about her view. One of the things she thinks that softer polytheists are unwilling to consider is the idea of a Deity so personally invested in you that they could become upset or even angry with you, and you would have to take steps to remedy the situation.

Being a hard polytheist who believes in Deities as very real and distinct beings and not archetypes or thought forms or imaginary friends has led to some tension. Especially because I believe in reciprocity and serving the Gods as opposed to having the Gods exist to give me cool stuff…I'm a really hard polytheist. I do not think of the Gods as interchangeable or generic. I see Them as incredibly distinct with distinct personalities. Their own agendas, Their own likes and dislikes. Because culturally I grew up with this idea of serving Them and doing as They ask, and if you say you are going to do it, you do it because They are so powerful. I grew up with a mindset that yes, They love you, but They will lay the smackdown if you screw up. I grew up with that as a matter of course. So I have some big issues sometimes when I see people kind of making light of or taking it really lightly, or being what I was raised to see as disrespectful. It's not like I would go and yell, but I will definitely make my feelings known when I see it.

So, I know that a lot of people find that an alien concept: The idea that a God can be pissed off. Especially when I hear people regarding themselves as on the same level as their Deity. Like "They want it done this way, but I'm not going to do that because I don't really believe that They could get upset." Or that They wouldn't be all fluffy and kind and happy all the time and always in a good mood. And the idea that also like, this kind of hubris that humanity is so special that the Gods are there to just give us stuff endlessly and grant our wishes without us doing anything. This idea that the Gods exist to be here for our self-actualization. I'm like, "really? Because that's not the way I grew up looking at it."

Santeria is founded on intense ritual service to the Orisha and the ancestors. Many rituals happen in a group setting, but Santerians have fairly intense daily, weekly, and monthly devotional rituals. Laura has adapted these rituals and this attitude to her relationship with Loki and other Gods she has come to know in recent years.

In terms of my personal practices there isn't a day that goes by where I'm not thinking about or doing something for Loki or one of the Orishas. It's a daily thing. It was always kind of the fabric of my life; "It's Monday, so I'm going to do something with Eleggua. It's Tuesday so time to say hello to Chango, let me lay out some offerings." With Loki, it's a daily thing because He's there every day and His altar is in my bedroom. I wake up in the morning and Their altars are the first thing I see. I go to sleep at night and Their altars are the last thing that I see. I tend them, I make offerings, I'll lay out food if I'm having something. Like today; I just went by the liquor store and part of it is, I'd like this but I think that my ancestors would like that, and the land spirits would enjoy this, and I think that I'm going to get this bottle over here for Loki and this is for Odin. That sort of thing...Laying out offerings, devotional practices, prayer, meditation...It becomes kind of a natural part of your everyday life, where you are conscious of Them and the exchange of energy deepens. If you have family and you live with family, you make yourself something and you ask them, "Hey, would you like some...?"

They may ask you to make things, ritual garb. Loki recently told me, "I need you to make me a certain kind of hat for you to wear to get yourself in sort of a headspace." He was very specific about it. I am not a crochet-er. I can, but it's really pitiful. He had me going to not even the regular yarn place. I was going into the cheaper yarn fabric store kind of chain artsy craftsy sort of place. I heard an "oh no. There is a specialty store that has really good wool and you need to go there." I'm like, really? He's like, "You'll come back here later because you are going to need A, B, C, and D from here." But going to the special yarn place to get the specific kind of yarn, and to sit there in front of His altar making this thing He wanted me to make even though it was painful for me to have to do it. Sitting there in front of His altar thinking about Him with every stitch. And praying with every stitch for, like, five hours, to make this very freaky kooky hat. That He wanted me to make. He has His purposes. It's stuff like that. Having your day hijacked because They're like, "hey, guess what I'd really like." Being open to that. Yeah.

So, it's kind of woven into a sort of every day thing. But I was used to that because I grew up around that and seeing my grandmother do that, and even my grandfather do that to a lesser degree. In our family we are also like that with the ancestors as well. So, every day I get up and I do something for my ancestors. Then I will go and do stuff for my Gods.

This level of engagement does, Laura admits, impact her normal work-a-day life…especially if one works in psychiatric nursing. She found that Loki had definite preferences about her working environment, and she says that He very much took steps to change it.

Loki really had a preference for that for two reasons: 1, because I had been injured badly and had my back broken and had two spinal fusions after being attacked by a patient; and 2, because I keep a really low profile at work regarding my personal beliefs. Especially with psychiatric nursing. I knew that this was not a career in which I could be like, "yes, and now I have to go because the voices in my head are telling me that They want ebboes." That's not one of those things that works out really great. And it could potentially, had I been open about my practices, could have led to an inpatient stay. Because they would not have—in that paradigm there really isn't any healthy way to do what I do. I never bought into [that paradigm] because that wasn't where I was coming from culturally. In psychiatric nursing I definitely had to pretend and keep very separate my work and my personal life. In a way that I am not as fearful about in medical nursing…

Working in a mental hospital was sort of like boot camp for shielding—it really is. If you take that home with you that will wipe you out. I had thought, prior to going to work in a psychiatric hospital, I had thought that I was very good at shielding and grounding and cleansing and doing all that. Even for me it was exhausting. The first six months, trying to keep that from following me home, and the energy of it, was just brutal. So, yeah, that part of it too. Mostly, it was also really frustrating.

Working in psych was really frustrating because there were a couple of times—and I was lucky I was able to help some of these situations—there were a couple of times where I was the only Hispanic staff person. And there were a couple times when we would get Hispanic patients who were very involved in Santeria and because they had shared their beliefs with the interviewing psychiatrist, they were slapped with a diagnosis of paranoid schizophrenia. And then I had to go and advocate and say, "You don't understand. This is a cultural thing. This is a spiritual practice. They are not delusional and they are not hallucinating. This is their belief. Unless you are willing to say that all Hispanics are paranoid schizophrenics, you're in trouble. I was actually able to get them to rethink those diagnoses based on that and the fact that if you have a psychiatrist interviewing somebody with their three years of college Spanish and the patient doesn't speak English, there can be a lot of problems with cross-cultural understanding and labeling incorrectly.

I threw down with a few psychiatrists over these issues over the years, which was professionally unpleasant. One woman came in and she had been sexually assaulted by someone. When she described this person, she said "es un Diablo: he's a devil." A very nice woman, not delusional at all, very anxious and upset because of what she had been through but not psychotic. I came into the nurse's station and I opened the chart and I saw this diagnosis of paranoid schizophrenia and I went to the psychiatrist and said, "what is this?" And she said, "oh, that woman is psychotic. She thinks she was raped by the devil." I was just like, "oh, HELL no," and I went and I talked with the woman. Then I went back to the psychiatrist and I said, listen: she was saying 'un Diablo' to tell you this is such a bad man. She knows it was not the Devil; it was a guy and I can tell you what his name is. It's not Satan, it's Jose, alright? She was just trying to express herself and you misunderstood her and you're gonna slap her with a diagnosis that's going to ruin her life." Very scary...Loki wanted me out of that.

Even though she was working in an awful environment, Laura acknowledges that it was difficult to let go. Her willingness to surrender her situation to Loki and trust that He was going to help her find something better was very difficult. This was the sort of difficulty that demanded faith on Laura's part.

It's hard to let go of certain things. When you are used to them and they are comfortable to you It can be scary. Part of the stuff with me is that He wanted me out of psychiatric nursing into another branch of nursing. And that happened, but in between there was a six month period of unemployment. That can be pretty terrifying.

Also, along the way, "oh by the way," the marriage had to go. That's a hard one. I fought to hold on to that even though it was not a good situation. It was a situation I knew and it was what

I was used to. Even though I was willing to settle for it, Loki wasn't willing to settle for it, and in the end I tried to cling on to the marriage even though He said it was going to go. In the end, it was my husband who walked out, but I knew it was coming. Part of it was because he couldn't understand or accept some of my practices or beliefs. He didn't understand it, he wasn't on board with it and I wasn't willing to back down from it. I knew it was a price I would ultimately have to pay, but boy I was kicking and screaming. That was hard.

Sometimes the Gods tell you something and you're like, "Oh, that's wonderful." Sometimes They tell you something is horrible, and even thought it's horrible and you hate it, you can't let go of it. [But] you can't let go of your faith, in order to try and fix something that can't be fixed...Part of it was you have to be willing to go. When the Gods tell you it's time to move on, it's time to move on. You can do it the easy way or the hard way sometimes. You can do it your way or you can do it Their way. The will give you a few opportunities to do it, and then They will intervene and make sure it happens one way or another...

I think that our Gods want us to be true to ourselves and true to Them. Usually there is a high price for that. Especially in our culture where people come to this path and they already have family and friends and careers and spouses, and sometimes not all of that can stay in place because the other people involved aren't going to understand, they aren't going to get it and you have to make some really brutal choices. Are you going to be true to who you are and true to who They want you to be, or are you going to cave? My hat's off to people who do that. Especially who don't grow up in a cultural context where that's an accepted and understood thing.

Laura says she really wishes that people understood that polytheism isn't a primitive, retrograde, superstitious precursor of modern scientific though that we should gratefully put behind us. The assumption polytheism is a lower rung on the evolutionary ladder than monotheism,, is very suspect, in Laura's opinion.

There tends to be a belief among monotheists that polytheism is something primitive and unformed and unsophisticated that was replaced when cultured people with sense outgrew their child-like tribal notions of the universe...I wish that they understood that it isn't some kind of primitive precursor to the natural evolution of becoming so wise that you realize that none of it really exists. There is a viewpoint that polytheism was sort of a step on the spiritual evolutionary path, up to the pinnacle of evolution of spirituality, which would be monotheism. And there is very much that attitude. Polytheism is something that primitive people who don't know any better believe. Polytheists aren't backwards or uneducated or superstitious. It's not coming out of that place. Polytheism comes from a legitimate place of connection and love.

Then, there is also a paternalistic attitude of pat, pat on the head, "isn't that interesting how delusional you are?" Like somehow our traditions are myths and yet the Bible is real...I wish they understood that there is a balance to understanding that you are a part of a spiritual ecosystem and that humanity is not the pinnacle of that ecosystem. In order to be in balance with ourselves and our planet and other people, we need to be in balance with our ancestors, land spirits, the Gods. There is such a thing as being able to respect the land that we live on and the spirit of the land that we live with, as opposed to trying to dominate it.

As a lot of these traditions—there are certainly a lot of traditions that are still alive that are still polytheistic and it's sort of an unbroken chain. For a lot of polytheists in the US, many of them find themselves in the position of coming to these traditions, especially the ones being called to European traditions where the chain was broken along the way. Getting right with our ancestors and having a strong ancestral practice is, to me, really key in rebuilding that. Europeans have not thought of themselves in that way for quite some time, and maybe that's why there is a disconnect in terms of relationship to the land, but everybody has an indigenous religious tradition and in every indigenous religious tradition on this earth there were several components. One was an ongoing relationship with their dead, an ongoing relationship and awareness of the sentience of the land and the land spirit, and the relationship to ancestral Gods, the Gods of that land, the Gods of that place. In trying to rebuild and reweave that, our ancestors are in a really brilliant place. All of us have ancestors who were polytheistic. Some of them were more recent, some of them you have to go a way back. Getting right with one's ancestors and establishing that kind of a practice and re-linking to that. They have so much to teach us about relationships to land spirits, relationships to the Gods that we think are lost and forgotten, but they're not.

We carry our ancestors with us in our DNA. We carry them

with us everywhere we go. We are the sum total of all their experiences and hopes and dreams and fears and all of their lives up to this point. They are a great resource. It's great to see more and more people who are polytheist having strong ancestral practices because that's a very important link back. Our ancestors have a lot to teach us about how to be in a right relationship with Them, our environment, and the Gods…if you go back far enough you will find ancestors who had particular devotions to particular Gods. That makes connecting with those Gods so much easier and so much more layered and nuanced and meaningful.

Caris

Caris, 42, undertook quite a spiritual journey to reach her present path of polytheism. Born into the Catholic tradition, Caris explored fundamentalist Christianity, Zen Buddhism, and Paganism before finally discovering Hellenic polytheism. One key aspect of her practice is that Caris does not expect the Gods to necessarily be interested in, or particularly needful of, human attention in general. In Caris' view, They are busy doing Their own things, but are open to developing relationships with specific individuals if properly approached. This mindset has lead Caris into a tremendous personal strength and self-sufficiency which she feels makes her involvement with Them, when such occasions arise, to be that much more powerful. This independence is very helpful, because Caris says there aren't many Hellenics to interact with in her geographic region. Despite her isolation, Caris honors the Hellenic Gods, and has developed enduring devotional relationships with some of Them.

In Caris' view, the very notion of such a supreme Deity as is found in near-Eastern monotheism is unreasonable at best and nonsensical at worst. She is quite pointed in her rejection of a single omnipotent God such as is worshipped by those religions.

> *The idea of a God with many faces almost certainly presupposes the existence of a God who is omnipotent, omniscient, omnipresent, and omnibenevolent. It just about presupposes that, and it doesn't make a lot of sense to me. The recent storms that have been going on in Missouri[§] really brought that home for me. I was talking to my boyfriend today—who is also a Hellenic, by the way—he said, "you know, when the storms first started happening, you heard a lot of people talking about faith and praying and "God's gonna save me. You're not hearing shit about that now. Have you heard anybody praying or talking to God or anything about that now? No. They're all looking for Their loved ones." It's like, okay, faith is not working, so let's go dig out the rubble. You start realizing that the monotheistic worldview, it is failing.*

Caris' definition of "polytheism" is short and to the point.

[§]This interview took place in summer of 2011, shortly after the massive tornado that decimated Joplin, Missouri.

"Simply put," she says, the word "polytheism" means "belief in more than one God. It's pretty simple. It means that you don't think that the world is monotheistic." In Caris' view, polytheism is more reasonable than monotheism.

> *The world makes a lot more sense when you've got a bunch more Gods and a lot of committee activity going on. That They're not omnipotent, They're not omniscient, They're not omnipresent, and They're not omnibenevolent. Bad things happen. It makes a lot more sense than a God who's everywhere. Polytheism also leaves a lot more room for those bad things to happen. Things that don't make a lot of sense do happen. The monotheistic worldview presupposes that that One God not only loves you very much and want what's best for you, which we can patently see isn't the case, but also that He actually wants or cares about you believing in or loving Him back. He's very jealous. I had boyfriends in high school who treated me better than that, though. Really.*

In her view, the divinity of the Gods is not problematized by tragedies and disasters, because They don't have control over everything that happens. Moreover, in her polytheist worldview, the Gods do not necessarily need or demand human worship. Caris also recognizes that polytheism allows for the Gods to just not be that overly preoccupied with human welfare.

> *Polytheism leaves room for the Gods to not really give a shit, and I like that. It makes me so much happier…That's a level of scrutiny I don't want to deal with. I like it that the Gods do Their thing, They're busy—like being the CEO of Microsoft or something and I'm doing my thing over here, and everything is going fine. Nobody needs anything from anybody, we just leave each other alone. I really like the idea of Gods who have Their own things to do. [Monotheism] is almost like having a really clingy boyfriend—you want Him to be able to go and entertain himself sometimes. You want Him to go have drinks with his friends. You want Him to have other people to talk to and stuff to do. And if He's just obsessed with people loving Him, that seems unhealthy to me.*

> *It's not that [the Gods] don't care, I mean, there's something to be said for people who want to have this big personal relationship with a God. But isn't that sort of like an addiction to a monotheistic sky-daddy in a way? That we just HAVE to believe that there is something much bigger than us that is totally wanting us to love Them and They want to totally love us back?*

Isn't that sort of the same thing happening? It's sort of refreshing to think that They have Their own stuff to do and are perfectly content to go do it without me. That idea fits the facts I've observed a lot better than the other idea does.

Another significant point in Caris' view of the Gods is that she does not necessarily see Them as ineffable. She says that, "If I really needed to understand why Zeus impregnated Io, I'm sure it wouldn't be all that difficult for Zeus to explain." Caris finds the Gods' lack of ineffability to be a positive thing, because when one views Deity as incomprehensible, they are less likely to puzzle things out for themselves. But if the mystery is knowable, then learning and searching become important ways to connect with the Gods.

When you have a God who is completely ineffable, then He isn't going to be something that you can completely understand at all. An ineffable God is one who, by definition, cannot be understood. He has His things He does for this reason and you will never, ever, understand it, so don't worry about it. It kind of advises you to check your mind at the door and not worry about it. I think you need to worry about it. I think you need to start puzzling it out. Why did Zeus impregnate Io? Why does He cheat on His wife? Why did these things happen? Why was Apollo hung up on Cassandra, what happened there? What was the reason for that? I think that though [the reasons] are a lot higher than that, I think that if we actually found out what that cosmological reason was, then we'd understand what it was. That's what I like about polytheism. I think it's much more of a Hermetic "as above, so below" kind of situation; They're not so far outside the realm of human experience that we would just never, never, never understand. Why did God let that 16-month old daughter get ripped out of her mother's arms in Joplin? Oh, He had a good reason. No, I don't think He did. I think it was just something really awful that happened. I don't think God had anything to do with it. If you believe in God, the Christian Deity, there is some ineffable purpose to a 16-month-old getting killed in a tornado. Not so nice. I don't think the Gods should be ineffable. If He was ineffable, I wouldn't want any part of it. And, oh, wait...I didn't. Guess not.

Her understanding of faith, however, is more complicated. Faith isn't a belief so much as it is "your hypothesis; you look how it's working out, you change the hypothesis to fit the facts you've observed." Her view of faith has evolved significantly since her Catholic beginnings and fundamentalist Christian experience.

I was a fundamentalist Christian for most of the first half of my life. At that point faith meant that you believed in something that had absolutely no basis in it. There wasn't any logic in it. You just had faith and prayed a lot and believed really hard that it would all kind of work out, but that's sort of like having faith that you're going to win the lottery, isn't it? I mean really. There is absolutely no evidence that you're gonna win the lottery, there is nothing that says you absolutely will win the lottery. You've never won the lottery before, but by God if you just keep thinking about it and have faith, you're gonna win the lottery. That's kind of evolved in the last ten years or so for me. For me, faith is a belief that is consistent with what you've seen before, and what you expect in the future. It's not so much a belief that something is going to happen regardless of any evidence to the contrary.

Caris' understanding of faith takes on interesting dimensions when it is applied in a polytheist context. In her view, the Gods' existence is not predicated on human acknowledgement thereof. Rather, faith often informs one's relationships with the Divine and guides who a person may ultimately become.

The Divine exists regardless of someone's faith in it. I have a strong faith in my spiritual worldview, but I don't think the Gods really give a tinker's damn whether or not people believe or worship Them; They're busy doing God things. I don't need faith in the world's banking systems, either, as long as they do their jobs. Faith is an emotion, and emotions can be so volatile. If it has a role at all, it serves to draw the seeker to the path that works for that person.

Even so, faith of a different sort plays an important role in Caris' practice. Rather than being a belief that the Gods exist, faith is a belief that the Gods are willing to work with you if you devote the time and effort to working with Them.

I totally believe that They are there even though I can't see them. I mean, Verizon is still there even though I can't see it, right? I think that faith plays an important role, though, I do. Belief in the Gods' system and what They want us to do, the sort of role They envision for us, especially in the Hellenic part is that you need to try to make a difference. That's super important. I think one can be an atheist and be a perfectly fine contributing member of society. The kind of person you are isn't predicated naturally by your faith, but your faith can help inform what you become. I think that there's going to be times when people need to lean on those Gods a little bit, for support or asking for things to happen. And the nice thing about it not being a magic sky-daddy is that, with the Hellenic Gods, if you are gonna ask for a favor from Them, you damn well better make it worth Their time. Why would They pay attention to prayer? What would draw Them from Their duties to look down upon this situation and do something about it? That's when, I think, They can play a major role. You find out what that God likes, you find out how to talk to Them, you find out what Their preferences are, what They like to be called, the kinds of gifts you should give. You make it worth Their time. If you make it worth Their time enough, amazing things can happen. And I think that that kind of partnership between people and the Gods—that you will give Them this worship, you will give Them this favor you promised, and in return They will think about doing this. I really like that. I like Gods who can be bargained with.

Caris grew up in a devoutly Catholic family that has generations of involvement with the Church. Unfortunately, her family's religion left her without any sense of inner peace. Her many attempts to seek out spiritual sustenance at one point led her to abandon religion altogether. The discovery of Paganism opened her eyes somewhat, but it didn't really speak to Caris' spirit.

It's kind of, well, it was definitely different. I started out Catholic. My whole family is pretty much still Catholic. I still have all these relatives that are nuns and priests and stuff. My grandparents are really staunch about it, too. I'm talking Lent, they fasted on meatless Fridays-all that stuff. They did all of that and I didn't know there was any other way to be religious. I began to get into more and more extreme versions of Christianity to try to find some sort of spiritual peace, but no matter what I did, I couldn't find peace. I converted to fundamentalism in high school and married a Pentecostal preacher when I was in college. Finally I realized how abusive that system was, realized that there really wasn't any kind of Christianity that made moral sense and fit the reality I could see all around me, and left the religion altogether.

I didn't know what else to do. I ended up in Zen Buddhism for a little while. I think it really helped center me a lot, it got rid of all those drama propensities you develop when you're fundamentalist. And from there, I thought that's not really quite hitting it either, and ended up looking into other Pagan traditions, but everything I knew about Paganism I had absorbed from different fundamentalist Christian authors writing about how bad Paganism was. Seriously. I think one of the first inklings I had about other religions was Bob Larson's Book of Cults. *Some of it was decently written, but I don't think most Christians realize how off-target he was about a lot of it. But at the time it was written, I don't think even Silver Ravenwolf was a cub back then. It was just a really long time ago.*

So there wasn't really a lot of information about Paganism and what you did have was middle-aged ladies wearing way too much eye makeup and a lot of beaten silver jewelry. (laughs). No offense. But that's all there really was back then. And I just thought, "Wow. That doesn't really make a lot of sense to me, either." So I went without religion for a long time. Finally, the guy I was dating was kind of looking into British Trad at the time and hiding it from me because he knew my general opinion of Paganism at that point. When it finally came out, we ended up in this Pagan group in our town, which had this huge, thriving Pagan scene at the time. It was awesome. But I didn't know a lot about it. I attended then just to meet people. But I wasn't really drawn into it...

While her discovery of Paganism was helpful, it wasn't until she discovered the reconstructionist movements like Hellenion that she began to seek out religion again. She was surprised and excited to find that there are people still worshipping the old Gods and Goddesses.

One day while driving to one of these Pagan meetings, I burst out to the then-BF, "If I could just worship Artemis, I'd totally do it, but nobody worships like that anymore. Everybody's all over this eclectic 'one God with a bunch of faces' stuff." He said, "I know some people who actually do worship that way." Suddenly I felt like my eyes had been opened for the first time. It was like walking into a Baskin-Robbins and seeing all those flavors, when all you've ever had was Neapolitan from the grocery store. I said, "Wait, like they pray to Artemis? It's not Wicca?" He said he thought it was different, and we could talk to them and find out what the deal was there. I never looked back.

One of the things that drew Caris into Hellenic polytheism in particular is that she has a personal connection to it. While she does not have any Greek ancestry, the meaning of her real name[*] is found in ancient Greek mythology.

My name is actually the name of a character from a Greek myth and I wanted to know where it came from, so I looked it up in Bullfinch's Mythology. I was like, 11. You want to talk about a heavy read? I was always interested in Greek mythology and it seems that it's been twisted into my life with every turn I take. There was a program I was in as a young child called the Athena program. The kids who were in it didn't even know who Athena was, and I was totally happy about that because I did. It made me really feel a part of it. It just seems that it was all sort of speaking to me all this time. I always felt drawn to Artemis, Aphrodite, all those Goddesses. When it came time to settle on something, and it became clear that actual, honest-to-Gods polytheism was a possibility even in this modern day, it seemed like the most natural thing to me. Considering that I'm nowhere near Greek in ancestry, I guess that doesn't make sense. It still felt very natural.

When asked if she'd had any personal experiences with the Gods that confirmed her belief in Them, Caris replied, "Kinda personal ones, yes." While Caris has no expectation that the Gods are always going to be engaged in her life, she has had experiences involving death and disaster that have validated her belief.

All of this really awful stuff was happening to my mother when I became polytheistic in 2002-3. My mom was battling cancer at the time and that's a really rough way to go...It brings up so many emotions. Right before she died, in mid-July, I found myself in the hospital chapel. It was one of that multi-denominational thingies that aren't supposed to be for any particular religion. The doctors told me the coma was probably going to last for a few weeks. That she probably wasn't going to wake up. Everything was fucked up. Her heart, her lungs, she was basically breathing with mechanical help and a billion drugs. I just prayed. I went to the back of the chapel and found a book where you can write-in your prayers. It's kind of a tradition for people to do that, I know now. Grief is a time when you write your prayers down. It's pretty well-known.

I happened to notice while I was paging through it how disgusted I felt. The book was page after page after page of "God, I trust you completely. We want to take grandma home with us this weekend." I'm like, no wonder God didn't weigh in. These people might as well just be praying totally at random. I was angry to see them basically demanding their God do things and "name it and claim it" in His name, as if they knew 100% for sure He'd do these amazing miracles for them, when I knew very well that He either wouldn't, or that the person would get better just thanks to modern medicine.

But I'd had so many things that had happened over the hospitalization that it was hard not to think that someone was watching out for my family. I would look out in the woods nearby and see the most weird bird behavior. I would tell my mom about it before the coma and she would say, "oh yeah. That's a mother bird, she's preparing her baby birds. Trying to make sure they're fed." And it would blow my mind.

So in the chapel, I wrote a prayer. I prayed that Artemis would take my mother as quickly as possible. I knew she wasn't going to wake up. Everything was too screwed up. I wrote that I was not going to pray for healing because I just didn't see how that could happen at this point, "but if You can end her suffering as quickly as possible, I think that everybody is going to be very appreciative. I will plant You a garden if You do this for me." Then I signed it and went upstairs. That day, she was dead. I was very grateful that she went without suffering too much more.

I was pulling her house together afterwards, and the first thing to happen was that the newspaper delivered a packet of wildflower seeds. They were doing a big "green month" kind of thing and everyone was getting packets of seeds; red ones. So, I was like, okay, I guess I am planting a garden. Very good. I planted the garden afterward and the flowers were very lovely. But the next thing that happened was, about a week after the death I was still getting the house together—My mom was a major pack rat. I was just, as you can probably imagine, pretty upset. I prayed to Persephone and said, "I just want to know that everything is okay, and that I've done the right things. I'd really appreciate some word from You to reassure me that my mother is safe with You guys and that wherever good people go when they die that she's there. I just want to know that everything is okay."

About four hours later, the derecho** of 2003 hit Memphis. Yeah, I'm serious. It was that day. It was the same day. Like, I'm getting up to go to the bathroom because my 18-year-old cat woke me up and the sky was emerald green. There was a

---

** Translated from the Spanish, the word "derecho" means "straight ahead." A "derecho" is "an hours-long windstorm associated with a line of severe thunderstorms. It's a result of straight-line winds, not the rotary winds of a tornado, hence its name. Steven A Ackerman, <u>Meterology: Understanding the Atmosphere</u> (Bolingbrook, IL: Jonas & Bartlett Learning, INC), 389.

bathroom under the staircase. I grabbed the cat and all but teleported into it. I ended up in there for about 2 hours, praying as hard as I could that nothing would happen. I was terrified to hear that the whole house—they say the house breathes. And it really does. It sounds like there is a freight train coming down on you. That derecho leveled most of Memphis. It took out almost every traffic light. I don't think very many people died--the newspapers made a big deal out of how few people even got hurt, but some people were out of power for months.

Across the street from our townhouse, the buildings were ripped apart to shreds. My mom's townhouse was totally untouched. The windows weren't even broken. And we got power back later that afternoon. I really think that prayer saved my life. I was smack in the middle of the storm's path. Right across the street there were houses ripped up and stuff torn apart everywhere. My mom's brand-new car that she had bought a week before her last hospitalization—amazing timing there—wasn't even scratched. Right across the street from all this stuff I was safe and my stuff was okay. I was like, Oh my gosh. So, I don't think the Gods seriously sent the derecho, I just want to say that for the record, but it's kind of hard not to fathom how this horrible thing happened so close to me, but I was perfectly fine and nothing bad happened to me and that the stuff in my freezer didn't even go bad. Kinda weird, don't you think? The timing is pretty interesting. Anyway, from then on, I was committed.

When it comes to her actual religious practice, Caris says that her tradition is very open. While some practices appeal more to her than others, she acknowledges that her approaches may change over time. What's important, she has found, is the small daily observances that keep her spiritually connected.

The Greeks themselves weren't really very rigid about exactly who they worshipped, so I don't see why I should be any different. I'm not drawn to any other tradition's Gods, like Isis, but I'm not closed to the idea. It just doesn't attract me at this time. I'm more drawn to the major and minor Hellenic Gods, as well as some of the other heroes and semi-divine beings in the religion like Aesclepius…

I find out what the two or three Gods I really feel drawn to like, in terms of epithets, in terms of incense to burn. I do find out what incense They like. Aphrodite—rose petals, for example. Things I think They would like, and those are the major things

I do. I don't practice any hard rituals or anything like that. I'm sort of the equivalent of a Sunday Christian, I think... Daily practices, I think there's stuff that everybody does in the Hellenic movement. Kiss your palm, say "Teletaí eisi téleiai. Khaire, Apollo!" *** I really like that. I like that the observances tend to not be dramatic and are more community-based. There is no Hellenic faith-based community up here where I live, which kind of sucks. I'd like there to be one. That would be cool. My ex-boyfriend actually turned in to some major kind of Hellenic high priest in my old hometown. It was so funny. So cool that it happened that way for him. And I admit: frankly, I'm kind of jealous. I would really like that to happen up here. Seriously: Wiccans and Norse gun nuts- that's it up here.

Although she has begun to explore having relationships with other Hellenic Gods, Caris' most significant relationships are with Hermes, Persephone, and Artemis.

I find Hermes fascinating because He has a background for problem-solving that I find very clever. When you feel like there is just no way, Hermes makes a way, and I really like that about Hermes. That is something that I really want to draw upon for my life. I want to have a God behind me who I can call upon if need be who can help me find a way out of something that has no way.

Persephone I find interesting because She is in this really, really weird situation where She gets drawn to Hades and becomes Queen of Hades, and yet She was just an ordinary girl. Well, as normal as one can be if one is the daughter of a Goddess, I guess. She still wasn't this huge Deity or anything, She was just this normal person out gathering flowers one day and then, "Whoa!" I think that what happened to Her is a testament of a someone getting caught in a situation that doesn't really look like it's that awesome, and you do the best you can with it and it turns into something really great. I also think that She is sort of an intermediary. Someone that can intercede for you. Hades just doesn't strike me as a very amenable God. He has lots of things to do. But Persephone, being basically a normal person, I think can intercede for you in those situations. The times that I have called upon Her, the neatest shit happened.

Artemis, again, I felt fond of Her all my life. The idea of some warrior huntress? WOW! That's totally cool. I really like that She charted Her own way. I like that a lot. She's so strong, and

---

*** Greek translation, "The rites are complete. Rejoice, Apollo!"

very independent; not married. Wow. In Greek society? How did that happen? I really like that She exists in the pantheon. I think She is important.

Sooner or later, many practicing polytheists must come to terms with the difference between their experiences of the Gods, and the myths about those Gods. Having abandoned a background of fundamentalist Christian literalism, Caris is unwilling to consider the myths as being literally true. The myths, for Caris, are metaphorical.

I have more of an understanding that mythology is not literal. Religion is, well, fundamentalists really do take all of that stuff literally. Seven days means seven days. We're not talking about seven thousand years; it's seven days. When you get into mythology, you begin to realize that mythology itself shifts and changes. The story of just who Aphrodite married and what happened, that changes depending on who you are reading. The best thing to take away from it is the general concepts. It's more of an allegorical thing, and I really like that, too. It's not dependent upon exactly what ancient Greek word Hesiod used, or Homer, or whoever. I love that. My understanding of that shifted away from, "yeah this really happened. She married Ares. No, She married Hephaestus, no wait, what word for "married" did they use?" Because there's no way whatsoever to take it literally without running into the same problems with contradictory accounts and decidedly ahistorical claims, I had no choice but to move to a much more metaphorical and nuanced view of the source myths. Leaving the literalist world freed me in a lot of ways to explore those metaphorical meanings.

Caris' view of the mythology as metaphorical also prompts her to read the plot points more critically. One thing that sticks out for her is the fact that the Gods are not meant to be role-models for humanity

Zeus cheated on His wife constantly. That's the thing everybody goes to in Hellenicism. Gods go a lot of things that humans aren't really supposed to do. I mean, Zeus LOVED seeing long-time married people. Everyone knows about that, everyone in Hellenicism knows the myths about that, but the stories also tell us that Zeus himself was not faithful. Well, what are you supposed to take from that? Are you supposed to take that it's okay to say that you want to be faithful but go out and cheat anyway? I don't think that's quite what they are driving at. I think the goal for people is that we don't have any great cosmological reason to stray, so we probably shouldn't. [Cheating] is divisive, in general. If Zeus wants to be divisive in

His household, then maybe there's a good reason for it. Not so much down here.

Caris has yet to incorporate the veneration of ancestors and land spirits into her practice. These are things that she is open to exploring at some point, but at present they haven't been a large part of her religious observance.

I don't worship the land or my ancestors largely because I haven't a clue how to do so or if either really care if I worship them or not. I know some Pagans are very drawn to those ideas and that's fine...I'm open to the idea but don't specifically include such things in my admittedly limited practice. I'd love to think that my ancestors can be contacted and help me if I need it. I've had some weird experiences after my mother died that make me feel like she might be helping me in my life. I haven't the foggiest how to deal with those experiences though. My mother asked me to remember her birthday every year and I do, and I light a candle on the day she died (it took a few years to realize I go through a major, major moody funk every year about a month before the big day, so these rituals help a little as a way to memorialize and move past those milestone markers). It pains me that I know so little about my ancestors though. I've begun assembling a family tree this past year—you probably know about that Census data that got released. I got curious and began fooling around with genealogy. I've been astonished at the things I'm finding with it. I'd like to eventually build a memorial of the lives of my ancestors, and maybe one day make a move toward reaching out to them. I've got friends who are way into Vodou and other very ancestor-worship related systems who talk a lot about how rewarding they find their practices. Like I'd venture to say most people do, I feel disconnected from my family line and wouldn't mind getting re-connected with the people in it.

I don't worship any nature spirits but I like thinking about them. I feel like I move through a world inhabited and resounding with such beings. I just don't know what they want, if anything, much less how I'd communicate with them to find out so I can give them what they want. It's an interesting idea. Ultimately I run into the same block I do with most other aspects of religion, be it Pagan or monotheist or whatever else—this problem of not knowing what will reach that other world's ears or how to know just what that other world's denizens want of me and mine.

Some polytheists have experienced conflict with other Pagans due to their emphasis on the existence and veneration of several, distinct, individual Gods and Goddesses. She admits that she doesn't necessarily understand the Wiccan view of Deity, and that the eclecticism often found in Paganism leaves her feeling alienated. These differences notwithstanding, Caris has decided that while disagreements might arise from time to time, these differences "aren't worth getting frictive about."

There are so many different ways to get to the Divine. There are so many different ways that you can express yourself spiritually, that when one person says, "Oh I know the way, I know how to do this, y'all need to listen to me, or we're gonna have some trouble," you're like, "what? How do you know?" I mean, did somebody write it on the sky? Are you positive? Did you see a pillar of flame? What happened here? How do you know?" Well, they don't. They don't know any better than I do. So, you do the best you can but I'm not going to get into a huge fight with someone over religion of any kind. It just isn't worth it. Because you are both fighting over something that you have no actual 100% proof of.

Wiccans are all kind of drinking something that I'm not getting in my cup. I don't know what it is. It's not that they're bad people, I don't want to characterize that they are bad automatically because I don't think that. It's just…such an eclectic worldview. That I am pursuing something that is a bit different than that, you get the feeling that they are like, "oh, you are so cute! Look at you!" You know what I mean? It's not condescension so much, but it's like I think that they feel like I am judging them for being more inclusive and eclectic and I feel like I'm more, in a sense—that they aren't getting what I am trying to say here: really, seriously, I like the idea of there being lots of different Gods. Again, not worth getting frictive about, but there is a sense of alienation there. It's like neither one of us has points that the other one can accept. It's not something really that I think can be met fully, because they're going, "There's one God with a million faces," and I'm like, "no, I think there are 12 of them. Or hundreds, and probably more." But I think They are distinct beings and Wiccans don't usually think that. They choose from what they like from both Paganism and monotheism. And that's fine if it works, but I can't do that. I just don't think that that kind of eclecticism works for me. Maybe it's that fundie background, I don't know…It feels like they are making stuff up on the fly, and I'm reading "Works and Days.'‡ It really does feel like we are drawing from very different sources. If they're happy, then that's cool. Whatever. It's just not something I can be happy doing. And it's why I didn't pursue Paganism until I found out about polytheism.

Caris doesn't have any sweeping statements to make about what she wished people understood about polytheism All she really wants is for people to be aware of its existence.

I just want them to know it exists. If I had known it existed years and years and years ago, in the mid-90's or so, I would have made that change a lot faster. I think a lot of people don't really understand that if you don't feel like the eclectic version of things is working for you, then there are all these people reconstructing all of these different faiths. We are so lucky to be alive in the modern age so you can find what works for you as a person, spiritually, out of all these different paths. I like that a lot. I wish people knew that.

---

‡ "Works and Days" is one of Hesiod's writings and when Caris was more immersed in the community, it was a standard with the others of her group.

114

Brian

Brian, 39, has been polytheist for over 20 years. While Brian has long identified as Pagan and maintained a solitary practice, he eventually joined a Gardnerian Wicca coven and worked with them for a number of years before once again splitting off into solitary spirituality. Though Brian works professionally in the IT field, his religious experiences have encouraged him to undertake postgraduate study of Western neo-Paganism in the context of gender and sexuality. One of the major concerns he has had regarding Wicca, which has been an abiding concern of his for decades, is the significance of gender roles and the hetero-normativity he feels is present in the religion. Brian's solitary religious practice involves regular devotional activities as well as study and meditation. He has established particularly close relationships with Athena, Sylvanus, and Hermes.

Brian's understanding of polytheism recognizes the multiplicity of the divine, but it doesn't necessarily arrange these Divinities into hierarchies. "I see polytheism as the belief in multiple divine entities either in worship or in partnership within a religious framework," he explains, "I said either in worship or in partnership because in some ways I don't necessarily see these things as a hierarchical relationship." According to Brian, one significant aspect of a polytheistic worldview is that very often, the human relationship with Deity "ends up being less of a parent-child relationship and more of a pragmatic understanding of your place in the world."

According to Brian, faith is "the belief part of religious involvement based either on affiliation with an official position of a given religion, or upon experience of a religion, based on its apparence." Yes, faith involves belief, but Brian recognizes that "there can be different contexts for [belief]. Either it can be as agreement with received dogma, which is probably less aligned with how I feel, or more based upon experience through practice or personal experience of the Divine." When describing the role that faith plays in his relationships with the Gods, Brian explains that "my faith and involvement with my Gods is quiet, pantheistic and respectful. It's not so much a belief as a recurring pantheistic epiphany punctuated by involvement with one or more Deities, who are like friends helping me along my way."

Brian had been raised in Christianity, but it never really appealed to him. It wasn't until he started exploring other cultures that he began to recognize his own religious leanings. His current path incorporates aspects of both polytheism and pantheism.

I began a spiritual quest as a child. Essentially I was raised in a Christian household, but I didn't have a lot of affinity with Christianity. Since my own views were much more pantheistic and I saw natural forces of this pantheistic worldview, I started looking around at world culture and world religious culture since about the age of eight, which sounds a little bit ludicrous but I was a precocious child and so I started reading everything I about a variety of world religions that I could get my hands on. A determined child with a library card is a force to be reckoned with. I ran through European mythology, Native American mythology, a lot of different things like Confucianism and Buddhism and became very eclectic. I just kind of got on with it for about another eight years or so. I just did my own thing in a very eclectic fashion. In a very pantheistic way but working with different aspects of nature. Gradually, I met other Pagans and they worshipped a variety of Gods. I saw a similarity between their views and my own, so I began to explore the names that they had given the forces, seeing Them at times as distinct and at times as forms of natural forces honored throughout the world by various cultures, backed up by my earlier research. So, I kind of did my own thing. And then I got to know people who were pantheists and polytheists and found that we had a lot in common and that advanced my understanding of where my spiritual life was going.

There are a multitude of thoughts and feelings that one might experience when they first embark on a new path of spiritual discovery. For Brian, the virtue of his polytheist approach has been that it allows him to experience profound epiphanies about his own interconnectedness with the natural world. A unique aspect of Brian's experience is that his interpretation of that experience draws as much upon Brian's background in science as it does on his spiritual explorations.

I think I have a fundamentally different spiritual worldview to people who would have a problem with science, so if my cosmology is that the world exists, that the divine exists, and that the world around us is the divine expressing itself in nature, then the laws of nature which are governed by the laws of science, are fundamentally not incompatible. We're just learning to better understand how all that works, and how it works in many ways for us and on us. Because I don't have a bizarre myth that says someone took some bits and stuck them together in a specific way, which science could perhaps deny, then I don't have a rocky relationship with science. I'm just coming to better understand how the divine has manifested itself through nature, because I am better understanding the mechanics of how nature functions...

There is a lot of scientific research, and I am doing humanities research at the moment, but my undergrad is in science and I do keep abreast of popular science magazines. I don't pretend I can crunch the kind of numbers that they do in astrophysics, but I do keep abreast of developments. There seems to be a part of the brain which regulates the difference between you and your environment. It seems that Buddhists in deep meditation do something that causes the brain not to have so much of a divide between the self and what's around us in terms of conception. They way they describe it—that sounded very clinical but it doesn't feel very clinical—because what it feels like is that the divisions, the artificial seeming divisions between self and the environment just seem to fall away. What I experience is a very great connectedness and I personally find it easiest to achieve that state when I'm out in nature. For me, it's almost naturally occurring. But I do wonder if I'm one of those people, and there do seem to be people with this predisposition, who just have these moments, like a finger comes down and everything lights up and all of the differences between me and what's around me just fall away, and there's a very beautiful stillness in that. It's very non-verbal. I knew someone once who said that some things are non-discursive. I think in some ways, this is. I read some accounts by Christians and scholars on epiphany, and they seem to be saying something very similar to what the Buddhist monks say as well. It does seem as if there does come a time when all of divinity merges and your place in that becomes the reality of what it is, rather than the strange self-centeredness of ego...

Brian does not "hold an extremely literal position" that anthropomorphizes the Gods as individual Divine Beings. Rather, he sees Them as "individual strands within a tapestry of natural forces." Brian explains that he relates to those strands "through my relationships with the Deities I honor in my religious practice."

The way I see it is that in many ways They are natural forces. I try to, because of the underlying pantheism of my approach, I see Them as part of a greater whole but with individual identities because They embody different and specific sets of natural forces. By natural forces, I mean this quite forwardly. For the purposes of my undergraduate work, I dedicated that to Athena, because I see Her as associated with knowledge and learning and the learning of skills and crafts. I thought that was quite appropriate to my undergraduate research. I made the work devotional as a whole and opened it with a devotional ritual to Her and I closed it with a devotional ritual to Her, so it bracketed my undergraduate studies. In some ways, I felt more inclined to finish them because I had contextualized my work within the relationship with that Deity…

I acknowledge that They may manifest differently to different people. I was actually chatting with a friend about this earlier in the week. We were talking about spirit possession in different traditions and how these things can be different. For me I saw this to be much the same way that different people's relationships are. Two people may know the same person, but they may have a profoundly different relationship with that person. And in many ways, that is how I see various polytheistic Gods as being. My experience of a given Deity might be quite different to the experience that someone else has with that Deity but that's because that's my relationship with that Deity.

Brian has long had a strong devotional relationship with Athena, but more recently Sylvanus and Hermes have become prominent in his practice. Brian has sensed the presence of Sylvanus in connection with the home he recently purchased. Hermes has come to be a patron for Brian's current postgraduate studies, occupying a similar role to that which Athena held for Brian's undergraduate work.

There is Sylvanus, who is a Roman Deity of the civilized forest, and for me that's very important. There are little things. When I was looking for this house, which I bought about seven or eight months ago, I arrived here and I really liked the house, but overgrowing the house were ash trees, and the ash was important to Sylvanus. That was just one of those little things that talks to you. But also, very near this house and certainly within a 15-20 minutes' distance is a National Trust wood. So it's a managed wood, and it's very close to here, so as part of and in recognition that it's involved with that, I can walk up to the woods, which also has ash trees. Sometimes it's about connection more than about specific deliberate acts.

I'm currently looking for a statue of Hermes because my postgraduate research is more linked to gender and queer studies and that kind of thing. I've been thrashing around trying to find a devotional statue of Hermes, and I'm failing utterly because either way I only find one that is ridiculously happy to the point where I can't bear to make myself look at it, which wouldn't be conducive to devotional work (laughs). I did find one but it's frightfully expensive. I think that what I need to do, and have done in the past, which is if I fail to find what I'm looking for I need to go ahead and make something. I'm quite good at crafty-type stuff. I guess the answer is that I can probably make something that is less hideous.

Brian observes a number of devotional practices both large and small. It is through these acts of devotion that he reconnects and recommits to his spirituality. He has found that acts of creation and the crafting of objects can be very powerful devotional practices.

I think some of them grew out of some of the things that I did when I was younger. When I started studying Buddhism, I taught myself meditation. I began a regular meditative practice. When I started doing more defined ritual work, I started doing things that would reconnect me on a daily basis with my spiritual practice. For instance, for a period of time I made sure I went into my temple—I kept a temple room in my house. I tend to spread things out in my home now rather than have a specific room for it. But I made a point every day of going into my temple room and changing the bowl of water to clean water. I have had times when I burned candles on a daily basis. Or I burned incense on a daily basis to specific Deities...

I do tend to follow the broader general Pagan year, but I have also just done things that were part of a personal devotional practice. In some cases, I mentioned that I kept a room devoted solely to religious practices and I had an altar. For periods of time I did different things in there. One of them was to go in every day and recite a self-blessing, which I found really useful. I have had periods of time when I make a point to change the water on the altar to clean water. I have had times when I made a point to bring incense—often stuff I had made. There are different things and it depends on what I am trying to do. Whether it is part of a devotional practice aimed at getting to know a Deity better and to understand Them better which might involved meditation or asking of an understanding and then seeing what comes out of it. Or it may simply be making myself go into the temple room or making myself go to the different things spread around my home that are devotional altars on a daily basis just to make sure I reconnect with my spiritual life…

There is a period of time I was working with a not very well-defined Horned God as part of my research into Wicca. I did make a statue and I do still have it I keep it in my bedroom. It hasn't frightened too many people. I have occasionally had people go, "oooh, that looks very strange" that occasioned comments on it but there aren't that many people passing though my bedroom so they don't have much opportunity. But yes, I think it does. It was certainly the culmination of a lot of devotional work to that Deity. I personally got a lot out of it. I think there is something about making something with your hands which connects you in ways that are quite important in terms of being human…

Like many other polytheists, Brian honors both ancestors and the nature spirits. These acts of ritual and veneration are important not only because they acknowledge the spirits, but because they provide Brian with the opportunity to reflect upon his relationship to Them, the contributions They have made to his life, and Their immediate presence in the world around him.

I see ancestors as people we should honor for their contributions to our lives, including biological ancestors and those within particular traditions. I set up an altar for Halloween, and those who have died, particularly those who died in the last year, are honored by me. It might be a full Halloween ritual, or it might just be a candle placed in the window for them, but it's my time to think of their contribution to my life, and to honor their memory.

In terms of nature spirits, I see them as naturally occurring parts of the landscape, and so I should honor them as part of the manifestation of divine nature. If I sense them whilst walking around in nature, I see it as important to be aware of, and polite to, the spirit of place, even if that means just quietly focusing on them and being still in their presence. It's not about having a ritual, but about being still and saying hello. If they want to communicate, they will. If not, I leave them alone.

Brian's understanding of the Gods as embodiments of natural forces has given him a very unique perspective. No less unique is his perspective of how the myths about these powerful natural forces relate to his personal experiences of Them.

Hermes is a really interesting one. So, you start with some myths around stealing things and some of the myths around sacrifice and some of the myths around the creation of Hermaphroditus. Then you start getting into really interesting things. More lately, okay, Athena was my patron Deity for my undergrad work, who should be that Deity for my postgrad work? Particularly given the themes? I came to the conclusion, along with quite a number of other people that because some of the queer connotations, He's actually quite appropriate to be the Deity that I research. That leads to, well, who should be the God or Goddess of the internet? That could be Hermes, it could be communication. I've heard different things.

I think what modern Pagans are struggling to do, and in some cases I think quite elegantly, in some ways in a really confused manner, is to find links with the modern world. So, I have cats, and like a million of other Pagans, I have statues of Bast in my home. That's very eclectic, because my religious practice doesn't really live out of Egypt. I find Egypt very interesting and I've read quite a lot about Egypt, but I have statues of Bast because She is the most obvious of the Goddesses of cats. So, from my research I see Hermes as really well-placed to the God of [the internet] because His role as psychopomp dovetails very nicely with that. He's very much about the other world, and communication, but also about strange things and wordcraft, in a very slippery and eloquent kind of way. But also about inclusion. You're talking about a Deity who combined with the Goddess of love to create something that was neither male nor female. That fits really well with the themes of my research. I think I'm very lucky that the Deity who is associated with that breaking of the gender binary is also a Deity of great eloquence. I think I could probably do much worse for my studies.

Gender has been one of the major points of friction that Brian has experienced in dealing with other Pagans. In some ways, his embracing of polytheism has enabled him to strip away the gender binaries he recognizes as integral to contemporary Paganism.

I started looking around at the Pagan community here and looking into various Pagan paths because I wanted to find out more about Paganism and its expression in terms of my own masculinity. So, I started looking and I was looking for a ritual framework that would allow me to accommodate the masculine as well as the feminine. Because I've been a big 80's Goddess boy and I quietly got on with that. But I got to an age, I guess about

30 at the time, when I started wanted to be around Pagans again because I'd been quietly been getting on with my own thing for ever such a long time. But I really didn't know what to do with my own masculinity in a religious context. So, I started looking into Wicca, which was a bit of a minefield, because although it did provide for a frame of reference for introducing a gender balance as such into my religious practice, it also provided a very convenient compulsory heterosexuality, which resoundingly clanged with my own internal spiritual landscape. I stuck at it for quite some time and was quite persistent. I have pretty thick skin, so I worked within a group into which I was initiated in the normal way that people are trained within Wicca, and I worked with them for a couple of years. Then I helped someone else run a coven for about five years. My work in the Craft stretches out over about eight years. Toward the end of it, despite my considerable efforts to struggle against really strong gender polarity and an underlying compulsory heterosexuality, I failed to convince my working partner, who was helping to lead the group with me, that we should "queer it up some more." After nearly half a decade of fighting about it, I stopped fighting about it and walked. Actually, that was one of the most instructive things I have ever done…

I talked to people for a while. I thrashed around for a while talking to people in the internet, on Facebook, and what I found, slightly bizarrely, was that people who were otherwise really right-on didn't ever think about what would happen if someone who is transgender wanted to join a group. It never occurred to them. People who vote liberal, who are socially liberal, who would never agree with discrimination in the workplace, who would work strongly against discrimination wherever else they found it, people who believe in gay marriage; it never occurred to them that a transgender person might want to join a coven. Or that people who are intersex and don't claim an assigned gender could want to join a coven. It just didn't occur to them. After enough of those conversations, I came to the conclusion about Wicca and the training and the way that people approach it and the way that it's taught that causes a bizarre tunnel vision on issues of gender and sexuality in a really weird way…

I think there is a real stream of expectation within Wicca that you are more than welcome to join as someone who is gender variant or sexually diverse. But what I have heard from a lot of people, so I know that I'm not the only person who has heard this, is that you have a "proper role" to play. I've been told, "So, yeah, you're queer, or maybe a bit of a camp bloke, but when you're in circle, you're a man, and that means you are attracted to women. That's your role to play and you must do that." And I'm just like, "what?" Help me out here but what is an appropriate gender role? Because I didn't think we had those anymore. I thought that we lost them with cupcakes and pleated dresses in the 50's. We still seem to have them and it's 60 years later and I'm not quite getting it. So, I think we have a role now of asking what an "appropriate gender role" is, and under what really old rock they found it. I've certainly heard this from other people who just bounced resoundingly off of Wicca. I've heard some real horror stories of people bouncing off of Wicca. Apparently I have extremely thick skin because I ended up in quite traditional groups. But, I've just heard absolute revulsion. I've also heard people doing what I've done, which is, go and work with it, try to be patient, try to stick it out, and try to get people's attitudes to change and eventually they just go, "okay right. You guys aren't interested in coming out of the 1950's, and you can justify that by any means, but I'm just not prepared to do it anymore."

For me, the word that really resounds, the term that really resounds is "internal spiritual landscape." If the things that are naturally occurring in my connection with my spiritual life, if there isn't any room for them in the tradition that I am working within then there is a conflict between the tradition and what it offers in terms of a spirituality, a cosmology, or maybe a theology and my internal landscape. And if those things are incompatible, then that is a relationship deal-breaker. I am not going to go along and attempt to share my spiritual life with other people in ways that are not in fundamental keeping with my spiritual life, because that's destructive.

If people were to understand only one thing about polytheism, Brian wishes that they would understand that it offers levels of harmony and inclusion unmatched by monotheist religions. According to Brian, one of the most important things that a polytheist view of the world has to offer is the possibility of harmony, diversity, and interconnectedness which are not feasible in the polarized dualism that characterizes contemporary monotheism.

There is a possibility for harmony in polytheism which is strongly different from the adversarial plus and minus of the dualistic good and evil as taught by monotheistic religion. In the polytheistic version of religion, various Deities have different roles in the world. Going back to my earlier tapestry metaphor, it's not black on one side and white on the other with both sides trying to win over the other or split the cloth. It's more a richness of being supported by each color and weave, making a contribution to the whole in which individual contributions are honored. I think that our society could learn from trying this approach more broadly from its attitudes towards diversity. I think in many ways, we've learned too much to speak in terms of polarity. I'd like to see us learn to speak more in terms of people's contributions, people's individual realities, and what they bring to the bigger picture.

Marcus Horatius

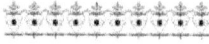

Marcus Horatius is 60 years old. There has never been a time in his life that he wasn't a practicing polytheist. Marcus' family hails from a small, isolated mountain town in the Abruzzo region of Italy. Remarkably, the village had been maintaining a vibrant and complex ancestral polytheism that worshipped the Gods of Rome and had not been molested by Christian authorities for several centuries. Christianity was present in the village and some people were Christians or a syncretic mixture of the two, but many of the townspeople observed the old religion. As an adult, Marco drew upon his family's traditions in his work with Religio Romana, a religious group dedicated to reconstructing the religion of ancient Rome. He has been a sacerdos in the religion since about 1989. In last several decades as the village has died out, the village's religious traditions have also began to fade. Marcus has kept part of the religion alive by adapting them to Religio Romana, thereby enhancing the religion's strong group ritual practice with traditions that are centered on the home and family. Marcus has devotional relationships with Jupiter, Ceres, Mars, Venus, Diana, Vesta and Janus, and he also honors the genii loci and the lares.

In constructing his definition of "polytheism," Marcus makes sure to include many different kinds of divine entities and not just Deities. According to Marcus, the Monist idea of a divine singularity that is the source of all things is a human-created concept that simply cannot account for the multitudes of divinity.

Polytheism is the belief in numerous spiritual beings, not just Gods, which are semi-divine—the spirit within ourselves being divine. But the higher beings are a multiplicity of Deities and above that there are usually hierarchies. Like, we would recognize the Deities of the earth. Or Deities of the world would be like, "the world" is more "the solar system," more than they think of it today. I guess there would be cosmological Deities, higher than what we would normally consider in nature, but I guess it depends on what traditions you are talking about.

Monotheism is a human construct and I don't—accept that possibility. The way I was raised, there was—there were higher Deities. We didn't know Them individually by name, but we knew Them collectively as a group of Deities and then we knew that the other Deities we usually prayed to, were Deities of nature.

Marcus does not really consider the Christian perspective of faith to be applicable in his practice, because it is unlike any concept he had been raised with. The closest thing to faith that Marcus learned as a child was the idea of "fides," which is a Latin term that implies trustworthiness, honesty, and uprightness in the keeping of agreements.* Fides involves more than simply the mental action of belief; it demands the actions of trust and the meeting of obligations.

I don't know that I would really understand the Christian meaning of the word faith, or piety. They're different from what I understand. Yes, "fides" is a Latin term that "faith" comes from, and it means the obligation of the superior to the inferior, in human relations as well as in divine-human, or between humans and plants and animals. We have a faith obligation to protect or nurture the world around us...

I guess a Christian view of faith is that you believe no matter what. Yeah, it's a matter of trust in your beliefs. We all have that. If you go to your Gods and say, "If you do this, we'll do that. We want a sign from you, otherwise I don't believe in you. I'll go to another God and ask Him." (Laughs.) I remember that from long ago. That's how we dealt with our Deities. And I remember doing that as a child. (Laughs.)

Marcus has the unique honor of being the only person in this study to be raised in a polytheist religion. His family comes from a small village in Abruzzo that managed to preserve their polytheism despite Catholicism's absolute dominance of the rest of Italy. His family brought their religion with them when the immigrated to the United States. In the 1980s, Marcus shifted from his family tradition to Religio Romana, which is the religion he practices today.

It was an Italian polytheistic religion of the countryside. My family came out of the mountain valleys of western Abruzzo. Which was actually part of the Papal states. But it was so

---

* The Latin word *"fides"* connotes promise, assurance, word of honor, engagement. According to Dr. John Paul Adams, Classics professor at California State University–Northridge, "Fides" was "an essential element in the character of a man of public affairs, and a necessary constituent element of all social and political transactions. *Fides* meant 'reliablilty', a sense of trust between two parties if a relationship between them was to exist. *Fides* was always reciprocal and mutual, and implied both privileges and responsibilities on both sides. In both public and private life the violation of *fides* was considered a serious matter, with both legal and religious consequences." Adams, John Paul. "The Roman Concept of Fides." <u>California State University, Northridge</u>. California State University-Northridge, 4 May 2009. Web. 9 Oct. 2013. <http://www.csun.edu/~hcfll004/fides.html>

isolated, nobody bothered them for centuries, apparently. So, yeah, some of my family were Christian. Some of them kept the old practices and put them behind Christianity, like [they] put the Christian statues in place of the other ones but still continue to practice. And then there were some who just openly did it the old way. That was my great-grandmother, Bisnonna She taught me and my sister some things. And my grandmother did. And my mother did. My aunts, and cousins, and whatnot…

Well, we identified ourselves as Roman. We did do that when I was a kid. There was always—we always accepted Roman literature as part of our heritage. My openly moving over to Religio Romana began in the late eighties. I'm under stricture by my tradition and the leaders of the tradition not to speak about the family tradition. But there was a time—when my grandfather got his citizenship. He decided that the whole family should adopt American holidays. Americans celebrate Christmas, so let's go celebrate. So he brought us to—all of his 9 children and their husbands and wives, and their grandchildren and all that—to midnight mass at a Catholic church. We walk in and there's a priest and maybe 5 other people. We set up in the back. We start opening up our food and playing our music and drinking our wine—we were celebrating. (Laughs.)…We kind of stunned them. We never did that again.

So, I got—in the eighties I got involved with some other people and I became a minister under the ULC in 1992. That's when we transposed family tradition to a more Roman one. Then we've been building on that and teaching about that. I have been a minister, or sacerdos—we prefer "sacerdos" instead of "priest" because that also has a different meaning…since about '89 or so.

There has never been any question for Marcus about whether or not the Gods exist. For him, the term "Gods" refers to many different kinds of Divinities. Although Marcus never really needed convincing that the Gods exist, he has had experiences with Deities and other spirits that added weight to his convictions.

When I say "Gods" in general—Gods and Goddesses—these include the lares, who are ancestors, the spirits of our ancestors. We have all these different beliefs about the afterlife. I've had experiences meeting with them, I guess you could call them ghosts. I've had exp—well, I've had experiences of something in the mortal body that isn't physical. I used to be a soldier, and I've seen people die. Violently as well as pleasantly, and there was a *particular incident where there was **something else** coming out of this person. And then yes, I've had visions of Goddesses. There are two particular Goddesses that I usually work with. I've seen other visions of Gods. I've had experiences where I've called upon the Gods. I was caught behind enemy positions, out in the Vietnam, you know, jungle. You better believe I prayed to the Gods...Things like that.*

Those kinds of experiences that make you think, "get me the hell out of here?"—I don't know that I've had those. I've had all kinds of things happen now and again. Well, we do some divination now and again which involves trance work. I don't know how you would take that being Gods or what They are—those are more like, well, they're trances. So you are going internally. I have had a near-death experience before, but I don't think that really shows anything in the way of Divinities or afterlife or anything like that. It was just kind of a shutting off of things. I guess there are a lot of things that have been experiences.

Marcus describes his relationships with the Gods as "personal relationships." The Gods are "like family" for Marcus, and he maintains devotions to several of Them. Several of the Gods have been in his life since he was a child. His relationships with the Gods are very much based upon the philosophy of fides, where Marcus gives prayers, offerings, and other devotions, and in return the Gods give Their blessings and support.

Jupiter is "a father figure," says Marcus, "the sky-father" who has always been in his life. Marcus has called upon Jupiter's blessings for everything from wise advice, to divination, to wine-making.

I talk to Him for advice, much of the divining is done under Him. Divining is done under a semi-trance state, so you work ritual to   get into that state and be with Him during the daytime. There are other Deities that we would do the same thing with at night. I don't know. Our meals—we always used to pour wine from our glasses onto the ground. That was always our tribute to Jupiter. We used to—once a year my grandfather used to slaughter a lamb for our special meal with Jupiter. The lamb's blood would go onto the vines as an offering there to Jupiter. Jupiter was God of my grandfather's grapevine, and when he made wine, and all of that. Pouring a libation of wine out to Jupiter at every main meal, it was like giving back some of the wine that Jupiter provided for us. My grandmother   had another relationship with Him. She used to do this thing where she had a garden, so she wanted Him to bring rain all the time. She would pick up the dry dirt and whirl around in the air, cursing at Him to bring rain and stuff like that. But mine has been more of a formal kind of relationship with Him. Yeah, I ask Him certain questions and I give Him His due and all that, and I have a little altar for Him outside. He struck lightning over my head one time, too. I kind of put out a little thing for Him then. He's one of the main ones I've worked with over the years, but He's the father-in-the-sky kind of thing.

Because Ceres Ferentina "is the mother of the family," Marco has been with Her all of his life. "Other Gods and Goddess have appeared and left at different periods in life," he says, "but She's always been there." Marcus identifies Ceres as his main Goddess.

Part of the family comes from a little town called Ferentino. Ferentino is in eastern Lazio. It's one of the hill towns so common to Italy. In ancient times it was home to the Hernici, allies of Rome after the demise of the Latin League. The town still uses its ancient designation SPQF for the "Senate and People of Ferentino." Its megalithic city walls were said to have been built by the sons of Saturn, over which are Roman walls, topped by Medieval walls. It was wiped out by the Ostrogoths in the fifth century, and then by the Spanish in the 1500's. My family ancestor, Sisto Dal Alatri, first moved there after 1665. The family traces back, as far as we can document, to Reale Valentino in 1013 CE.

Outside Rome, Cerés Ferentina was the patron Goddess of the Latin League at the little town called Ariccia—I don't know if you've ever heard of Lake Nemi. Well, at Lake Nemi, the sanctuary of Diana is on one side of the lake, and on the other side is Ariccia, which is where the Latin League had their sanctuary for Ceres Ferentina. She is a—She is kind of Goddess of the earth. There is the Mother Earth, who is Tellus, and then Her daughter was Ceres. Ceres is the produce of the earth, so She is associated by the Romans with wheat, but She is also associated with all kinds of plants that grew out of the earth. Ceres is from the Latin gere, meaning "to bear" as you may bear a child. Ferentina is a diminutive form of Ferona, from "fere" meaning "to bring forth. Ferona is a Goddess concerned with the well-being of young animals and children, in the same way that Ceres is called upon to protect young plants. In a sense we are the sons of the earth, sprung up from the land, so there is that connotation with Ceres Ferentina. She is like the divine matriarch of the family, Ceres Ferentina. Because I work so much with herbs, whether foraging for them or growing them, She's also a Goddess of my little garden. My Hortus Cerreri is dedicated to Her.

Marcus has had a very long relationship with the God Mars. His mother dedicated him to Mars at age 4. His relationship with Mars has been very familial ever since.

I was dedicated to Mars at the age of 4, so I've been with Him for a while. I've had all kinds of relationships. He was like my big brother when I was a little kid. I remember my first pair of shoes, when I was, like, 6. I remember running into the bedroom and going to the shrine and showing my shoes to Him. He's like my big brother even though I had another big brother. He was there often enough throughout my childhood. Then when I was in the army, I called on Him quite a few times, actually. Well, my own son went into the army after a while, and I called upon Mars again: "All these years, I've been worshipping you. You'd better protect my son now or I will never do anything for you again." (Laughs.)

Venus is a Goddess with whom Marcus has had a somewhat rocky relationship. He recognizes Her as a Goddess who brings children and thereby ensures family happiness.

Every time I get a statue of Her, it breaks immediately. She must be mad at me. (Laughs.) Oh, well. I haven't' done a lot of work with Her, but She is a Goddess who provides children to keep the family happy. I've had a few children and now I'm looking for grandchildren someday. I don't have a close relationship with Her, but I have worked with Her sometimes as She is called upon for the family and for children and things like that.

Marcus' experience with Diana has, as would be expected, involved forests and the creatures who live there. One such experience with a forest creature occurred in a very unexpected place.

Well, Diana is a Goddess of the forest and forest animals and such, and Her and Silvanus who is a God of the forest as well, since I go out into the forest and do foraging for different things—for herbs and whatnot—I pay my respects to both Diana and Silvanus. I've had—I've run into deer who lead me places. I run into other animals. A baby raccoon one time I remember, would lead me up to some place. I assume that was sent from Her. The strangest thing that ever happened was the day—I don't live in New York City, mind you, I live in Ohio—but it is still strange to see a deer in my backyard. This little deer came up the alleyway and into the backyard. She came up to the pine tree where I have my little altar for Diana, and she made this little bow and she turned around and walked out. And it was on the day of my son's birthday. Mark that down as another kind of experience with the Gods.

Vesta is a Goddess Marcus has a lot of experience with. As the Goddess of the hearth and house-holding, he honors Her often for the good of his family.

She is the Goddess of the hearth, the center of the family. It's kind of literal. When I was young we still had the old wood-burning stoves back then. That fire always kept burning and that was the center of the family. I still pay my respects in more of an abstract sense, now, but I have a little shrine for Her in my kitchen so I can pay my respects. Mostly when I'm doing house chores. I might burn a little incense to Her or say good morning or whatever.

Marcus has a daily devotional practice to Janus, the guardian of doorways. According to Marcus, there are actually two versions of Janus, one minor and one major.

Janus…. Well, every morning I wake up, I go outside while the sun rises, [and say] "I rise with you, I drink with you;" it's an old ritual. Of course He's like the guardian of the front door. There are like two different Gods actually. The minor God is the God of doorways, and there's a number of different things done with the front door to protect the entrance. And then there's the cosmic, or more cosmic one, one who is the opener of the way, the one who opens the day when the Gods enter the world. Every morning He is greeted—the more cosmological one.

Both Marcus' family tradition and Religio Romana honor the spirits of place. In these traditions, the spirits of place are called geni locii.

I live in Ohio, so I assume the geni locii here are Native American. So I offer them something that would be appropriate for them, but I still do it in a Roman way. There is a particular one where…There are places I would go to, where I come upon these spirits. I think the weirdest place I've ever been was out in Oregon. where there was three of us. Two of us stopped and said, "there is something wrong here." There were no spirits that

I could feel.

It's normal for me to go into the woods or along the ocean or something like that, and to start feeling spirits around me. Those would be what I call the geni locii. They, again, could be ghosts for all I know. There is this one place I got to where there was this white girl who was taken there by the Indians and eventually killed there. There is a hostile spirit there. Any time I go there it's kind of like, it is running around screaming at me to go away. It's not her; its' somebody else. So, it's not a regular kind of forest spirit. On the other side of the river there's another kind of spirit who has always been helpful in sending me messengers and showing me things and places to go and things like that. There's friendly ones and not-so-friendly.

Marcus says that Religio Romana calls the spirits of the dead-in-general "Manes." In religious practice, these spirits will be classified into more the specific categories of lares, larvae, and lemures.

There are the evil manes who are called larvae, and the lares [who] are the spirits of family members who have evolved to a higher state of spirituality. They're not Gods yet, but they are disembodied spirits who watch over the family, protect it, that sort of thing. Of course, there would be other spirits of the family who are not so good. They did not manage to evolve. They might come back to the family. We always had that belief that you are reincarnated back into the family...Besides family lares and the evil larvae, there is another category of Manes called lemures. Not necessarily evil or good, but not family. They roam the earth searching for someone to offer them rites, and thus become a lar. We have some festivals for them, placing out offerings for them, but never invite them into the house.

I remember my aunts talking about—like there'd be a dog or a cat come by, and they'd say, "Oh! That must be uncle so-and-so. He's as skinny as him, he has the same overbite." (Laughs.) There was also that kind of idea floating around. But the lares would be beneficial spirits. And they are family.

When asked how the mythology compares to his experience of the Gods, Marcus explains in no uncertain terms that there is no relationship whatsoever. First of all, Marcus explains, the myths modern people ascribe to the Roman Deities are Greek in origin and are about the Greek Gods, who are not the same as the Roman Gods. But more importantly, ancient myths are irrelevant because Marcus didn't grow up learning about the Gods through myths. His family

taught him about the Gods through the oral tradition of "veglia"**
which are stories, songs, and other folklore that intricately interweave
things like folktales, herbal lore, family in-jokes, and stories about the
Gods and other spirits.

> *The myths are Greek. We don't really—I mean, we accept the
> myths as allegories. When I was younger we had what we called
> the veglia, that's one of the words my great-grandmother taught
> me. The veglia is a bunch of stories. They're like fairytales,
> they're history, they're family tales, there's practical knowledge,
> and she used to work them all together. She might take a
> fairytale and work into it some lore about a particular herb.
> And the next time you would hear the same fairytale, it would
> be all different. I mean, the whole storyline could be different.
> Myth is a living thing. It is always flowing and changing. So
> when you talk about the myths, if you are talking about the
> myths of the Roman and Greek Gods, well, which myths?
> Because those were—once they are written down, they're not
> myths any more. They're stories.*

> *They are just so different from the veglia that they don't connect
> with me at all. As far as what the myths have to say about the
> Gods, I don't think they were really talking about the Gods
> anyways, not experiences I would have. They can—the myths
> can inform you when you are doing trance work and you see all
> these visions and whatnot, then you might be able to relate some
> of those back to myth to help you recognize some things. Other
> than that, I don't know. I don't have any relation that I can
> think of between the myths and the Gods.*

> *I'll give you a story, a typical Italian veglia. Two women go by
> this house every day. They look inside, and there's a garden. The
> one woman says we should go and pick some of those vegetables.
> I bet she's not there watching. "Oh no, we can't do that" says the
> other woman, "I'm pregnant and if she comes out I can't get
> away." Well, they keep watching the place, they see a watchdog
> and give him some meat, and they give some milk to a cat, they
> give some seed to a chicken, and they go into the garden and they
> gather up all these vegetables. On the way out, they see this little
> mushroom. A woman stops to get the mushroom and pick at it.
> And out comes this witch. It's the witch's ear! The story goes on,
> but the witch's ear is the name of a particular kind of
> mushroom. From there, you can go into telling about that*

** "Veglia" seems to be related to an Italian word meaning "vigil," or "watch." When you
consider the vital spiritual knowledge and cultural wisdom contained in Marcus' family veglia,
it makes sense that these are stories a listener should vigilantly pay close attention to.

particular type of mushroom, what you can do with it, a little of the lore about it, you can take that little bit of fairytale and mix it into another fairytale, all kinds of things like that… And they would make it like "OH, your aunt so-and-so, she was pregnant. And her and her friend went over here and did this." They used to play with it all the time. It's kind of fun. It's a sing-song type of speech when they did it… That's how the veglia works.

Marcus has experienced a small amount of friction within the Pagan community because of his emphasis on polytheism. While he doesn't mind being called "Pagan," the word had different connotations for him growing up that it does for contemporary people. His occasional conflict with other Pagans has largely involved theological differences with Wiccans. On the other hand, Marcus' encounters with people from indigenous African and North American cultures have been very amenable.

It depends what you mean by "Pagan." (Laughs.)…I don't care if I'm called a Pagan. We—the family—never considered ourselves Pagan. We don't really have a word for our own tradition. It was just the family tradition. But "Pagan" was those Christian peasants who worked out in the fields. That wasn't us—we didn't do that. We're not "Pagan" in that sense. When I was young, nobody knew what a Pagan was, in the modern sense of the term…Nobody believed Pagans existed. It wasn't hard for us—we didn't know.

"Pagan" as it's used today most often refers to Wiccan, and if that's what they mean, then no, I'm not Wiccan. I apparently don't get along with too many Wiccans. Wiccans come from Christianity and no matter what they may think of themselves, they still think like Christians. So, when I pointed that out a couple of times, "that was like, a Christian point of view you have there"—and they got very upset because most of them I've met have been reacting to Christianity for some reason. They have problems with it. They don't like to be seen as Christian. "Christian" is, I guess, a bad word to them. So, yeah. If you include Wiccans, then yes, I've had a hard time with some Pagans. But most of the time, no. I don't have a problem with them. No.

American Indians—I've dealt with a number of tribes in the southwest and the northern plains. I found that their views of things are a lot like ours. I met a fellow once from Africa. He was telling me some of his folklore stories and I was telling him some of ours, and they were the same stories, there were just different names of characters. If they're a "real Pagan"—it depends how you qualify that term, "Pagan"—I've gotten along well with them.

Growing up, Marcus says that he never really experienced too much friction because his family is polytheist. He surmises that because they were also Italian immigrants, whatever difference his family showed was explained away by the neighbors as being an ethnic cultural difference. It wasn't until he joined the army that he experienced religious conflict as such.

I never really had any [conflict] when I was a kid about it. I lived in Cleveland and Cleveland has a lot of eastern Europeans. If they noticed anything strange about us it was because we were Italian. When we moved up to the suburbs, everybody was Protestant, and they were like, "they're like that because they are Catholic." Whatever the excuse, people will put names on you anyway. They would make their own justifications for whatever they thought was different about us. They never really did say anything.

The first time I was ever really confronted about what my religion might be was when I was in boot camp in the army. I think that's it. On the first Sunday, they said "All you Catholics off to the right, and all you Protestants off to the left." Which left two of us. The first sergeant gets up on the dais and he leans up over and starts screaming at this little guy who's standing next to me. "What's your problem?" Well, the guys says, "I'm, Jewish." The sergeant says, "you can choose right or left, but you're going to chapel today." Off he goes and I was left behind. And then [the sergeant] says, "what's your problem?" and so I told him, "I'm a polytheist." He just started stammering, "well…you go off and do whatever it is that you people do." So for the rest of boot camp, I went over and sat under an oak tree. I didn't have to go to chapel. The army said that I was Buddhist. That was the first time I have ever been confronted with it: "oh, I have to declare what I am?" (Laughs.)

One of the major religious struggles Marcus has been facing is the effort to get Religio Romana officially recognized as a religion. This struggle hasn't quite been easy in the United States, but it has proven to be a major headache in Europe, especially in Italy, because the fascists historically have appropriated Roman mythology in much the same way that the Nazis appropriated Norse mythology. Religio Romana faces a struggle to distance itself from nationalism and bigotry within its spiritual homeland.

In the United States, we had to go through a couple of court cases back in the nineties, to get recognition of Religio Romana as being a legitimate religious tradition. Eventually we had a couple of local communities incorporated, so we have kind of won that now. Now we're looking at Canada, which has a five year process, different requirements and whatnot. We are in negotiations right now to be incorporated in Sweden…registered as a belief society. Europe has been real hard to get any recognition in at all, so this might be a back door for us.

They don't have a corporation law in Sweden, they have a tradition. Anyone can form a corporation and whatnot, but the only ones who have to register are a belief society other than Lutheran. It has to do with the fact that they passed this law allowing religious freedom, so you're free to believe in something else but you have to register it if you want to be recognized as an organization. But if we're recognized by Sweden, and Sweden is part of the EU and a signatory of the EU's constitution, then we would have to be recognized in other European states as well. That's a real problem in Italy, where Mussolini had [identified fascism with] Roma antiqua, and neo-fascists and skinheads still use the Roman religion as a front for bigotry. It's been more of a political struggle at this point to get recognized. We were encouraged by what happened in Greece, but that has to do with national pride, which in Italy, it worked kind of just the opposite for us.

Marcus has faced other conflicts due to his religious background. Particularly annoying are the are anthropologists and academics who simply refuse to believe that any group of Europeans, much less a village nestled in the mountains of the Papal States, could have maintained a polytheist culture from ancient times until today. Yet the most difficult has probably been Marcus' effort to honor the wishes of his tradition's elders back home in Italy and allow the religion he grew up with to perish.

Oh. I know there's a lot of Italians who would like to know about my family tradition, too. I've been approached by—what's his name—Kurtzman—I think that's his name. There are a couple of people who approached me, and told him about me, so they wanted to find out more. There's some question as to whether there was an Italian tradition of [polytheists that] managed to survive. There are records of it up to such and such a point, but what my family has to say about it is yes, we survived. We came over to America sometime in the 1890's. It survived over here in part. Of course it is also changed, I would assume. I don't know. There is that structure and some of the—well, most of the elders are dead now. I'm 60 and I'm the last generation of them anyways. So, the old ones are gone. The ones that remain—the leader, I think he just prefers that the whole tradition die out. So they don't even want me talking to anybody about it.

It might seem strange that a group of people would choose to let their ancient traditions die out rather than allow them to continue in an altered state. Marcus recognizes that it is difficult to explain this situation to outsiders. But the elders of Marcus' tradition feel that the issue is just as much about social responsibility as it is about cultural integrity.

Not all of my ancestors are the kind of people that you would want to be reincarnated into anybody. It has to do with some of the beliefs that we have...It's also a family tradition, so there's that. I think a lot of that is involved in this decision. But it's also that—this is the sticking point for a lot of people, but it's common with these kinds of old traditions—in order to be in the tradition, first you have to be in the bloodline on both sides. Then you have to be trained. Well, family came over to the Americas, we don't have a lot of people who are married back into the bloodline. That's one big factor. And then you have to be trained, so you have to have somebody who's willing to train you. It's dying out for that reason. There's just not enough of us left, and I think they prefer it that way...There's a dark side to our tradition that they want to die out.

Yet, Marcus has found a way to incorporate some of his family tradition into Religio Romana in a way that does not violate the wishes of his elders. The religion of ancient Rome had civic rituals but it also had a private home-based practice. Marcus is translating his aspects of his family's practice into a home-based practice that members of Religio Romana can use.

That is one of my things now with the Religio Romana. I can transpose some of my tradition and some of the ideas to the Roman, to some of the people who are coming in to Religio Romana. That is a way to translate it, preserve it, in a sense. In a sense, because some of the family aspects will preserve my tradition—the family aspects of the Roman Religion—and I can easily transpose between the two. And that allows me not only to have our tradition to be preserved, but to allow it to evolve. If it is to survive, any living tradition has to evolve a little bit. Traditions grow. A living tradition will evolve and grow in time…We do have a long history of lot of material to base our ideas on, because we are reconstructionist. There is the philosophy, the myths, the rituals, as ancient as you can get, so, I think we would be in the position to teach others who are interested in rebuilding a polytheistic Western tradition.

One thing that Marcus wishes people understood is that the notions of monism are not the only religious philosophies in the world. There are more ancient ones that, one of which is polytheism. Yet, Marcus also notes that polytheism can incorporate a cosmic-level of monism even while affirming the independent existence of individual, distinct, Deities. And polytheist religions, Marcus reminds us, have always primarily been family practices even in cases that the religion was state-sponsored and state-supported.

Polytheism just seems natural to me! I get so many instances of this "one-ness" that comes out of the Christian idea, which comes out of Platonism, which in turn goes back to Pythagoreanism. Sorry, but there are more ancient philosophies than just that one—they didn't all believe that. I was pretty much raised on the Involuti, which, they had their own version of a single God, kind of. All the Gods are facets of the one great mind, or something like that, is how it is as a philosophy. We always thought of that "great mind" as the "Involuti." I don't know if you have a word in English for that. But the Involuti is like the "council of the Gods" sort of thing.

The Involuti are like, I hate to use this word,--kind of like "the matrix." Not the movie, but the real meaning of the word "matrix;" the web of divine energies that creates and formulates our destinies and all that is controlled by the Involuti, who are above it. Yeah, "Involuti" in the English language means the same as "convoluted:" intricate interconnection of things. That is one of the meanings in Italian for involuti, but we mean it for the higher [cosmic] Gods.

I've always understood my polytheism to be a family tradition. When I look at the Roman religion and all the emphasis that is put on the state religion of ancient Roman Empire and whatnot, the real religion, when you actually get into it and start studying it, it is a family religion. It's focus is on Vesta, the Goddess of the hearth, and on the lares, who are the family members. It's very family-oriented. Even though we have so many Gods, all the other ones I really know about, all the other ones I've interacted with, all the other polytheistic traditions, are basically the same way: a family tradition.

You know, I look at India now and then, and it's really amazing to me. There is a whole culture there, where some of it is so much like what we were doing all the time when I was a kid. The rituals, the different places they have, sacred places, the different Gods. That, to me, is a beautiful culture. Sometimes I really don't understand this Christian society we're in.

Shadow

Media producer Shadow has been a polytheist for over 30 years. Having been raised in a nominally Christian home, Shadow worked his way through Pentecostalism, Catholicism, and Wicca before discovering the Kemetic religion. Contemporary Kemetics are dedicated to reconstructing as much as is possible the religion of ancient Egypt. "[T]he religion of Ancient Egypt was always an urban and state-sponsored religion," he explains, "and it was (and in reconstruction is trying to be) highly structured, hierarchical and organized, and with a defined moral code." For these reasons, Shadow explains, the Kemetic religion "does not fall within the usual definition or contemporary notions of [the term] 'Pagan,'" * and he does not in fact consider himself to be Pagan. Today, Shadow proudly serves his Deities and a growing congregation of fellow Kemetics as the Chief Priest for the Per Ma'at Kemetic Temple, which he founded. In addition to his priestly duties, Shadow maintains a structured Kemetic ritual and devotional practice. His duties as priest call upon him to serve all of the Kemetic Deities, but he is specifically a priest of Aset-Nebthet (Isis-Nephthys) and his personal, intimate devotions focus mainly upon Them.

According to Shadow, polytheism is "the concept that there is more than one God," but that They are "not necessarily all equal Gods." These Gods "may be worshipped in different ways," or perhaps some "may not be [worshipped] at all." The Gods "may or may not care" about being worshipped, or about humanity. The Kemetic religion proceeds from the conviction that the Gods are willing to engage with humanity and will do so under specific ritual and spiritual conditions. Shadow recognizes that the efforts to reconstruct ancient Kemeticism are intimately linked to this understanding of polytheism, but he also recognizes how in a roundabout way, the original Kemetics' influence upon Western Christian mysticism has also influence contemporary Kemetic practice.

Kemetic religion today is still being defined, I guess because we are making an attempt at reconstruction, to the extent possible, of deep religious practices done in ancient Egypt, which was the

* Shadow Mihai, HSH. Personal electronic correspondence. 29 June 2011. Web.

land of Kem in the Egyptian tongue, therefore it is "Kemetic." Really, it's a process of construction, although with Egypt you have more of an ability of finding out and constructing what was done. Usually in what we call reconstructive paths, it's a process of actually constructing, because we don't really know a lot. So we're trying to recreate or create something relevant today using what has been done in the past within the Egyptian mythos. There's a lot more evidence of the way things worked because we do have a 3-to-4000 plus years history prior to Christ, so I guess that's about 6000 years ago. That's generally the basic timeframe. It's a little bit complex. We have to pay attention to things like temple practice, stuff which in a lot of other reconstruction religions doesn't exist because they didn't use temples, necessarily. And they didn't have the kind of complex hierarchical structure that the Egyptians had, which we've seen is married with politics as well... The Greeks wrote something—the Greek and the Egyptian historians wrote something, called it the book of Hermes, or Hermes Trismegistus, the book of thrice-great Hermes, which is purported to be a collection of spiritual and magical books taken from Egypt. It probably is, at least in part, and it was done around the third century C.E. And that influenced Christian mystics throughout the ages, which in turn influenced the founders of the Pagan movements in the western world including the freemasons, and the people who created Thelema and the Golden Dawn, which in turn influence people like me, who are trying to reconstruct Kemetic religion from the ground up. So it kind of came full circle in a way.

Shadow's understanding of the word "faith" is complex and somewhat different than the conventional understanding of the term. By and large, he recognizes that the word faith is a "new testament Biblical term" that indicates belief without evidence. For him, such belief is insincere. Shadow's conception of faith, in his personal Kemetic context, is that it involves spiritual knowledge gained from religious practice.

"Faith is the substance of the things hoped for and the evidence of things not seen..." In other words, faith is created through an experiential kind of process where you have some kind of knowledge but that [knowledge] doesn't necessarily function because it's about something that you don't ordinarily see. It's not something that you normally can count on as something that you learned like mathematics, but it's sort of the same thing. You [do] get some kind of knowledge through a process, either

*meditation or a kind of spiritual practice, about your spiritual
walk. It's more than what might normally be considered when
you would say, "I take it on faith." "I t you" or "my faith got
me through it," That's a little bit more close to what I'm talking
about. Sometimes when people talk about faith it just means
that, well, I believe it without evidence. People say that all the
time, they believe without evidence. That's hoping or wishing and
it's a very insecure concept to me, that kind of faith. That is
not, to me, what faith is. Faith to me is more of a direct
spiritual kind of knowledge. When you think about it, you
take all of mathematics on faith anyway. When you think
about it there's not really any proof of mathematics, or of
physics. I mean you can prove physics from moment to moment to
moment, but the kind of faith I am talking about you can prove
from moment to moment also.*

Shadow explains that it took "a very long process of spiritual
searching" before he found the Kemetic religion. The Catholic
Christian context held strong appeal because of its elaborate ritual
structure, but Shadow found the theology to be problematic. It was
when he discovered Kemeticism that Shadow found a fulfilling and
enjoyable balance of polytheist theology and strong ritual structure.

*I was never really happy, I guess in the Christian faith, the
protestant Christian faith. Nothing ever seemed to work for me.
I gravitated towards Catholicism. My family background is in
orthodox Christianity, but where I grew up we didn't have any
Orthodox churches. I gravitated towards Catholicism. I really
liked the ceremony and ritual of it which when I attended
masses and stuff like that, it would always have an effect on me.
At particular points in the ritual, and very specific spots in the
Mass when it was done right, I would have particular feelings
and so that was kind of the first step towards Kemeticism.
Although I never really—it just didn't really work with me, for
the Christian concept of salvation and that stuff. At the same
time, I always had this—I described it in the written portion of
the interview—I kept having these visions of a female face and
it was really bizarre. Really, really bizarre; I would look at a
wall and the space would pop up. It was always the same face.
It went on for years and years and years.*

*Again, at the same time, I finally moved into—I finally got
tired of not having anything interesting…I started trying to
make contact with who I thought, divinity-wise, was working
with metaphysics. I was always interested in the paranormal,*

and in ghosts and stuff, although ghosts and those things never really manifested. Magical kinds of things. I started experimenting with mentalism, and witchcraft and those kinds of things to see what kinds of facts they would have. They are very, very, very connected. These two experiences kind of flowed together; it was like one night I realized—or I was told, by someone whom I interpreted as Isis. She kind of led me along into this sort of neo-Pagan path into Wicca. I kind of gravitated towards what is called Egyptian Wicca.

In Wicca, I met people—Ellen Cannon Reed had just died several months before—I had met people who were left in her coven. I guess her husband moved away, but I'd met a few other people. So I met these Egyptian Wiccans and most of them went into other areas after Ellen died. A couple of them went to Hellenic Paganism, but those things didn't work for me as well. I guess the experience, my personal experience, is that the closer I got to the person of Isis, the more drawn I was to more formal Kemetic practice which is very different than what is done in normal neo-Pagan practice, in terms of its formality, but also in terms of its particular moral codes and whatnot. It's very...I won't say strict, but it is formal in a way that most people aren't attracted to. It's my observation that people who get closer and closer to Egyptian Gods are attracted to it more, and get more out of it when practic[ing] in an Egyptian context. I would say my observation of people who are in Hellenic Paganism get more out of it when they practice and what they understand is the way that the Greeks did it as well. It just seems more natural. There are systems. There are magical systems and religious systems and they kind of work within themselves. I guess that's how I can explain it. I guess I can also say the Gods like to be worshipped in a certain way, and They're used to it in a certain way, it just works and flows better that way. And in this meandering way is how I was drawn to Kemetic practice. Now it just seems like the right way to do things. I get more out of it.

Over the last thirty years, Shadow has had many personal experiences which confirm for him that the Deities exist, and that many of Them welcome our engagement. Sometimes these experiences happen during religious ritual, but others happen in a more spontaneous way. In Shadow's view, it is important not to get preoccupied with worrying about whether it really is the Gods communicating with you, or just a self-generated psychological response. The important thing, he says, is to be open to invitation and to initiation.

> The process in any of these religious paths is initiatory. By which I mean there's rituals and things you go through, very specific things. It doesn't matter whether it's Wicca or whether it's Asatru, but definitely in the Egyptian context, which draws on some of the Hermetic practices and set ritual steps, and ritual is designed to create a psychological effect. When you do it right you have a psychological effect. But you also have a metaphysical affect. Or, to put another way, just because you're having a psychological effect doesn't mean you're not talking to the Gods. Both things happen. In my prior experience, I had really great moments when I was in a Pentecostal church, or as I said, anytime I am in a Catholic mass there is something that happens at a particular point in the mass which I can't put my finger on that is happening. Although I have those moments, they don't compare to the things that happened, the things that I've gone through in Kemetic practice. I would come commune, in my instance, with Isis-Nephthys, the twins. The point of becoming a priest in Kemetic religion is to become partly possessed by and coexist with the particular Deity that you are working with. The concept of Deity is also a little bit different. We call it Netjer, and that concept spans both what a western concept of God would be, as well as a principle of nature, an active principle of nature, and even an abstract principle like justice. It's a very complex thing. The point is, that at some point you have an experience where you invite that particular God into you. They have already invited Themselves more or less, otherwise you wouldn't invite that particular Deity, and They are with you all the time so you always feel Their presence.

> There are other specific times when I had audible experiences and saw faces. One day, I asked Her who She was and She said—She audibly said—"I am the Lady of the Waters. Come to me and you will create something never seen before." That happened a long, long time ago and I can feel it right now. She showed me this visually. I can see these black and silvery waters flowing. I didn't know, when that experience happened, I didn't know that one of the names for Isis is the "Lady of the Waters." It's not an often-used name. I found it several weeks later as I was looking through trying to track it down, that it was one of Her names as well. It sounds so simple and yet it's such a profound moment, because it was actually audible. I've had a number of things like that happen. These are the

experiences with Netjer either that I sought or that that came to me within the context of being on the path of Kemetic practice. So I have no doubt that these personages are hearing and They want to talk to us and for whatever reason—I don't know how to think of it but I guess, we as sentient beings are kind of reaching into Their realm back and forth and I know that we're part of Them anyway. It makes some kind of sense that They would want to communicate with us, and vice versa.

In his home, Shadow keeps a ritual shrine for the Kemetic Deities which is tended daily according to Kemetic tradition. He also sets time aside for devotion and service to the Deities on a weekly basis.

In my personal practice, I have two kinds of things because I came through Wicca. I often informally do something that is very witch-like, I suppose. I'll go out under the Moon and I will draw a circle, which isn't something that is normally thought of as Egyptian, but they did do it outside of temple space. I will invoke the Goddess in a very Wicca-like way...That's one personal thing. One other thing that I do is to keep a shrine in the Egyptian manner where the God is installed in the statue through something called the Opening of the Mouth ceremony so that there is a part, a place in your own home, where the Deity is always present. And that is more formalized and you daily make devotions and burn incense and things like that there. There is daily practice. Either a prayer will be taken from some of the scriptures, or other books from ancient Egypt, or something that I've done myself. And there are different times of day. It's all very fluid, I would say, a lot more fluid than people would think...Tuesdays are usually the day that I try to do something specific, I specifically set aside time beyond the regular devotional times. There's always an offering of either incense or food or something like that. There is always a prayer of worship and there may or may not be prayers to ask assistance, although not usually in my case. There's always some adoration and prayer and communing every day, as I said.

Ancient Egyptians honored myriad diverse Deities, many who originated there and many who were adopted and syncretized from other cultures. This, plus thousands of years of syncretic mythology have posed an interesting challenge for those working to rebuild the Kemetic religion. The tremendous wealth of archaeological and historical information about Heliopolis prompted Shadow to adopt the Heliopolitan Ennead as the primary Deities of the temple. Shadow also honors Heliopolitan Deities in his personal practice.

> *Egyptians had just tons of different Deities. However, throughout their history, there's always a nonet—there was always nine in any particular area that were supreme Deities of the Temples. They included Re and Horus and Isis and Osiris and Nephthys, and then depending on the time and location, there may have been Atum, Sekhmet, or somebody else in there who were also considered to be part and parcel of the Creator. The Heliopolitan Ennead is the group of Gods who were worshipped, organized in Heliopolis, which was the main center. We work with that in the planning stage because most of the archaeological information from Egypt, the works that you find, are very more complete around where are the Temples of Heliopolis were. There is more information about ethics, there is more information about hierarchy and things like that. We can extrapolate from that. It hardly matters which Ennead you work with in reconstructing the religion. We base a lot of what we do on that group for pragmatic purposes. But that doesn't mean that they are exclusive. There are Deities within that group that I personally do not connect with. Atum, for instance. And there are other Deities who I would work with that are not in that group. I don't think Bast is in there either, come to think of it. Enneads were very important throughout the history of Egypt. So it's a hierarchical kind of planning kind of thing...It just occurred to me what an odd term "work with" is. I think that is a peculiarly neo-Pagan term. (Laughs.)*

When asked about whether he honors ancestors in his personal practice, Shadow explains that the ancestors played a major role in ancient Egyptian religion and that they are very important to contemporary Kemeticism as well. He is very clear that it isn't about worshipping the dead so much as it is about maintaining one's connection to them.

> *Contact with ancestors is part and parcel of Egyptian approach to religion. The whole concept and the whole thrust of Egyptian religion, and in fact their very societal structure for a few thousand years, was not because they were obsessed with death, but because they saw that death continued on into another form of life, and they continued their relationship with the ancestors. And it's a very important, integral part of the religion to continue to connect with your ancestors. Especially the recent ones, to speak with them, and to help them along, and to ask their guidance. So, yes. We do that all the time. It's also a very*

natural religion. You might not think of it that way because it was urban. The central aspect of the Kemetic religion was always Ma'at, which means truth, beauty and balance. It's a complex term, but the purpose is to achieve balance in every part of your life, I suppose, and so that necessarily implies a natural and holistic approach to life, including your diet and your exercise and what you do daily. The a'ku, which is the word for ancestors—the a'ku, our predecessors, are extremely important for the Kemetic religion. It's not a worshipful thing, it's not that you worship them. Outsiders, people who don't understand religion, would say that it's ancestor worship, and it has nothing to do with worship. You don't worship the dead, but you would continue your relationship with them, which is an entirely different thing.

Myth does not play an etiological or eschatological role in Shadow's religious practice. Rather, he has found mythology to be instructive about the personalities and character of the Deities he honors, and an opportunity to know Them more deeply.

My experience of the character of the Gods is very close to what one might expect when one reads the myths. In terms of character, in terms of presence, feelings you get in the presence of a certain Deity, or communications you might get. I don't think the myths are literal, particularly in the Egyptian context. They are very specific, and they develop characters well. For instance, Seth has always been a controversial one, who later became, in the Christian context, associated as a devil. But Seth is a very complex character who did some very bad things. The central lesson I got from Seth is what happens when your will is either completely unrestrained, or you need to rely on it alone. Seth manages to kill Osiris and chop Him up, because He wants to become the Great One. He fights with Horus to lead the Ennead. He does these really mean and evil things sometimes, and a lot of what He does is destructive. But on the other hand, the other myth that you hear about Him is that at the end of the day, when the forces of chaos and destruction are about to overwhelm the forces of creation, and all of the Gods cower in fear, the only person who stands between Them and utter destruction is Seth. Seth stands and says "I will not permit it." This God is a complex God, ruled primarily by one thing but [who] has a lot of personality traits that go with that. Those myths, when you put them together, really do sum up a particular kind of character. In my experience, all of these myths sort of define different characters. They are...not necessarily archetypal but they are definitely different particular persons. My experience in dealing with individual forms of a Deity is that the myths really do reflect those persons in a way.

One of the things Shadow wishes people would understand is that they are probably more polytheistic than they realize. Christianity, for example, is actually a very polytheistic religion in Shadow's view. The concept of honoring multiple Deities might not be so challenging for people to grasp if they would recognize this.

You see here's the thing, I think most people are polytheist, regardless of who they are. I base that on an observational experience of how they practice in their daily life. If you're a Catholic, and you're praying to a saint, you're a polytheist. So regardless of what the dogma is, what you do in your practice reflects something that means something different to you. I think it's more natural. It's way more widespread, because it's more natural than being monotheist. The Egyptians are often called monolatrists in that they tend to see the Gods as aspects of a Creator, or it is easy to infer within their myths and structure that the worship of any God is the worship of the Creator. It's just—I think it's pretty well impossible to connect with something you can't conceive of. Or that you can't, by definition, communicate with. You can't connect to an all-powerful all-knowing being unless that being puts itself in a container that you understand. And so that's what polytheism is about to me. Christ the son, Jehovah, the Father, Sophia the Holy Spirit, those are definitely three completely different containers of what may or may not be a single Deity. I think people need to chill out a little bit about polytheism. I don't think it's a big bone of contention for anybody, I don't think anybody talks about it very much. I've never had anybody bring it up outside of Pagan circles.

Shadow, fortunately, has not experienced too much friction due to his emphasis on polytheism. However, his viewpoint as being not monotheist yet also not Pagan has given him an unusual perspective on the relationship between Christianity and contemporary Paganism.

People forget, or they didn't know, that Wicca structurally was developed through Christian mysticism. When I mentioned that to some people, even some old guard Wiccans, I got a very hostile reaction. (laughs). It just was. Gerald Gardner structured Wicca after Masonic practice and that's just the way it is…

People in church don't talk about other religions generally speaking. They almost never talk about Pagan religions. They don't go round out of the blue saying things about how they feel, that they dislike the witches or that they don't like Hellenic Pagans. It just doesn't come up. It got very tiring for me personally, attending an event held by what we called the Santa Clarita Pagan Network. I was their representative on the local interfaith council, which of course is populated by Christians of the various types. I found it very tiring to have to attend our weekly meetings among the Pagan group, and within minutes somebody would start talking about how dumb Christians were or they would make some kind of snipe out of the blue, as if that was what we were all their for. It just became really tiring for me.

But the other thing is that my close friend who is a Baptist in upbringing and religion, would attend with me. She would never say anything about Paganism or anything like that. She didn't complain. When you start complaining about people's religion, it hurts them, you know? Especially in the other contexts where you may or may not know that she is [Christian]. Eventually everybody did know it and it did not make a difference. So these people were just being very insensitive and upsetting.

So I have to say, if you can't set aside your feelings about a religion, it is because you find something really attractive about it. I was Pentecostal for a number of years, and I really, really believed in some of the things they were saying. When I saw that some of the leaders were clearly just using local people to get a bunch of money, or they didn't really believe what they were saying themselves, I was extremely disillusioned. Having seen that, I had to leave. I was really hurt by the disconnect between what they said and what they did behind closed doors and even in front of people. But, it wasn't for me anyway. I don't go around talking about it and saying how evil Billy Graham is. I believe that a lot of these people are very sincere and doing what they think they should do, and they make their living a certain way, and they are entitled to a living, and all that stuff. But if I am obsessed with them, and that's all that I can talk about, why am I studying another religion? Maybe I should make a difference in the religion that is really obsessing me. So that was my complaint with the Pagan groups. I eventually had to stop bringing my friend, and eventually I just stopped, because somebody would always say things that would hurt her feelings for no reason.

That said, I was a representative of the local Pagan group on the interfaith council. We got together to meet as a group of religious leaders to do some good things in the community. We gave food to the hungry, we found places for the homeless. That kind of stuff. And we tried to understand each other's religious positions. They were always very good and very open.

In Shadow's experience, individual Kemetics may or may not feel an identification with the larger Pagan movement. There are many reasons that he does not. Some of these reasons are related to contemporary socio-political factors. Others have to do with the interesting parallels that Shadow has found between ancient Kemetic religion and the Judaic and Christian monotheism that came later.

I don't consider myself a Pagan for a number of reasons. One of which is small-p political, partly for the reasons I just told you and partly because...in the general Pagan movement I see a lot of people attracted to it not because they find something in it, but because they find no rules in it as a movement. I find a lot of people glom onto New Age, Wicca, or Teen Witch kind of stuff, these experimental things, because they don't have to follow any kind of ethical path. That, to me, is the opposite of what spirituality and religion are about. Or at least what religion is about. A spiritual path by itself may or may not have particular ethical guidelines. Religion has very definite ones. I find a lot of people who like to stay in the Pagan movement stay there because they don't like to be told what to do. They kind of react against that. Kemetics generally don't feel like that...A lot of us [just] don't consider ourselves to be Pagan.

The other thing is just structural. [Kemeticism] doesn't conform to what you might call a Pagan religion, the religion of the heath and the hill and whatnot. I will add that there is evidence that Judaism was based in large part on ancient Egyptian religion. So as Christianity can be seen as a kind of variant of Judaism, we can say that it as well derives from Egyptian religion. So if Christianity is not Pagan, neither can Kemeticism be Pagan...it's a very hierarchical religion, even though where we are now we don't have a group of temples. There's a number of us...it is hierarchical and respectful and very, very concerned about how things ought to be done. Not to say that you cannot do things in many different ways, it's just that the structure is important because what comes out at the other end is determined a little bit by the structure with which you begin. So we don't really conform [to Paganism] that way.

Also, the other thing is, the more I learn and the more I

read—you have to learn how to read Egyptian hieroglyphics—the more you read and the more you know about Christian and Jewish religion the more you suspect that it was based on things that were taught in Egypt during the time that the Jews for there. Things like the 10 commandments. You can find corollaries much older, what we call the negative confessions. There are 42 negative confessions in Egyptian beginning with the words "Thou shalt not…" or they actually said, "I have not done" this or that. Magical stories: the parting of the Red Sea could have been lifted from a particular magical text that predated the Hebrew. In that story, one of the priests magicians parted the Red Sea in a particular way. Many of the stories do that.

Plus, the concept of a single creator as well, even though the Egyptians have many Gods. They still have a single creator, Atum. So there are all these allegories. I tend to see that it flows in a certain direction in terms of time, it had to go from the former to the latter, not the other way around. In terms of Christianity too—because I have an Orthodox background and a Catholic background—the actual image that you see of the nursing Madonna and Christ, [which] you see throughout Europe, even up into Moscow and St. Petersburg, are often taken from preexisting friezes or preexisting sculptures or preexisting mosaics of Isis nursing Horus. In particular, as far north as Moscow where they had a temple of Isis. Or in Sweden, there is a very famous black Madonna, which was built over a temple of Isis. They just say She's the black Madonna and She's feeding Christ. There are all of these pictures that are very familiar to us as Christians, and they're just lifted from that. You can actually find archaeologists and Egyptologists who made the observation a hundred years ago. So I tend to see this not as a Pagan thing. I kind of bristle at the term a little bit. It doesn't bother most people, but I find Kemetic religion really doesn't connect with what other people think of as Pagan. That's not to say we don't connect with people in the religious reconstruction movement.

Also I tended to see, as I was moving [from Wicca] into Kemetic practice…there was a perceived "we're different from you" kind of attitude on the Kemetic side. In coming into that, I would say that that's true. Some of them do, I would say. This [also] is why I say "tends to." Some people do tend to think of themselves as Pagans. It depends on if you are practicing Egyptian Wicca or strictly Kemetic practice. Some people use the terms loosely.

Perhaps one of the significant difficulties Shadow has experienced as a result of his religious practice is facing the ethnocentrism and bigotry he encounters in the attitudes of scholars who write about ancient Egypt. To combat this, Shadow learned hieroglyphics and does his own primary research whenever possible.

> *When all you are left with is archaeological and Egyptological things which are very chauvinistic, it is a bit bizarre. Because you find there's Wallace Budge, who has this overwhelming love of the Egyptian context but this chauvinistic view of the "savage minds" of Egyptians. In one breath, how can you say, oh, that's what their structure was, or this political idea here, and then call them savage mind in the next because they have a polytheistic mindset. The fact is, Budge didn't understand what the Egyptians were saying about life after death...Right up until today. There's a disconnect. I don't think anybody studies in Egyptology for very long without falling love with the society or the art or the culture, and yet they still somehow in their minds and what they write, say that these people were primitive. It just doesn't make sense. And you can't interpret these things if you have that mindset. The interpretation just isn't going to be correct. You cannot do it.*

Ceisiwr Serith

Pagan author and scholar Ceisiwr Serith has been a polytheist for 35 years. Ceisiwr identifies as an Indo-European Reconstructionist. He belongs to the Nemos Ognios, a protogrove of the Druid organization Ár nDraíocht Féin, or ADF. The grove meets weekly for ritual, education, and ritual, and they hold seasonal rituals to celebrate the eight Neo-Pagan holidays. He works with Deities from the Roman, Irish, Proto-Indo-European, and American pantheons, but says that his closest personal relationships are with the Gaulish God Cernnunos and Manannán Mac Lir.

Ceisiwr defines polytheism as "the worship of more than one Deity." He wishes to note that in this definition he is "very specific about the **worship** of more than one Deity rather than the **belief** in more than one Deity." For him, the word "faith" would "simply be referring to belief. The acceptance of something in a religious context perhaps with less evidence then one would have in a non-religious context." For Ceisiwr, practice is more important than faith when it comes to polytheism. In fact, he says that faith plays no part in his religion because he believes that "Paganism is about doing rather than believing."

I think Paganism is about doing the right thing. That aspect does fit in with the whole nature religion thing, I suppose: Where are we now? What is appropriate for now? How do we do things that make the world a pretty place, an appropriate place? I do a lot of work in Proto-Indo-European religion. There is this concept in it, "Xártus" The word comes from the root "xar-"* which means to join together in an appropriate and beautiful manner. The word "harmony" comes from it, actuall. "Xar-" is to harmonize. The pattern that the cosmos forms in the Vedic religion, "?ta," you might have run across it somewhere. So the idea that the universe is supposed to be a pretty place, a well-put-together place, means that our job is to fit it together as well as possible in our lives. Our job is to act virtuously, to learn, to worship... and "belief" doesn't really enter into that. I don't really care what the beliefs of my plumber are, as long as he does the plumbing right. He could even have crazy ideas about

---

* The "x" is pronounced like the "ch" in the German "Bach."

plumbing. But if my plumbing works, I don't care. I see the
universe as being that way. It doesn't really matter how I believe
things are, as long as I'm doing the right things.

Originally raised Roman Catholic, Ceisiwr's path to polytheism
began when he was in high school. Perhaps nobody was more
surprised than he when the fantastical, exotic, mysterious, and
somewhat fraudulent identity he built for himself as a teenager
became a significant part of a deep and sincere religious identity.

Back in high school, which was in the mid-seventies, I was a
newcomer to the area. It was an area where everybody had
known each other since kindergarten. So I was an outsider. So
I made friends with the other new kid. One day, we were
building this structure in the woods—a big stone circle. Not big
tall stones, small stones. In the shape of a circle, a triangle, and
a pentagram. It's a long story as to why we were doing that, but
as we were doing it I said, "this looks like a witchy symbol. We
should be the school witches." And he said, "OK." So we
decided to set up a fake little coven to have some sort of identity
within the school. We'd be the school witches. So I decided to do
some research on the subject, and I got hooked. I had been
studying mythology since I was in the second grade, and I
remember thinking at the time, "how come nobody worships
these Gods anymore?" So I did have that in my background. I
started doing Wicca when I was in high school. Years and years
later, I ended up getting involved in ADF. Through that, I got
out of Wicca—it just fell away. I became more of a
polytheist—a hard polytheist—than the Wiccan "all Gods are
one God" sort of stuff. So basically I got involved in it through
fraud. (Laughs.)

Ceisiwr came strongly to identify with the ADF because the
organization emphasizes many of the things that are important to
him. According to Ceisiwr, the ADF has helped him work to become
the person and Pagan that he most wants to be.

I'm a big fan of ADF. Ian Corrigan says that we don't
proselytize, but we do recruit. I think of myself as being a semi-
recruiter for it. I really like the group. We've been around for a
long time now. It emphasizes a lot of the things I care
about—the importance of ritual, the importance of virtue,
which is kind of a nice thing to hear. It isn't just "an it harm
none do what you will." There are things you really should
aspire to be like. That's actually a really important part of
Pagan ethics. It isn't a question of "thou shalt," or "thou shalt

not," it's "thou shalt aspire to." It isn't "don't do this.' It's "be honorable." That is something you have to work at all the time: what's the honorable thing in this situation? Be wise. Okay, what's the wisest thing to do in a situation? It's a constant engagement with the world instead of just a, "this is good, this is bad" sort of a thing. I see that as more of a Pagan approach to ethics and morality. And that's an important part of ADF as well. I think it was Ian Corrigan who classified Druidic Paganism as being composed of piety, study, and virtue. That really appeals to me. Worshipping the Gods in the best and most appropriate way. Learning as much as you can about the way things are. Living a virtuous life. To me, that sums up my goals as a Pagan.

Ceisiwr has had experiences with the Gods and Goddesses which have convinced him that They are real. "I've heard Them," he explains, "I've seen Them—like, physically seen Them—and there have been the various kinds of visions, and that sort of thing."

The one that was probably the most striking one was when I was in college. I attended Holy Cross—a Jesuit school. It's on the side of the hill. Further up the hill, there's a fair amount of wild area. One day I decided to go do a ritual up there. So I was up there and I was doing some praying, I forget exactly what I was praying about, but my incense went out, and I heard, literally, "enough." And I said, "no, no, I'm going to continue to do more of this." I tried lighting the incense again but I could not get it lit. Finally, I gave up and started walking down the hill. And as I walked down the hill, I saw a rock on the ground that said, "pick me up." So I picked it up, and I brought it back to my room, and just sort of set it up in my room. I didn't know what it was or why I should have it. The ritual had been dedicated towards the antlered God Cernnunos. A couple months later, the friend from high school was visiting. I told him the story, he didn't know anything about Cernnunos, and I told him that the stone wanted to be picked up, and he said "well, yeah it's got a stag and it." And when I looked at it, there is actually the outline of a stag in high relief. And that part of the stone was the part that had been faced down. I hadn't seen it when I picked it up. It was a very powerful day. I actually physically heard something, and I was given this stone that had a stag on it, that I could not have seen when I picked it up. Though that's probably my most impressive story.

After being spoken to by Cernnunos, and then "sometime later seeing Woden and Manannán" Ceisiwr realized that that the Gods are separate, distinct individuals. "But it was only years after that," he says, "that I started to make offerings rather than do magical forms of ritual, and as result discovered that different Deities answered differently and had different preferences." Ceisiwr's historical research and personal experiences with the Gaulish Cernnunos have led him to conclude that this God who he honors in his practice differs significantly from the Cernnunos who is honored by Wiccans.

> *The Wiccan God that they sometimes call Cernnunos is a God of maleness, of sexuality, of the wild, of animals, whereas the Gaulish God has no connection with sexuality and is most likely not a God of animals and the wild. He's more of a God of bi-directionality, a God of the in-between, who has a fairly large role in commerce. Actually I wrote a paper on this. I presented it at the Harvard Celtic Colloquium. It got published in the proceedings. It's a particular Deity I know a heck of a lot about. The Gaulish one.*

Manannán Mac Lir is another God Ceisiwr honors. Ceisiwr says that his visionary experience with Manannán prepared he and his family for significant, life-altering events.

> *He's been one who's given visions. He's sort of a God of in-between as well, like Cernnunos is. One of my other impressive experiences was at a ritual at a festival. There was a woman who was supposed to be doing this sort of guided meditation thing and we were all supposed to be following along with it. I hate guided meditations. I feel like I'm in kindergarten and imagining or something.*

> *So I decided to basically go off on my own. So I ended up with these visions of snakes and water: the whole import of these visions is that all hell was about to break loose, but things were going to be okay. I opened my eyes and discovered that I was standing directly opposite a shrine of Manannán Mac Lir that was outside the space. He's connected with water. In Indo-European Gods, snakes are connected with water and also with chaos. About a month after that, my wife's company merged with another company and the headquarters was going to be moving to Iowa. She ended up getting another job, we moved to another state, we ended up in a house we absolutely love in a neighborhood that's great. So, essentially He gave me a vision of all hell's about to break loose but it'll be okay. Then all hell broke loose; but, it was OK.*

Ceisiwr says that his relationship with the Gods "varies depending on the Deity." According to Ceiswr, "the Deities are individuals, and as such have Their own personalities. That means that some prefer to be related to in one way and some in others." Brighid, in his experience, "is very friendly, and my relationship with Her is somewhat familial," whereas his relationship with Cernunnos "is harsher." Generally, he relates to Them "in terms of reciprocity, my relationships with Them being established and maintained through prayers and offerings." Ceisiwr is very engaged with his religious practice and makes a point of doing devotional work and making offerings every day.

> *Some of what I do are morning prayers. I have several shrines, and my main sacred area is at the stove, because the hearth is a central part of the Indo-European religion. So my main shrines have always been near the hearth. At one side of it, I have an icon that I painted myself, of the Goddess Brigid, and an oil lamp, with a small bowl of water, and a small silver bowl. And to the right of my stove, I have images of Gods, Ancestors, and nature spirits, specifically the patrons of the members of my family—the Gods and Goddesses who are most connected with Them and also I have a lamp there. So I start up on the left of it, where the Brigid stuff is, and I pray to Brigid as I light the flame and Her lamp. I will also offer Her milk—She gets milk from each of the cartons of milk that I use. So it's not like a once a week thing, it's whenever I open a new carton. I pour it in the little silver bowl. So I pray to Her and I take the same match and I transfer the fire to the oil lamp over the other shrine and I say, "the altar is lit form the hearth." And then I do a little prayer setting up the cosmology. Then I do a general prayer to the Gods, the ancestors, and the nature spirits. And then I have a bowl there, and I offer a hazelnut, a walnut, and an almond, that that I may be wise, be strong, and be prosperous. And then I blow out the oil lamp at that shrine, and then I go blow out the lamp on the other shrine. Actually, the entire ritual is on my website*

Like other members of the ADF, Ceisiwr makes a point of honoring the Deities, ancestors, and nature spirits—which are referred to as the three kindreds. He says that the ADF honors ancestors and nature spirits "because the ancient Pagans honored them. We make sure we include all three in our practice."

> *[Ancestors] are in the main shrine. I have images of my lineage. I have an African woman holding a child because we all go*

back to Africa. I've got a statue of Lincoln, Jefferson, and Chester A. Arthur, who is actually my favorite president. Those are to represent the cultural ancestors. I have a shell from one of the shots that was fired at my father's funeral that represents my more recent personal ancestors. I tend not to do too much directly with them, except for each year at Samhain, but they are mentioned in my daily practice.

Nature spirits are something I'm not really—I don't really spend that much time with. I probably should. I do occasional walks in the woods and give prayers as I go. But I do that largely in the context of my Grove that I go to. We actually do a fair amount of stuff there with the nature spirits and the relationship between culture and nature and the real relationship between the tame and the wild. How we need to make nice with it, but that they have to make nice with us back. I don't really see Paganism as being the big nature religion that a lot of people do. If you look at ancient Rome, for instance, the average Roman living in an apartment building in the middle of Rome couldn't give a squat about nature spirits, but he was still Pagan. I'd like to see a recognition of that. In fact, if I lived in a city, I think I'd be writing a book on urban Paganism, and not the urban Paganism about "oh look! You can still be Pagan I the city because we've got parks and we've got trees growing in them," but rather, "hey! You can still be a Pagan in a city because there are statues of Mercury and Minerva around here." That kind of thing. The city itself has a kind of spirit. A city is as natural as a beaver dam. So, I'm not really that into nature spirits. Although I recognize and I honor them.

The underlying philosophy of Ceisiwr's practice is reciprocity. This is the idea that humans and those whom we honor are in a two-way, interactive, mutually rewarding relationship. Each gives and each takes and the give and take are predicated on love, devotion, and respect.

One thing that just popped into my head about that's important about what I do, it's pretty central to ADF, the idea of reciprocity. The idea that we give, They give. It's not like, well, we've given to the Gods and now They're obligated to give back to us. It's more like if you invite someone to your house for dinner. They now have a social obligation to invite you back to their house for dinner. It's not a law. It's just the way that hospitality works. If you go back and forth, inviting each other back and forth, you become friends and you develop a relationship, and after a while you stop keeping track of how many times who has been at whose house, because you are just friends. As I see it, at least one of the goals of Paganism is to be that way to the Gods. Now, certain Gods more so than others because some Gods don't like to think of Themselves as your friends. But still, that back-and-forth when you make offerings, that's you inviting Them to dinner. Their inviting you to dinner is Them giving you blessings in response. But it doesn't come out of a necessity for following rules, it comes out of a friendly relationship that's been established and maintained through this exchange. That's an important part of my practice. For years, beginning in my Wiccan days, I didn't do any sorts of offerings and did very few prayers. I did magic and that kind of stuff… I don't do any magic any more. I discovered that prayers and offerings work just as well.

Myth has proven to be an interesting issue for Ceisiwr. "A lot of the Gods I worship," he explains, "don't have myths or myths connected with them that we know of. Cernunnos, we know nothing about; the proto-European Deities we know nothing about." That said, Ceisiwr does have clear ideas about reconciling his personal experiences to the lore that does exist about his Gods.

I general, my experiences of the Deities has lined up enough with the lore that there isn't really a problem there. We don't, or shouldn't, look at the lore as if it's a canon. If you read, for instance, the Greek myths, you'll find that Euripides does the myths one way, but they're still found differently in Homer, and Aeschylus tells a slightly different version of it. So even in ancient times there was a sense that there was a general outline of the myth but that you could make some changes here and there, but there was never a sense of scripture. We have to really be careful about viewing a particular text as scripture especially since in our living culture we don't have a lot of those variants. So, as long as it stays within the general framework, if we look at the myth and pretend it's Homer, and pretend we're Euripides, then we're cool.

You have to stay in the general framework, though. I wouldn't, for instance, worship the Morrigan as a Goddess of love. On the other hand, I know someone who's worshipping the God Lugh as a God of work projects because one of Lugh's jobs in the second battle of Mag Tuired was to take everyone's talents and meld them together to win the battle. My friend, who also belongs to Ár nDraíocht Féin, sees that as very applicable to being in a job

situation with all these different talents and responsibilities and
you have to accomplish a mission.

If there is one thing that Ceisiwr wishes people understood about polytheism, it's that polytheism is no less reasonable than monotheism. In fact, there are cases where Ceisiwr thinks polytheism is more reasonable than monotheism.

> *[I]t's just as reasonable a position as monotheism. In many ways I think it's more reasonable, because it avoids some of the problems that monotheism has. Like, the problem of evil. If you've got a single, omnipotent, omniscient, omni-benevolent Deity then why is there evil? But if you've got a bunch of Deities, well, They all have Their priorities, They all have Their interests, and They're not always necessarily watching over us. So, you don't have that question. Are you familiar with John Michael Greer's book A World full of Gods?... He deals with those questions.*

Ceisiwr has from time to time experienced some tension in relation to his religion. Yet more often than not, when he has ventured out and gotten into discussions about his religion, the conversations have been cordial and respectful.

> *In general, people have either been intrigued, or as uninterested in my religion as they are in anyone else's. People don't really like to talk about religion. At least, not in my area. So it's not an issue. People might be like, "so what do you do?" and I say, "well, I write." What do you write?" "I write about ancient Paganism" "oh, that sounds interesting, so tell me about it." So I talk about what I write about. It comes out as a result—I don't necessarily say "well, I'm a Pagan, too." But it becomes fairly clear as a result of the conversation that I'm a Pagan. It just flows…the conversation just flows. And that's cool. So no, I haven't had any conflict. Now, I will point out that I stay at home. My wife goes to work and I stay at home and I take care of everything and I write. So I don't have the day-to-day interactions that other people have...So there aren't as many possibilities for conflict that others might have. I just haven't had any myself.*

Paul Bjorn

Paul Bjorn, 23, is an American graduate student living in Scotland. He has been a polytheist and Heathen for 11 years. Paul differs from many Heathens because his practice is solitary in nature. Having never lived in an area where many other Heathens live made it difficult to share rituals or holidays with anyone. Despite the lack of Heathen fellowship, Paul has maintained devotional relationships with Thor, Tyr, and Odin. While he honors and affirms the Gods and Goddesses of all religions, the only Gods he prays to are the Germanic ones.

"When I use the term polytheism," Paul explains, "I use the usual textbook definition that it is the belief, and—I don't like using the word 'worship' because it has inferred connotations behind it—but the 'reverence,' we can use that word—of more than one, well, technically, more than two Deities." According to Paul, "faith" is basically "the belief in something without the most standard form of evidence as we understand it—physical evidence, I guess." In any case, Paul says that faith doesn't really play a role in his relationships with the Gods.

Faith is, it's kind of a—well, "I don't know if there's something there, but I will believe that it is without evidence one way or another of it." How I see faith, is that I see faith as a little blind, and a little, at times, naive. How I've always approached things—I'm pretty much a skeptic at heart—I've always approach things from different perspectives. Everything, on these different perspectives that I'm looking at—certain aspects of life, I see as little actual evidence for there to be just us or some totalitarian supernatural entity.

Originally born into a Catholic family, Paul found himself drifting away from Christianity at an early age. Paul discovered the Norse Gods when he read the Eddas as a child. The epic scope of the stories felt very familiar and it wasn't long before Paul felt a connection to the Norse Gods. After a brief time studying Wicca, Paul discovered Heathenry.

I come from a very Latin American Catholic family. My mother is from Nicaragua, and a very strict Catholic so I grew up Catholic, as she thought that would be the best way to go.

Well, if you know anything about Latin American Catholicism, it's very much an almost Pagan religion without the benefit of wanting to call itself that. So I just—well, I actually have read the Bible because I used to be a huge, huge a reader when I was young. So I read that, and it sounded to me like—exactly like I all of these other stories that I was reading. My elementary school had a fantastic library. It had a ton of books from the 1800s and the early 1900s. So probably by the time that I was ten, nine or ten, I was reading things like the Eddas and Beowulf.

And so by the time I got around to reading the Bible, it sounded like they were very similar in tone, not necessarily in content. How they went about saying things sounded similar in that sense. So I continued to read all of the sagas, and things like that. For some reason, they just seemed to click a little better than the Bible and everything that I was being told that the PSR…PSR is like a, kinda like, a Sunday school. When you're Catholic, you have to complete PSR in order to be confirmed Catholic.

The stories that I was reading in the library in my old school, they were clicking a little better than the stories and PSR and everything that was being told then and in church. I just decided to look a little more deeply at it because people had this strange fascination of saying, "Oh, it's a myth, it's not real." And I was always like, "well we believe that now because of our thinking about it. These myths that I'm reading were believed by people just the same way that the myths in the Bible are believed by people." So I went from that angle and started looking at other religions. Of course I started learning about Wicca. The gateway to Paganism is Wicca, as so many people like to call it. Me knowing my way around history a little bit, even at that age—I was about 12. I did finally get confirmed, to appease my mother. So I started learning about Wicca, and getting into that a little bit. That only lasted for a few months because I kind of knew, "oh, well, this is not old religion, it's new religion masquerading as old religion." And so then I was kind of jumbled a little bit. I didn't know exactly, spiritually, where to go until I was actually like, "Well, what stories are you reading? What tales actually got you interested in this?" I started looking at everything from a Germanic angle. Finally, I was doing a little more research—thank you, the Internet—and I discovered that there was actually reconstruction Paganism, which I thought was absolutely fantastic. So I looked into that, and it was an instant click for me. And so many words, that's how I came to Heathenry. (Laughs.)

Paul finds Heathenry to be spiritually fulfilling because it demands a high degree of self-sufficiency. According to Paul, Heathenry makes it possible to be a good person and contributing member of society even if you choose never to engage the Gods. He also believes that those who choose to interact with the Gods can still be enriched even if they only see Them as Jungian archetypes. Paul shares that he maintains a shrine to three of the Gods with whom he feels a strong affinity; Thor, Tyr, an Odin.

Well, what I find most fulfilling about Heathenry is that everything really is on you. You can be the best Heathen that there possibly is, and never talk to a single God. Not that I have anything against that, or any other way, but it has philosophical aspects to it, that seem a little more realistic. It seems a little more real, like it's really properly functioning in society more than a lot of—mainly monotheism. Monotheism would like to mold us to being one way, when it's really, I feel, philosophically, it should be this way. Mainly, the outlook on life, the outlook on the realities of the part of us that's here. I personally tend not to think of the afterlife, because I will get there when I'm going to get there. So, there's no need for me to actually think about it until I'm about there. That's mainly the imagery that's called up.

Some Heathens, for instance, only believe that the Gods are a Jungian archetype. And I'm completely fine with that, as long as somebody gets something out of what these Deities represent. Societies need the hero, they need to have a wise person who knows a little more than what they seem to ever say. The [Gods] are all very real, whether people what to say, "oh, They're actually physical, superior beings," or if They are energy, or They're just archetypes.

I actually do have a shrine to three: Thor the protector of humanity and also a God of fertility. I have them kind of set up in a semi-circle. Thor is in the center. To Thor's left is the God Tyr, God of justice, also the old sky God in Indo-European thinking. [He's] one-handed, justice, and war. And then to Thor's right is Odin, who is the current sky-God. He's now the chieftain of the Gods; He's the wisest and He's also the God of wisdom, the God of magic, and also a God of death.

While Paul acknowledges the possibility that some of the

Gods and Goddesses, for instance Frigga and Freya, might be one and the same, he largely acknowledges the Deities to be separate and distinct entities. His experiences have been quiet, personal, and intimate, but they have convinced him that the Gods and Goddesses do exist.

> *Sometimes I go a little bit back and forth on it. For instance, there's the whole idea that the Goddess Freya, and the Goddess Frigga, are, for example, the same Goddess—and really, that just depends on how I am looking at things. I can see it their way, depending. But there have been just these few times, when something has been going on in my life. Let's see here—just certain times when things are going wrong in one aspect of life, whether I'm in a little bit of danger here, or I'm being, or have been horribly mistreated by friends or coworkers or what-have-you. Then you just get this sudden little tap or ping, and you think okay, there's something there, and it just feels like there's a little more than me against the world. I think that's when I realized and started to accept that Deities are there, as opposed to some all-concerning force.*

Paul admits that he's "not the best at keeping solitary ritual," but he does fill the offering bowl on his shrine to celebrate the holidays. One of the most significant parts of Paul's religious practices is regular prayer to his Gods. Nothing fancy and no dead languages, just conversation and honest interest in engaging his Gods.

> *Really, I just use words to communicate: I talk. That's really all I do. I don't do any ritualistic, formulaic, whatever, and I certainly don't try to speak to Them in old Norse, as some Heathens will. I assume that They understand English just as well. So, really, my prayer is a little more just, "well, here's what's going on with me. Here are things I'm going to try to work on." On occasion if I do end up asking for help, or any outside assistance, I'll always give some sort of offering, like, it's typically some kind of drink that is usually the easiest because everything else, something solid, I feel that I would like to burn it, but in a city that's not always the easiest thing to do.*

While many Heathens incorporate their ancestors and the wights into their religious veneration, Paul has been somewhat reluctant to do so. It isn't that he doesn't want to honor his ancestors, but rather that the interfaith divide between Paul and his Catholic ancestors is quite daunting. Also daunting are the challenges of relating to the spirits of a foreign land where you are living as more of a guest than as a citizen.

I would very much like to incorporate ancestors in. I just—I still get this little weirdness sometimes when I'm, for instance—both my grandfathers are dead. One of them just passed away last year. So, there is just a little certain weirdness about the whole ancestor side. Me, I don't have any hang-ups for anybody else at all. That's just—its personal at this point for me. Knowing my one grandfather, I don't know if he would exactly enjoy that part of it. I know he would enjoy being honored in his own sense, but being very of Latin American Catholic as he was, I don't know if he would enjoy the entire context. And as far as the land spirits, yes I actually, normally made offerings to the land spirits back home. I haven't done it here. I haven't felt connected enough at all to do it here. But back home, I actually have a tree, an evergreen that I planted specifically for the land spirits. It was sort of a little focal point for them to be like, "oh well, right now, out here, I can offer you guys this tree. So yeah, I used to do something every holiday for the land spirits back home.

Paul's reading into the myths and stories of the Norse Gods started when he was young. As he has gotten older Paul has decided that it is more important to consider what principles the myth is trying to convey rather than affirming them as literal truths. In Paul's view, myths are inspired stories that can powerfully inform personal experience.

Well, there's always a little bit of sorting between "here's what the myth says, and here's what the myth is trying to accomplish." Sometimes things do borderline on the slightly absurd at points in time. I don't know if I actually want to use that word at this point in time, but it's the only word that comes to mind right now. Certain things, like for instance, Thor's crossing a river, and one of the giantess [who] is trying to kill Him goes into the river and just starts menstruating into the river to fill the river up and drown Him…That myth borderlines on the, "well that's a little strange," if we actually think about that 100% literally. I try to take these myths with a little bit of a grain of salt, try to see more what they are saying than what, in print, they are saying. Seeing how all that goes, just clearing the weight of the story and clearing it down to bare bones, "this is saying this about these specific players in this mythic drama. All of that becomes very consistent.

For instance, I have some excellent ability to avoid car accidents. For some strange reason. I do not know [why]…It's a very good thing. But, realistically, I probably should have been in several, but I manage to skate free of them. Knocking on wood so I don't curse myself now. Sometimes it's, for instance, we don't actually get thunder storms here, but back home we definitely do. And I specifically remember this one night. I'm driving along the highway late at night. It starts raining a bit. A deer quite literally pops out into the middle of the road, because deer are absolutely stupid. So I swerved and this deer, it does not look like it is going to be moving, and I'm too close to get my car away from it enough. Since it was raining, it turned into a little bit of a thunderstorm. But just a huge crack of lightning just streaks across the sky. And spooks the living hell out of the deer. The deer just bolted in the opposite direction that I was swerving. That whole concept of the myth of Thor, Thunder God protecting humanity—at that point in time in all the myths I'd read, His weapon was lightning and that is the instrument He uses to protect humanity. Just right then and there, it was like, "Okay." That's a bit of a click, when all these myths are stripped of the dramatic effect right into the real and imminent world.

Unfortunately, Paul has experienced friction with both Pagans and non-Pagans because of his Heathen religion. Paul's friction with Pagans is rooted in his affinity for academic research and reconstructionism combined with his rejection of esotericism and magical practice. His conflicts with monotheists have been very painful, ranging from ostracism to physical confrontation to being disowned by his family.

Issues with non-Pagans have been a little more brutal, so to speak, than with Pagans. With other Pagans, for instance coming from the side, so to speak, of Wiccans. They have this concept of, say—Deity can really be anything because as it turns out they have a very, very, different outlook on life and reality than, say, a Christian would, or a person who is reconstructing a religion would have. They're very much rooted in ceremonial magic, which was a big, big Christian heresy—Catholic heresy, specifically. So that's their angle where they're coming from, and unfortunately they don't want to see it as such. They want to say that "well, this magic and these practices that I am doing are that really old, and in fact the original religion of humanity," when anyone who actually does any academic research…If somebody does academic research on it [they] can start to see the historically recent origins of it. Normally what ends up happening when an argument comes up, [is that] they'll have some idea of how your faith or your religious belief, your philosophy, came from them. I can understand that they want to legitimize their ideas as much as they possibly can, but when someone will tell me, "oh, what you believe really comes for me," it's a little insulting and a little condescending. I've gotten that a few times.

Also, people of generic Neo-Paganism and eclectic Paganism—it doesn't have to be Wicca, they can be whatever kind of eclectic ideas that, I guess, are the Pagan nature. They'll also tend to believe more strictly into, say, astrology, and numerology, and reiki, and things like this. They will automatically think, if you go to a Pagan festival—when you start talking and they start talking about their astrology work and whatever, just all their things that they've come up with, their readings and numerology, and what-have-you, and it seems sometimes that they get a little offended because I don't believe in any of that. They kind of expect a little more that all Pagans, all Heathens, all people who are not monotheistic, would believe in all of these different concepts, and I don't. I really don't. I don't believe in them at all. That is sometimes a little bit of a conflict as well. I'm sure there are other types of things…but those tend to be the main conflict areas.

As far as people who are not in Pagan, I mean, really, it's all too common. I've been confronted, on more occasions then I can actually count. I used to have someone in one of my choirs that I used to run. A very, very devout Pentecostal. Pretty much every week it would be something… I mean really, I've encountered both tolerant and really intolerant Christians, Muslims and Jews. I encountered the full spectrum of that. Some of them don't care at all and are fine with it, and some actively think that I'm going to burn in hell unless I change my ways. But I guess that's just the way it is sometimes.

Paul wishes people would understand that polytheism is a real and reasonable worldview. "I think mainly I would like people to actively realize that it is a legitimate form of thinking," Paul explains, "A legitimate philosophy that just because it's older and it went away in certain parts of the world, that doesn't mean that it was wrong or primitive." Paul says he believes that "more people need to see it as this is just as fulfilling, just as in italics "real" to humanity as any other of the mainstream religions that are out there currently." Polytheism is a living, valid worldview, Paul, believes, and not a dead, primitive one.

Tess Dawson

For 14 years, Tess Dawson has been devoted to reviving the religion of Natib Qadish, the religion of the ancient Canaanites from whom Abraham sprang. There are not many qadishuma and those who do practice don't live in the same area. As a result, much of Tess' work has been with building online communities. In addition to moderating online discussion groups and serving as web admin for informational resource sites, Tess maintains a temple to the Gods and Goddesses of Natib Qadish in her home. Natib Qadish draws heavily from the traditions and practices of the ancient Late Bronze Age city of Ugarit, and does not, according to Tess, fit into the values, practices and priorities of the modern Pagan movement. While Tess serves all of the Qadish Gods in her capacity as priestess and temple-keeper, she has had personal experiences with Ilu (known as El in Hebrew), Athirat (known as Asherah in Hebrew), 'Athtart (known as Astarte in Greek or Ashtoreth in Hebrew), 'Anat, Ba'al Hadad, Choron (also spelled Horon), Rashap (known as Reshef in Hebrew), Shapshu, Yarikh, Nikkal, Yamm, and Kathir-wa-Khasis (also spelled Kothar-wa-Hasis). She is especially close to Athirat and Ilu.

The concepts of "hard" and "soft" polytheism have been circulating in the greater Pagan community for a while. Tess is very clear about which one she thinks is a more accurate definition of the term, which she also believes applies best to her practice.

> *Polytheism means the worship of more than one or two individual and separate Deities. I have seen some folks make a distinction between "hard polytheism" and "soft polytheism". I make no such distinction. "Soft polytheism" is actually "monism": a belief that many Deities are facets of one Deity or one "energy." "Hard polytheism" is just polytheism. I hear phrases such as "soft polytheism" versus "hard polytheism" used more often in the Pagan community/communities than I do among polytheists.*

For Tess, the word "faith" connotes both belief and religious identity. While she accepts the latter definition of "faith," she rejects the former because hers is not a belief-based religion.

> *The word "faith" is a tricky one. It is often used synonymously with "belief," or sometimes it is used as another word for*

"religion." I practice a "faith" in that I have a religion, but as for "belief," I would go a step further and say I have knowledge that the Deities exist, just as I know air exists though I cannot see it, and just as I know there are penguins in Antarctica though I've never been to Antarctica. Beyond that, I have had experiences which have proven to me the Deities' existences.

Tess says that faith, insofar as it connotes belief, does not play a major role in her relationships with the Deities. Rather, she says that it is her knowledge and her experiences with Them that guides her.

Knowledge and experience of the Deities plays a strong role in my relationships with the Deities. "Belief" is a wishy-washy word and doesn't fit in well with the experiences I've had. The Deities have given me proof of Their existence—thus any "belief" has given way to knowing, and I honor the Deities as the Deities They are.

Faith is a tricky word. In reviewing the definition of faith, I'm led to other words such as belief, trust, religion, set of beliefs, and loyalty, all of which cover different concepts. In some respects, since I've had an experience where I've been visited by a few Deities, I don't find faith (i.e. belief) vital because I know what I've experienced: I know that there are Divine Beings, even if I don't always readily experience Them with my senses all the time. I have faith (i.e. trust) that most of the Deities do what They can most of the time to benefit humanity or assure the proper workings of life on earth and the workings of the universe. My faith (i.e. religion) is something that I've developed over time and will continue to develop, as a means to honor the Deities and as a connection to other people who honor the same Deities in a similar fashion, and as a way to relate to the world beyond.

For most of her early life, Tess was nominally Christian. She says that she "transitioned away from Christianity," because she felt "little connection to the religion' and "disagreed with some of the dogma." As she grew older, she sought spiritual connectedness through contemporary Paganism. Tess grew dissatisfied with Paganism because her interaction with the distant-seeming God and Goddess still left her longing for a personal, intimate connection with the divine. Tess worked through a period of agnosticism before discovering Athirat and building the traditions that would eventually lead to her recreation of Natib Qadish.

Originally I was raised Christian, which I remained more or less for about eighteen years. I was then considering an eclectic Wiccan-based non-specific spirituality for about five years before I heard Athirat's call and took up Canaanite religion.

As a budding eclectic Pagan, try as I might I had no connection, no relationship, seemingly no interaction with the typical Wiccan perception of The Goddess and The God, i.e. The Goddess and The God are the two main Deities and all the other Deities are aspects or archetypes of these two polar Deities. I found the idea of simply worshipping archetypes (as some Pagans do) impersonal and unsatisfying, and in some respects it felt atheistic to me. I could not (and still cannot) understand worshipping a symbol that exemplifies a role or a part of the human experience. At one point early on I believed as some eclectic Pagans do that all Deities are part of one Source or one over-arching divinity but later I came to realize that these ideas of archetypes and/or system of dualtheism or dualism, or monism did not accurately fit my growing perception of the Deities...

By winter 1998 I had nearly become officially agnostic, thinking that I felt the divine ever present in my life but maybe there was just no way that I could have that personal relationship that I had thought and hoped was possible. I prayed, like I often did, addressing my prayer to the divine realm and hoping there was some sort of prayer-forwarding system that would shunt my prayer off to whom and/or where it was supposed to go. I asked "Is anyone out there? Does anyone care?"

I received an answer: "I care." I had thought that this could simply be my answering myself, so to confirm the communication, I asked if She—for the voice was female—had a name. She answered with Asherah—the Hebrew Goddess of the Iron Age, earlier known as Athirat to the Canaanites of the Bronze Age. I had never heard of the name before, and I was surprised to find that there indeed was a Goddess with this name and She belonged to a pantheon I had never heard of previously. I had never examined the polytheistic religions of Canaan and Israel—I had never thought to, since much of my experience with Paganism was based on Celtic or Norse Deities. Her presence answered some of the vague, unformulated questions I had in my mind but had never fully examined, such as what was the Pagan past before the Bible, if the people of the Bible indeed had a polytheist past...

When I had an experience with Athirat—a Goddess I did not know until that experience—it was the turning point in my perception and belief that the Deities are completely separate beings because I was visited by one specific, individual Goddess. In researching the Canaanites and their Deities, I have found that my experience of the Deities as multiple and individual is similar to how the ancient Canaanites viewed their Deities.

Tess is a Canaanite reconstructionist, a qadish. As such she is devoted to the Deities of that pantheon and has active devotional relationships with many of Them.

I experience Ilu as a quiet, generous presence, often like a warm, heavy, strong hand on my right shoulder. He is head of the pantheon, and the father of most of the pantheon. The other Deities revere Him for His status and for His great wisdom which is said to equate in its vastness with the number of silver hairs in His beard.

His daughter, 'Anat, on the other hand, is a powder keg. She's the Goddess of warfare. Earlier scholarship characterized Her as being sexually licentious, but later scholarship has pulled back from this view. In my experience, She's got a hot temper, but She is utterly loyal to those She considers friends. In the ancient texts, She destroys all of Her comrade Ba'al Haddad's enemies. At one point, She is filled with bloodlust and runs out of enemies to kill, so upon Her return home, She lines up and slaughters Her furniture. I love to think of Her fresh from the battle and covered in bits of upholstery. She can have a sense of mischief to Her, and She is also the adolescent who bursts into flame at matters She considers unfair. I had a dream once that I believe involved Her: She had tattoos, piercings, long black hair (possibly in dreadlocks). She winked at me as She passed me in a mall parking lot. She is a Goddess who burns so fiercely that it is difficult to be in Her presence for long periods of time.

Ba'al Hadad, the storm God, is a Deity with whom I've had lesser experiences, but each time I see an opening in heavy storm clouds, I'm reminded again of the Bronze Age tale of how the craftsman-mage God Kothar-wa-Khasis creates a window in Ba'al Hadad's palace so that He may rain His blessings upon the earth.

Kothar-wa-Khasis, the craftsman and mage God, provided powerful weapons to Ba'al Hadad in His fights against Yamm. Kothar-wa-Khasis inspires the technology that improves humanity. To that effect, I believe He once "healed" my refrigerator; and I've been known to call upon Him for technical difficulties including computer issues.

Rashap is the God of plague, warfare, healing, and protection. The Egyptians also honored this Canaanite God and there is a decent amount of Rashap's iconography in Egyptian sources. He is dark, foreboding, swift, passionate, and has a sense of humor that is difficult for humans to understand. He is life and vitality, and He is also the force of wasting which leads to death.

When I experience Choron, He feels often as a cloaked presence. He cleanses away misdeed and He protects people from inappropriate magic. He is associated with venomous creatures—snakes and scorpions. I see Him has having a special connection to the horned viper. He is powerful, but subtle.

'Athtart in the ancient texts often accompanies 'Anat, especially on hunting trips. 'Athtart is a Goddess of justice, balance, and treaties, and to some extent divination. I sense Her presence as calming, young, sweet, rational, thoughtful, and kind. She often seems to know the best way to resolve situations.

Shapshu is the sun Goddess who has a strong association with horses. She is said to burn off the "fog" of poison and contamination. Because She is Ilu's messenger, and because She travels from the above world of the living to the House of Freedom in the underworld, She can carry messages between the worlds.

Yarikh, the moon God, marries Nikkal in a Bronze Age text celebrating the occurrence of a human marriage. Nikkal is a Goddess of the fruiting orchards said to grow ripe and full with the fertilizing night dew of Her husband Yarikh. I experience a delightful coolness about Them, as Their mysteries quietly take place in the darkened hours.

Yamm is a boisterous sea God. In the ancient texts, He demands that Ba'al Hadad submit to Him and He sends messengers which He instructs to abstain from the regular courtesies of bowing. He is said to live in a silver house below the waves. The arguments between Yamm, Ba'al Hadad, and Mot (the God of death) balance the world between sea, fertile land, and desert. If any one of Them reigned over the entire world, the world would be in peril. It is the tension between the three Gods that holds the world in an ever-changing ever-dynamic state. Yamm is difficult to work with because of His primordial, chaotic nature. He does not care about the fate of humanity. However, I have had a suspicion that He will sometimes avoid hitting His followers with hurricanes dead-on.

As one who is actively working to restore the ancient polytheist religions and bring awareness of pre-monotheistic Gods, Tess has had occasion to interact with Gods who are not Canaanite in origin. She has had experiences with the Egyptian Anubis and the Celtic Brigid; more recently she has had experiences with Dionysus and the Thracian God, Sabazios.

On rare occasion, I have had experiences with the Egyptian God Anubis; this dovetails nicely with Canaanite religion since the Canaanites sometimes honored Egyptian Deities and the Egyptians included Canaanite Deities, such as Rashap, in their pantheon. I once had an experience with Brigid in a meditation or a dream: I saw myself as a little girl lost in a department store and She offered to help me find my mom—I see this as symbolic of my feeling spiritually lost and Her offering to assist me in finding my own matron Goddess. Also on rarer occasions, I believe I've had brushes with one or two Norse Deities.

More recently I had a haunting dream about a white horse and rider piercing through the clouds and riding out of the north. I remember more dreams than not since I've been working on dream recall and study for many years: my recall rate when I work on dreams is at least about 90%. (I've challenged myself and I've remembered at least part of a dream every night for the past month and a half.) This dream of horse and rider had a different quality to it than most of my dreams, a stunning, frightening, real quality. I had the dream on a new moon. The next new moon rolled around and two days afterwards, I had another dream—this one involved a procession, and as They passed by me on Their way into the north, the celebrants passed me a small piece of paper with the name "Sabazios" on it. I found a friend who is a devotee of Sabazios and learned that the dream of the procession and the dream of the horse-and-rider were connected and indeed symbolized Him. I knew nothing of this God and yet, the horse and rider imagery came through.

Later, I had a dream of Dionysus—again the dream quality was different from my other dreams in that it seemed more real. This time, I was possessed by the Deity and felt as if He had volition over my body and I could only make suggestions as to where and how to move. Despite the strangeness of the dream, it had a comforting, pleasant quality to it. I was lucid dreaming in the dream: I was aware I was dreaming, but there was little I could do to change it, and I had the same sensation as I awoke and the sensation took a few hours to wear off completely. I have been surprised to learn of a connection between the two Deities through interpretatio graeca of Sabazios and Dionysus. I don't know if the last dream, the Dionysian-like one represented Sabazios or Dionysus, or both. I look forward to figuring that out.

When asked about the level of correspondence she has found between the mythology and her experiences of the Gods, Tess says that "my experiences and the typical ancient mythology stack up surprisingly well." Sometimes the correspondence is surprising, "when [it] happens with a Deity I did not know or study before 'meeting'." Such was her experience both with Athirat and Sabazios. Tess explains that "I often rely on ancient accounts of the Deities to test, measure, or both, as to whether or not I've had an experience with a Deity." Overall, Tess finds that mythology isn't the definitive word on the nature and personalities of the Gods, but it is helpful for determining whether you are dealing with the Gods or with your own mental projections of Them.

Tess describes her relationships with the Gods as "organic, open, honest, humble, respectful, a state of being in gratitude." Tess' interactions with Them more often than not involve a grateful acknowledgment of Their presence in the world. While Tess does find herself periodically chatting with Them throughout the day, she says that it is when she sets aside special time to meditate upon her Gods that the communication becomes more interactive.

There are some that I feel I am in a loose communication with more frequently more than others, such as Ilu and Athirat. There are some that I pray to when specific needs present themselves—such as for technological items not working, I'll initiate contact with Kathir-wa-Khasis. There are some Deities who I acknowledge at certain times of day or during certain weather: Shapshu for sunshine, Yarikh at night, Nikkal when fruit trees blossom, Ba'al Hadad in stormy or rainy weather, Shachar at dawn, Shalim at dusk, and so on. And then there are some who just flat out make Their presences known to me through dreams, meditation, visions, or interesting incidences in regular life.

Communication in the past has been more one-sided on my part—I often address Them periodically throughout the day. However, since I've allowed more time in meditation and as I observe my dreams, this has allowed space for my listening and making communication more dynamic instead of static. Sometimes I have a difficult time honoring the information or communication I'm experiencing, thinking it is a daydream but of late I've been writing down what I think I might receive and allowing for the possibility of open communication and the possibility that I've received a divine message. Writing down what might be an experience gives me an opportunity for the communication to be affirmed or dismissed at a later date, by unrelated or unsolicited responses from others than are in-line with what I experienced, by events that transpire that appear synchronic or in sympathy with what I experienced, or through some information or research that I find later but didn't know earlier which confirms the experience.

Ancestor veneration was a minor feature of ancient Canaanite religion. Tess has incorporated it into her religious practice. This has not been without difficulty, as she has ancestors who are not particularly appreciative of her qadish religion. She has also adopted ancestors as "spiritual" kin, whose values and actions inspire Tess.

I have a small ancestor shrine I've built and set next to a small set of refinished shelves which serve as my Deities' shrine. I honor the ancestors each day alongside my Deities with incense at each meal I have. On holidays, on special occasions, or when I feel it is needed, I will offer food and drink at the shrines as well. I am fairly new to ancestor worship, but they seem to be responding well. I dreamed that two ancestors I didn't know well showed up to greet me, and it turns out they are early 19th century cousins to some direct relations in the family tree.—I knew of their names from doing some research but since they were indirect and distant cousins, I hadn't given them any thought. I do now.

Sometimes I have difficulty with honoring the ancestors considering that a few of my ancestors were reputedly in the Crusades. I just have to take a deep breath, and ask for the ancestors who would be comfortable with my polytheism to come forward. I have specific ancient ancestors who are reputed to be biologically related (but I have my strong doubts) who I honor at the shrine as spiritual kin—"Jezebel", Dido, and Solomon. I also honor Ditanu, the legendary ancestor of Canaanite kings.

Tess has an intense and complex ritual practice to honor and commune with her Gods. Her fairly lengthy and detailed account depicts the intricacies of intense devotional involvement with her Gods. Tess believes that it is important to note, however, that this level of engagement is not necessary or expected of everyone, and that her practice is this demanding because she is a qadish priestess with religious obligations to her Gods and responsibility for the spiritual well-being of the community in which she lives. That her surrounding community is largely Christian is not the point; in Tess' view, the Gods are generous enough to give Their blessings to humanity regardless of whether humanity is humble enough to be grateful for those blessings.

This kind of devotional activity is not for the layperson and certainly not for a beginner; I would never expect a neophyte or even a seasoned practitioner to do what I do. I am a priest at a temple, caring for the Deities in this way so that a layperson, a regular, average, everyday devotee of the Deities, isn't obligated to do so. This is how it was in ancient times: most people had small devotional corners or shrines in their homes where they would leave what offerings they could and honor as they could. The priests at the temple would make offerings on behalf of the city for the community's collective good. The temple I keep is dedicated to the Canaanite Deities. When I have other Deities outside the pantheon whom I would like to honor, I place Their images on my shrine instead. My shrine is in my living room; it is not in the temple.

In an average day, I wake up and I fetch my notebook to write down what dreams I've had in the night and morning. I've practiced dream recall and interpretation for about twenty-four years, and dreaming is an important practice in Canaanite religion. Lately, out of curiosity, I challenged myself to remember dreams for as many consecutive nights as I could and right now I'm up to thirty-eight days in a row.

After jotting down quick notes about my dreams, I will wash up—face and hands, or just hands—and put on a plain hand-sewn linen shift (needle and thread, no machine), and a long plain scarf over my head. I keep my shoes off. I stand outside the entrance to the temple I set up for the Canaanite Gods; the temple is located in my home. I turn on the light in the temple room, and I use the sacred oil I prepared ahead of time to cleanse myself outside the temple. The oil is comprised of olive oil, drops of myrrh essential oil or pinches of powdered myrrh resin; sometimes I'll add another essential oil or two such as cedar, marjoram, or cistus/labdanum. I anoint my forehead in a crescent and disk or an eight pointed star, or just make a sweeping motion across my brow with my ring and pinky fingers of the right hand, and I anoint my hands.

I anoint a clean incense holder before I take it into the temple. I have quality incense sitting near the temple entrance—this is important because cheaper incenses have dung in them. I choose the incense that I believe is appropriate for the day—usually it's myrrh incense. Myrrh was a very important healing and offering substance to the ancient Canaanites. I will daub a little of the oil on the incense stick as well to purify it before it goes into the temple.

I pause for a moment outside the temple, then enter the temple with my right foot. I have a lighter set up on a small table that separates the inner sanctuary from the outer sanctuary, and I light the incense there. I step into the outer sanctuary and I pause for a moment. Then I take a step with the right foot into the inner sanctuary. I approach the altar and I softly ring a brass bell on the altar, then I knock on the cabinet which serves as the niche that holds the Deity images. (The bell dispels any evil spirits, and the knocking is for politeness.) I open the cabinet and bow before the Deities with the incense. Often I will anoint the Deity images, as well. Then I bless the Deities and ask that my offering will bring Them shalamu (peace/wellbeing), na'amu (pleasantness/charm/grace/beauty), and that it may strengthen Them. I put the incense in a holder on the altar, and then I kneel and place my forehead to the floor. If the occasion calls for it, sometimes I will do this seven times. I stand, leave the cabinet open, and back out with my right foot staying in front. I back out before the Deities because it is rude to turn a back to Them.

After I leave the temple, I change into a robe or a tunic and a different scarf for my head and go check my email. I try to avoid actually replying to my email before I've been awake a little bit longer. I'm not a morning person. Sometimes I will make a little breakfast and some coffee (sometimes I postpone breakfast until I've made a second trip to the temple). I listen to music, but I try to be conscious that the music can sometimes filter into the temple room, so I do not leave the radio on [during] commercials. I have a shrine to the Deities and the ancestors in the living room, and before I eat breakfast, I put some incense there at the shrine and I bob my knees then bow deeply before presenting the incense.

When I'm pretty certain the incense has run low in the temple, I will clean myself up and put back on my linen shift and scarf, cleanse again with the oil, and reenter the temple. I kneel and put my forehead to the floor before Them, rise, ring the bell softly, then close the cabinet. I will then take the incense holder with ash out as I leave the temple.

I spend the rest of the day in various activities from correspondence, to writing, to researching, to language learning, to deep meditation. I am becoming more conscious of adding in exercise in the day, as well. At lunch, again I will go to the shrine (not the temple) and give incense to the Deities and the ancestors. If I'm eating and I'm in the room, I like to give Them something to "eat," whether that be food and drink, or incense, or both. I do the same at dinner. In the evening, I return to the temple room to bow outside the temple and turn off the light for the night. Before I go to bed, I will revisit my dream notes and write down the dream as I recall it in a dream journal, if I hadn't already written the entry earlier.

As I go to bed, I will spend several minutes in prayer before I go to bed, and sometimes I will ask a question before falling asleep which I hope to have answered in my dreams. Then I wake up in the morning and do it all again.

There are some days where I can't go inside the temple for issues of ritual purity, so I turn on the light in the temple room and leave an incense offering at the entrance of the temple, then go about my day as usual.

Tess has experienced a tremendous amount of friction between herself and others due to her philosophy of polytheism and the nature of her practice. The friction takes different forms depending upon the others in the discussion. Interfaith dialogue, according to Tess, has also proven challenging.

Sometimes being a polytheist is difficult in interfaith discussion because there is an attitude of "it all comes from one Source", "it" being Deities, or "manifestations of the divine." This is a form of generic monism prevalent even in groups that are supposed to promote interfaith understanding and dialogue. This doesn't work for polytheists and only promotes a false idea that religions all support a monist view.

I often feel I have more friction with Pagans than I do with non-Pagans because I'm more likely to speak about religion with them than with non-Pagans. I have been in many a conversation where other Pagans tried to convince me that I was misguided: that all Deities were a manifestation, aspect, or archetypal energy of The Goddess and The God, The Divine, or that at some point They all emanated from one Source and thus They are all One. I've more than once been patronized with the attitude that "right now you just don't understand that all is

One, but one day you'll grow and learn." It's frustrating.

When I further explain that I really have experienced the Deities as individuals, I get a look as if I'm a strange primitive exotic person from a faraway land and a faraway time. And sometimes I just get completely blank stares.

Sometimes I feel that polytheism is looked at—even by Pagans—as less theologically evolved than dualtheism or monism, or an inadvertent monotheism. Polytheists of historic culturally-based polytheistic religions such as Natib Qadish, Religio Romana, Romuva, and so on used to be considered as part of a wider Pagan movement, but it is becoming increasingly apparent that these historic, culturally-based polytheistic religions are quite different from the Pagan movement.

A sizable portion of the Pagan movement seems to prefer a Neo-Romanticist view, championing theories of Jung, Freud, and J.G. Frazer, as well as the preceding Sturm und Drang movement. Paganism as a movement is also becoming dualist, monist, non-theistic, or even self-focused, as opposed to the historic culturally-based polytheistic religions which are centered on the Deities first and foremost, and upon community and ancestor veneration second. Polytheists who have had experiences with Deities recognize that a conception of these Deities as non-Deities/non-Divine (as in the form of Jungian archetypes), and subsequent treatment of these Deities in a way that is inconsistent with honoring a real Deity, is wrong.

There's really no getting around that. A genuine experience is life-changing and one can't go back to thinking "it's all in my head" or "They're all facets" afterwards. To do so, and to see others do so, feels like the greatest of disrespect. And to see others give lip-service to our Deities while worshipping archetypes or focusing consistently on the self or the Deity as a symbol of oneself, is quite wrong in a polytheistic religion. Non-polytheists sometimes have a notion that believing in many individual Deities as actual Deities is somehow superstitious or unevolved.

There has been a great deal of friction lately because of the polytheists asserting that the Deities are actually Deities, not symbols, archetypes, aspects, or facets of something else. It's as if stating this kind of boundary in our religions is somehow broaching a taboo subject to the modern Pagan movement. It seems more acceptable to be so relativistic that our brains fall out rather than to have boundaries, beliefs, and religious standards. Discussions have gotten more than just heated.

In Tess' experience, there has been vehement debate in the Pagan community regarding the working definition of "polytheism." In her view, polytheists who belong to a historically-based reconstructionist group have one definition of polytheism, but many of those who are generally Pagan and self-identify as polytheist but do not participate in reconstructionist religions have very different views of what polytheism is. Conflict has erupted whenever the two sides attempt to broach a discussion.

> *Another trouble arises when people decide to "self-define" as polytheists. Polytheism means the worship of many separate individual Gods. If someone holds that there is a power higher than the Gods and worships that higher power, and the Deities as manifestations of that higher power, this isn't polytheism—it's monism. Just because a person "self-identifies" as a polytheist, doesn't mean their beliefs actually fit the definition of polytheism.*

> *So further conflict breaks out between the polytheists and the "self-defined polytheists" who think the polytheists are being exclusionary and mean spirited. It's a massive transition to go from being born, living, and breathing in a dominant western cultural bias of monotheism into a practice of polytheism. Some folks haven't fully and deeply understood yet what it is to be a polytheist. And not everyone has (or has yet had) a life-changing event where they have experienced the Deities firsthand.*

> *I grapple more with opinions of non-polytheists regarding polytheists. It is difficult to educate dedicated monotheists who believe in only one God that mine are not merely fairy stories. But at the same time, it is more difficult to chat with a "self-identified polytheist" who is really a monist. I have difficulty, too, in interfaith situations where the members of the program claim that "it all" (i.e. every version of God and every God) comes |from| one Source. We are often so acculturated to a monotheistic mindset that it is very difficult for many people even to begin to understand a polytheistic perspective, let alone to live one.*

Tess worships the very Gods and Goddesses who were abandoned by the descendents of Abraham, whose culture was the cradle of all 3 of the near-Eastern monotheist religions. More than once Tess has pondered what it would mean for the safety and well-being of the people of Israel, Iraq, Jordan, and other Near Eastern nations to defy Judaism, Christianity, or Islam and embrace the old Gods of their ancestors. The March 2013 public beating, rape and murder a Syrian Pagan woman named Yana, at the hands of rebels spurred to action by her radicalized brother, is precisely the sort danger Tess is concerned about.[*] As of January 2013, Pagans in Syria and Egypt who had been participating in vivacious online discussions uniformly fell silent and have not been heard from since.[**] Another Canaanite polytheist, Ben-Il who lives in Lebanon and contributed to this research project has also fallen silent and all attempts to reach him have failed. Tess' concern is very valid and very relevant.

> *Another concern I have regards a polytheist's safety in some communities, [in the] local U.S. and abroad. I wonder how other polytheists cope with the possibility of danger in some monotheist communities. Since I venerate Deities from a near-Eastern pantheon, I cannot help but realize that the response to my ways by the communities that live in the Near East today could be dangerous. There are Pagans and polytheists in these countries and they must be careful in their ways since the local governments only accept monotheistic religions—specifically Christianity, Judaism, and Islam—as socially and even legally acceptable. How can polytheists ease tensions between ourselves and monotheists? Can a polytheist ease tensions with monotheistic communities when certain communities or individuals in those communities refuse to tolerate difference and react in violence? It doesn't matter to me that other people believe I'm wrong, but it matters a great deal when intolerance occurs [which] then results in discrimination or violence. There's a big difference in tolerance and agreement and you don't have to have agreement to have tolerance. I don't expect others to agree with my religion, but I do expect and hope for tolerance. In what ways can we protect ourselves from intolerance and discrimination, or even from hate-related violence? In what ways can we promote diversity in a non-provoking, non-threatening way when just the thought of polytheism is enough to provoke a small number of people to great conflict and even violence; when sometimes the mere discussion of polytheism is not only distasteful to some but taboo to others?*

Tess is less concerned with whether or not people have a better understanding of polytheism than she is with whether or not they would simply stop devaluing it as superstitious atavism. She also wishes that the Pagan community would accept the concept of

---

[*] Pitzl-Waters, Jason. "The Fall of a Syrian Pagan." Web log post. The Wild Hunt. Jason-Pitzl Waters' The Wild Hunt Blog, 21 Mar. 2013. Web. 18 July 2013.

[**] Schulz, Cara. "In Syria and Egypt, Pagan Voices Fall Silent." PNCMinnesota Bureau. Pagan Newswire Collective, 13 Jan. 2013. Web. 18 July 2013.

polytheism as the worship of many individual Deities rather than the worship of archetypal facets.

> *I think it would promote useful discourse if some would cease to devalue polytheism, or view it as "primitive" or less-evolved. I find it particularly interesting that N. Wyatt directly addresses this bias in his work, <u>Word of Tree and Whisper of Stone, and Other Papers on Ugaritian Thought</u> (It's a 2007 book from Gorgias Press): "We have from the start to try to rid ourselves of instinctive feelings of aversion, superiority or scorn, which may be engendered by the convention of our own culture, that monotheism is somehow inherently superior to or more moral than polytheism as a conceptional form; or that 'idolatry' is somehow inherently evil."*

> *Believing, experiencing, knowing the Deities as individual Divine Beings doesn't make the concept or the one who holds it unenlightened. Sometimes I even sense an attitude that some think that polytheists are making up their experiences, imagining them, because these experiences do not fit into the more socially-acceptable philosophical molds, or that polytheists are a misguided fools who play "let's-pretend." I find these attitudes and misconceptions less than helpful in honest discussion and discourse.*

> *I also feel a lot of pressure, strangely enough, from the Pagan community, to conform with or agree with the idea of all Deities as facets of one over-arching divinity (a concept of monism, or even a modified monotheism), or the idea of all Deities as representations of The Goddess and The God (dualism). Or lately, the idea has evolved regarding worshipping the Deities as Jungian archetypes: this is backwards since Jungian archetypes are philosophical constructs, not Deities. It would be helpful if others could try to understand that a belief in polytheism is a belief in many Deities, not in one Deity with different faces and not in two Deities with different faces.*

Devin

Devin, a 42-year old IT professional, has been a committed polytheist for four years. He says that he had always "had the feelings" that the Gods and Goddesses are real, but that it wasn't until he discovered Asatru that he could find a concrete expression of those feelings. While he is an oathed member of an Asatru kindred* in Minnesota, his family decided to found their own kindred, which they have called Bauernhof. While he honors many of the Aesir Gods of the Norse pantheon, his fulltrui, or patron to whom he is primarily devoted, is Heimdall. Because his family runs a small farm on their property, he also has a devotional relationship with Frigga and with the Vanir Deities Freyr and Freja.

Devin doesn't necessarily have a personal definition of polytheism, "but when I talk to people and I say I'm a polytheist, I just usually say it's the belief in multiple Gods." He finds the question of faith interesting. "My wife and I were talking about the movie Contact the other day," he says, "that whole faith thing. To me, faith is—faith would be the belief in something. I guess I don't really put an 'undying' or an 'absolute' on it, but I think it's just the belief in something..." Devin finds that the role faith plays in his relationships with the Gods isn't really about belief. "My faith," he explains, "is validated when I honor the Gods/Goddesses of my folkway."

Devin grew up in a provisionally Christian household that wasn't particularly religious. His journey into polytheism, like many others before him, began with an exploration of Paganism. Yet it wasn't until he finally made connections with Heathens that he found his current path.

I've always been, I mean I grew up in a Christian household, not a hard-core every Sunday we go to church type thing. My dad talked about being Baptist and my mom talked about being Lutheran, I think. I went to a Christian elementary school for two years, so it's kind of, I would say it's—this is a generalization—our household was more of a typical Christian household. In that they proclaimed to be Christian but y didn't necessarily go to church or that kind of thing. When I grew older religion just kind of fell by the wayside for me. I've always been a very strong nature person, liking to spend time outside and things like that.

Paganism always resonated with me, but to me I just considered myself quote "Pagan" unquote without really understanding what that is. You know, I kind of did a lot of research on the Wicca path and the Druid path and even some Native American religion, even some Buddhism. Some things like that. I just decided I had a calling from nature and the strongest thing to me was Druidry to me, initially. In Minnesota where I used to live, I can't remember the name of the group but it was basically like the Minnesota Pagan group or something like that. I was investigating the Druidry side of it, but I never found other Druids. I never even really found other Pagans. So it was all this virtual world for me. There was this event that happened every month called the Heathen Family Brunch. I spent 6-8 months trying to find a way to make that event. To actually go when the event was occurring. When I finally managed to do it, I went to this person's house. They were all Heathen…I showed up, and immediately from meeting these people and listening to their history and their beliefs and their lore, it just clicked. I just basically walked into a home that I had been missing from for 38 years. That's kind of how I found my faith, my path.

Oftentimes in Pagan discussions, the terms "Heathen" and "Asatru" are used interchangeably. Devin clarified what these terms mean to him and how he uses each.

I think, to me, I think "Heathen" is a general term that people who honor the Northern European Gods sometimes use. I would say that Asatru is more of a specific—I'm trying to think of how to explain this really—more specific to the Vanir and Aesir. I think Heathen or Heatherny is sort of the generic "we can worship the Aesir, the Vanir, the Norns, the Jotun, across the board." That's my opinion…It's interesting because you will find people who will call themselves Heathen, "I'm a Heathen." And then you will find people who will say, "I'm Asatru." Then you find people like myself who, in my opinion, I mean, I guess, Heathenry to me is, you know, an encompassing the belief and honoring of the Northern European Gods, and then Asatru is more dedicated to the Aesir and the Vanir.

Generally speaking, Heathen groups tend to be organized into groups called kindreds, which convene for the purpose of fellowship, holiday observances, and worship of the Gods. Devin's involvement with Asatru is very much influenced by the desire to participate in a kindred.

[I] went to that Heathen brunch they were actually having it at the Volkshof hof. I oathed with them over Yule of last year. For that, I have been with them as sort of an associate member for a year, so it's been a year and a half, going on two years now that I have been affiliated with them. When we moved to Colorado, because they are in Minnesota, when I moved to Colorado to take care of my dad, there were some kindreds but they were an hour plus dive away, and things like that. So my family and I formed our own little kindred, which would be Bauernhof. That's kind of how we have Volkshof and our own little family kindred.

It is one thing to decide to raise your family in the Asatru religion. It is quite another level of dedication to convene your household as an official kindred. Devin's family's decision to become a kindred came about from a desire to be open to others.

I also wanted to, well, we discussed it but we didn't want to feel like what we had was potentially closed to people. Because as a Pagan, this person kept saying, we're having Heathen Brunch. If that person hadn't kept after me to show up and always let me know where it is, and things like that, I would probably still be floundering in the quagmire of Paganism. To me, it's sort of that we didn't want to have a closed type of environment where we're just a family, an Asatru family. We didn't want to feel like other people—if we met people who were interested in the Northern Gods, who were interested in the Lore—we didn't want to feel like we couldn't invite them in. That was sort of why we did it.

The idea in the olden days was the kindreds were different families who were bound together, probably because, from the research I've done, there's safety in numbers. Resources. If there's a creek of fertile land, then you're going to have people want to occupy that. My understanding is that kindreds are just big clans of different families who banded together. Basically they became one big family. Because these other Heathens opened their doors and arms to us, and said "come on in, you're more than welcome," I sort of felt like we had to have that same type of—what I consider when I've met other kindreds—a Heathen attitude that's basically until you're proven otherwise you're basically kith. There's not this predefined judgment.

Contemporary Heathens of all kinds have distinguished themselves as being different than and separate from contemporary Paganism. Their insistence on hard polytheism, their devotional study of the "lore"—the epic poetry and mythology of their Norse and Germanic forbearers—and their embracing of the nine noble virtues, have created a distinct religious culture which Devin finds deeply satisfying.

I used to have this belief that Paganism was, well I used to equate Paganism with Christianity from an umbrella standpoint. You know how in Christianity you have Baptists and Lutherans and Mormons—how many ways can your worship their God and this Jesus Christ guy? I used to look at Paganism as being like that umbrella of Christianity. Under that you had Wicca and Druidry and Heathenry, etc. I used to think it's just a different form of Paganism.

When I went and met Volksohof and sat down and talked with them, Sara sat down and explained how the Northern European people honored the Northern Gods- Thor, Odin, Freya, and they have their own pantheon and their whole life is dedicated to honoring this pantheon. It just clicked. I can't really put my finger on what clicked, but when she explained it to me, it was the Gods calling and saying, "you're home. You're one of us."

What drew me was I think that, and the lack of ambiguity in Heathenry or Asatru. It was: here is the pantheon and here are the Gods, here's our lore, here's the history of how the nine worlds were created, how the Joatun were created. Here's how things will go through and how Baldur will die and Ragnarok, the whole nine yards.

It was so "there," versus Druidry and Wicca, and some of the other nature-based religions that I read about and did some investigating in. They were just...very ambiguous. And just kind of, "I'm sitting here looking at a fruit tree and that could be a God or Goddess" in Druidry or Wicca or something, and none of that really felt right. When I learned all about the Heathen pantheon, it was like, this is my family.

Some of the things I like about Heathenry is that they are not as occult or obsessed with the spells and the this and that. You don't have to be a seer or a shaman to commune with the Gods or have a connection with the Gods. You don't have to fully understand the runes or be able to read the runes to be a Heathen. I'm interested in the runes but they don't call to me a strongly as a lot of other things. That doesn't mean I can't commune with the Gods. There are hundreds of ways to do that.

I don't really have any other questions or anything like that. I think it's just great that this was focused on polytheism vs. Paganism.

Heathens place a high priority on honoring the wights, or spirits of place, and the ancestors. When asked if Bauernhof honors them, Devin insists that this is the case.

Very much so…I think the reason is that we don't put our Gods on a pedestal. To me, the Gods aren't on pedestals, they are our ancestors. The Gods are our ancestors and we are direct descendants and relations of Them. If you don't honor your ancestors, then you really aren't honoring your Gods. The same thing with the Vanir and the land spirits and the house wights. They're all part of the pantheon. And, you know, the Gods created the earth and everything and if you don't keep everything happy, bad things are going to happen.

Of the many Norse Gods who are honored by modern Heathens, Thor, Odin, Freyr, Tyr, and for reasons seemingly unrelated to the religion, Loki, are the most widely worshipped. Devin, however, has always been drawn to the watchful and steadfast Heimdall. As a nature-lover, farmer, and outdoorsman, Devin recognizes the blessings of Freya, Freyr, and Thor.

Probably some of it is that being a father and husband, the whole protector role. I'm not an in-your-face guy. I'm not the first person to volunteer to do some outspoken role. I wouldn't be one to get up in front of a crowd and recite the Eddas. I wouldn't be down to do something like that. Thor, Odin, and Tyr—They are upfront Gods who are in-your-face. I'm not that type of person. But yet if you need a cord of wood chopped, I will go chop some wood. If you need this done I'll do this. I tend to be kind of a behind-the-scenes person. Reading about the pantheon and all the different Gods, the whole protector, "critical person but not upfront" role of Heimdall really called to me. When I think about protecting my family and being a watchman, that just clicked.

We grow our own food and try to do as much as we can off of things that we make, build, [and] grow, and those are the Gods and Goddesses. Thor is kicking the Jotun's tail all winter so we can get spring back. Freya's a Deity of fertility, as is Freyr, and so because of that we feel like we have a connection. We honor Them and we hope that we honor Them well enough so that They can help us with what we need.

According to Devin, his relationships with the Gods is "constantly evolving and changing." Part of this is learning to recognize when the Gods are letting you know something. Part of it is learning more about the Gods and how to connect to Them. It is this connection with Them that confirms for Devin that his Gods are real.

> It's a day to day thing. On some Days, all the Gods will talk to me. Every day I get up and I ask—it sounds cheesy—but I ask the Gods to provide me with direction and support and strength to face what comes up. You don't always get an answer; you don't get an answer like, "here," but you'll be doing something and an idea will click and you'll be like, "Wow! Freya just told me something." Then, the evolving part is just learning more about the Gods and Goddesses every day that I am reading about Them. Learning about Them and myself and what I feel I have in me that is a connection to those Gods and Goddesses. Like, taking care of the land and trying not to be wasteful and things like that.

> The Gods are real, and the books are real, and it's been passed down from generation to generation. That, and like I said, when I read about the Gods and what Their purpose is and what They stand for. I see Them there and I see Them in me. That's the connection and the proof that They're there. If They weren't, I wouldn't feel that calling or that connection to Them.

An important part of life for Bauernhof kindred is the ritual honoring of the Holy Powers. Devin presides over a monthly ritual, or blot, to honor the Gods and the passing of the seasons. Devin feels that it is important to formally acknowledge the Gods, ancestors, and wights and thereby demonstrate your worthiness to be in Their company.

> Our biggest thing is the blot. They happen monthly. They are usually to honor a God or Goddess or a group of Them and they revolve around typically something within the year. Ostara is the rebirthing of Midgard and fertility and the growing season coming back, breeding like rabbits (laughs). Then the harvest where Odin comes down and takes the worthy to Valhalla and the wild hunt where He is hunting for those souls. Yule is the same thing. The celebration of bringing back the sun. They all tend to revolve around things like that. We honor all the different Gods, but there are specifically Gods that you are going to honor during a specific blot. From a day-to-day standpoint, we're always trying to honor Them. We have an altar in our

house and we are always leaving food and snacks out for the house wights. When we go out, we leave stuff for the land wights to protect our crops. We do that on a day to day basis. Those are some of the things we do.

It's offering and acknowledging that the entities of the Gods and the wights are there. They are like us. They need acknowledgement and sustenance. The acknowledgement that They are there. Our honoring Them and attempt at being, not so much worthy, but worthy of being Their followers. I don't like to use the word "worthy" because as an Asatruar, one thing that I like about it, is that it's a shame-based religion versus Christianity which is more guilt-based. As Christian, you are supposed to feel bad because this nice guy was killed for all your sins and yet you are still going to be a piece of crap and not do anything right and every day you all you have to do is ask His forgiveness, etc. In Asatru, it's shame-based, in that if you do something wrong you should feel shameful about it, because you are dishonoring your ancestors, your kin, your kith, your clan, the Gods. So, to me you should feel good about yourself and the good deeds you have done, and the oaths that you fulfilled that you stepped up to. You should mimic the Gods, and basically be like Them. To me, my Gods lead by example. They don't demand obedience. Like with Heimdall, He is constantly ever-vigilant, ever-listening. Tyr, He's always making those decisions of "is this the right thing to do? What must be sacrificed?" Things like that. I look at that and I feel that I need to follow that lead. Step up and be like the Gods.

In Devin's view, Heathenry is about honor and integrity. There is no place or need for the guilt and obedience that he feels is so common in Christianity.

I look at the two and I see how kindreds versus congregations act. I sit down and say, "Here is a kindred, here is a congregation; here are the things we do, the core that we follow, here is what Christianity does. A lot of the things they do don't link up, but the biggest thing that stands out to me with Christianity is that whole vicious cycle of "I'm not good enough. Please forgive me. Now I feel good. But I'm not good enough," that whole thing. Our nine noble virtues are Hospitality, Courage, Truth, Honor, Fidelity, Discipline, Industry, Self-Reliance, and Perseverance. To me they are the one thing that links up between Christianity and Heathenry. Those noble virtues are somewhat like the ten commandments...Hospitality goes back to why we formed the family-type kindred vs. just being an Asatru family. The hospitality that we have felt and that we feel every time we meet another Heathen is something that the Gods want us to have. To open our hof, our home, to people of the faith or people who are interested in the faith. That's the thing that I'm trying to instill in my children. Leading by example but coming up with, "Well, what do you think Tyr would do," or "which of the noble virtues is this?" Things like that. I try to live by them.

While Devin would welcome an increase in the prevalence of Heathenry, he would never endorse evangelizing the nine noble virtues or any other part of Heathen values. He thinks it is better for people to discover it on their own and join in learning and fellowship of their own accord.

Another interesting part of the calling to Heathenry is that one of the things that drives me nuts is the big p-word. Proselytizing. There was no proselytizing with Heathenry. Even the reading I would do about Druidry and Wicca, there seemed to be a little bit of—I don't want to say "we're the best" sort of thinking—but there always seemed to be a little bit of competition between the different paths. I don't feel that way with Heathenry. There are lots of Heathens who have their opinions about Wicca people and Druids. Polytheism, to Asatru, is about the Gods. It's about our kin and the Gods. If you don't feel the calling it's no big deal. You're not going to burn anywhere or rot anywhere like that. They're just not in your calling. To me, I like that there isn't a judgmental—well there are some things that are judgmental in Heathenry—but if you don't come choose to follow our path, or you don't hear our path or our calling, there's no "you're not looking hard enough." There is none of that. I like that. We don't do like one of those religions that believes there is only a certain amount of space in Heaven. I like that we're not tasked with converting all of the world and trying to get everyone to believe our things. It just goes back to, it's about the Gods and our relationship to the Gods, and that's it. That actually does call to me about the religion.

When asked if there was anything he wished people understood about polytheism, Devin answers, "that we are not evil devil worshipers/human sacrificing folk, etc." He feels that if they opened their minds, people would see that polytheism is not really that spectacularly odd after all.

[A]s much as I give my sister crap about this, we don't hunt the

neighborhood looking for animals and children to slaughter. It sounds stupid, but typically when I meet a monotheist—and this might be a generalization—but a lot of monotheists, when you start talking about multiple Gods, the first thing that pops into their mind is the occult or Satanists or something along those lines. I just wish people could be more open minded. Why can't there be more than one God? Why are people so closed about this and think there can be only one?

Edragon

For forty years, Edragon has honored the Gods of his Welsh ancestors. More recently, he became the founder and director of Dragonstone Hill, a protogrove of the contemporary Druid order Ár nDraíocht Féin. The morning of our scheduled interview, Edragon could not speak with me because he was in the midst of handling a catastrophe; his family's bakery business had caught fire during the night and burned to the ground. The chance to speak about his experiences with the Gods and his relationships with Them was of such importance that Edragon did not wish to put the interview off. Despite his loss and the considerable demands on his time and attention, Edragon insisted on completing the interview that very evening, which he did. I am very grateful to him for this decision. What is most clear from this interview is Edragon's powerful faith that his Gods and ancestors would give him the insight, understanding, and opportunities to overcome this tragedy.

Edragon says he first embraced polytheism by "studying varied forms of mythology," which led him into "realizing the practicality of the Goddesses and Gods and Their ascribed duties and responsibilities." His understanding of the concepts which underpin polytheism are rooted in the same practicality.

> *My definition of polytheism. Well, "poly" meaning many, "theism" meaning many Gods and Goddesses who may be ascribed to different tasks, areas of life; overseeing different aspects of the, I won't say the Earth or the world, but different aspects life. You have Epona, for example, who looks after horses and mules and so on. You know what I mean. Various tasks and duties…I don't know if it's a good answer or not, but my description of polytheism is the theology which would believe in many different Deities. Gods and Goddesses as opposed to one God.*

Edragon's discussion of the term "faith" was also very informed by this practicality. He thinks that one must feel that the Deities are real and believe They exist if one is to have a relationship with Them.

> *My understanding of the word faith, which is something that*

has always led to a lot of discussion…I think it's pretty simple in one respect: belief. Believing, having the confidence and believing that say, for example, if you asked one of the Deities to teach you something, that you would have the belief and the confidence…to know that [it] would be taken care of. You believe that it will. Faith is knowing that. Faith is a feeling of confidence that you can go to the Deities, [and] that you can rely on Them to look after and take care of certain things. [It's] certainly reciprocity [as well]. But faith is knowing that They're there, it's real, it's all part of "what is."

Edragon's path to polytheism began as a response to two vastly different conversations he'd had with religious leaders. The study and thinking he undertook following those discussions led him to the conclusion that each individual human being is a contributing part of a vast natural realm.

During an afternoon many years ago with a Tibetan monk, and talking about all sorts of different things it was really quite fascinating. In regards to talking about Jesus-and-what-have-you, his response looked upon Jesus as, "what a wonderful prophet, what a great human being, what potential power, what a beautiful being to have been sent to mankind." I came away from that and I was really happy. It was kind of like, you know, this guy can accept these things and it's good. A few weeks later I was at a Catholic wedding and had the opportunity to sit at the same table as the priest. In conversation, I said, "so, what are your thoughts on Buddha?" And I thought the man was going to throw holy water on me. It was as if I had now blasphemed, you know? He's going to cut my tongue out and dunk me in holy water because, you know, how could I bring something like this up at his table. And I found that very annoying. And I started questioning, well, what is the problem here?

The more I would study, the more I would read and delve into things, the further back I got and the more I started to realize that, before the advent of what we call modern religion, the tribal people, the ancient people, were pretty much sharing the same things. [They were] aware of the seasons, aware of their place in nature, [had] respect for both themselves and nature. Not being governed by a powerful authority that would dictate over them and tell them what they must believe and what they must not believe, and what they should fear. And, learning also about my background and my heritage at the same time, and realizing it was very strongly Welsh and looking into the Welsh teachings. I've also looked into the Germanic and Norse. I've studied Latin for many years in school, so I read the Roman and Greeks. You start to see there were all these pantheons that are very similar... the household Gods take care of the same things in all of these pantheons. Some are more powerful and some are more flamboyant and some are more subdued. But, They're all there. And the overriding tone seemed to be, man's place in nature, so I said, "you know, what was wrong with the old stuff? What was wrong with the ancient ways?"

So I started to adhere, what would you say, "go back." I mean we've all seen that T-shirt picture of Stonehenge and the message underneath it reads, "Give Me That Old-time Religion." And it made more sense to me. It made more sense to me to pay homage to a Deity which something pertained to. For example, Lugnasadh celebrates Llew and the harvest. The more I got into it, the more I became aware that each time of the year we were honoring a different Deity because of the things that were brought to us from Them and how it coincided with the earth cycles and the nature cycles and it just made a whole heck of a lot more sense. It evoked more of a closeness, more of a secure feeling in myself.

Edragon's choice to embrace polytheism was only the first step on his current spiritual journey. Through his reading and pondering of Welsh mythology, Edragon felt pulled toward contemporary Druidry. Eventually, he joined the Ár nDraíocht Féin. Looking back into his family history, however, proved to Edragon that his interest in esoteric practice and ancient Welsh religious traditions was actually a family tradition—of sorts.

My grandmother, who was Welsh, was a member of the Gwydion Order, her maiden name was Price. She had a three-times removed uncle, Charles Price, who was a self-proclaimed arch Druid in Wales. Also, my family on my father's side, you know, evolved into being English but actually was Flemish. That family, whose last name was Drake, came from Flanders in the 1170's and on the order of Scotland and England, set up a conclave called "Drakerage." For many years the lineage followed down through very boring very straight-laced but the names remained the same and so on and so forth. But in the 1700's, I don't know the year exactly so I'm just going to guess 1790, during a lot of religious intolerance, some of my ancestral fathers were instrumental in the secret meetings which later evolved into a Masonic order, and many of the principles of that Masonic order were to protect many of the principles and precepts of the Druid Order. So, you know, it's for lack of a better word, it's sort of like Reagan's trickle-down economics. It became trickle-down theology. So all of this just came natural and the more I did this, the more I felt confident that, you know, this is where I belong…The lifelong teaching and learning of our place in the universe, in the world, with man, and with nature. The constant learning and understanding of how it all works. The discoveries along the path about ourselves. Just seemed to be a lot more pure and rewarding to me. And I have found it to be that way.

When asked to discuss the experiences that he has had which convinced him that the Gods, ancestors, and land spirits are real, Edragon explains that it's the subtle, small, unobtrusive things which have been most convincing. Many of these experiences were not instances where Edragon asked for Divine intercession, but rather for insight and understanding to get through difficult times.

In Druidry, we're well aware of the ancestors, the Shining Ones, the noble dead, etcetera. I have found [that] by nature, whenever I may be posed with a problem, it's not necessarily the Deities I call upon. I find that I commune a lot with ancient ones. i.e.: grandfathers. What would they have done? Things that they would have said. Here we have this group, this gathering place here we call Dragonstone Hill, where our matron Goddess is Rhiannon. So many times I have just sat quietly and consulted, you know, said, "here is my problem. Bring me an answer," so to speak. Maybe that day or sometime later there will be a "eureka!" moment. I know it sounds corny. But it's like, "yeah. Okay. I see that." A sign or something. Nothing happens by coincidence.

I may be thinking about something and saying, "you know, maybe Rhiannon could you give me some guidance on this." Someone will come along an hour or two later and way to me, "Hey. Did you ever think of doing this?" And I'll say, "Wow. There's the answer." You know? I just believe that's how it works. You can say it's answering prayers or what have you, but that's how it works. I mean, not that you are going to go out and do that all the time. But we also have strong leanings toward Manawyddan--the strong steadfast, silent type of character. I find myself lots of times, saying to myself, "Manawyddan, please give me some of your foresight and strength to get through this difficult time." I think the presences have been strong. We had a beautiful ceremony at Imbolc, we had the candle-lighting for Brigid, we involved 20 people with lighting the candles and the energy was just so great. The feelings were just so warm and everybody was just captivated and blown away by it. So, how else would you describe that?

Over the years, Edragon has built relationships with the Deities Llew, Arianrhod, Rhiannon, Manawyddan, Pryderi, Nantosuelta,* Epona, Robor** and Grannus.*** Some of these relationships have come as a result of his role as director of Dragonstone Hill. Others have evolved through his personal religious practice.

I've worked with Llew. Sometimes I have worked with Arianrhod, but we're a bit hesitant only because of the way She sort of ended up with things. But She is a very powerful figure. We have a spring, and three years ago we dedicated it to Nantosuelta. Nantosuelta is a Goddess of nature, the earth, and fertility, what-have-you, and moreover, we believe or have the understanding that springs bring forth the waters from deep within the earth. Some would call them the tears of the earth, and some also would carry away any problems to the earth. And what we do at the spring, and what they do in Britain, for example, is people will come and say their prayers and they will tie a ribbon to one of the nearby trees asking Nantosuelta to maybe bless their garden or protect them from fire—of all things considering this morning—if they are looking to have children, the look for blessing in that they could bear children, become pregnant. They will [put] their feet in the spring. They may sip from the spring, they may take the spring water and drip it over them, asperse themselves with it. Nantosuelta plays a big part. It varies, you know.

Yule we get to be a little different. We become more Scandinavian. We incorporate the ancient feast of the warriors,

---

* "Nantosuelta" means "winding river." She is a Gaulish Goddess of fertility and the home, and is often depicted as carrying a stick topped with a tiny house. Charles Russell and Patricia Turner, Encyclopedia of Ancient Deities (Jefferson, N.C.: McFarland, 2000), 336.

** Robur is a Gaulish oak God. The only known instance of His name being used is from an inscription found at Angoulême, Charente, France (CIL XIII 01112) where He is invoked alongside the spirit of place (genius locus). Russell and Turner, Encyclopedia of Ancient Deities, 405.

*** Grannus is a Gaulish healing God associated with springs who was eventually syncretized with Apollo and worshipped throughout the Roman Empire. John Thomas Koch, Celtic Culture: A Historical Encyclopedia, vol. 3 (Santa Barbara, CO: ABC-CLIO, 2005), 844.

which has pretty much become what the Christians call Holy Communion.$ Several years ago. I was hesitant at first. I was thinking, "wow. Everyone is going to think I want to perform communion?" But there was the ancient feast of the warriors in which wine was offered as the blessing from the lady of the land, and bread was from the lord of the land. As you passed the chalice, or as you passed the bread, you would pass it on to the person next to you, "may you never thirst." "may you never hunger." And they would respond, "I give thanks to the lady of the land, I give thanks to the lord the land." We had about 85 people the first time and they were all delighted. They were all really touched and felt really connected and really close. But, you know, those are basically the main Deities that we will pay attention to. Many of them creep in. Like Epona. We have horses here so Epona is a big one. Robor, the God of oak trees. Grannus, the God of healing. Gosh, there's just so many.

It seems to come a whole lot easier when there are different parts of the year. We're more in tune with who's up and doing what. Somebody might say, "this year we should pay more attention to Brigid." Or someone will say, "you know, don't forget Belenus[†] at Beltane." Someone will say "you've talked about Epona but what about Epos Olloati[‡]?" You have all these different things come in. As I've said before you find that there's all kinds of Gods, there's just hundreds. So, what I often do, or what I often encourage, actually, is if someone's got a piece, if someone wants to do something about Cernnunos and May day: great, do it! They want to do the Green Man, they want to do Cernnunos, Belenus—do it.[†] Bring it. We all join in on it. But we had selected as, because of our horses, because of our Welsh adherence, because of the powers that Rhiannon had to travel between this world and the other world, She is a very strong figure and we decided that She would be our matron, and Manawyddan would be our patron. For the same reasons—for His strength and His steadfastness. That's basically why we did that.

So many Gods come in; one [member] came in one day and said,

$ Edrgon draws this conclusion based on his own research, although other historians would disagree that the feast of the ancestors is the origin of the Christian Holy Communion.

†Belenus, "The Brilliant One," is a Celtic God of light, the sun, and healing. Known in Ireland as Bile, he was primarily worshipped in Ireland and Aquitaine. Michael Jordan, Dictionary of Gods and Goddesses (New York: Facts on File, 2004) 48.

‡The Celtic Epos Olloatir is a male horse Deity often seen as a male version of Epona the Horse Goddess or as Her consort who was sometimes depicted as a Centaur. Tadhg MacCrossan, The Truth About Druids (Minneapolis, MN: Llewellyn Books 2005), 8.

"What about Rudianus§?" "Is that the guy with the Italian restaurant down the road?" And they said, "No, no, no. He's a God of war. A war God." Okay, I'd say, "What should we do?" and they'd answer, "Can we talk about asking for help and peace and guidance for our guys in the service?" I'd say, "sure, you know?" and I think that's the big thing. Never to close out what someone may bring in.

Edragon has found that the spirits of nature play an important role in the continued well-being of our planet. The ancestors, he says, play an important role in the continued well-being of humanity. Both nature spirits and ancestors are an integral part of his religious practice.

The nature spirits are all around us. We're in a wooded very rural area in northeastern Pennsylvania in the mountains. Nature spirits are everywhere, you know from an insect to deer and bear roaming by. Fish in the pond or the creek, the way we incorporate them is that we incorporate them and we asking for Their blessings. We ask them to bring us any gifts or guidance they may have, and in return we offer our protection and respect.

In regards to the ancients, we all have our ancestors. Oftentimes in our modern society these elders who have passed away get pushed into the background. We try to keep them alive, by asking them for guidance and understanding, and helping us to remember Their ways. And in return, we give respect and honor, and we will give a sacrifice of fruits or some drink.

Samhain is a very big day here, where it is of course geared wholly toward the ancestors. What we will do at Samhain is we will have our ritual which ends with procession through a vale, and as we go through we are told by one of the attendees, "you have now left the darkness and are moving into the light." At that time, the person is handed a lit torch. We surround the pond, and we may have 100-120 people. It's quite a moving scene to see all these people with torches at night. There are some readings. Then we do what we call the "Calling of the Ancestors." Where people will randomly call out the names, whether it's a person—some will call out pets, horses, dogs, what have you—some will holler out the name of someone and maybe four people on the other side will laugh because they remember

---

§Rudianus is a Celtic war Deity who was worshipped in southern Gaul, often depicted holding aloft a severed human head. Ian Armit, <u>Headhunting and the Body in Iron Age Europe</u> (Cambridge, Cambridge University Press, 2012), 84.

them. Some will call out a name and others will cry. Others will have all they can do to call out the name of this ancestor, but it is a very cleansing sort of experience. After which we have a huge sort of bonfire. Which we use to send all of our energies off to them. We also will set a plate at the table for any visiting ancestors. We light candles and put them along the roadway and in the windows for traveling ancestors to find their way. One of the most moving things that we have been doing is that we set aside a table where folks will bring photographs of those who have passed away. It's a real moving scene to see a table full of photographs for people, and the response it brings. It generates an energy. Which, for lack of better words, puts you in direct connection with the beings.

And you know, even in Christianity—I won't say it verbatim—but there's a little lesson of as long as you remember me in your heart, I will never die. I think it's sad the way society says, "Well okay. Aunt Harriet is dead. Grandpa's dead. Goodbye"…If they would just take a moment and realize that—I mean, there are times when I'm up against things and people are up against things, and people will say, "what would my grandfather have done? Or, "my grandfather had a similar situation, and he did this." Whether it was dealing with people or building a house, or whatever it might be: fixing a car. Whatever it is, you're communing with Them. So we hold Them in high esteem and in great honor and we will do tribute to them and we will ask for Their blessings and thank Them for being among us. That's what we do. We will incorporate the nature spirits and the ancestors and of ours we thank the shining ones for their blessings. We'll ask them for an omen, we'll sacrifice to Them, we'll make a sacrifice of very nice whiskey on the fire for example. Things such as that. Pay honor and tribute and thank them. So all three aspects, the nature spirits, the ancestors, and the shining ones are very important to us.

As was the case with his polytheist Welsh ancestors, Edragon has rituals and votive practices to honor his Gods, his ancestors, and his land spirits. Some of these rituals are group celebrations he partakes of with Dragonstone Hill, and others are rituals he does on his own, at home.

I have an altar in my office. It's a typical Druid altar. It has your well, and your fire, and your tree. The tree has a little dragon statue with it. It has a pole made of American Edison, a medicine pot which is sort of a hollowed out stone. Simple rituals asking for guidance, peace, understanding, and thanking Rhiannon and Manawyddan because They are the patrons of Dragonstone Hill, for Their strength and guidance. Sometimes it's a simple lighting of a candle and a clearing of the air with a bell, a little sacrifice of some whiskey on water, that sort of thing. Sometimes it's leaving small gifts. A lot of times little prayers and rituals done in my head and in my heart, so to speak, are done on the property. We have many standing stones and I will go, for Rhiannon, for example, I will leave birdseed on the stone or pieces of bread for Her birds, if you will. Pretty much again, asking for peace and understanding and guidance. The ability to commune with the ancients and those who have passed on, etc. for understanding. Right now, I'm asking Pryderi, and Manawyddan, and Belenus to deal with what this fire is. I've also asked Nantosuelta because She is a Goddess of fire and could She help protect my family from the fallout of this fire, so to speak. That sort of thing. Understanding where it's come from and what it's about.

Edragon recognizes that there are significant differences between the Gods as he knows Them, and the way that They are portrayed in the myths. Edragon recognizes that myths are sacred narratives with many powerful layers of meaning and that their importance lies in their ability to evoke wonder. The issue of whether myths might be literally true is far less important than the fact they are stories that inspired the imagination, as well as reverence and respect, for enormous forces which humans could not easily understand.

You know the myths, I personally feel—and I might get Joseph Campbell-like here—but the myths really had to be sensational. They had to be because otherwise people wouldn't have paid attention. Certainly They deserve the attention and respect for being the Gods They are, but They also had human characteristics and They lived among the people. Their deeds had to be magnified. These were the teachings. These were the examples of how to behave. How to solve a problem. How to deal with an adversary, for example. How to be fair. How to be strong. How to deal with strength and weakness and so forth. This is, I feel, [is] what was governing the ancient people. These stories, these myths. The tolerance and the patience of Bran, for example, when all that was going on, trying to be fair. Eventually, or course, having to go and rescue His sister. But overall, you see, "Wow. I want to be like Him, or I want to be like Her." You had role models. That's how I see it.

Now in the real world, I guess if you want to put it that way, in today's world, it's like, well, okay, we all kind of know that Mars isn't flying across the sky, and some of the things, like, we could try that, but I don't know how we could keep Bran's head alive on a platter for years, you know. Or any number of things. Or, you know, we could try like the dickens to throw people into the cauldron of life and see if they bounce back out. But now we're coming back around to faith.

You sort of have to feel in your heart and feel in your body that these examples, well, MAYBE they really did happen. They're not happening now, but we have these wonderful examples [from] which to draw and grow and learn. And you know, actually, if you look at it in that point of view, you can look at Christianity the same way. We can all go down to the pond this afternoon and try to walk on the water. We're all gonna look pretty silly after a while. We'll be covered with mud and soaking wet. But who's to say that didn't happen, somehow? Who's to say Bran's head wasn't alive on a platter for all these years? You know, who's to say? But in the meantime people have great inspiration and we have these great stories and it was just like, well, ya know, Bran got His head cut off and it sat on a tray for years and He guided Them a back to the island of the mighty. And everybody was fine after that and He died. Oh. Gee. Okay. But when you take it and say, "Oh! This is what happened. This giant man walked to Ireland across the sea and towed His ships behind Him. You know what I mean? Wow!" And, "where can I get a cauldron? Maybe when I'm about to croak, maybe my wife and kids will throw me in it and I can come back out." You know what I mean?

I don't mean to sound facetious, but it's hope, it's inspiration. And we're talking also, unfortunately, of people from different times when life was much simpler. You've got the great stories of Llew and all He could accomplish and the things that He could do. And His spear! I mean, you know, thinking back nearly 3000 years about a spear that hit its target and returned. That was something that today is no more far-fetched than Star Wars. I think the mythology was very important because it made people aware that there was an existence, or an energy, or a force, beyond themselves that may have to be reckoned with. That may have to be appealed to and understood, for [people] to grow and to interact among themselves peacefully and with examples and with some sort of guidance.

When asked whether there was anything he wished people understood about polytheism, Edragon says he wishes that Christians would recognize that they practice a form of polytheism themselves, and that many of their traditions come from ancient polytheist practices. If they would recognize this, Edragon believes there would be better relationships between Christians and Pagans.

In Christianity, you have the Father, the Son, and the Holy Ghost, you know, the trinity. They try to pass that off as one, but it's not. I think they should, people should realize and understand that many modern religions have come from polytheism. You have the Germanic Eostre, from which we get Easter. Saturnalia from the Romans turned into Christmas. I mean all of these things have been cooked down from polytheism. And they're all incorporated in one way or another. You know, I just feel it might help if they understood the history of, say, Christianity. The simple principles of divide and conquer. You have to assimilate the peoples somehow. The best way to assimilate was to incorporate their religion. So a lot of what has boiled down to monotheism today came from the polytheists, by incorporating it and cooking it down…

But when you start to dissect it, I mean, you know, the questions I'm always fielding: "well, you know, it's pretty cold and nasty out here, why were the shepherds out in their fields. Landing time isn't till February when we celebrate Imbolc. Why do they do this at Christmas? Well, it was Yule and Saturnalia and the great incorporation of so much polytheism and I really feel that people, before they should be so critical they should understand where they came from and where their beliefs were handed down from. I would like people to understand this, and not be like, "well, I can't talk to her, she's Wiccan," or "I can't talk to him, he's Roman Catholic.

I'll give you a good example. I officiated a funeral back in April. The people who had the loss are neo-Pagan. They said to me, "could you do something for our mother?" I said to them I certainly would. Now here's my concern. My concern was that there are a good many elders in this group and they were Lutherans and Methodists and a few United Church of Christ people. And these were elder people and I respected that. I said, "You know what, do you have a minister also? I think this should be shared. You have your desires and wishes and they will have theirs. You don't want to offend the elders." They thought that was a good idea. So there it was, the day of the funeral, and there's the minister and he says to me, you wanted to talk to me? I said "sure." He said, "Now, what denomination are you with?" I said "I'm clergy of the Druid order." He said, "Oh. You know, two weeks ago I was at a seminar at this place and we went to this other place and they have standing stones and all this stuff. Alright. Yeah. Back to the source!" And we hit it off really well and we did the funeral service and we complemented each other. It was almost a high, if you can believe it; it was almost a high doing this funeral service. He was with United Methodist and here I was with the Druid order and we complemented each other so well. People were just blown away and delighted by the ceremony by the ritual and so forth. He did a gravesite thing, I did a gravesite thing. And it was just amazing. He talked about going off with the Lord and the Father and I talked about going to the place where you will be purified by smoke. It was almost surreal in that both were the same. I think in answer to your question, the realization that things aren't that far off as we would like to think, and the prejudices should be put away. Because basically we're all in this together. The ancients were right. Maybe the moderns were right to a degree and somehow they need to come to a meeting point. That's my thoughts.

I think that we're living in a very interesting world. I really feel that there is a lot of confusion, dissention from and among the modern monotheism. I'm finding an insurgence and curiosity. I received an email from a young man last week who said, "I'm looking forward to coming to your next event because I'm wanting to convert." I thought that was so funny. It struck me funny because 2000 years ago you were converted anyway. Can you convert back? I guess you're going to re-vert. So, I may soon be in the business of re-verting people But I'm finding people looking more and more into the aspects of neo-Paganism, whether it's Wiccan or Druidic or what-have-you. I think that's very interesting because there is a new, stronger realization that we are part of this natural world and we have done things to our natural world that hopefully can be remedied. People, I think, are feeling that. Trying to understand where, you know, that there's more to it than dressing up and going to church on Sunday, paying your $15 dollars in tithes and you're "off the *hook." It's, you know, spending time in a nature space and understanding the things we've talked about, like the ancestors and the importance of Them, having respect for what is happening around them and seeing an understanding. Maybe some people will seem off-the-wall and they'll sit and tell you that "I spent 3 minutes today talking to a squirrel." Okay. That's good. I'm also happy and I think there will be a resurgence, more of a growth.*

A lot of people want to get a better understanding of the ancient Celtic world. We've had so much of this shamrocks and green beer routine that I think that's kind of worn out. Radio stations have asked me to do spots on St. Patrick's Day. I say, "Excuse me. You do not know who you are talking to. Do a spot exonerating St. Patrick, or St. Columba for that matter? These guys were sellouts. They were scoundrels. I've always made it a point to tell people who the snakes really were. "Oh. St. Patrick drove the snakes out of Ireland." You know who the snakes were? That's the nickname the Romans gave the Celts because their houses were half underground. "Oh. Really?"

But I mean, finding out what it's all about. Finding their place in nature. That's what it's all about. There are many Deities that people can feel a connection with and pay tribute to and grow from, [who help them] understand more of their own substance, and makeup and how they fit into the world. I think that's going to be important for the future because you will be more cognizant of the world and nature. And hopefully, too, they will have respect for the other religions so that everybody can cohabitate peacefully. And that's pretty much it. What I have found at our gathering is people wanting to grow and feel more connected. A place to be and to be a part of, where they can participate and not just sit and be washed over. So I think that's important. And, I hope that your work gets out there and really gets people thinking and understanding...

I also want everyone to know that people should not be afraid of Druids. We're not wearing pointed hats and waving magick wands and turning people into whatever. It's not the Harry Potter routine.

Ann

❊❊❊❊❊❊❊❊
∙ ∙ ∙ ∙ ∙ ∙ ∙ ∙ ∙

Ann, a professional diviner of Greek descent, has been a practicing polytheist since 1985. For years she maintained a tradition of honoring the Deities of ancient Greece privately while continuing to attend Greek Orthodox services with her family. During that time, Ann says she "had to struggle with finding ways to be true to my faith while working within the cultural framework which would allow me to be seen as a member of some 'fringe' group."* Although Ann's religious practice is largely solitary, she is a member of the Hellenion organization that promotes the revival of ancient Greek religion. Currently, she is working to found a Hellenion proto-demos in her area of Louisiana. While she acknowledges and honors all of the Greek Deities, Ann says that she feels closest to Hera and Hestia, and has a strong connection to Poseidon.

For Anne, faith is not simply a matter of belief without evidence. For her, faith "plays a very strong role in my relationships with the Undying Ones." Faith is about "[k]nowing that there are different forces in the universe that affect our lives." This knowledge is "more visceral, something that's down in the gut, under the belt. It's there; it's literally a part of me." Her understanding of the term polytheism is similar to her outlook on faith; according to Ann, belief alone does not make a polytheist. For her, polytheism means "[w]orshipping more than one God." She distinguishes between "a soft polytheism where people say all the Gods are one," and hard polytheism "in which, for example, the Roman God Jupiter is not the same as the Greek God Zeus, even though They're very similar." Anne identifies as a hard polytheist. In her view, regardless how one identifies, their polytheism is defined by their honoring and worshipping of the Deities, not their belief about the nature of the Gods.

Ann comes from an ethnic Greek background. Even though her family is Greek Orthodox, they still took pride in the myths of their ancient ancestors. Ann grew up with these stories and as she grew up, she really began to identify with those Deities.

I come from an ethnic Greek background, so I grew up with the stories of the Greek Gods you know? The stories of the heroes

---

* Ann H. Personal electronic communication. 17 July 2011. Web.

like Hercules, Theseus, Jason. I grew up with those stories, and I would feel actually pulled to the Gods in the stories. I mean, I remember when I was either probably in my early teens, it was, when the original "Clash of the Titans" movie came out, and there was some definite sense of recognition, despite the cheesy animation, which I thought was cheesy even at the time. When I was young I felt most drawn to Athena, but as I got older, I felt like it wasn't right to honor just Her and not the rest of Her family. Now, this understanding developed over time. For many years, I was either actively involved in the Greek Orthodox Christian faith, or trying to reconcile the understanding that had been growing in me to the faith that I was raised in. I finally said, "You know, Jesus is a God, but He's not mine." When I finally said that, and said, "I do know—I'm listening," to the Gods who called to me, the Greek Gods, there was a sense of "Well, finally you've come home. What took you so long?" It's one of these things that, with somebody who has experienced it, you don't need to explain it, but if you try to explain it, you can't.

Ann walked the spiritual tightrope for about ten years. It wasn't until after her father passed away that Ann "came out" as a Hellenic polytheist to her family.

Both of my sisters were very accepting and understanding at first…I have [recently] had some degree of conflict with one of my sisters because of it, as she is now trying to "convert" me back to Christianity – which is something that absolutely will not happen…My mother didn't even bat and eye when I wore a Poseidon T-shirt in front of her, with the name Poseidon in Greek letters. My sisters are both Christian. And just so she knows she has the option, I'm going to be introducing my 15 month old daughter to both Christianity and my faith. I've seen enough pain that people have gone through, when they feel like they're being forced into an option they don't like. On the flip side of this, I've seen a lot of fanaticism, because they are not shown other options or are constantly told how bad the other options are. It's like protestant evangelicals saying that Roman Catholics are going to hell because they don't believe the same things, even though, at the heart of it, there is the belief in and worship of the same God. The best way I"ve seen, and the best way I'm figuring, is to raise a child in our faith, but give her information about others. If she feels drawn to another as she gets older, that will be her choice.

Over the years, Ann has had several experiences that convinced her that her Deities are real. These experiences have ranged from a sense of emotional fulfillment in response to devotional offerings to sudden, dramatic meteorological shifts.

> *As far as specific instances, I definitely remember when I started making a daily offering of coffee to Hestia, Goddess of the hearth, how every morning when I did that, from the first pot of coffee brewed that day, there is the sense of peace, very much a sense of "come sit down and have coffee and a cookie." It's funny, because one time we had a friend visiting us, and I wasn't feeling well and I slept in, and he got the distinct impression that there was someone behind him clearing Her throat and suggesting, "would you make a cup of coffee for me?" and he told us about this. I couldn't say that I was surprised in the slightest. I mean, in 2010--let me give you a little background. I'm a member of an organization called Hellenion, which is made up of Hellenic polytheists. Every month on the second Saturday of the month, they do a libation honoring various Gods, and it's a rotation throughout the year. Last May 2010, on the second Saturday, was a libation honoring Apollo. The skies were partly cloudy, it seems like it was threatening rain, and it was kind of breezy. I had been meaning to actually sit down and say an offertory prayer—write it out—for Apollo. So I did. Literally within 5 minutes after I finished it, the sky cleared up entirely. That, for me, is like, "OKAY, Yeah. Apollo is listening."*

Ann has the distinction of honoring two Goddesses who are not typically well-represented in the mythology or the literary adaptations thereof. Hestia rarely is written about or commented upon. Hera has been demonized as a vicious, petty, jealous, materialistic woman scorned. In Anne's experiences, these Goddesses are loving, wise, and generous with Their blessings. On more than one occasion Ann has felt moved to write about Hestia and share her experiences with this Goddess.

> *It's almost like Hera and Hestia are, They feel—I have a feeling very much that even though They're not my physical mother, They are both standing in a mother role to me, and Poseidon is in a father role. It's not something that I can really explain, except to say that all of humanity is Their children, and there are certain children that acknowledge the relationship…With Poseidon, I always feel very connected to water in general and when I'm really, really stressed and I take a*

hot bath to relax. It always seems to work better when I put sea salt in the water. It's nothing as specifically concrete as with Hera.

My perception of Hera, my understanding of Her, is that Her problems with Zeus' infidelity were not because He stepped outside the marriage bond. Because in the time that those stories were being first set down, it was not uncommon for a man to have a wife and concubines, a wife and mistresses, and everybody acknowledged that. If there was honesty about it, there wasn't much of a problem. The way the stories are is, He was sneaking around behind Her back and not honest. She's not always vindictive to the female parents of the various offspring of Zeus. She was not vindictive to the mother of Hercules. Actually, in Greek, His name is "Herakles," which honors Her: "Warrior of Hera," essentially. Persephone is Zeus' daughter by Demeter, and obviously Hera had no problem with that. Which to me, would imply that one or the other had clued Hera in that this was what was going on. For me, it's not a matter of infidelity; it's a matter of honesty. And even in the modern day, those in a polyamorous relationship would not be upset about overstepping the marriage bounds, if all the parties are adults and consented.

Part of the reason that I think Hestia has so little traceable references in ancient literature is kind of really simple. You don't write down things that everybody knows that are commonplace. We don't write those things down. There are very few references to Her specifically outside of the Homeric and Orphic hymns that are dedicated to Her individually, or ones that reference Her by name but are dedicated to all the Gods. One of the two Homeric hymns honoring Hestia, it shows that without Her there is no banquet. Offerings are made to the Olympians, but there is no meal on Olympus where She is not present and honored. According to the stories, one of the reasons She is welcomed everywhere is that She is the only Olympian God, period, who did not engage in warfare. She was the soldiers when they were going out away from the hearth, and then returning to the hearth. The hearth was the center of the household. If the hearth is the center, then the household and the greater community revolve around that hearth. Even in ancient Greece, there was a central hearth to Hestia, like there was in Rome to Vesta. When people went from one city to establish another, they would actually nurture coals from Hestia's fire to establish in a new city, linking the two communities together.

You don't find that a lot in the literature, because you don't write down what everybody knows. If everybody knows it, you don't feel the need to talk about it or write about it.

Ann's personal practice involves making frequent small devotional offerings, and it also involves observing as many of the Hellenic holy days as she can. Ancestors are also a part of Ann's practice, and she honors Them through ritual feast days.

With Hestia, I actually keep a candle going in my house, as a symbolic hearth because we don't have a fireplace or anything like that. For mother's day this year, I made a point of doing a small ritual honoring the mother of Apollo and Artemis, because it's the second Sunday in May that is Mother's day. The Hellenion libation calendar that they have, Artemis is in April and Apollo is in May, so it seemed to me to be appropriate, on Mother's Day, to honor Leto, and all of the other mother Goddesses—Hera, even Mother Earth Herself. I posted that I wanted to do this on a yahoo group that I'm part of. Somebody made the comment that it was a way to incorporate what is essentially a secular holiday into a religious practice. A modern sacral holiday being corporate and given additional meaning besides saying, "bring your mother out to dinner," sort of thing. I did get at least one comment that it was a really neat idea…

I honor my ancestors as part of my religious practice during specific festivals such as the third day of the Anthesteria festival (in the spring) and the Genisios festival (in the fall). I also hold personal memorials to them on the anniversary of their passing each year.

Another significant aspect of Ann's practice is service to the Deities through writing, research, and crafting. Specifically, Ann wishes to help build the tools and the resources to help people who are called to work as oracles for the Gods.

A number of years ago there were two articles that appeared on Witch Vox, one of which was "Hestia, the Overlooked Olympian," and another one was about Hestia and Ares as partners in social change. Both of these were essays and articles that I have written…

One of the things I'm noticing is that except for things like Halloween, there aren't a lot of mainstream articles about polytheists that get put out. That leads to, in a lot of ways, a sense of fear of the unknown, and people accepting without any sort of knowledge the Pagan=bad or polytheist=bad mindset because there isn't even close to equal treatment. Right now, I've been steering through my Facebook page and there are several Wikipedia entries on polytheism that they are considering pulling because there's almost no newspaper-based backing of facts. It's not necessarily intentional discrimination in the cyber world, but it seems to be almost a nasty feedback loop.

A number of years ago, I actually encountered a scholarly article online about a Greek alphabet oracle that in a lot of ways could be considered similar to the Norse and Germanic runes. Basically, I decided—I have been thinking about this for years and I finally decided to get off my ass and do it—What I actually did was create a physical, tangible, set of the Greek letters, writing down from the article the keywords, numeric values, and meanings that were given in the article for each letter. I'm also in the process of working to get some more modern keywords that go with the particular letters that can specifically convey to a more modern reader or audience what the particular letter would be all about. For example, the letter P, or Pi: the keyword is "many" but if you read the long description, then the letter means "perseverance." Because it talks about many troubles before you get to your goal.

Even if it doesn't catch on as the next big thing in Paganism, it's not something that shouldn't be revived. There are people who, around the country and even around the world, are feeling called to be oracles for the various Gods and Goddesses, and this would be yet another tool they could use because very few tarot decks have any sort of really Greek symbology, things that are based in the Greek mythology. If you are using the tarot as a part of this, sometimes there is a translation issue.

If there is anything that Ann wishes people understood about polytheists, it is that understanding divinity in the universe boils down to perspective; it isn't an issue of right or wrong. Just because people may be polytheist doesn't mean they are mentally deficient, insane, or dedicated to a countercultural lifestyle on the fringe of society.

As human beings, we are human beings that can completely understand the divinity in the universe and polytheists understand the Divine differently from monotheists, but it's not saying that either polytheists or monotheists are wrong based on their perceptions. It would be like two people who are neighbors, one who is Catholic, one who is Methodist, and agreeing to disagree. Just because someone is a polytheist doesn't make them a nut or a fringe member of society. There are people who are software designers, doctors, lawyers, around the world and in the US, people who are highly educated and polytheist. A fair percentage—probably a fair majority at this point in time—are called to polytheism as adults. We are only now starting to see a second generation of Greek polytheists in the United States, even though in Greek culture there are a lot of things—things that to me [seem to be] fairly obvious folk practices that take on a Christian veneer which are taken from a pre-Christian era in Greece.

Ann has faced challenges in working to establish a Hellenic proto-demos in her area. Some of the challenges exist because it is hard to locate other Hellenic polytheists. Another issue is that in her area of Louisiana, the occult shops are geared toward Santeria and Voodoo with Celtic and Norse offerings every now and again, but very have little to offer Hellenics. Fortunately, none of Ann's difficulties have been the result of conflict with other Pagans due to her emphasis on polytheism.

One of the major challenges is in connecting with people in the New Orleans area who are Hellenic polytheists. I'm sure there are more, but if I don't have contact information for person X, Y, or Z, and they don't know I exist, it is hard to find community. Especially since even when there are occult stores here, the vast majority of them are geared towards Voodoo and Santeria. There is a bit of Celtic and Norse mingled in, but it's primarily geared toward African traditional religion. Considering the history of the history of the area, I can understand why. Voodoo is, quite frankly, indigenous to the area. I have had practitioners of Voodoo who are glad to participate when I do a libation and have invited me to participate if they do a public ritual, so it's not that there would be a "oh, you're THAT kind of Pagan" attitude.

[U]ntil there is enough of a communication base between various individuals who are Hellenic polytheist or Asatru in a specific area—the Asatru tend to be a little bit better organized—But until you can establish enough communications in an area, it's hard to get things going. When I was moving—for a while after Katrina and before coming back to New Orleans, I was living in northeast Alabama. There was a Hellenion community in Atlanta. There still is. But a four-hour drive to go to ritual can be difficult. There was a local ADF grove, who I could at least do some seasonal worship with, because they use the Celtic 8-holiday wheel of the year. They are very accepting of the fact

that I was not going to be a member of the ADF, but I would join in because you can still honor your own Gods in a different place, and in fact that is one of the things that irritates me with some of the more fervently reconstructionist within the Hellenic community. Some of the more fervent reconstructionists would be appalled by even the idea that someone who follows the Greek Gods might also make offerings to the Voodoo loa because They are the spirits of the place. It would be like, if I was living in the country, making an offering to the dryads or the spirit of the meadows or whatever. For me, these are who are the spirits of the place, and you honor Them along with the Gods. For me, it's a no-brainer but it's something I sometimes have trouble explaining to people.

Erynn Rowan Laurie

Poet, priestess, elder, and independent Pagan scholar Erynn Rowan Laurie is a force of nature. She has been a major figure in the emergence of Celtic reconstructionist Paganism, but her practice is by no means limited to Celtic parameters. Her introduction to the esoteric realms began at age 12 through studying astrology and Tarot. She went on to serve as an Eclectic Wiccan priestess for many years before coming to her current polytheist practice, a significant aspect of which is Filidecht. Filidecht is the mystical poetic tradition of the ancient Celts, but due to a lack of primary source material, it has been difficult to discover the corpus of practices upon which Filidecht was based. From 1995-2001, Erynn studied Siberian shamanism, and has adapted many of those techniques to help recreate Filidecht for contemporary poets and seekers.

"I was raised in Protestant Christianity with a fairly evangelical, Southern Baptist bent," Erynn explains. "I was a Buddhist for a while, and then became a Wiccan." Although she has been a Pagan since 1984, Erynn followed a "more or less duotheistic" path for the first several years. Then, "from Wicca I moved on into the idea of Celtic reconstructionist Paganism as a polytheist" she says, "and have been much happier in that world." It has been over 20 years since she came to her current polytheist path. Currently, her practice includes polytheist, animist, and shamanic traditions.

I practice several traditions. I primarily identify as a Celtic reconstructionist Pagan practicing filidecht (the art of sacred poetry), but I am also a Mystes and Luperca of the Ekklesía Antínoou, and I attend the local Shinto shrine. In the past I have practiced Wicca (both eclectic and as an initiated Alexandrian 2nd degree) and I have studied Ulchi shamanism with a member of the Ulchi tribe of southeastern Siberia. While I do not practice Afro-Carribean religions, Hinduism, or Kemetic traditions, I have cordial relations with particular Deities and entities within those traditions, often through friends who are practitioners, and my work tends to be very much animist and localized in the Pacific Northwest.

I am currently mostly solitary and am in the process of attempting to relocate overseas. I'm a member of Neos

Alexandria and have contributed to some of their work. I also have longstanding individual ritual practices that are primarily animist and/or Celtic. I meet occasionally with the members of the Ekklesía Antínoou when people are available for ritual.

Rather than focus on a single pantheon, Erynn honors individual Deities from Gaelic, Shinto, Kemetic, Greek, Roman, Afro-Caribbean, and Hindu cultures. Animism is also very important to her practice.

There are a number of animal and plant spirits that I work with on many levels, both as allies in the spirit worlds, and for divination and other work. They are primarily represented physically in my work through the use of images or actual parts of animals that include skins, feathers, bones, claws, and teeth, that help me connect more strongly to them when I'm doing my work and journeying. Some spirits, like salmon, are intimately connected with multiple cultures and serve as bridges from one place to another -- among the Gaels the salmon is and embodiment wisdom, often the specific wisdom of the oldest of spirits and ancestors; in the Pacific Northwest, salmon is plenty and wealth, giving itself to the people in an act of complete generosity; in Siberia the salmon is an ancestral spirit of one of the Ulchi clans. In all these things, the spirit of salmon bridges continents and cultures and offers its knowledge to people everywhere in northern hemisphere coastal regions, or where the salmon migrate inland via riverine systems to spawn. For those who are in desert areas or tropical and southern oceans where salmon are not found, they can offer their knowledge through Otherworldly contacts found during journeying.

Erynn does not have any single ritual template guiding her interactions with her Holy Powers. She says that her relationships vary "wildly from one Deity to another." The number of Divinities she honors and the vast cultural differences between Them has necessitated that she have very distinct, individualized relationships with Them.

My relationships with Brigid, Manannán, Ogma and Airmed are very close and longstanding; I consider Them patrons and teachers and I have worked with each of T for a long time. I do regular ritual with and for Them and keep altars for Them in my home. Ogma was a major inspiration in my study of the ogam and was a huge presence as I was writing my book on the topic (Ogam: Weaving Word Wisdom). I have been a flametender for Brigid since 1993, when Her eternal flame was rekindled. Airmed has been a very healing presence and was one of the Deities who originally led me into the Gaelic pantheon to begin with. Manannán has been an important gatekeeper to the mysteries and aids me in moving between the worlds.

Many of the Deities in other pantheons that I honor or work with tend to be Deities of wisdom, poetry, writing, and music. These are things with which I tend to surround myself, and the pursuit of wisdom is my spiritual goal, so it makes sense that I would gravitate to these Beings. Athena, Djehuti and Seshat, Sarasvati, and Ame-Uzume-No-Mikoto are all Deities who are concerned with writing, wisdom, and the arts. My relationships with Them are not as close as with the Gaelic Deities, but They are very fond and amicable and I ask for Their aid as well as those of my primary Deities when I embark on a big project that falls within those realms.

Some of the "Deities" I work with are more in the manner of demi-Gods or heroes, like Suibhne or Fionn (think Heracles or Achilles in Greek culture). They are never specifically stated to be Divine, though they may have some distant deific ancestry. Both of these are exemplary poets, both are dwellers in wilderness, and Suibhne has specific resonances to the problems of those with post traumatic stress issues, having gone mad in battle; for me, he is a healing model and a figure that offers some positive reinforcement to the idea that one can be damaged but still have useful skills and talents that are valued in society.

Other Deities and entities have simply showed up at the doorstep and found a warm welcome. I've always been of the opinion that when spirits come knocking, you open the door and offer Them hospitality. Some of Them like it well enough to stick around and help out, and so I have a practice that, on the outside, looks very eclectic culturally but which is in its essence tightly focused in several directions thematically.

Erynn doesn't spend time discussing the particular meanings of "polytheism" and "faith." Neither concept is as relevant to her spirituality as religious practice is.

I'm not so much centered around faith and belief as around experience. I've found that I don't have to "believe in" the Deities to feel Their presence in my life. When I speak to Them, when I listen to Them, They offer rewarding and fulfilling experiences in return. They have come forward with guidance and advice, and have been healing and enlightening presences in a broad variety of circumstances. They have been the pillars of my life through very difficult periods and my recovery through some really terrible experiences.

Erynn was pretty solidly Wiccan in her view of Deity until a Goddess came forward and changed her mind. Erynn was a bit surprised to find that different Gods and Goddesses had different expectations than the Goddess of Wicca.

When I was originally practicing Wicca I was, like most Wiccans, working with "The Goddess" in magic and in circle. Airmed was the first of the individual Deities to come to me, and She said that They weren't all the same, They didn't all want the same things, and that what She wanted was not Wiccan. She wanted me to learn Irish. I've since done translation work in Old Irish, and sung in a Scottish Gaelic choir, though I can't hold much of a conversation in the languages. These seem to be sufficient for Her at the moment. She wanted me to study Gaelic mythologies. She introduced me to Brigid, who introduced me to Manannán. It was Her influence that led me to begin the studies that would become a part of the nascent Celtic reconstructionist movement.

Airmed is the Irish Deity who is primarily associated with herbal healing and plant knowledge. She is the daughter of Dian Cécht and the sister of Miach and Octriuil, who all tended the sacred well called Slaine (health) during the Second Battle of Mag Tuired. Given that She is the one who sorted and identified the healing herbs that grew on Miach's grave, and that Dian Cécht scattered those herbs, I've always seen Her as a sort of patron of lost knowledge that can be regained through study and mystical means. The well of Slaine brought back those who were mortally wounded to full health, and this feels like another metaphor for the reconstruction or restoration of what is mostly gone.

Since that time, I've had many encounters with Deities who were quite insistent that They were not a part of some amorphous singularity that can be addressed by any name—They feel it's sort of the spiritual equivalent of "hey, you!" and that it isn't particularly respectful. Thor and Loki are very vehemently insistent that They are NOT the same Deity, thank you VERY much.

The shift from a soft polytheist view of the Gods as being merely facets of a single Godhead to a hard polytheist view of the

Gods and Goddesses as separate, distinct, entities can be quite an adjustment. Especially for someone whose priestly duties are very invested in working within the soft polytheist framework. Erynn has found the change to be very rewarding because it allows her to work more closely alongside her Gods.

> *It was a difficult but freeing sensation. The thought that I would have to do more work to get to know individual Deities was a bit intimidating, but I felt that it also created extremely valuable opportunities to get to know those individuals much more deeply. I could call upon Deities who had particular likes and skills that had something to do with my own, and felt that I might actually be able to develop better and stronger relationships within the spiritual worlds because of it. Things in my spiritual life became much more focused and sharply drawn, and their results in my everyday life became more plain and obvious.*

> *In being Wiccan, I'd initially substituted Mother for the Father of the Christianity in which I was raised. The expectation of omniscience, omnipotence, and omnipresence was identical, if softened and feminized somewhat. In discovering localized and individualized Deity, I found myself much more able to connect with something and someone far more personal, with individuals who had been neglected for hundreds or thousands of years and who responded with enthusiasm to someone who acknowledged Them as whom and what They are. I found much more complexity in polytheistic individual Deities than I did in a great, overarching monist Deity; complexity is something that fascinates me and draws me in.*

> *I've found that Deities with particular interests in me as a person or in the things I'm interested in have a more vested interest in working with me. There's more focus of attention on our relationships than I felt with any overarching Deity who had to have its attentions scattered everywhere all at once; the feeling is much less fragmentary when a particular Deity with an interest in poetry comes to help me out with something than I had when I was trying to call on The Goddess to come help me with a poem. I also feel that my work and my devotion are more personal and meaningful to Them, as They have fewer devotees than any "generic" Deity, whether "God" or "Goddess."*

Erynn has experienced a degree of friction with others because of her emphasis on polytheism in both belief and practice. She does recognize that there may very well be an underlying connectedness to all and all beings—both corporeal and non. Yet

Erynn also finds that it is as disrespectful to ignore the individuality of different Deities as it is to ignore the individuality of different human beings.

Sadly, this is fairly frequent. Non-polytheists assume that I simply haven't "got it" yet, that I'm either blind or stupid or not evolved enough, and that monism is the True Underlying Reality of the Universe™. I think it's arrogant for them to assume that their view is the only correct one and that my lived experience is invalid.

"Humanity" may be one conceptual whole, but it still doesn't mean we aren't all individual human beings with individual bodies and lives and thoughts and desires. I don't answer to "Djuna" or "Pradeep" because I don't have any idea that you mean me when you call out that name. You have to call me by my name, and in a language I speak, before I'll know who you're talking about. It's the same way with Deity, in my experience.

They assume they know my Deities, can call on Them by any name they like, can assign any random set of attributes to Them, that they can invoke any of Them into a circle together, and assume everyone will get along just fine because They're all just the same Deity soup anyway. A lot of these same people are of the opinion that Deity is really a psychological phenomenon, and that it's all in our heads; I think that's inherently a non-polytheistic attitude to have—it seems entirely non-theistic, period...

As a result of her views, Erynn has experienced some difficulty in working with other Pagans. Part of this is due to what she regards to be the 'default settings' of Paganism.

I often find it difficult to work with other Pagan groups because of this assumption of deific monism. They're happy to allow that Deity comes with many names and faces, but the "thousand faceted jewel" metaphor gets way too much use. It's not a case of all paths lead to the top of the mountain, because some of us are walking on paths that lead to the seaside, or through deep forest, or even out into places beyond this planetary sphere. There is no singular mountain on our planet, there are many continents, and all paths lead where they lead, yet this concept seems almost impossible for some folks to allow.

In Pagan community discussion, Wiccan language and monistic models are regarded as the default—circle casting, four elements, The God and The Goddess are all seen as "generic" to everyone

Pagan, though it is getting slightly less so these days (mostly because reconstructionists and other polytheists are speaking up in greater numbers). These assumptions make it nearly impossible for polytheists, and for reconstructionist Pagans generally to feel heard.

Within reconstructionist communities, I also sometimes experience frictions with people who believe that reconstructionists should stick with one pantheon and one pantheon only, even though we are all polytheists. I've always felt that one of the beauties of polytheism is that it allows us to seek and understand Deities from different cultures without having to claim an exclusivity. One can be a polytheist henotheist, who worships a particular Deity exclusively, but why should the rest of us be forced to conform to a restrictive model because some people are uncomfortable with stretching beyond the limits of one particular cultural tradition?

Beyond the scope of the Pagan realm, Erynn has experienced some frustration in her attempts to share her viewpoints with Christian and Jewish colleagues.

Non-Pagans, of course, have no idea about Paganism most of the time anyway. I've done interfaith work and the Christians and Jews I've worked with almost never have the first clue what I'm talking about. The monotheist assumptions are truly disheartening, and the idea that there can be only one answer to any question makes it even more difficult. Even the ones who want to understand have a great deal of trouble putting aside the monotheist lens through which they view the world—I can either be wrong or just misguided, but I can't have a valid view of something true about the world, from their perspective. There is something so profoundly alien about polytheism to most monotheists that they often find it completely unintelligible.

Despite having felt some disappointment in working with other Pagans, Erynn remains excited about and engaged in exploring new aspects of polytheist practice. There are questions that she grapples with, and her efforts do not fail to yield solid spiritual insights.

There are questions that come up in reconstructionist groups sometimes about things like "if you have cultures in proximity with storm Gods, who's in charge of the storms? Is there some sort of jurisdictional shift when you move from one place to another?" It's interesting to consider, but I'm not sure it's actually a relevant question when it comes to practice, given that each individual polytheist is going to be speaking with the storm God that they're closest to.

What I find more interesting as a question is how well do Deities from different pantheons and cultures work together? How do They negotiate Their interactions? How do They share Their followers when people are drawn to multiple Deities from multiple cultures? Within a particular mythos, we often see tribal and familial disagreements and animosities, but how does that work between Deities of different cultures?

When one worships the Deity of a particular river, how does being in a place where that river does not run affect one's spiritual understanding? Sarasvati helps me with this, as She was originally a riverine Deity whose river no longer exists—She took up many other associations and spread far beyond Her initial place and powers, becoming important not just in Hinduism but also in Buddhism and Jain religion and, eventually, to western Pagans who may know little or nothing of Her original contexts and forms. I think it is, or at least can be, the same way for any other Deity associated with a particular thing or place in a specific location. Manannán may be the first king of the Isle of Man, and a sea Deity of the North Sea, but He is also found in every wave in every ocean, and in the mists that rise in every valley.

In my experience, there are some Deities—like Antinous, for instance—who seem to act as envoys and negotiators, or bridges between cultures and pantheons. Way-openers of various pantheons often seem to act as diplomats, if you will, and I have seen at least some anecdotal evidence that people who revere these way-openers tend to be a little more open to working with Deities of many cultures at the same time because they understand the crossroads and the mists where Deities introduce Their followers to other Deities for different purposes, from opening contact to "cross-training" for new techniques to bring home to Their own pantheons.

One thing Erynn wishes people understood about polytheism is that, "No, we don't actually believe it's all the same thing down deep. Our experience is different than yours, and that's all right. It's not a threat that we experience Deity and the Otherworlds differently."

Amy Blackthorn

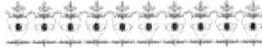

Criminal justice professional Amy Blackthorn was 11 when she first heard the calls of Diana and Hecate. When she got older and began working with a coven, the Morrigan and Herne joined her practice. Today, 20 years later, Amy is the leader of the Wise Woman Tradition of Green Witchcraft. When asked to describe her relationship with these Deities, she says, "They are my spiritual family. I devote to Them, I leave offerings forThem, and talk with Them regularly...my practice is daily. My Hearth is my home's heart, and as such, I have an altar—used daily—in my kitchen."

"Interaction on a regular basis showed me," Amy says, that "the Gods have separate faces. After working one-on-one with different Deities through the years, you get to know Them as They are, rather than as we would hope They would be." In Amy's view, polytheism isn't only the belief in multiple Gods. It is a religious philosophy which allows you a wider range of religious expression. She also makes a strong distinction between polytheism as she practices it, and the polytheism she has encountered in her interactions with Wiccans, who she considers to be "syncretic monotheists, rather than polytheists." Amy coined the term "syncretic monotheism," which she defines as "Seeing the Divine as being many facets while coming from one wellspring," to help differentiate her understanding of polytheism from what she finds to be the more pervasive Pagan ones.

> In my teaching, I have a lot of students come to me who have read several books that more or less say the same thing. They define Wicca as, almost as, a syncretic monotheist faith rather than a polytheist faith. I get a lot of, "God is one big diamond and I just see one little part." Well, the way I see true polytheism is we take that big rock and we smash it into a million little pieces and everybody gets to take a piece home with them. Deity is not just one facet. If I had to eat one dish for the rest of my life, I think I'd get bored. Polytheism gives you the opportunity to decide not only what your faith is and how you can best express that to other people, but how you can celebrate that part of yourself without limiting yourself to one dish for the rest of your life...

When asked about the role that faith plays in her relationships with the Gods, Amy admits that, "Faith is a tricky word, because faith implies lack of knowledge. I KNOW my Gods. I don't feel or think They 'might' be out there somewhere. I know." There is nothing nebulous or simply hopeful about faith, in her view. Faith prompts action, because gives us the desire to better understand ourselves and our relationship to the world around us.

Okay. It's not—faith isn't just having someone sit at the other end of the room and tell you what they believe for the rest of your life. Faith is going out and experiencing what you think is out there. I mean, the point of religion is not just to give you a bedtime story to feel better at night. It's to give us a better understanding of who we are and where we want to be in five years. And, in theory, in the other side of this life. Faith isn't just the idea that there is something out there but it gives you a more specific idea of where to take that next step. A lot of people when they go through their job training, they are looking for, okay where's my promotion? If you are sitting in a room because someone told you to sit in a room one day out of the week for the rest of your life, are you getting anything out of it? It's not just, "okay, I went, I sat here, I get my little checkmark in the book today." It's "this has meaning." If you don't feel that tingle in your gut that says "I'm here for a reason"—that little tingle in your gut that says you are here for a reason, that's faith to me.

Like so many others before her, the first steps of Amy's spiritual journey into her current polytheist practice were guided by books on Wicca and witchcraft. "I started with Cunningham at 11," Amy explains. She recalls the frustration she had felt when asking problematic questions in Christian Sunday school, and the subsequent satisfaction at taking the steps, entirely on her own, to learn new things and discover a different set of religious beliefs. Amy is quick to point out, however, that her pride and satisfaction did not come with an accompanying sense of "coming home" to beliefs that made sense.

I hear so many people use the phrase, "coming home" that I feel like it's gotten trite. I felt that I had come home probably three years later, at 13. I read everything I could get my hands on from 11-13 but it was exciting in a way that wasn't based in the reality of what Wicca is. I was excited by what I read, but I wasn't seeing it for what it was, I was romanticizing it. When I turned 13 and I was in a place where I was more responsible and emotionally mature, I decided to do my self-dedication ritual. Before then it was something I thought about, but there was still a part of me that felt that it wasn't real, so I didn't bother. When I had grown up enough to realize this was no longer a religious fantasy, but the reality for many people—I got my head on straight, approached it with the reverence it deserved, and Dedicated.

When it came to the church, I spent so much time as a child apologizing for what I thought. My parents used church as free babysitting to sleep off a Saturday night hangover, not as spiritual fulfillment. I took church very seriously from about five because of the fire and brimstone speeches I got from the pulpit. I can remember being in second grade and going to Sunday school and getting in trouble with the woman who's in charge of Sunday school because I asked her, "if God is loving and forgiving, and understanding, then why were all women cursed with menses and painful pregnancies as punishment for Eve's sin? Why are all women punished for the act of one?" I got into so much trouble for that. It wasn't that I was being flippant or that I wasn't taking it very seriously. The woman who was in the Sunday school, I got the feeling that she had never thought about it that way. But because she never said to herself, "well, I never thought about it that way," I got into trouble.

So reading Cunningham at such a young age when I'm trying to find my own identity, when I'm trying to find where I fit in the world, having someone (even in a book) say, this is different but that doesn't mean it's wrong, it really gave me a sense of—accomplishment is the wrong word, but not by much—to be able to find something on my own...Satisfaction that a parent didn't have to hand me or feed me [this], a clergyperson didn't fill my head up with something just so there's something in there. It was something I came to on my own. I was actually pretty proud that I had taken the step to find what I believed. It wasn't even that I was questioning what I believed because I'd been going to church since I could remember but knew I didn't believe that...I didn't have a chance for the coming home that some of the other people express when they changed faiths. I didn't need to come home, because I didn't realize that I wasn't home. I just finally figured things out.

As she grew up, Amy began to interact more and more with the Divine. As her personal practice and knowledge grew, and as she began working with different Goddesses and Gods, Amy began to understand that whatever underlying connection these Deities might have, They still had very distinct personalities, very distinct ways of engaging with the mundane world, and very distinct expectations of the humans who sought Them out. It became patently obvious over time that the Goddesses and Gods were not just facets of one Divine Godhead; each was a Divine Being unto Herself or Himself.

> [Cunningham] gave me that whole "God is a big old diamond and everybody sees the different sides." But in working with the Divine, and working with individual Goddesses and individual Gods, you get to the point where you understand that... While I understand where people get the "different sides" point of view, in working with Deity and individual Gods and individual Goddesses AS Their own personalities it is clear that yes, They are all Divine, but They are all completely different personalities. I understand where people get the "we're all one," and "kumbaya," stuff—its' great. But when you look at the way the Gods behave and the way They've been worshipped, They're all so very different. I mean, Kali Ma and Durga are light-years away from where Aphrodite is. Sometimes They maybe have similar associations. Different Gods and different Goddesses are associated with similar things. You can have a little list of, "these are all the Goddesses of love," But They are completely different personalities, and to [treat] Them any less than that, I feel, would be disrespectful. It's white-washing. Every religion, every culture, has differences for a reason. Everyone comes from a different place. I explain to my students the same concept by warning them not to invoke separate pantheons in the same circle without serious scholarship and research. These cultures may have warred for the last thousand years and by bringing Them into the same circle, these disparate cultures clash in a way isn't beneficial to your Working.

There isn't much philosophizing or conjecture behind Amy's sense of spiritual reality. Her understanding is based on hard knowledge gained from a harrowing near-death experience. Yet attempting to explain this to others, particularly her devoutly Baptist family members, is very challenging.

> I got into a little argument with my sister-in-law a couple years ago. She is from a Baptist background and sincerely believes that anyone who not only isn't Christian but isn't Baptist and almost to the point of going to her church, is going to hell. In an effort to save my soul from what she believes to be eternal damnation, she asked my husband and my mother and my adjacent people

what I believed to fortify her argument against me, rather than asking me what my faith is and what faith is, in my definition. She just decided that these were all the things that it meant. She knew in her heart of hearts that what she had read and been told was going to happen to us all when we died. And my point to her was, I died about nine years ago. I was clinically dead for about three minutes. I know what awaits me when I die. When you look at the word "faith" it does imply doubt because you're not sure. You have to be understanding of what you think is going to happen but you don't have a way to prove it. In my way of thinking, I proved it by being clinically dead, seeing what I believe is what happens in the afterlife. At that point, it's not faith anymore. I feel that it's knowledge because whether it's some hallucination brought on by a near-death experience, or the real afterlife, I no longer have doubt.

I had been interested in looking at near-death experiences and trying to understand what went on before I had my own understanding. I've a very skeptical person by nature. It seems funny that someone who believes in magick and hocus-pocus would be a skeptic at heart, but I was. So when I was in a car accident, I was able to regain consciousness and be awake and alert and aware of my surroundings about 24 hours later, and I asked my now-husband, "when I was in the car, with the blanket over my head and unable to see anything, was this where the ambulance was parked? Is this where you were standing? Is this where your friend Ralph was? Is this where the police line was? Is this where they landed the helicopter?" My husband confirmed, yes, yes, yes, and by the way how did you see that? You were facing the wrong direction and had a blanket over your head and they scooped you into the helicopter ad you were gone. There is no way you could have seen any of that stuff. I told him I had been floating outside of my body, which if I had to say was about 30 feet above the scene.

Looking at the scene, not being in my body anymore, I remembered flying over the desert and talking to, I guess what would be my spirit guide and saying, okay, what happened? I was supposed to be home. I'm supposed to be home now and I'm not home." I was given the choice. Stay dead or come back. It was explained to me that my body was broken, broken, and it was going to be hard. Did I want to come back, and if so, why? And it wasn't a choice for me at that point. I knew I wanted to help people; I was in seminary school for three years when I was in the car accident. I was already halfway to becoming a minister.

I knew it was important for me to come back and continue that work. The next thing I know, they are getting me out of the car, stuffing me into the helicopter, and getting me back to the hospital.

Confirmation of one's belief comes in many forms. For some people, there are enormous, powerful experiences that confirm their beliefs. For others, a series of outrageous synchronicities leads up to an undeniable confirmation. Yet despite having had a powerful near-death experience validate her convictions, Amy's confirmation that the Gods are real and involved in her life had been established years earlier. Amy explains that prayer, meditation, and ritual undertaken to connect with the Gods brought solid confirmation which her near-death experience merely validated.

What means so much to me is the fact that through prayer and meditation and ritual, we meet and interact with our Gods on a daily basis, weekly basis, monthly basis, you know, depending on your path and I guess how devout you are. You have the opportunity to meet and talk with and work with the Gods on a one-to-one basis. Not like, "Hi. My name is Amy and how do you do," you know, "we're gonna go have coffee." It sounds a little, it sounds funny when you come from an outside monotheist standpoint because a lot of monotheists are used to going to church and praying and some feel that some of their prayers might not be heard. But prayer and meditation and ritual give you the opportunity to work within yourself to get confirmation. To know that They're there. To know that They're there for you.

Devotional activities are a very important part of Amy's religious practice. Rituals and ceremonies are important, as are prayer and meditation. Yet as Amy has discovered, even mundane activities like gardening, cooking, and washing the dishes can become devotional, when undertaken in the right frame of mind. But in order for any of this, all of these activities must come from, and seek to connect back to, the spiritual place inside one's self.

My favorite personal meditation is gardening. It is devotional. It is therapeutic. Gardening is putting back some of what I have used from that same earth, continuing that cycle. Esbats can be solo or with the group depending on the schedules of the month. Solo Esbats include a nicely prepared-from-scratch meal, candle lighting, and a personal connection with the Gods. If I have a need I'll work magick after my meal, outside if the weather is habitable. Esbats are lower key in my life. Stop, appreciate what you have, give thanks. Sabbats are more involved, it is a group affair, with potluck meal, robes, masks and ritual theatre.

A few years ago, two other High Priestesses and myself were lamenting that though we adored our coveners or students, we missed being able to participate in ritual. We decided to have a Samhain celebration with three HPs. Each of us came from a Tradition with a history of Aspecting (A religious partnership between Gods and people that involves a form of voluntary possession for the purpose of delivering insight and messages. i.e. Drawing Down the Moon) at Samhain. So we decided if each of us Aspected a different Deity we'd have the opportunity to meet and receive guidance from two Deities.

My daily observances are small and personal: "all acts of love and pleasure are my rituals." So lighting incense and feeling connected to a Goddess I work with while going about my daily life is personal ritual. Dishes in the kitchen are meditative, and I contemplate the Gods. Softly singing favorite chants while working at my desk is centering. Rituals needn't be orchestrated productions every day. They just need to be meaningful to you. All of the gold chalices and thousand dollar wands won't get you to a spiritual place inside yourself. Only you can do that. Ritual is all of the above.

Because of the way my tradition is set up, we celebrate astrologically. It's a couple days later then most Wiccans would celebrate their holiday. I can go out and have fun with people I know in the community...We can go out and have ritual, maybe have a girls' night with some drinks, or just have a cookout. But there's also the astrological dates, because they are a slightly different observance than most of my community, I can have that as personal time. I can sit on deck and pray. I can work out in the garden. Working in the garden, just growing your own food, is a really great way to commune with nature... There are so many polytheists I know who are like, "I practice a nature-based faith but that doesn't mean I actually need to go outside. I'm just gonna stay in my mom's basement."

In Amy's view, ritual in particular occupies a unique place in polytheist religious practice. Ritual demands that you set aside mundane concerns and focus on the spiritual matters at hand. In a modern society which emphasizes constant digital connection and demands a multitasking mindset, ritual affords the opportunity to unplug and re-dedicate.

Honestly, when you look at individual psychology, our rational thinking brains get so easily bored that ritual gives you a chance to see and smell and touch and move and do things that aren't just…that are more engaging. It helps keep your interest. It helps keep your little brain that is worrying inside about your checkbook, your kids' soccer game, and everything else, and it puts it outside. Ritual is supposed to be a time outside of time and a place outside of place. By keeping your brain engaged in the singing or the drumming or the writing rituals or even just sitting with some incense and taking a deep breath deep inside yourself gives you a space to be away from all of that. Where it's okay to put daily life down for an hour or two hours even if it's just 8 times a year.

Amy recognizes that there are "Samhain and Beltane" Pagans who, very much like their "Easter and Christmas" Christian counterparts, seldom partake of the religious practices of their faith. She admits that she doesn't entirely understand them, nor does she understand the mindset of those who do not engage in devotional activities. She raises the interesting question of why it is that large group rituals are seen as important enough for even the least religious Pagan to celebrate occasionally, but daily practices to reconnect with your faith are not seen as necessarily or particularly desirable.

The observance is great, but I think the daily stuff is a little more important sometimes, because when it gets to the point where you're not…if you religion isn't there for you on a daily basis, then what is it there for? My parents when to church on Easter and Christmas, but they sent us every week. It was portrayed as something you do when you're a kid, but when you're a grownup, it doesn't really matter anymore. If faith isn't that important to you, it should be. Well, I personally I feel it should be one way or the other. You either have it or you don't. That one or two times a year when you take your faith off the shelf and you dust it off and you show it to somebody else and then you put it back in the closet—it's like religion was a waste of time for them.

Religion plays such an important part of Amy's life because when she completed her advanced training with a Dianic coven, she decided to "hive off" and form her own within the Wise Woman tradition of Green Witchcraft.

Once you have been in a particular group for a while, once you have gone through not just the training, the emotional development that comes with the training to lead a group, you are kicked out of the nest, in a loving and supportive way...Once you've gotten to the point that your high priestess feels that you have learned all you need to learn, it's "hey, time for you to go teach some new people! It's time for you to hive." Then, you would leave the coven you're with and start your own. You're still free to come and go, come back to the mother coven for rituals or for advice or for visiting. They have become your family. Years and years and years of working with people pretty closely, they are your family.

The Wise Woman tradition of Green Witchcraft originated in the Dianic tradition, but the emphasis is on the individual's place within the vast natural realm. The devotional practices of connecting with nature are key to the tradition.

It started as an offshoot of the Dianic tradition, or the Dianic way of thinking. The great thing about the woman who founded it is that this is more about being able to connect with "here," wherever "here" is. The plants that grow in your backyard are a form of divination through everyday life. It has to do more with connection and less about the bells and whistles of rituals rather than keeping faith just for, or just through, Diana. It's less angry feminism and more, "be in your backyard. Be in your own space. Just be at one with it." It doesn't have to involve spending $80 on some crazy wand that was blessed by so and so whody-wooty. It's about, "go out in your backyard. Take a walk in the woods." It's about being comfortable in yourself, and being yourself in nature, even if that nature is a potted plant on your apartment patio.

The structure of Amy's coven is similar to those which espouse the theology of a "triple Goddess," a great female Deity who has three archetypal facets of the Maiden, Mother, and Crone. Therein, each facet bearing the likeness of a Goddess from an ancient culture who symbolizes the functions of each facet. Unlike many of those groups, however, Amy's coven recognizes the individuality, separateness, and uniqueness of each Goddess, and distinguishes the actual Goddess from the archetypal role that She is gracious enough to take on for the coven's work. Amy's coven has built relationships with Diana, Hecate, and The Morrighan. Occasionally they will work with Gods like Herne. Her personal relationships with each of these Deities have strengthened the work she does with her coven.

Diana is the maiden not only from the traditional standpoint but from Her role in mythology and practice. She wanted to be the "virgin" in the way that "virgin" was originally meant. Not, "someone who has never known the touch of a man," but a woman who is "of Her own self." Independent: "I wanna go over here today so that's what I'm gonna do." It's important that no matter how old or young a person is, they are able to say, "I can be an independent person. I can have independent thought outside of work and family and school and everything else. She was one of the first Deities I got to know as young girl and I felt a very close connection to Her wild nature. She hunted, She ran around on Her own terms. To a preteen without a stable home life, being independent seemed like the most incredible, freeing thing in existence.

The Morrighan became part of my group because of my previous tradition experience. The Morrighan was the head Goddess for part of the year in my tradition, before I moved to the Green Witchcraft Tradition. I developed a strong relationship with Her and it actually worked out really well. I had problems as a younger person, finding a strong female figure to help push me out of my emotional nest, out of my teens and into [being] an adult, having a home and making a family. It sounds funny, but having a Goddess of war and death who's got your back is actually very empowering.

Hecate is another of the first Goddesses I started working with as a young lady. At the tender age of 11, I found my sister's book in her book bag. She was 14. I was 11, being the snooping younger sister sharing a room. And, I found a book. It's funny how this book written for 30- and 40- year olds made sense to this thinking 11-year old. It just happens that we were working with mythology and learning about myths when I found something that was telling me that everybody's myths, everybody's religions and viewpoints of Gods, were religions, in the same way that my parents sending met to church; these are Gods too. Hecate was one of the first Gods I started working with, through that. She appeared in a fictional series I was reading at the time, and I was thrilled to find that She really existed in this new faith, and not just in the fictionalized version of Her. We've been together ever since. She has Her own shrine in the kitchen where I do most of my Work and worship.

As far as our group goes, everyone is free to work with the Goddesses that mean the most to them. Not to the exclusion of the Gods, which is pretty much how it is in a lot of Dianic sects, they're kind of "He's a God, and we're not gonna do any of that." Gods are certainly welcome. It's just that I didn't have a lot of experience working with individual Gods, so They're not necessarily the focus. But I make sure that my students know that the God we might be working with is not just a backup dancer.

One question Amy has grappled with is to determine what role myth plays in her relationships with her Deities. Certainly, myths are important sacred narratives that give insight about the Gods, but Amy also sees they are so fantastic and impossible that the Deities seem almost utterly unapproachable. The best way to deal with this discrepancy, she has found, is to approach Them anyway and give yourself a chance to really interact with Them.

I read a discussion last week, and some people in the community have been discussing this, so it's funny that this comes up. It gets to the point where it almost feels like... you're reading about these Gods and They're so big and They're so overblown and They're our personalities and our flaws magnified to the point where They seem so big. If people are made in the image of Gods, and we have flaws, then hey, guess what, maybe They do, too. So what changes is, well It's almost like reading about a celebrity in a magazine. One of those crazy gossip rags. And then, having lunch with Them. The gossip rag has to make it sound big and important and imposing, otherwise the readers wouldn't read. But when you get Them in a one-on-one, well... They may still have flaws because people have flaws and people made in the image of the Gods have flaws. But They know so much more than we do. They've been around just about forever. The things we have issues with, the things we need guidance on, the support we need emotionally, They can be there for that because They've seen it, and been it, and done it. It's not necessarily, "Oh my goodness, let's cower before a Deity." You have to approach Deity as a respectful friend. Not bowing and scraping. It's important to have respect. But not as a loss of respect for yourself. And They understand that and They appreciate that.

Ancestors and land spirits have grown increasingly important to Amy's personal practice. These were things she had been taught but had not begun to incorporate until recently. Fraught familial relationships posed a challenge at first, but Amy has worked through her misgivings and begun to connect with her ancestors. She has also began to leave ritual offerings for the spirits of her land. The important thing that Amy keeps in mind is that she is building reciprocal friendships, rather than working relationships.

Certainly I have. More recently than I had expected. It is something that I had been taught. Maybe when I was around 18, the coven I was in worked with ancestors and spirits. Because I don't really like my family it was a little harder to work with them. Abusive grandparents, adoption of my mom, etc left me leery of "ancestors," but it's gotten to the point now where I've worked with some friends in slightly different circles where land spirits and the spirits of your ancestors are a given. That actually made it a little easier to work my toe into the pool of working with more spirits in addition to working with and having the reference of my Deities.

The land spirits of our home and our property, that's just been a few months now. Once a week under the oak tree in the backyard, I have a little glass, I will put some grain alcohol or maybe some candy out there for those spirits. I'm actually burning incense right now. It's a very personal thing, sort of, "Hi! How ya doin? I know you're here. I'm here, too I just wanted to say, Hi!" instead of a big production of "I want to appease the spirits! Give me a better job!"

Unfortunately, in teaching and working with the public, I get a lot of, what a friend of mine would call, "fair-weather witches." The sort that say, if something bad comes up, I will just throw a spell at it and that will make it all better, but I won't touch my altar or think about the Gods again until I need something." That just makes you a shitty friend. If you have a friendship with someone, and you only call when you need them, that doesn't make you a good friend. So as far as the land spirits and my ancestors, I look at it more as a friendship than a working relationship. "I'll call you and we'll have coffee. I'll leave you a gift and you'll know I'm thinking of you without it being a big production where it takes five hours to light a candle.

Amy has on occasion experienced friction with others due to her emphasis on polytheism. However, being unwaveringly rooted in her own, hard polytheism made it easier for her to accept other viewpoints. Since becoming an adult, the work she has done with the community has had a significant impact on her willingness to peaceably disagree with others.

Because I started younger, I got a lot of the "there there, little one. You'll grow out of that one day," from a lot of the people I knew, even in the Pagan community when I first started dealing with the public. But once I found my own identity within

Paganism as an adult, I knew that I was a hard polytheist, and not syncretic monotheist. I knew that this was what I felt...I came to the point where I was already comfortable within myself and I didn't need a sandwich board. When I've dealt with other people who are more the "big diamond," it didn't feel necessary to argue with them about it. It was more of a "that's great, that's wonderful. I'm glad you found something that works for you. Have a nice day." If I had found some of that when I was a little younger, it could have been a problem due to the lack of maturity. By the time I started dealing more with the community and dealing more with one versus the other, it was already to the point where I had the respect of my peers from my experience and working public outreach that it wasn't really questioned. It was, "Okay great. Everybody goes home happy." I agree to disagree in the best way possible.

There isn't simply one thing which Amy wishes people understood about polytheism, there are several. The first is that hard polytheism isn't a threat to anyone else's belief system. That said, she also wishes that Pagans from all belief backgrounds would begin to engage in practice that is meaningful to them, and not feel driven to seek validation of their spiritual convictions.

I think the biggest detractors for hard polytheism are monotheist Pagans, not Christians or people from other monotheistic faiths. It gets to the point where you spend so much of your time defending who you are that we start to feel like we have to defend ourselves all the time, even from each other. I wish more monotheists or syncretic monotheists understood that hard polytheism, that real belief, isn't a threat to them. I don't want to tell anybody that they're doing anything wrong. I don't want anyone to see that my practices are better than anyone else's. I just want to be left alone with my Gods. Everybody has the right way for them. I don't—I would never, ever, ever, tell one of my students that any one path is any better than another.

We get a lot of people new to Paganism who are unfortunately under the impression that you start out as solitary, then you join an eclectic coven, then you join a traditional coven, and then you get some super secret gold star that nobody knows about it. That's not it. Some of the most incredible polytheists, syncretic monotheists I've met, some of the most incredible Pagans I've worked with, were solitary and did what meant something to them. They worked with their Gods and that was good enough. They didn't need a gold star from anybody else. They did their work, and they formed incredible connections and bonds with their ancestors, with their Gods, and that was enough. It shouldn't be about who got a gold star this week. It should be about that emotional connection that drives you to do things. Not just for the betterment of yourself but for the betterment of the people around you, whether they have the same beliefs as you or not.

Herakles

For over 40 years, Herakles has secretly worshipped the Olympian Twelve. Having been born into a Christian family and currently living with his Mormon siblings, Herakles has known from an early age that well-being of his family relationships depended upon his silence. Because he lives in a small desert town in the Southwestern U.S., Herakles has worshipped in relative isolation from Pagans or other Hellenic polytheists. It wasn't until 2010 that Herakles discovered the existence of contemporary Paganism through an online community. He discovered this project because the call for interviews had been posted on that community's forum by members of that community. Herakles' interview for this project was the first time in his life that he had ever deeply conversed with another person about his devotion to the Olympian twelve.

Herakles defines polytheism as "A belief in more than more than one God and Goddess." He views faith as "believing in something you can't touch, see, feel, or hear. Believing in the intangible." Herakles says that when he first discovered polytheism, he felt "a kind of 'coming home' to a belief in the right way for me. It was as though doors which had been closed to me were now open and I could see the glory of my Gods and Goddesses." When asked about how he maintained faith in the Gods during all those years of silence, Herakles responds that, "faith plays a very important part in my relationship with the Olympian Twelve." He characterizes this as an "inner faith," and explains that "while I didn't have anybody to guide me or help me along," he says, "I at the same time didn't have anybody that would deride and try to convince me that I was worshipping the air-quote 'Devil.' So I felt strong in myself that my worship of the Gods and Goddesses was important." Herakles adds that "it brought me some sense of inner warmth and satisfaction."

Herakles first recognized he was polytheist in his early 20's. After pondering his spiritual leanings, Herakles says that he "just knew the Gods and Goddesses were real separate and very distinct Deities. It is hard to tell of the affirmation beyond a sort of epiphany." Like many other polytheists, Herakles first discovered the Gods through reading books on classical mythology.

My folks were in the military so we moved a lot. We were never in any one place to go to any one church: When I did go, there was something that I felt was missing while I was listening to the sermon. It just didn't feel right to me. And I started reading some books of the Odyssey and the Iliad. Bullfinch's Mythology. A couple works by Plato and Hesiod and there was something in there when they were talking about the Gods that seemed to make a connection with me. And I started to feel, well, a closeness to the Gods of Greece. In my early 20's I more or less became a polytheist.

Prior to his commitment to polytheism, Herakles did feel moved to prayer, on occasion. But these experiences, he says, had very mixed results.

This was during high school. During that time I hadn't really quite set myself on the road to polytheism. During woodshop, if I remember right, I think I said the following prayer: I wasn't directing this to anyone in particular. I was trying to make a bookcase. You know, the obligatory bookcase. I was saying, "I pray that this comes out right." Whoever I was praying to decided, "let's have a laugh at him" and one side ended up being shorter than the other. So, I didn't make an A or a B. The teacher was kind to me and gave me a C, for originality.

Today, Herakles honors the Olympian Twelve. Over the years, he has built very different relationships with Them, and feels closer to some than to others.

I have a relationship with the Goddess Athena...I have called on Her a few times when I needed some wisdom. I believe She answered me. And sometimes I believe She wanted me to find the answer on my own. I also feel, I don't know, a closeness, an affinity, with Zeus. Kind of look at Him as a father-type figure. There have been a couple times when my own father and I were not getting along and I would pray to Zeus to give me some understanding of what a father is going through, and maybe partake of a little of His wisdom. Those two are the main ones. I have said prayers to, well, I had a chance to go on vacation to Hawaii, and I said a prayer to Hermes that I would have a safe flight, and it went well...But as to having a connection with the other Gods and Goddesses, I would say that Zeus and Athena were the two that I felt closest to.

During the Vietnam War, Herakles took up regular prayer to the Goddess Athena. His prayers weren't necessarily for victory, but for wisdom to dawn upon the Generals and politicians who were driving the fight.

> *Although Ares is the God of war, Athena never lost a battle. And so during that time, and even when there was a chance that I would be going myself, I did say a long prayer to Her. And also to Ares, but primarily to Athena that She would give our men wisdom and our generals good stratagems to keep our men safe and defeat the Viet-cong. And even during the recent conflict, the two wars with Iraq. I did say a prayer. I think Athena has been working overtime on that.*

You're never too old for love. Herakles still seeks the wisdom of Aphrodite in such matters.

> *Ah yes. Goddess of love. I have prayed to Her and not only when I was in my 20's; in 30's 40's 50's and 60's also. Well, I think She did answer my prayers, because...the women I was being attracted to were not right for me. I know that the movies I've seen about Aphrodite always have Her as mainly involved in the sexual aspect of love. But I think She is more than that. She is the Goddess of love—pure, [or] sexual, any aspect that you can think involving love. She is the epitome of what love means. And I still pray to Her that I will find someone to be with in a long-term relationship.*

Herakles' lack of outdoorsiness left him feeling little connection with Artemis. The one time, Herakles says, that he did find need for prayer while enduring the great outdoors, he feels that it was Poseidon who helped most.

> *Well, I haven't prayed that often with Artemis. I was never much of an outdoorsman. So, my father never took me out hunting, when a prayer to Her would have come in handy. The one time when my father did take me out was to do some fishing. At the time, I was maybe 8 or 9, maybe older, maybe younger. But we were in a boat and my line got caught under a boat and for a second I thought I was going to be pulled over into the water. I didn't know how to swim. And I said up a prayer: "I don't want to go in the water." I was afraid of drowning. And I think maybe, well I know this is a stretch, but now looking back I think maybe Poseidon and maybe also Athena calmed my fears that I would be all right. But as I said, I wasn't an outdoors person, so I didn't pray to Artemis...*

The sun-God Apollo is also known for healing, knowledge, and oracular revelation. All three of these seem to have come into play recently in Herakles' relationship with Apollo.

Well, I have to say that I may have prayed to Apollo a couple times when I was having some problems even before my current health issues. I was, I would say the most recent one was last year. About December of 2008 and into January of 2010. I was having some health issues and I was praying to Him...I didn't pray that He would cure me, but what He did was even better. I went to my primary doctor about this problem. He said, well, I think you need to see a specialist. So I went to see a specialist over in Sun City. Anyway, I told him about what my primary care doctor said and he told me, "okay." And he examined me. So he examined me, you know breathe in, breathe out, cough here, cough there, turn left, turn right. And he said, you know, I want you to have some x-rays. So he sent me back and took a bunch of x-rays. And he says, "also you need to have a cat scan." The clinic where he as at also had CT. So I went and had a CT scan. And I waited about forty minutes afterwards and he came back and said, I found a mass in your colon. I want you to go to the emergency room right now: I am going to call over there right now and have them all set up, I'll tell them you are coming. I don't think this is something you can put off. And, well, I went to the emergency room. It was over at Banner Boswell in Sun City. And I told them, and they of course had to do their own tests. The gist of it is that the next morning, I went in for the operation. I had to have part of my colon cut out and they had to reconnect it.

So if I hadn't prayed, and if Apollo hadn't gotten me to go to my primary doctor, I might have, well, yeah... This is not Apollo's, like when something goes wrong people often say, well, it's Christians, Muslims, Jews might say, "oh it's the Devil's fault." But what happened the rest of the year, I never put on onus on Apollo for what happened. I had to have a colostomy bag. I had to wear that for about 6-7 weeks. It was a total disaster mess to the max. Fortunately that was reversed in April. Unfortunately I developed a hernia for that, which was repaired the last day of September. Unfortunately, about 50 days later, I was I the hospital again, this was another Banner facility. Turned out that an ulcer I had had burst and burned a hole in my stomach.

It gets better, if you can believe it. Three days later I was released from the hospital for that operation. I was back in from a second ulcer that was bleeding. I had lost a full unit of blood. I was in ICU for two days and out for four. Then, I developed another hernia which was the operation to repair it that I just went through a month ago. But I think that if Apollo had not quietly, said something…He didn't come right out and say, "This is Apollo. Go to your doctor," like you see in movies. But if He hadn't gotten me to go to the doctor in the first place, you'd be having a very, very, very long distance conversation.

Herakles says that he has never felt the need to call upon Dionysus. "There was a time," Herakles says, "when I would have a few drinks, but thinking back on it even when I knew of the Gods, I never said a prayer to Him. I guess it was that I never felt a need; I never felt a need to call on Him."

When, as a child, Herakles could see his family beginning to have difficulties, he prayed and knew that his prayers had been heard. When he became a polytheist, he came to feel that both Demeter and Hera heard his prayers and helped to help alleviate his family's strife.

Yes. I think, well, I have said a prayer to Hera and Demeter when it seemed that my parents were having some problems with their marriage. When my mother was pregnant with my younger sister, I said a prayer that the pregnancy would go well. And [I prayed] again when she was pregnant with my younger brother. Both of those times, I six, with my youngest sister, and about nine with my younger brother. So I wasn't praying specifically to Demeter, but I think She was watching out, and saw that maybe I was a potential believer. Like I said, when my parents were having marital problems I did pray to Her that the marriage would hold and they would be able to work through their problems. I think She answered me. They were married for 59 years…Lately, I would have to say that I have been saying a prayer to Hera that if I have a future home that it would be stable and blessed and the She would show me just a fraction of Her divinity in that my relationship would last. If not as long as my parents, then as long as I'm still on this earth.

Herakles hasn't prayed to Ares that often. When he has, it has been regarding the need for strength, wisdom, and strategy in America's military actions. Yet when he was younger, Herakles recalls an instance where Ares' help was very much in evidence, even if Herakles himself was too young to realize that. In retrospect, Herakles also believes that Ares hasn't been portrayed in myth and literature as fairly as He deserves to have been.

Ares. Well, like I said when we were talking about Athena. I did pray to Him that He would help our soldiers in battle. Personally, I never called on Him. Okay now, I'm trying to remember now. A lot of these situations which I think the Gods helped me with even though I wasn't at that time an air-quote "believer"...There was a time when I was, well, twelve or thirteen. This was shortly after we, my family, had moved to Arizona. I was in the last year of elementary school I came into conflict with the class bully. I don't know whether it was Ares who helped me or Athena, but I was able to talk my way out of being physically put into a trash barrel. I'm not a physical or violent person, so I don't know whether push came to shove or fist came to face what I would have done. If I would have become overly violent. I hear that people who are the quiet type can become excessively violent when pushed. So, not wanting that and not knowing what would happen, whether I would go overboard, I managed to talk myself out of getting dumped in the trash can. At the time, I wasn't praying to any God or Goddess in particular, just speaking whatever came to my mind and whatever I said worked. But to pray specifically to Ares, I have not done so...

From what I have read in the Iliad and from some things I've read about I Hesiod, Ares was sort of given short shrift. He was the God of war, but He wasn't that popular with the Greeks. I think there is a place for a God of war. The Goddess Athena was excellent in strategies and leadership. But sometimes war is violent, war is bloody, war is something that you don't want to leave to a namby-pamby God.

Herakles prefers the Greek pronunciation of the name, rather than the Latin "Hercules" which is most popularly recognized. The name Herakles translates roughly to "warrior of Hera," which is entirely appropriate given the labors which She assigned Him. Herakles feels tremendous affinity and admiration for this God "because of the trials He had to go through." The God's story is an especially powerfully myth for Herakles.

I know that He killed His sons. To atone for that, He was given into service to His step-brother who was King of Thebes, and it was at that time that He had to perform the 12 labors. And there He was, His madness was gone, and He went on with His life...But at one point, Deianeira was worried that She might be losing Herakles' love, and the centaur, who was not a nice centaur, gave her a cloak and said that "if you give Herakles this cloak, He will love only you." And She was desperate that Herkles would leave her, so She said, "Here, Herakles, my husband, here's this cloak." Herkles was pleased *to get that gift from His wife. So He puts it on, and the cloak was poisoned and started to, I believe, it started to burn Him. And He tried to take it off, but it was, like, stuck to His skin. The more He tried to pull, the harder the skin clung. And He built himself a funeral pyre…He had a bow that He gave to a companion…and told Him to use it in the cause of justice. Herakles laid himself on the pyre and His mortal flesh was burned away and His immortal flesh rose up into Olympus, where He was greeted by His father Zeus, and His step-mother. This is one, I believe, what I remember, I believe that Hera went through a pseudo-pregnancy and Herakles came out from under Her gown and from that moment He was the son of Zeus and Hera. Zeus gave Herakles His daughter Hebe for wife. The young man went on to use that bow in the Trojan war.* *

At present, Herakles' polytheism doesn't have much in the way of ritual practice. He does not have ceremonies to honor the Gods, the ancestors, or the land spirits. One of the side-effects for being so isolated for so long is that it has been hard to learn about what contemporary people are doing to recreate ancient practices.

I think it's primarily because I never knew what rituals were appropriate or what rituals were…my knowledge of the Gods and the Goddesses and how They should be worshipped and what forms of sacrifice were needed isn't strong. I think I remember something I saw in a movie, one of the Steve Reeves Hercules movies. When they were having a celebration I did notice that before they drank the wine, they would pour some of it out onto the earth. I think this was an offering to whichever God they were praying to.

I was never into any type of ancestor worship. Now, my older sister, and she is doing a genealogy of the Moses family and her married name, the Thomas's. She's found that there was a Moses who came over to the US in about 1690 in Massachusetts and another branch of the family form German came over in like, 1750. I know that the Asians go in for ancestor worship, but I never felt a calling in that direction.

When contemplating the way that the Gods are portrayed in the myths, and the way that he has experienced those Gods, Herakles concludes that "there is a lot more to the Gods and Goddess then there's dreamed up in Homer's philosophy." For Herakles, the Gods

---

* The young man was Poeas, Herakles' chief steward. Poeas' son Philoctetes inherited the bow and fought with it during the Trojan war, during which the bow of Herakles was instrumental to the success of the Greeks.

are immense, ineffable.

> *It is, to me, inconceivable for a mortal, no matter how brilliant, to say "this is what the God Hermes is, or the Goddess Aphrodite, or the Goddess Hestia, or any God or Goddess. There is so much more. They are an all-encompassing truth and light. They are each individual, each unique, each in Their own light. I'm without words to describe Them.*

Herakles has labored long and silently to avoid conflicts with those who would not understand his views. He hasn't experienced any real conflict with Pagans or non-Pagans on account of his beliefs. Yet, Herakles is quite pointed in his refusal to use the term "Pagan" as a self-descriptor.

> *Well, the term Pagan, whether it's with a small 'p' or a capital "P" is in my view, a derisive term used by, in my small circle anyhow, Christians, as meaning anyone who isn't Christian, who isn't a believer in a one Deity, that they are outsiders. Even like country bumpkins that just don't know better, and if they knew better then they'd be worshipping this one God. While there is a website I have become familiar with called "The Full Circle—it's a Pagan website—and even there they use the term as not derisive, but most of the people on that site call themselves Wiccan and they are worshipping the earth Goddess. I don't know that much about that aspect of their faith, but to me, I am first and foremost in my belief and my faith, a polytheist. I am not a Pagan. I am not a Christian. I am not a Jew. I am not a Muslim. I also am not a Zoroastrian or a Buddhist or a Hindu. I know that the Hindus are somewhat polytheists themselves and they have many Gods they worship, but my polytheism is for the Olympians, primarily. I do honor and have great respect for the Gods of Egypt, but the Deities I worship are the Olympians.*

Herakles doesn't have a laundry list of things he wishes people understood about polytheism. More than anything, he wishes that people would take a less sinister view of it.

> *It is not worshipping "a" or "the" devil. It is not consorting with demons or anything like that. It is worshipping a family of Gods and Goddesses that brings satisfaction, warmth, a sense of [being a] part of a greater whole…I would also say don't judge a polytheist until you have worshipped his Gods. My Gods are as real to me as any person whose God is real to them.*

Helix

Blogger, editor, and seminary instructor Helix has been a practicing polytheist for over 14 years. She is an initiate in the Anderson Feri/Faery* tradition. In her tradition-specific practice, Helix works with a mentor and occasionally meets for group work with other Faery practitioners. She is also active in her local Pagan community and attends sabbats with an eclectic Wiccan coven. Through her work with Faery, Helix came to have relationships with the Star Goddess and the Peacock God. Independently of Faery, Helix has also built relationships with Kali, Isis, and Brighid.

Helix's definition of polytheism is pretty straightforward.: "Polytheism is the belief in many Gods, straight up." But for Helix, belief alone does not a polytheist make. For her, devotion and ritual practice are implied in the definition, even if they are not explicitly stated.

I tend to add to that definition that it includes religious practice, that it includes honoring, or devotion to, many Gods. Because I believe that belief is not really sufficient to make a polytheist. If belief is not really integrated into some kind of religious life and is just sort of disconnected, then I feel that there's no point in talking about it. I actually have run into folks who are not religious, they're not even particularly spiritual, but they allow the possibility that there are many Gods, and probably are—but it's just not relevant to their lives. A Buddhist will sometimes be technically polytheist, like yes, there are many Gods, but we don't do anything with Them. They don't give offerings, they don't worship, they actually sometimes find the Gods to be a distraction from religious practice. So belief alone doesn't seem to be a useful definition of polytheism, it needs to be both a belief and a practice.

For Helix, 'faith" isn't a belief that the Gods exist. Faith is the conviction that her personal experiences are real, and that her connection to the Gods is real, even if there are times when she can't sense Their presence.

* The tradition's name was originally spelled "Faery." The preferred spelling of "Feri" came into use during the mid-1990s. In 2010, a schism happened which split the community into two major groups. One has retained the "Feri" spelling, and the other decided to reclaim the Andersons' older "Faery" spelling.

I had a really interesting conversation with Galina Krasskova at one point, and she said that "Faith is what gets you through when you can't sense the Gods." Even if I have tangible experiences of my Gods, even on a regular basis, there will be times where it seems that They're not there. Faith is what comes in to get one through those times—faith that those experiences were real, that they continue to be relevant, that they will be repeated, that the current state of feeling no particular spiritual presence is a temporary one.

Faith isn't a word that Helix often uses in reference of her religious practice, because in general it is associated with belief-based religions. Practice is more important to her religion, in Helix's view, than belief is.

"Faith" is not a term I use very much because it is so strongly associated, especially in the States, with belief-based religion. Christianity is very focused on having correct belief, but that is certainly not the case for many religions around the world. Practice is much more important to a many religions then belief, and I think in most contemporary Pagan traditions, practice is more important than belief. Belief and practice are also very connected. It's not like there's a clear dichotomy here. But I tend to use the word faith to mean a state of having belief, and not to use it to describe more practice-based religions. I'm going along with what I feel is the general American usage is of the word faith, and when I do that, I know that there are other definitions of that word. For example, some people use the word "faith" to mean religion. But I think that that can be potentially misleading.

Raised in mainstream Christian life, Helix wasn't exposed to Paganism at an early age. Her frustration about the theological claims of Christianity is what led her to explore other religions. Surprisingly, it was other Christians who pointed out that Helix is Pagan, and those Christians encouraged her to explore that.

Let me think about how far back to go. (Laughs). I was raised as a Protestant Christian. I was raised Methodist. I have nothing bad to say about that. When I was in college, I started to get frustrated with the way that a lot of Christianity seemed to make exclusive claims, like, you know, Christianity really is the one and only way. Liberal Christianity has a tendency to not do that, to be more inclusive, to be more open to the wisdom of other religions. But I was frustrated with the exclusive claims in Christianity as a whole, because that view just seemed ridiculous to me. I started exploring Unitarianism and women's spirituality, but I actually ended up at an extremely liberal Methodist church, which was GLBT-welcoming and earth-centered. They use a lot of Goddess language in worship, and I was pretty comfortable there for a while. But after attending for two or three years, the people there started to tell me that I was Pagan. Not in a, "You're Pagan, so get out," sort of way, but more "This is what you are and how fabulous to have you here" (laughs). And I was attending Pagan festivals at the time too, and reading, and I was aware of eclectic Paganism.

I moved to another city for graduate school, and at that time I shopped around for churches, but none of them was as cool as my last church. I thought, "Maybe it's time for me to actually look for a coven. I've been wanting more magical training. I've been wanting to get more serious about this." So I spent about 2½ years visiting all sorts of local groups. I studied with one Alexandrian coven for about six months, but nothing quite clicked or fit right. Finally, a friend invited me to her Reclaiming tradition witch camp. And when I talked to her about what I was looking for in terms of training, she said I should study with T. Thorn Coyle, who wrote Evolutionary Witchcraft and is a Feri initiate. (The Feri tradition is sometimes also called Faery or Anderson Faery – the two spellings reflect a division in the tradition that, over time, is evolving into two separate traditions. I prefer "Faery" now, but in the mid-2000s, the philosophical differences that have divided the tradition hadn't quite come to a head.) At that point, I was kind of desperate! I pulled about 30 people together, and we organized one of Thorn's distance apprenticeships.

I did that for about two years, for the length of the program, and I continued to study with Thorn in advanced training for 2 or 3 years after that. At which point, I got very tired of distance training. Distance training does have a role. I teach classes online, so I think some topics and skills can be taught really well in a distance format. But for the purpose of studying initiatory witchcraft, distance training didn't have the intimacy or the personal relationship that I was really looking for. I moved across the country a couple of times. I finally connected with a different Faery mentor in person and studied with him for about another year, until I was finally initiated. And that takes me up to the present.

When she first started exploring Paganism and for a number

of years afterward, Helix embraced soft polytheism. It wasn't until she started exploring the Feri tradition that her view shifted to hard polytheism.

> I started out as more of a soft polytheist, by which I mean that the Gods were all aspects of one Divine source. I think even when I was still attending a Christian church and I would have these palpable experiences of the Holy Spirit, I would feel physical sensations like tingling, especially around my head, or just a sense of presence, or a sense of being moved by love or wisdom—rarely anything I could see with my physical eyes.

> Then when I was in college, I started having experiences with a presence that I eventually came to call Kali, which was the closest name I could find for the images that I got from the presence. The impression I got from the presence was that the name was perfectly acceptable. I worked quite a bit with that entity and with that presence in my life for several years. I feel like the Gods come and go, sort of like friends. Your relationships wax and wane. Some of them are very long-term, some of them become very important, and at other times they ebb. She hasn't had as much of a presence in my life since my mid-twenties.

> I continued to have that kind of experience while studying with Reclaiming for a bit, going to camps, and in general Pagan circles. But it was really when I started studying Anderson Faery witchcraft more seriously that I started to have experiences of much stronger personalities than in my earlier years. Much more of a sense of a very separate being, you know, not "Ah, the universe is turning this particular face to me because of my needs and who I am"—because that was my attitude at first. Instead, I was getting a sense that some of the presences I had been experiencing were as unique as the human beings around me. They seemed much closer than those more diffuse experiences that I had earlier, just much more—I don't know, it's hard to describe. Much more distinct.

> In particular, before I was initiated, I had a peer group of people studying Faery who I was working with, and one of us had gotten an intuitive tap to look into the Egyptian mythos, especially Isis. So we were doing research and looking at Her epithets, feeling very intuitively through that process, like this Deity was very much trying to contact us. Eventually, we had a sense that the entity that was tapping us was sort of a primal Isis. We connected with a form that had existed before the very large diffuse Isis that was worshipped throughout the Hellenic

world and developed into the cult of the Virgin Mary, a form from before She had been syncretized with a bunch of other Goddesses including Hathor. She's a very primal, maybe even nomadic Deity.

So we collected all of this information, and received a certain amount of gnosis just doing the research process, and finally we got into circle and called a very specific list of titles and epithets and invoked Her. I got the strongest single sense of presence that I'd ever had, totally terrifying and exhilarating. We got very, very strong images, and some words, and it felt like the top of my head was coming off... a lot of different physical sensations, and when we put out offerings, I visually saw something moving over the offerings as if to accept them, saw with my eyes as opposed to just my mind's eye. So that was profound. I think I was already a polytheist at that point, but I hadn't had many of these kinds of experiences—they had had a lesser impact. This one was notable for how powerful it was and for the relationship it formed afterwards. The sense of presence lingered as we continued to work with that Deity, and I continue to work with Her now. It was definitely a turning point for me.

Religious practice can come in many forms, from large group rituals to individual meditation and everything in between. Helix has found that daily devotional practice is a powerful way to maintain her connection to the Gods.

Most days, I sit down on my altar for a few minutes. I do some prayers for self-alignment and for cleansing, that sort of thing. I usually pour out water or blow a bit of energy into a stone and leave it, or I light a candle. I have a number of Gods that I honor at my altar on a regular basis, and I often make these little offerings every day. I don't necessarily sit there and give Them my whole attention for my entire time at the altar, but I leave Them a little something, I sing Them a little song, I do *something* every day or every other day just to say, "I remember you, I'm thinking of you, here's a present." I tend to think of interacting with Deity as being like cultivating a relationship with a person. People don't become friends unless they call each other up regularly and say hi, or give each other little gifts, take each other out to eat, have each other over and drink tea, stuff like that. So I feel like the attention I give these Beings at my altar is my daily maintenance of those relationships.

When asked to describe her relationships with the Gods, Helix explains that They are "somewhat like a friendship or love relationship." Like all friendships, these relationships are made strong through regular engagement, "the reciprocal giving of gifts and favors, sharing experiences, asking for and receiving advice." Helix does not see the Gods as her superiors, but as "people with different abilities and forms." She does acknowledge that some relationships are "very formal, however, for Deities who are accustomed to being treated like human kings or queens." She recognizes the devotional and educational aspects of her relationships, but does not consider herself "to be fundamentally a 'servant' of the Gods."

Although there is room within the Feri and Faery traditions for many different Deities and many are in fact honored in the tradition, The Star Goddess is perhaps the Deity who was had the greatest impact. Helix admits that she holds a monistic view of the Star Goddess, but she does not assume that this grants her the license to view the Deities simply as interchangeable facets of the Star Goddess.

> My tradition's theology is unsystematic, like most Pagan theology. Not all Feri or Faery witches are going to agree with what I have to say. But there's no dogma in Faery. My understanding of the Star Goddess… This is one area of my theology in which I am kind of a monist. I usually prefer not to anthropomorphize the Star Goddess, because to me She is the fabric of being, and in some ways She's more like "the void" or "nothing" then "something." But She's pervasive, and all beings—including Gods and human beings and everything that is—are a manifestation and emanation of Her.

> So I have retained some of that soft polytheism, but the difference is that I take the individual Gods as seriously and as separately as I do individual human beings, in my practice and how I treat Them. Just because I think that everything is an emanation of the Star Goddess doesn't mean I think you can treat everyone exactly alike and interchangeably. With the Gods, you can't treat one love Goddess exactly the same way that you treat another love Goddess. They're separate beings… Just like you can't treat your sister exactly the same as your best friend. They're different people.

> To me, the Star Goddess is also a lot like the kabbalistic concept of the unknowable God who is all potential. We often refer to Her as God Herself to emphasize that She is both masculine and feminine and everything in between. One of the founders of my tradition, Victor Anderson, would say "the clitorophallic

God Herself"… So, She is everything. Many Feri witches do work with Her in a much more anthropomorphized way, as a specifically personality-having Goddess. But that's not usually the way that I work with Her.

Another very important divinity in the Feri and Faery traditions is the Peacock God. Through her work with the Peacock God, Helix began to understand both the freedom and the consequence of moral choices, and how these choices impact one's ability to maintain spiritual autonomy.

Many of the people in my tradition work with the Peacock God, who comes originally from the Yezidi people. The Yezidi are an ethnic group who live in Iran and are horribly persecuted. They have their own religion, and the Muslim Iranians really don't like them—the think of them as devil-worshippers. One of the stories the Yezidi have about the Peacock is this. Long before the Yezidi were a people, there was once a shepherd standing by a swamp. As the shepherd stood, a spirit of good, a sort of angelic being, threw down a peacock from heaven, and the peacock lay broken and bleeding on the ground. The shepherd saw this, and he took the peacock home to his cave and tended to His wounds. In the morning, the peacock was fully healed. Then the peacock said to the shepherd, "As a reward for what you have done for me, I will implant the great conflict in your heart and in the hearts of all your descendants." And He went away.

The way I understand the "great conflict" is knowledge of good and evil. Basically, it's a different telling of the story in the Bible of eating the fruit of the tree of knowledge—developing the capacity for moral choice—and this is why the Peacock was thrown out of heaven by "a spirit of good," for whom the possibility of choosing evil is a problem. Moral choice was the gift of the peacock to the shepherd, who then became the progenitor of the Yezidi people.

The Peacock God, in my tradition, is connected to the principles of pride and spiritual autonomy. We have a principle of not submitting our life force to others—which is not to say that we can't be in relationships with unequal power dynamics, because nearly all relationships have them. Power dynamics are not inherently unhealthy. But we cannot choose to be slaves or otherwise permanently give up our autonomy, and the Peacock God is connected with that. He's also a spirit of beauty, because of the gorgeous peacock feathers—He shows us how to be beautiful and proud of it when we go out into the world, how to hold ourselves like kings and queens. But the Peacock God can also be a trickster, He can have even be destructive if His influence isn't properly balanced in a context of love. The shadow of pride is arrogance. I don't want to say too much more about my tradition's theology right now, but Cora Anderson, one of the founders, published several books on the tradition, and Victor Anderson was also interviewed a number of times while he was alive. That's where I'd point anyone who wants to know more.

Helix has had a relationship with Kali for a number of years, although that relationship isn't as active as it once was. From Kali, Helix first began to recognize that the Gods are simultaneously immense, all-encompassing, transcendent forces, and immanent, individual, personal Divinities.

That's not a very active relationship for me right now, but when I was younger, She was the first non-Christian entity I had a relationship with. And, again, Kali was just sort of the best name that I could come up with for Her, and the response that I always got with that name was, "That's an acceptable name." But I often got imagery from Her that didn't quite fit with the Hindu Kali, and I was reading quite a bit about Kali at this point. One of the things that's interesting to me about Kali is that like many Deities in contemporary Paganism, She can be very large and diffuse, or She can be relatively small and personal.

In India, Kali is worshipped as one of the creators of the universe. Her black skin represents the void of space from which all things come. Her tongue sticks out because She's enunciating the Sanskrit syllables that bring creation into being, and at the end of time everything will be devoured by Her and the universe will return to its original state of potential. So She's big on that level, and associated with Being itself. But She's also worshipped almost like the Virgin Mary. Some of Her devotees have a very personal, very loving, very caring, sometimes protective relationship with Her, where they will lovingly wash Her image and bring Her offerings of food and flowers. I particularly remember reading about a devotee who did not like the imagery of the belt of severed arms that is usually around Her waist. She said, "I don't like the idea of men's hands on Her, because She is ultimately a virgin; She's complete in herself, a woman unto Herself." I thought that was very interesting…

My relationship with Her moves back and forth between an intimate relationship where I feel very personally spoken to, and experiencing Her as a vast natural force that's just completely beyond my comprehension. I think that pops up in other religions, too. If you look at the Jewish tradition, you get God as the creator who is very transcendent, very outside the world, who speaks creation into being. But you also get God who walks in the Garden of Eden in the cool of the evening and talks personally with Adam and Eve. So there's that difference there, too. You know, the very big Gods who are associated with the ALL, and these very personal Gods who sit with you in your living room. I think that polytheism is an orientation towards that smaller, more intimate form of Deity, but it doesn't exclude having a relationship with the larger ones.

Brighid is a much-loved Goddess who has garnered many devotees, one of whom is Helix. While many honor Brighid as a healer or mother, Helix has also worked artistically with Her.

Just briefly about Brighid. I've worked with several different Gods as healers, but I've worked with Her both as a healer and as a poet. She is one of the easier Deities to be around. Some of the Deities I work can be fierce and scary and difficult, and Brighid has a comforting side, which is nice. The Star Goddess can be very loving, but as I said, I don't often work with Her in an anthropomorphized way. She's usually very big, but Brigid can be like my mom. She has a fierce warrior side, too, though. One of those nice things about polytheism is that it's like having a broad range of friends, you don't have to go to any one Deity for all of your needs.

From her study of Faery witchcraft, Helix learned the importance of ancestors, land spirits, and elemental spirits. She incorporates all three into her religious practice.

Well, I developed both of those after beginning to study Faery witchcraft, and I've noticed that there are definitely some forms of witchcraft that draw more strongly on historical roots than others. The more that I've studied the witchcraft branches that consider themselves traditional witchcraft, the more important it has become to work with the land spirits, the ancestors, and the Fey. I don't know if I really distinguish between the land spirits and the Fey. They're pretty much the same thing to me.

Ancestor work is just fundamental, without my ancestors I wouldn't be here, literally and physically. Their history and their experiences affect me today…partially because we have the same

DNA; there are a lot of hereditary traits that are passed. And secondarily, because patterns in families repeat themselves, and that's just a psychological fact. There is a wonderful counseling tool called the geneagram, by which you chart emotional patterns in your family over generations, and that's been a really revealing tool for me to use. Trauma patterns tend to repeat themselves in families until somebody resolves them. In my Craft tradition, I've been taught that if you resolve a trauma pattern—or a problem or a complex or whenever word you want to use for it—for yourself, you resolve it for your ancestors and heal the entire ancestral line. So some of the work that I do is for healing myself and my ancestors, so that my descendants don't have to suffer from the same repeating patterns in my family line. So that's one of the points of ancestor work.

But more fundamentally, it's just about knowing myself and connecting to beings that love me and are interested in my well-being in the world. My ancestors are out there rooting for me. And they have love and they have wisdom to share if I reach out to them. I would say that my ancestors are not as strong a presence in my life as Deity, but I haven't been cultivating that kind of relationship for as long. I definitely have had some strong ancestral contact; it's just a process. My dad is an amateur genealogist, and his research has been really helpful to me in learning a lot more about my ancestors. He has wonderful stories. I just find that enriching. As for the land spirits, again, I don't have a relationship with them that is as strong as with Deity.

I've done some interesting work with the emergent spirits of cities. I live in Boston right now and I find it a very difficult place to live. Cities have an aura or energy field, and I always feel the plane kind of hit that aura when I'm flying into Boston—my stomach lurches, or sometimes I get weepy. Boston is angry and driven and dirty and overcrowded—there are a lot of exciting things going on here too—but that negative energy is very strong and it comes out in the constant road rage and the miserable expressions on people's faces when you ride public transportation and such. I don't really have answers about how to work with an angry Deity, because the spirits of cities are pretty big, and I found that Boston—well, she's difficult. She seems really angry at having millions of people living in a space that was originally designed for, at most, hundreds of thousands. My being aware of the city's energy helps to keep me from getting swept up in it. I try to keep myself relaxed and calm, not get swept up in the crazy Protestant work ethic that everyone seems to be driven by here. I also leave offerings for the spirits that live in my yard. There are some, but I'm not entirely sure that there are any responsive spirits who live there consistently. I live in the middle of the city, in a very urban area, and I do have a little yard with plants and trees, so I try to make it a friendly place for spirits to live. I haven't gotten very much response. I don't know. It's a rough neighborhood. So, I do the best I can, frankly.

It's not like I feel that the presence of humans drives all land spirits away—but really densely populated areas, especially where people are leaving trash all over the place, and there a lot of fights, and they're just constantly occupied by humans who are putting out a lot of negative energy, I find it can be really hard to contact the land spirits. It's a lot easier if I go out, even just to a farm, but even better if I go out to a place that's not regularly occupied by human beings—then it's a lot easier to sense them. I was in Ireland recently, and we visited some places where there was such a strong sense of the presence of the land spirits. This kind of uncanny quiet, and a sense of losing track of how time was running…we went to some forests that were just soaked in fey energy.

Mythology plays an interesting role in Helix's relationships with the Gods. According to Helix, one of the most important things she does when beginning a new relationship with a Deity is reinterpreting that Deity's origin myth.

Often when I contact Deity for the first time, the first thing that happens is that I receive a retelling of Their origin myth. And I think this is just me, this is something that I'm interested in and that's why I tend to get this particular information. But I often get a series of images that relate to that Deity's most famous myth, with a different interpretive spin. Very interesting. The first time I ever met Persephone in ritual, I got a spin on Her origin story that had a very dominant/submissive vibe…and also strong sense that even though She had not gone to the underworld willingly the first time—or not entirely willingly anyway—that as the relationship developed in the underworld, it became Her who really has the upper hand over Hades.

I don't know if it's mostly that the Gods change—though I think They do change—or that They reveal different parts of

Themselves to different people. Maybe it's both. Victor Anderson, one of the founders of my tradition, used to say that the Gods come to us wearing Their party hats; They dress up and present Themselves in a given ritual or to a given person in a way that is appropriate for that person in that context. So, the stories change. I do find that when I contact a Deity that there is some kind of relationship between how the Deity is and how They are [presented] in the myth I already know. But They usually have something to say about those myths. It's the same as when you're meeting a person for the first time. You may have heard stories about Them, but how They strike you in person may be quite different.

Helix hasn't personally experienced much conflict with non-Pagans regarding her emphasis on hard polytheism, because she hasn't felt moved to explain her beliefs to them. Helix prefers to maintain a useful and open dialogue, which she has found often involves discussing soft polytheist views of Deity.

I have spent a great deal of time around liberal Christians, and I just haven't felt like it was particularly important to really explain polytheism to them. Like, hard polytheism vs. soft. Soft polytheism is usually immediately graspable to them. There is a fairly famous Protestant theologian named Sallie McFague, and she's done some great work around the idea that people need many images of the Divine. They need multiple images of God. And of course, she's a monotheist, but she believes in experiencing God in many, many different ways: as a mother, as a father, as a nurturer, as a warrior, all these different ways of experiencing God. But she thinks of it as God revealing him/herself in many different ways to many different people at many different times. Whereas, hard polytheism is more that the Gods are indeed separate, not one God revealing Him- or Herself in many ways. They're different Gods.

So I've often talked about soft polytheism with liberal Christians, and they usually understand that instantly. That provides a place to dialogue fruitfully. Many liberal Christians are also panentheists, even if they don't necessarily know that term. They think that the Divine is in the world as well as beyond the world. I'm usually talking to liberal Christians about our shared areas of interest: environmentalism, GLBT rights, civil liberties—all that good stuff. There's usually not a lot of reason to try to go into my actual practice and the way I think about the Gods, because it would just confuse them. I don't think it would really teach them anything helpful. Because that's not the way that they experience God, generally speaking. So, if somebody asks me very directly, I'll certainly tell them about my practice, but it's not usually something I bring up

Liberal Christians especially are suspicious of direct gnosis— if you're saying "such and such Deity told me this and that," they'll take it as a mental illness. And they associate hearing the voices of Gods with fundamentalist Christians: "God told me to…" I don't know, "beat up my Muslim neighbor" or whatever. They associate hearing the voices of Gods with violence. They're open to the idea that one receives general messages from God about love, but if you're actually having conversations with the Gods, liberal Christians are like, "Do you need a psychiatrist?" (Laughs). I don't usually find trying to have that conversation worthwhile, because I don't feel it will benefit either of us to go into a full explanation. I feel private about my practice. Even talking about it here feels a little bit vulnerable. I made the comparison…that my spiritual practice is kind of like my sex life. I may talk about my sex life to certain other people who are interested, but I'm not going to go out and discuss it with just anyone. It's just—to me, it's kind of asking for trouble. It's not necessarily going to lead to greater understanding, at least not at this point…I try to be a positive face of Paganism for non-Pagans, and part of the way I maintain that credibility is by not pushing them too far, too fast with information that they have no context for.

Conflicts regarding polytheism have erupted from time to time in the Pagan community, but Helix recognizes that it is much more important for Pagans to remember what all they have in common and respect each other rather than to overemphasize their differences.

I am a little annoyed at how much trouble folks are going to separate soft from hard polytheist in the Pagan community right now. I think that there are valid distinctions to be made, and it's an interesting discussion to have, but I feel like the hard polytheists spend a lot of time poo-pooing the soft polytheists for being fluffy-bunny, wishy-washy, blah, blah, blah. I don't think that's helpful. I always think that infighting within minority groups is a waste of energy. Even though I have a hard polytheist practice, I don't think that the soft polytheists need to be dragged kicking and screaming to my supposedly superior point of view. Part of that is because I have some flexibility along that range, there are ways in which I look at the world and a soft polytheist way, and ways in which I act in a hard polytheist way. So one of the things that I wish Pagans would understand about these distinctions is that I don't think the line between hard and soft polytheism is actually obvious and clear. I think there's a range there that has to do with behaviors.

The other thing is, I feel like I do associate certain kinds of polytheist practice with being kind of nuts. I don't do what the Gods tell me to do, simply because They're Gods. I take messages I get from the Gods as seriously as I would take advice from friends, and the degree of trust I put into each of Them is based on how much of a relationship we've had, and what kinds of experiences I've had with Them in the past. I take what I receive with a certain amount of salt, and I submit it to discernment. That's the kind of relationship I have with the Gods. I do feel like there are definitely Pagans out there who may or may not be receiving messages from various entities, but they have not vetted Them well. It's like taking advice from your crazy alcoholic friend. It's not good. I feel Paganism really has a long way to go when it comes to emotional maturity, as a movement. That makes me reluctant to discuss my practices too openly.

Kiya

Kiya, 33, works as the editor for Immanion Press. She is syncretic and eclectic in her approach to religion. Her "primary public affiliation is with Egyptian reconstruction (or Kemeticism)." Some of her Kemetic scholarship was published as <u>The Traveller's Guide to the Du'at</u>. She is also a student in of the Blackheart line of Feri, which she characterizes as "ecstasy-oriented, liminal, and spirit-work driven approach to the Craft rather than the more common fertility-and-polarity focus of Wicca-derived traditions." Kiya's "personal practice" is a Craft tradition which is "increasingly broad-based." It features "fairy-faith elements," and is informed by her "interest in trying to rediscover old European spirit-work practices, particularly from the areas from which my ancestors came." Kiya primarily works with are Hetharu (Hathor), Set, Wepwawet (Ophois), Khnum, Nut, Djehwty (Thoth) and the Feri Powers. Kiya explains that "I also honor several other Powers, though for the most part that is 'I honor Them' rather than 'I work with Them.'" Her household acknowledges the Celtic Gods because one of her husbands is a Celtic Pagan. "Of late," Kiya says, "among the most important parts of my practice has been dealing with the linked realms of the ancestors, the nature spirits, and the Good Folk."

Kiya's religious practice is well-balanced between group rituals and personal rites. Her ritual circle "is an ecumenical group." Her group is made up of "a Celtic recon fostering with Taoist mysticism, a neo-shaman with training in lineaged Crow tribe spiritual practices, an environmentalist-spirituality Reform Jew, and someone probably best described as a seeker with Heathen leanings." The group is newly formed and still building a shared ritual praxis, although each member has individual responsibilities to take care of. Kiya's Kemetic practice "is largely solitary," although she does at times include "one of the children who is old enough to participate in rituals." While her practice is solitary, Kiya does see herself as involved in the larger Kemetic community because her research "[supplies] a broader community with ritual practice." She considers her Craft line to be her "extended family" and attends gatherings with them, making a special effort to attend the major yearly communal gathering which draws members from as far away as Germany. Kiya explains that she does share significant parts of her spiritual practice with one of her husbands, although they "do not share a specific named religion." He is part of her newly formed ritual circle, and Kiya says that their shared practice "draws from threads shared between our religions, our personal inclinations in relationship, and our mutual support."

Kiya's not sure that she's "ever not been a polytheist," but notes that it "hasn't always mattered." For her, there just wasn't a time when polytheism "didn't seem like an obvious and intuitive response to the world." She was raised in a monotheist household, but religion wasn't terribly emphasized. "My basic assumption of polytheism," she says, "became a matter of more active belief when I was fourteen or fifteen." In church, Kiya listened to Bible stories "in which people were visited by their God, who had messages or guidance for them," and her reaction was that if she was going to have a God, she says "I wanted one who would take a personal interest in me, too."

> *I was raised sort of generically Christian. Neither of my parents are particularly religious, but my father's form of non-religion is Anglican and my mother's form of non-religion is Catholic. I attended a Methodist church as a child, and we celebrated Christmas and Easter more or less secularly. My drift away from mainstream religion was completely unremarkable and largely uninteresting to my parents.*

> *Some of my earliest religious thoughts were of feeling isolated and a bit alienated in a Christian church service, and figuring that if that God didn't want to talk to me, I should hold out for a God that did...Interestingly, I recently was reminded that when I was maybe about eleven or so my father gave me a tape of some Andean folk music, which included a praise song for the Andean Goddess, Pachamama. I think that was one of the first serious confirmations I had that people still cared about the pantheons. This realization has led me to honoring Pachamama monthly, in thanks for the way Her people guided me.*

> *I was introduced to modern Paganism sometime around the age of fourteen or fifteen—in 1992 or 1993—through some introductory Wiccan outer court books. I was nominally polytheist and attempting to wedge it into duotheism from then on, eventually settling into genuine polytheistic practice in my early twenties...I just find—and found—it much easier to deal with a theological system that's structured in a manner that appears to make some sense. Monotheism feels profoundly paradoxical in improbable ways to me, ranging from the cosmological through the biological, and does not appear consistent with the universe I observe. Now, a form of*

*emanationist monotheism that produces a wide variety of lesser
Powers could be consistent, but at that point the original
emanating power becomes effectively irrelevant.*

The idea of belief doesn't play into Kiya's definition of
polytheism because she "hate[s] hate the Christian-hegemonic
obsession with 'belief'." She defines polytheism as "a religious
practice that honors...multiple Gods, most particularly one—and/or
its associated theological structure—which posits multiple Gods of
similar levels of power and effectiveness." She is also careful to
distinguish "between systems with one 'ultimate God' and then an
assortment of Gods and Powers which are significantly lesser in
capacity than the ultimate one."

"Faith" is not a word Kiya uses much, and she is willing to
define it only so far as to say that the word faith connotes "trust." On
the occasions in which she is pressed to use the word "faith," she only
does so in a context where she's "thinking of the Greek verb 'pisteuo,'
in which 'faith' is the verb, is itself an action or thing done,' as
opposed to "the more passive English construction '[to] have faith'."
Because of its connotations of belief, Kiya does not "typically use the
word in its meaning roughly synonymous with 'religion,'" because she
does not "think it appropriate to describe Pagan religions with that
terminology."

> *"Faith," when used to refer to Gods, is most often at least
> connotationally talking about the process of maintaining belief
> and trust in the existence of that God in the absence of evidence
> for Their presence. And that as a process doesn't really have any
> particular role in my practices. However, on the level in which
> the Gods are immanent and essential to the function of the
> cosmos in some way, the fact that the cosmos behaves accordingly
> is sufficient demonstration of Their existence as to move it out
> of the realm of "faith" in this regard. On the level in which
> there is personal mystical, ecstatic, or otherwise observational
> experience of the God in question, likewise, "faith" seems an
> inappropriate word.*
>
> *In the case of the divine Powers where I have a personal
> relationship, that faith is maintained in much the same way it is
> maintained with more simply corporeal entities: I have faith
> that people I know will behave according to their natures, that
> they will keep their agreements, and so on.*
>
> *I have maintained shrines and made offerings to Powers where I
> did not have a personal relationship; in those cases I placed faith
> in the expectation that my gifts were received. In one specific*

case, I have a moderate level of belief that the assistance I was petitioning for was given to me, but there was no ecstatic revelation.

Upon her introduction to Paganism, Kiya did spend some time honoring the Goddess and God of Wicca. Her first inkling that there might be separate, distinct Gods came because she discovered that although the Goddess she worked with didn't mind being worshipped in the abstract, her God most certainly did.

I went through a period, primarily in my teens, of trying to deal with religious things through a pop-cultural Wiccan framework, with The Goddess and The God and all that structure. My Lady did not object to this structure per se, but the God that I perceived as present in my important mystical work was having no part of it. For a while I tried to get access to that divine presence primarily through pursuit of … shall we say unstable and not well-chosen relationships. Looking for a theophany of a God of chaos in a boyfriend does not lend itself to stable relationship, I found.

I eventually drifted away from that model, though I didn't stop trying to make it work in some fashion for quite some time. I tried several systems without finding one that really clicked, until I stumbled across the Egyptian reconstructionism and found not only a coherent polytheistic theology but that I could match my experiences of the Gods to specific names within that theology. After that point I gave up on trying to do the Wicca-ish duotheism thing entirely, with a great deal of relief.

Kiya is somewhat reluctant to discuss her relationships with her Gods. This reluctance comes, in part, because it is difficult to describe the ineffable. But even more to the point, Kiya feels that these relationships are very personal and very private and generally not open for discussion.

As I've gotten more and more involved in devotional mysticism it has become more and more difficult for me to be comfortable talking directly about the Gods and my personal interactions with Them.

I have in the past assembled immense lists of 'God as…' roles that I am familiar with from historical studies and the practices of other people, mostly because I knew people who could use the help shaking free of assumptions of what it means to be a God and what the relationships are between Gods and people.

I have simple devotional "I make this offering just because" relationships with some Gods. I have relationships where I feel that I am doing the work of that particular God in the world in some fashion. I have more engaged familial relationships with Gods. I don't know, there's a wide range of potentiality and sometimes it's hard to explain things, which is I suspect part of why it's becoming increasingly inappropriate for me to talk about it.

This reticence to discuss her Gods extends somewhat to describing her ritual practice. Because the time and energy demands of being a parent are so great, Kiya does not observe many ritual practices. A primary consideration for Kiya is how to make her day-to-day life a devotional offering to her Gods.

My formal rituals are largely in the Egyptian reconstructionist mode, commonly attempts to adapt ancient liturgies and temple ritual to personal use. I do very few formal rituals…Most of my honor-and-communing is done with action within the spheres of interest of my Gods: as a mother with important familial ties to a mother Goddess, I honor Her in part by raising my children well. There isn't a lot of space in my life for ceremonialism, even if I put a lot of value on it, just because the demands of being the primary caregiver are so immense.

Myth plays a role in many people's relationships with the Gods. While Kiya says that "I have never known a myth to be 'wrong,'" she has "known understanding of those myths to be misleading."

Myths are funny things. And, within the context of my Egyptian affiliation, we have very few surviving myths arranged in story format. That narrative focus was imposed on the scraps we have by the Greeks, who also reinterpreted some of the stories into a more Hellenic form.

The thing about myths is that each of them contains nuggets of understanding about the Gods, which can be unlocked like puzzles over time and experience and with a good understanding of the structure of the story and its imagery. But that's not going to be complete, because each puzzle is a facet; each mention unlocks a different piece, and then there's the next level of puzzle, that posed by the many facets thus revealed, and so on.

Kiya reveals that she has at times experienced conflict between herself and others on account of her polytheism. Some of her conflict has been in relation to other polytheists.

My experience with religious discussions with non-polytheists is that they are very, very heavily engaged in a monotheistic paradigm. Including people whose actual identification is as atheists. Thus…they frequently refuse to engage with or acknowledge contributions from polytheists.

I was once asked—by an atheist—"What's the point in worshipping a God that's not omnipotent?" and I was left with this vast chasm between anything that made sense to me and what must make sense to that person, and not the slightest idea of how one might manage to bridge that gap. As if love, or personal relationship, or honoring a power because They have the virtues of Their flaws and the flaws of Their virtues, or respect for the principles that a God puts forth meant nothing compared to theoretical wish-granting capability. I just…I left that conversation because there was no way to have it.

Right at the moment, I feel much more in conflict with other polytheists because of the things that they assume that polytheism necessarily also means, such as lying about people with different theological positions, or insufficiently dogmatically correct approaches to the same theologies, and otherwise being an asshole, so I'm not sure I can answer that usefully. If I set that current-moment frustration aside, I will note that I have a lot of default baseline disaffection from much of the Pagan movement, though that is not merely a polytheism thing. I don't have a lot theologically in common with the most common expectations of what Paganism means, and it's too exhausting to deal with it, so I mostly don't.

When asked if there was anything she wished other people understood about polytheism, Kiya answers, "That it's actually polytheistic, for one. That it's not 'the mother Goddess who is Jesus in drag', or 'the Lady and the Lord' or 'all Gods are one God and all Goddesses are one Goddess' or that kind of thing." Kiya recognizes polytheism to be "a system in which there are a plurality of figures and personalities out there, and gender is one minor trait about which They may differ, just like ordinary embodied people."

Elaine

Elaine, a 27-year-old video game designer and writer, has only recently come to identify as a polytheist. Her training in philosophy is integral to her materialist worldview, and it wasn't until she began to explore the more psychological aspects of religion that she became comfortable with it. While she has certainly learned a lot from Jung and Hillman, Elaine stops well short of identifying the Gods as simply being archetypes. It's true that she has found it very important to retain an intellectual agnosticism and objectivity regarding any literal view of the existence of the Gods and Goddesses. However, she also recognizes the significance of the emotional and spiritual connections she has with Them and honors Them despite her rationalist perspective. She has found that there are certain questions better addressed to the spirit than the intellect, and her actions proceed from that conviction. Elaine regards writing as a sacred vocation and thinks of her work as a writer as being very much devotional in nature. Elaine's primary relationships are with Artemis, Hermes, Apollo, and Dionysus, but she honors other Greek Deities and Egyptian Deities as well as the Deities of Thelema,* which she has been studying for several years.

In terms of her understanding of the word "polytheism," Elaine emphasizes the plurality and multiplicity inherent in the term. She recognizes individuality even as she acknowledges an underlying connection between the Deities.

> *I guess the concept of the Divine in plural would be how I personally understand "polytheism." I know that there are probably some polytheists who don't agree with me on that. But...as a philosophy major I think of it in terms of "the one" and "the many" question, it would be the Divine in terms of the many. Seeing it in terms of that particular way...I am Hinduesque regarding my stance toward the Divine. I don't think Jehova and Zeus are in any way *interchangeable*, but I believe that experientially, some people experience the Divine as*

---

* The Greek word for will is "thelema." As such, Crowley thought it would be the perfect name for his magico-religious tradition. Thelema, Crowley believed, would carry humanity out of the age of Osiris, characterized by restriction, repression, and the worship of a dying, slain God, and into the age of Horus, characterized by the freedom to develop and enact one's "True Will" and the worship of a resplendent young solar God. Henrik Bogdan and Martin P. Starr, <u>Aleister Crowley and Western Esotericism</u> (Oxford: Oxford University Press, 2012), 5-6.

unity and others as plurality.

Elaine defines faith as "as a decision to accept a premise, an idea, even though you may have some ambiguity about whether it's valid or true or not." Her understanding of the term is greatly influenced by her readings of Richard Rorty and William James.

> *Richard Rorty is a pragmatist. His pragmatism means that faith actually doesn't actually matter all that much to him. It's about the value of the idea in the idea of practice itself. So, for me, just sort of going through all of this extra theological thinking that I have had to do to accept my religion and practice it, that was sort of an important concept. Because I grew up with "faith," but it just wasn't very helpful. It sort of seemed to be a roadblock. So for Rorty, I think it's…my understanding of what he's saying is that the value of the experience of the Divine is important. There can be more than one experience and it can even contradict itself...Essentially, I'm of the William James school regarding faith. It's as good as the "cash value" of the experience.*

Elaine first came to polytheism through her writing and her love of literature and ancient philosophy. As a writer, Elaine says she recognizes a certain plurality in her own personality, and so the idea of the Divine also having many distinct personalities made a lot of sense for her.

> *I'm a writer, and I have a writer persona, I guess. I don't think of myself as actually being one person, which I realize is probably a little bit strange. But that's sort of how it's always been to me. When I was really young, I got really into games of pretend and things like that. So the idea of there being multiple Gods just made a lot of intuitive sense to me. Later on, how I got into polytheism, in the—for lack of a better word—Pagan sense; I was aware of Paganism. Like every other person in the Pagan world I was into Wicca for like, a month, when I was fourteen and so I sort of vaguely knew about it. So it was sort of only recently in the last few years that I realized that there were polytheists per se. The reconstruction movement wasn't something I was aware of until I happened [up]on it on the internet and then did a bunch of digging…*

> *For a long time I was very drawn to metaphorical and philosophical depictions of the Gods, such as Robert Calasso's "Literature and the Gods" and Nietzsche's "Birth of Tragedy." This took a very spiritual, religious tone for me, at*

times. So the Gods were part of my thinking before I began calling myself a polytheist, and my experience as a polytheist is still flavored with that poetic sensibility.

Elaine's relationships with the Gods are influenced by her understanding of stories as sacred things and the act of storytelling to be a sacred event. For Elaine, storytelling is similar to religion because both are deeply related to how humans make meaning of their lives.

Some of the myths just seem really—I think sometimes that followers of Hera must really have a problem with that because in so many of the myths She's portrayed as an this unrepentant bitch. But that can't be the only reality, and there's more to the myths than that, too...Often I've found that I have my own insights about Them, my own experiences with Them. The myth may not make sense in light of my experiences right away, but a year down the line, I'll have some other experience or insight. I try not to discount myth. The one thing I like about polytheism in general is that the Gods are so incredibly complex and multifaceted. There are so many layers and you can never really get to the essence of Them. I try to not get too hung up on it. I try to let the Gods speak to me about who They are.

I have a lot of theorizing that I've done about why stories are sacred, but I don't really "know," I just sort of feel the sacred when I'm experiencing a story. Jung is sort of helpful in that he describes how the stories can be expressing really deep experiences you've had that can't really be described in any kind of direct way. A lot of these deep experiences are Divine in nature. I don't really know what that means, or how we know that they're Divine, but it's definitely a sense that you get. There's also another layer in that. I guess that stories—especially mythological stories—are so...they just seem to reveal something about the inner workings of the universe. I think that's something we've always associated with religion. The idea that religion can reveal this hidden structure that's there or these hidden forces at work that are there. And I certainly think stories can do that sort of thing too. And then there's also how the closest thing I have ever come to a conversion experience was when I was studying the romantics. Their idea of Divine inspiration is also very influential for me. Again, that's not really something that we can intellectually describe. It's just really very much like being overcome by a muse of poetry. I think that...we derive meaning from the same techniques we use to create stories: editing memories, preserving very vivid or unusual memories, connecting memories together. I think that has to do with their sacredness, though at the moment I do wonder if "the sacredness of stories" isn't a bit cliché. Storytelling can also get in the way of experiencing something on its own terms. But more to the point, I suppose that in this sense, I'm very drawn to Alan Moore's imagery of the world as a story the Gods create. You can put me in his camp on these matters, at least.

When describing her experiences with the Deities, Elaine pointedly divides herself into the roles of agnostic philosopher and religious practitioner. More than anything, her splitting of perspective demonstrates that the spiritual power of polytheism is not based on belief, but on practice.

I definitely had, well, I have my philosopher hat that I put on sometimes and in that sense I'm definitely agnostic. I don't know for sure. But when I'm a religious practicioner, I can definitely say yes to that question, in the sense that I definitely had experiences where it's nothing that I could have ever imagined and I felt that a God was responding to me or talking to me or communicating with me…I've definitely had experiences, and I have definitely had overwhelming experiences that have confirmed for me that if nothing else, this is definitely a path worth pursuing.

Elaine's practice involves the veneration of several Deities. She admits that "[t]rying to understand how to fit all of these Gods into my life is challenging. Generally, once I've established a relationship, I feel quite guilty if I don't keep it up." One thing that helps is that she sees the Gods as being more or less Divine people, and thinks of Them as friends. In these friendships, "certain periods are more distant than others, and often, when the time is right, one of us will reach out and revisit the connection anew." One of the oldest friends Elaine has is the Goddess Artemis.

Artemis is really an important Goddess to me because She is the first Goddess I ever felt a connection to. Probably really the first Divine figure I felt a connection to. For a lot of personal reasons. When I was really young, I was really into Peter Pan, so when I found out about this Goddess who never wanted to grow up, who ran in the forest with the crazy retinue of nymphs and huntresses. Like, that seemed really cool. This one actually, I think, counts as an experience. I dressed up as Her for Halloween one year. I felt really weird the whole time I was dressed up as Her. It was like, I acted very different. My mom noticed that I was...not that I was acting like Artemis, but my Mom noticed that I was acting very solemn. I definitely had this sense that I was doing something important or that I was doing something very serious. That dovetails very nicely with the fact that Artemis is a Goddess of independence and She is very self-possessed and self-contained. So to me She was always, well, first. In my own practice I honor Her first before I honor the other Gods. I'm not sure why that's important. I always go to Her when I'm experiencing self-doubt or I'm feeling this need to return to the core of myself.

Athena is another Goddess Elaine reveres. As an artist, Elaine doesn't necessarily identify strongly with Her, but she honors Athena for governing those aspects of life that are important to a healthy, well-functioning, community.

Athena I got into, I felt really close to Her in my teens when I was discovering philosophy. She, well...I don't have as many direct experiences with Her. I definitely studied the great classics in college and that was really important to me, and She rules over that whole endeavor. She's always a Goddess of heroic patronage. Which is important to me in certain ways. I, like, for me when I do "Athena" acts, I read philosophy, I try to do something important for my community, I try to be brave. I also really like Her because She's the Goddess of heroes, sort of. She takes them under Her wing and inspires them. That's something I really enjoy about Her. Doing that sort of think, like, trying to make my community a better place and being brave are important to me.

I'm not as close to Athena as I once was, though I wouldn't be surprised if that changed. As my path in life becomes more set down that of an artist, I'm drawn to Gods that are, in certain respects, Her opposite (being as close to Dionysos as I am now, that's somewhat inevitable!). But I'm very fascinated by Athena, and the cultural circumstances of Her worship—for instance, the scene where She's invoked in the Oresteia has so much to say about gender, justice, the evolution of society. That's probably a somewhat weird basis for a relationship with a Goddess, but there you are.

She's also important in my life because She isn't directly relevant to a lot of my stated ambitions. Community, ethics, and law are a part of the life of anybody who has a place in society. It seems to me that polytheists in older times would have had a God to govern every aspect of their lives, and now people tend to focus more on a few Gods who inspire them. I'm sure that's fine in some ways, but the presence of a Divine... Power? Potentiality? Dimension? Not sure what the word is... can be a very potent thing to experience in realms that aren't as significant to you personally and I try to cultivate it. Athena reminds me of my duties to the greater world, the greater community.

Elaine's relationship with Apollo has posed some strong personal growth challenges for her. Although her relationship with Apollo isn't easy, Elaine says that He is absolutely crucial to her work philosophically and artistically.

Apollo is a really...He's a God that's very concerned with purity, and I'm a very messy person. This makes things a little difficult...I came to Apollo through Nietzsche's "Birth of Tragedy." The Apollonian/Dionysian dichotomy. It was a pretty influential idea. Apollo's sort of an art God to me. He's very exacting. I do have that part of me is extremely perfectionist about my writing. When I pray to Apollo it doesn't really help that perfectionism. It's hard to describe. He's very orderly to me, He's very interested in abstract, beautiful forms. That's not something I totally believe in. I do find it compelling. Through Him I met the Muses and that is something that I do when I write. I try something that gets me into the headspace to write. I actually have a little ritual to help me do it, where I invoke the Muses, and He's a part of that.

Apollo...is a good example of a God I don't entirely get along well with some of the time. That probably sounds far more presumptuous than I mean it: what I mean is just He represents forces I wrestle with, and sometimes that means I wrestle with Him. He can be kind, compassionate, and He's exquisitely beautiful, but He is also aloof, harsh and prescriptive, and honestly quite frightening and awesome—in the traditional sense of the word.

But it's as fortunate and productive as a relationship with a friend who is very different from me. A lot of the tension arises simply from the fact that we are not the same, and learning how to cope with that is very productive.

I think that merits some explanation. Sannion from the House of Vines website once said something that struck me: "the Gods are basically people." That sounds simple, and in some ways it's reductive, but I think it's true. Bhakti in Hinduism describes the various ways we can have relationships with the Gods in terms of fundamental human dynamics. Going from

Christianity, where you had this very specific relationship to Jehova, to polytheism, one of the things that really meant a lot to me was the freedom to approach the Gods in a way that felt natural. To be able to think of my relationship to the Gods as friends, as parents, as teachers, or even as a child, which bhakti describes—the plurality of that—is very poignant to me. It's less prescriptive, more flexible and spontaneous and natural.

So I don't feel bad about saying "I struggle with Apollo." I don't think it reduces His divinity one whit. Because He really is an incredibly significant God to me, absolutely crucial. He plays a huge role in my writing life: I've struggled a great deal with discipline and focus in that arena, and Apollo's lessons, ones of the importance of order and piousness, are ones I need to learn to succeed.

Given her understanding of Apollo, it isn't surprising that Elaine's relationship with Dionysus also has Nietzschean connotations. However, Elaine has found that Dionysus supports her creativity in ways that Apollo does not.

Dionysus is really awesome. He's so faceted. The more you learn about Him, the more layers unfold. He is very much a God of experience to me. I'm not able to convey Him very well. But I've definitely had some of my stronger spiritual experiences of Him. Pretty much every aspect of Him is important to me. Like, the God of intoxicants, the God of boundary breaking, the God of the Theater of course. He's very accessible to me. Apollo is harder to reach. Dionysus always seems very close at hand.

Ever since I read "The Birth of Tragedy," I've continued to return to Him, because much of what makes Dionysos Himself is what inspires my art. Intoxication, ecstasy, making suffering meaningful in the face of the threat of nihilism— it's a very Nietzschean interpretation of Dionysos, of course, but I think that is completely relevant and substantiated.

There's an interesting story with respect to that. Most people I've met have patron Gods. I think that is fascinating, and probably says a lot about how people in our present day and culture relate to Deity. I've never felt I had one, so I asked about it, and got the very strong impression that a patron was not for me. I asked several times, and then finally went into a trance state to ask. The answer I got was "your patron is Agathos Daimon"—meaning my own personal spirit, which has evolved, in my own understanding, into a somewhat Jungian thing.

Well, Dionysos and I got very close, and it turns out one of His epithets is Agathos Daimon. He's not my patron, but He is a guide in a way the other Gods are not. Some people have a very master-servant relationship to the Gods, but I don't. Not because I see *any* problem with that, or because I think I'm worthy to have anything different, but because I feel the very distinct sense that the Gods want me to succeed in my life as a writer. So Dionysos is not my patron in that He does not tutor me, tell me what to do—though I will do what He asks—or shelter me, but He is extremely generous about being present for me. He's Beatrice to my Dante.

I often feel very unworthy of this. I try to make up for it in my way—for instance, in February of this year, I threw a huge bacchanal, not overtly religious but clearly quite inspired by Him. People were incredibly receptive to this party, incidentally—far more people showed up far more enthusiastically than any other party my host had ever thrown. I roused up a chant of "Evohe, Evohe!" No one I knew there was overtly Pagan, either! It goes to show you how resonant the Gods are, even with people who don't explicitly believe in Them. I do what I can.

Hermes' varied interests, perpetual travel, and skills with communication have made Him a constant in Elaine's life. Paradoxically, Hermes is so present and so much a part of her life that it is difficult for Elaine to point to any one area and identify it as being specifically influenced by Hermes.

Hermes is also, sort of along with Artemis, I really relate to Hermes. Being a writer. And I enjoy travel, I have my fingers in lots of different pies often. Hermes can be the God of whatever you are doing at practically any given time. He's also a very accessible God, I suppose for that reason. I'm pretty flighty and pretty communicative. He is definitely similar in that respect. I guess because He's the messenger of the Gods I never really have trouble connecting with Him. Whenever I have anything urgent where I feel I need to communicate with Them, I speak to Him.

I don't have a whole lot to say about Hermes, simply because there's no huge story there, but He's an enormous part of my life. Part of it is because His interests are so varied, and part of it is because He really is a messenger figure for me, and part of it is because I'm pretty classically Mercurial: I love writing, making connections, researching new things, etc.. One of Apollo's epithets is "distant," and Hermes is the opposite of that: always close at hand, and usually quite good-natured about it. One of the things I enjoy about my relationship with Him is that it's highly practical and off-the-cuff: I still observe some of the traditional rules regarding miasma and the like, but I suppose I "feel" that Hermes "likes" a lot of off-the-cuff devotional activities. We've had some fun moments together. The first time I saw The Barber of Seville and heard Figaro's aria, it was actually quite a religious experience: I really felt Hermes in that music.

Whereas Apollo helps Elaine with those areas which she has difficulty mastering, Hecate helps her discover those areas she has trouble facing up to. Hecate is also integral to Elaine's connection with her ancestors.

Hecate is kind of mysterious. I'm still learning a lot about Her. To me She's sort of a counterpart to, She's related to Hermes. I mean, She's the Goddess of crossroads and travel. I have a private magickal practice that I do and She obviously is very important to that. She is also someone who...every month, [I do] the meal for Her. And I do that because I feel like when I communicate with Her I'm acknowledging parts of myself that are very difficult but that She can deal with. Aside from that, I don't know Her all that well.

I celebrate Hekate's Supper on the Dark Moon as a way of honoring Her and all Chthonic powers, including the ancestors. That monthly ritual has brought us quite close over time. Hekate is a riddle: She is in some ways almost as accessible and close-at-hand as Hermes, but in some ways veiled and remote. I have had some very intense visions about Her, though. One of my earliest experiences as a polytheist involved praying to Her... I was really struggling, at the time, with how to set up a ritual and what kind of mindspace to be in as I prayed, and She gave me some very explicit instructions, some practical ("use frankincense when you pray") and some philosophical ("a ritual is a space you enter in which everything is momentarily sacred"). As with Hermes, I'm not rambling as much about Hekate because there's not a huge story there, but I consider Her to be one of my most significant deific relationships.

Elaine draws from many sources in her creative life. Her religious life is no less varied. In addition to the Greek Dieities, Elaine has built relationships with Odin, Freya, Baldur, and of course, Saga.

Odin is fairly recent. I'm in the process of trying to learn more about Norse culture and myth in order to communicate with

Him better. But I was sort of feeling a lack connection for a while. I do respect Him when I honor the other Gods, but I don't feel particularly connected to Him. A few years ago, before I even really knew all that much about the traditional practices of any culture, I was like "it would be really nice to have a sort of a father God. If anyone is out there and sort of willing to do that for me." And Odin sort of popped in, like, "Hello." Which I was a little wary about because He's a badass motherfucker. He's pretty scary. But He is incredible appropriate. He keeps the mead of inspiration. The fact that I'm devoted to my writing is something He enjoys in me. He's pretty supportive of that. He knows I need to focus on that and that I can't do anything crazy for Him—at least so far. He's definitely...I've had a few thunderstorm experiences where I felt Him especially strongly. He hasn't asked anything huge of me; every time I have questioned Him if there is a greater role He wants to play in my life, He always answers that I need to focus on my work. But knowing Him it's just a matter of time for the other shoe to drop.

Freya I stumbled upon one day. I found this picture of Her and I felt immediately very drawn to it. Then I looked Her up and found out that the reason why was basically because of everything hhe is. As with Frigga, She's a Goddess of Magick. The Goddess of love. This very fertile and giving Goddess but also, because I'm not a mother myself and don't really every intend to be one, She is a Goddess of a lot of womanly things that don't have to do with motherhood at all. She just sort of made perfect sense for me to honor Her and try to learn from Her. So much of what She has domain over is what I'm interested in...I kind of syncretize Freya with Aphrodite, who I've grown much closer to. Whatever I see in either of Them overlaps significantly enough that I often conceive of both of Them as a unity. Make of that what you will!

I'll elaborate a bit on Aphrodite because that's interesting. My idea of Her was quite influenced by Homer's Iliad, and I thought of Her as being a much more... shallow, I suppose? ... Deity than She actually is. She won me over with Anne Carson's translation of Sappho's hymn, and ever since She snuck Her way into my life with lots of chance encounters, references, and UPG.

Baldur is like a Jesus that makes sense to me. He's sort of...I don't consider Him to be the same sort of person as Apollo or anything. But I do share a similar sort of reverence to Him as I do Apollo. I normally don't interact with Him until Christmas time, or right about now during the summer solstice when the birth and the dying of the sun become especially meaningful…I also syncretize Baldur and Apollo somewhat. This is another "ticking time bomb" relationship. I feel drawn to Baldur, and I'm sure there's a reason for that, but He hasn't made it known what that reason is again.

Saga is interesting. We don't know that much about Her to begin with, but because She is an important figure to Odin and because She and Odin share stories, I felt really compelled by Odin to pay special attention to Her. She's one I try to speak to each time I write. I find Her to be very welcoming and giving.

For the last three years, Elaine has undertaken a depth study of Thelema. She includes the Thelemic Deities Nuit and Hadit in her personal religious practice.

Conceptually, They are who They are within the system of Thelema. Because I'm pretty new to Thelema and my understanding is pretty basic. Nuit is space. Hadit is time, or motion. Nuit is the welcoming, huge circumference of everything and Hadit is the secret that can't be revealed. On a person level, I understand Them in terms of other things, the associations I have with Them. Nuit is very similar to a figure in Percy Shelley's Prometheus Unbound named Asia. Hadit is sort of like Prometheus, but I don't do things with Himas much. Asia is sort of this concept of the animating love of the universe, like when the Romantic poet, or Prometheus, is able to forgive His tormentor and see the world anew and feel connected to it. Hadit I have less of an investment in because I know less about Him.

In addition to the Egypt-inspired philosophies of Thelema, Elaine is also interested in the Deities of ancient Egypt. She has devotional relationships with Isis, Thoth, and Horus.

Horus is a Thelemic Deity. I've actually begun to revere Him because of that. I guess I sort of exaggerated when I said I wasn't connected to the Thelemic Deities. They sort of make sense within Thelema and then I sort of see Them differently in polytheism and Thelema. I've begun to feel close to Horus through the stories in the Book of the Law. It's hard to explain, except that I felt, upon reading the book of the Law, that Horus deserved more attention from me…I see Horus in conjunction with His Thelemic-Deity-counterpart, so my reverence for Him is not particularly historical. Engaging with Him is almost entirely on those terms.

Isis is sort of a strange story. There was a particular character of a queen in a story I read that was really important to me back when I was 11 or 12. The character was sort of inconsequential but She left a big impression on me. It was about this queen who is incredibly regal and strong with magick whose husband had died and She was trying to resurrect Him. That character's story really left a mark on me. Sort of similar to the Odin story. Frigga is amazing and all but I really didn't relate to Her. And I was sort of feeling like I needed more of an authoritative female force in my life. I started randomly discovering more about the Egyptian Deities. Again, that character, just the feel of Her story and how it dovetailed with Isis so well that I felt like I'd known Her all along.

Thoth is really remote and mysterious but I'm interested in magick and I'm interested in writing. I [knew I] was going to have to interact with Him eventually. He is, well, I'm interested also in Greco-Egyptian syncretism. I find that really interesting. I find it interesting that He is connected with Hermes in that context because He and Hermes are absolutely nothing alike to me in a lot of ways. Thoth is a lot more reserved. He's also a trickster and He's also very good with language. He sort of, like…Hermes will help me out if I'm in a bind or something. Whereas Thoth is more of a teacher to me…I'm a practicing magician, so Thoth is a guide for that, basically. Thoth, unlike Hermes, is quite remote to me in certain ways. Not inaccessible at all, but… strangely aloof, difficult to understand.

Elaine admits that her understanding of the Gods isn't limited to personal gnosis, history, and mythology. Because she acknowledges storytelling as a Divine activity, Elaine takes literary and even pop culture ideas into account when exploring her relationships with the Gods. The three Deities of whom this is most true for Elaine are Morpheus, Prometheus, and Viridios.

Morpheus is a being…I'm not sure if He is the same as the Greek God, but I do a lot of dreaming and dreamwork. I've met a shapeshifter in my dreamwork a lot of times who sort of told me that He wanted certain things to be done for Him, and to be spoken to in certain ways. In return He would teach me certain things about dreams. That one is a bit more mysterious, but that is sort of how I communicate with Him. I was a bit hesitant to say this explicitly, but since "pop culture Paganism" is such a big debate in the blogosphere these days I suppose I will admit that my idea of Morpheus is hugely inspired by Neil Gaiman's The Sandman. Judging by the recent art of Morpheus I've seen, I'm not alone in that.

In terms of Prometheus, I try not to get too caught up in the myth. The Prometheus in the Pandora myth I don't really relate to. I focus on the aspects of myth that I do connect with…He's the romantic Prometheus- the Prometheus of Byron and William Blake and Percy Shelly. And to me He's everything that the Romantics embraced. A belief in humanity. The willingness to rebel against even the Gods for perceived injustice. It's easier to admit to being inspired by 19th century poets than a comic book character! But nonetheless, I would not have come to Prometheus except through the fact that He is such an important literary figure, not only to the Romantics but all the way down to modern authors like Camus.

Viridios is a name that a lot of people use for the Green Man. He's sort of a convenient name for me for this very deep archetype that has been a big deal to me for a while. I don't really think He's, maybe He's a facet of the Green Man or something. When I was young, as I mentioned, I was really into Peter Pan, who has a lot of mythic resonances. Later on, I was really into Puck from a Midsummer night's dream. Viridios is the name I use for this sort of green, sprightly trickster-y youth in the forest who runs around and is forever young and that kind of stuff.

Elaine maintains a regular devotional practice to her Gods and has built her own festival calendar around venerating Them. But the most important devotional activity she does is her work as a writer. For Elaine, stories are sacred things and she views her writing as a sacred vocation.

Right now, I'm throat-deep in a three-year magic system and focusing very strongly on my writing, so all I do is the Deipnon/Noumenia/Agathos Daimon day. This doesn't feel like enough, but nothing ever will!… The most important devotional ritual for me is my writing, which I associate with the Gods. I've had a really hard time writing. It's only in the past year when I've involved Them more that I've been able to break through a lot of fears and anxiety, writer's block and difficulty and actually write. I approach it really, really ritualistically. Like, I sit down and meditate and I say a prayer to the muses and Gods of writing. I actually received an oracle once that told me that I should collaborate with the Gods. So since then—well, it depends on what story ideas are going on in my head. Like, when a particular God is related to Them. But before I write I'll actually invoke whatever Gods seem appropriate and begin writing. That's the most important one to me. I also celebrate traditional Hellenic rituals. I have festivals that I celebrate on my own. I have a festival for each God that really means something to me. Usually I will have a brief ceremony and pray to Them, and typically because it feels right to me, I try to do something in Their name, or perform some action for Them. That helps me feel really close to Them…

One thing I do is have a special tarot deck set aside for divination with Them, the Thoth deck. I use it only on those special days. I always ask if there is something the Gods, or a particular God, would like me to do for Them, and try to use my intuition to determine what it is. Usually the answer is "take care of your shit," so for now, at least, I think this is enough.

In addition to the Gods, Elaine honors her ancestors and the nature spirits. Ancestor veneration is relatively new to her, but she has overcome the challenges she met in creating her ritual practice. Honoring the spirits of the land came somewhat more naturally for Elaine than honoring Deities did.

A couple months ago I was reading an article about how Ancestors are incredibly important but aren't incorporated enough, and I was like, "Oh. I feel bad now." The bond isn't particularly deep at the moment. One thing I did when I began to incorporate ancestors into my practice is that I keep a candle on my altar for my ancestors. I also have a candle that I keep for those who I call the "Dead Poets," which is from that movie, but it honors the lineage of artists, writers, and poets who've gone before me. I think that's made a lot of sense to me, and it's how I'm beginning to understand ancestor worship. So it's sort of, like, I had some trouble with it until I realized I could have one candle for my physical ancestors, and another candle for my spiritual or artistic kindred spirits throughout the ages. Aside for honoring them I haven't done anything else with that. I definitely have felt close to land spirits. Unfortunately I don't live in a city where there's any nature—at all, really. It's pretty bad here. But I do live close to a park and I have always since I was really little connected to tree spirits. I've made a point of going to the park and sense them/be aware of them. I think that's pretty much all I can do at this point until I move somewhere that there's actual trees. But I would really like to explore that in-depth one day. I think it's really awesome.

Thus far, Elaine has not experienced too much friction about her emphasis on a polytheist religious practice. While Elaine has witnessed the conflicts between hard and soft polytheists online, she has been careful not to be drawn into those arguments in her real life. Even so, the arguments she has seen in blogs and articles have at times left Elaine feeling torn about the relevance of literal belief in her personal religious practice.

I see a lot of those fights, but I'm really careful about who I talk to. They don't have a huge stake in it. Their focus is different. They're very accepting of whatever I say for the most part. Not that there are a lot of awful Thelemites out there. For the most part, they really honor personal experiences. That's one thing I really like. I also think that it's because the only formal group I've ever been a part of, it's been during the past couple months, I also joined Neos Alexandria, it's Greco-Roman publishing group. It's much more informal. It isn't too active right now, unfortunately. But one thing I like about it is that the premise is syncretism. They don't get too hung up on differences which I think are kind of like splitting hairs. Both of those groups have been really nice. Honestly, I've had some interactions with Asatru, and they're sort of famed for being more conservative. But they haven't had problems with anything I've said, they haven't even had a problem that I worship Odin and Freya outside the context of Heathen culture. I guess the answer is that I choose my friends carefully and I've been very lucky. I know that theologically, too, a lot of the ideas I have about Jung strike polytheists the wrong way. I don't mind that because I think their defensiveness comes from this position of, like, you know, "the Gods are real, They are separate from us and They're autonomous," And I totally agree with that, just in a non-literal fashion. I feel like, in spirit, where it counts, as far as their experiences, we are very similar and I feel like there's no use getting into some silly argument over theology when I feel that what we have in common is what matters.

Basically, I think that your intellectual beliefs, your ideas about how the universe works and such, can be separate from your devotional practice, and that you can accept and consider on their own terms multiple, superficially-conflicting experiences with Deity. An amazing friend of mine, Arda, calls this "polygnosticism." I think it's ridiculous, and unwarranted, to expect everyone to have faith in literal, independent Deities. We live in a confusing and ambiguous world. I just don't fucking know if there are objective, literal Gods or not! Perhaps I haven't had the right experiences. But I love Them, and I feel Their presence, and I am compelled to revere Them. I honor both my desire for philosophical inquiry and open-mindedness, and my desire to revere the Gods, and quite frankly, it is extremely presumptuous of anyone to think my Gods have a problem with that. Some of the people in that debate were asserting as much, contrary to the opinions of agnostic types who have consulted with their Gods, and have been told by Themn, to the best of their understanding, that it doesn't matter. I honestly don't know why those hardliners want to discourage any sincere practitioner from giving the Gods the reverence They deserve. Given the diversity of opinions on the nature of Deity in the ancient world, I don't think that's historically substantiated, either.

At the same time, a lot of "pop culture" Paganism seems to me to be quite superficial and shallow. Not because they're worshipping Batman, exactly, but because it seems more along the lines of playing with "imaginary friends." It's complex: I'm the last person in the world to think imaginary friends are silly, and a lot of my "communication" with the Gods takes place in the form of pretend-conversations, in the form of the way They inspire my art and my characters, who are as real to me as human beings are, sometimes. But I feel that you need to have some discernment. Whatever "Deity" means and has meant, it is something overwhelming, powerful, and awe-inspiring. So while in the grand scheme of things, your conversation with Hermes during your commute may be *a part* of your overall communication with Him, you may be best served to be conservative and consider that an attempt on *your* part to understand Him and what He is trying to say to you.

When asked if there was anything she wished people understood about polytheism, Elaine explained that she wished it were easier to talk about it, in general. General culture is so clueless about polytheism, it seems, that there must always be this huge discussion about what it is and why she chose it every single time the topic comes up.

I wish that it were easier to just tell someone I was a polytheist without there being this big discussion about it. It just feels like there is a big gap. People don't have an easy way of grasping it. I feel like every time I say anything about it there's this huge discussion that has to involve my relationship with my mother, my beliefs or non-beliefs in materialism, atheism, Christianity. I just wish people would focus on the experiences. I wish our culture respected religious experiences more. I think from there it would be a lot easier for them to grasp polytheism. It's hard to answer that question because it has been so difficult to get over the initial hurdle of someone being in shock and even feeling like they wanted to laugh at what I was doing. It really feels like there's a gap that and it's unfortunate. I think all polytheists have really good reasons for believing what they believe, and I just wish it was easier for other people to understand how polytheists come to their conclusions.

Raven Kaldera

Raven Kaldera was four years old when he first heard the Gods speaking to him. At age 8, he set up his first of several Goddess shrines. After discovering Paganism as a teenager, Raven began to formally and intentionally embrace a more polytheist spirituality. Many years later, Raven underwent gender reassignment surgery at the behest of his Goddess, Hela. Since then, his transgender identity has become integral to his work as a shaman[*] and author. Raven's work for the Pagan community differs significantly from his personal practice. He is a founding member of the First Kingdom Church of Asphodel, a community of eclectic Neo-Pagans who meet for activities and events at Kaldera's Cauldron Farm.   In his personal practice, Raven is a Northern Tradition Pagan who nonetheless also has a devotional practice for non-Norse Deities. Kaldera has found that each side of his practice enriches and informs the other, and that the balance he finds in walking between them strengthens his role as a leader and elder in the larger Pagan community.

Raven's definition of polytheism is fairly straightforward. Raven defines polytheism as "belief in multiple Gods. Very simple. Belief and an active worship of in some cases, yeah." For Raven, the distinguishing feature of hard polytheism isn't that it provides a suitable or more convincing approach to the Divine, but that it gives a vital frame of reference for his experiences. "For me," he explains, "polytheism has been less about 'Okay, I'm looking for a faith that suits me,' and more about 'I'm looking for a faith that makes sense of what I'm already experiencing. This is what is already going on. What explains this best?'"

Raven defines faith as "believing when there is no—when you have no personal proof." He also gives a supplemental definition of the term, which "means your religion, your 'faith.'" The struggle Raven experiences isn't about deciding whether or not the Gods exist or

---

[*] The term "shaman," when used in a contemporary western context, has become increasingly embattled due to Westerners' insistence on appropriating and redefining it according to their own tastes. Raven admits that he would prefer to use the ancient Norse word for his spiritual practices, but unfortunately that term, and much of the practices associated with it, were decimated by Christian incursion. While the word "shaman" seems to have originated in North Asia, it has come to be regarded as an umbrella term for spiritual practitioners who employ altered consciousness, esoteric techniques, herbal healing, drumming, and other forms of indigenous spiritual technology for the purpose of negotiating with the spirit realm on behalf of the clan, tribe, or community. Alan J. Barnard and Jonathan Spencer, eds. The Routledge Encyclopedia of Social and Cultural Anthropology (London: Routledge, 2011), 638-641.

whether They are talking to him, or even if he is in the right line of work. Belief in the existence of the Gods is rendered irrelevant because his personal experiences with Them have given him knowledge that They are real. "For me," he says, "I have no doubt that the Gods exist. I can't turn Them off." The hard part for Raven is always trusting Them, especially when the things They ask of him are particularly difficult.

> For me, because—and I've said this repeatedly—for me, because I talk to the Gods, I never question that They exist. For me, that's ... I don't know if you've ever seen the movie Constantine, but it's the moment where the guy's talking to Gabriel and says, "Well, I believe." And Gabriel says, "No, you don't believe. You know. That's different. That's not faith." For me faith has been not been about whether They exist, or whether They're speaking to me, but whether what They ask me to do and what They ask other people to do is always for the greater good, and if what They ask to me to do is always for my own good even if I can't see that at the moment. So my problem isn't believing that They exist, it's believing that They are always doing the right thing... That's a hard one. "Are you good?" Well, not so much "good," but "Is your vision really that much larger than mine, and are your goals that much more potent and effective than mine?"

Many polytheists came to their path only after their experience with conventional Neo-Pagan practice led them to the conclusion that the Gods are real, distinct, individual beings. For Raven, the reverse was true.

> I came to polytheism long before I formally came to Paganism. When I was in the fourth grade, I was building altars in the basement to Gods. All I had to go on was books of myths. I didn't know anything about the Norse Gods. I was building altars to Egyptian and Greek Gods because that's all I knew about. The first big altar I built – we went to see the Tutankhamen Exhibit in D. C. when I was a kid. It was the first time it came to D.C. And this is dating me, but I was in the fourth grade when that happened. Way back in the 70's. (laughs) As my souvenir, I bought this enormous poster of Selkhet[†] who is actually a death Goddess. I took it downstairs and hung it on the basement wall. We had a finished basement. Part of it was the kids' play area, I basically kept my toys there

---

[†] Egyptian Goddess of fertility who healed poisonous stings and bites, Selkhet also guarded the tombs to protect the canopic jars that held the corpse's intestines. Patricia Monaghan, Encyclopedia of Goddesses and Heroines (Westport, CT: Greenwood, 2009), 36.

where we played. And I was just moved to put a box under it and cover it with a piece of fabric and start putting things on it. My parents wouldn't let me light candles, although I did anyway. I stole birthday candles and lit them. It just seemed like the right thing to do, I was going to build this altar to Her and I didn't know who She was. Then She talked to me. Just for a moment She gave me the sort of "Ding! Hello!" But even that was like, "Oh my God! This works! You can build an altar to something and it will speak to you!" (laughs) So I built a row of them. "I really like Artemis from the myths. I'm gonna build one for Artemis. I'll color a little picture and I'll put it on there." So, this is me in the fourth grade making rows of altars in the basement to Gods. At that point clearly I was believing in Them. I wasn't even sure what you were supposed to do. I didn't know about offerings or anything else like that. I just sort of made a pretty altar, and would sit in front of it and hope to hear something. So, I was a polytheist that far back.

I did not run into neo-Paganism until I was in high school and my first boyfriend was the oldest son of a BTW high Priestess. He basically sneaked me into his coven at 14, which would never happen today without my parents' knowledge. I mean, I'm incredibly glad they did that. That wouldn't happen today because everybody's too worried about covering their ass. But thank Gods that they did that. I really needed that. But that was my first introduction to "Paganism: The religion." I was like, people do this besides me?

My first experiences that I can remember were back when I was four of five. Hela would come to me in dreams. I didn't know who She was and I was very clear that She was the Dark Lady. I was very clear that the face She put on was not Her real face. She put on a face that was kind of like the face of one of the figures of my storybook-kind-of-things. It was the feel of when adults get to say, you know, "You don't get to see this." In dreams, She would take me places. She would say, "Hold my hand, don't let go," and we would go places. I didn't understand what it was for. Mostly, She seemed to be showing me off to various people who didn't like me much. But She would also—She would talk to me. She would only come for short periods of time, and She would say, "Study that. Learn that." I'm like, "Okay!" I thought it was because, well, I had this idea that I made up. When I was in the first grade I was making up this whole story where I was some lost member of Their family and I was going to become this kind of great important thing, some superhero sort of thing like that, and I was getting training to become this sort of superhero. (Laughs.)

In the intervening years, Raven has had many experiences with the Gods which made him unwaveringly certain as to Their existence. As he grew older, the painful things he experienced at the behest of Hela drove him to become spiritually stronger and more powerful.

Then, of course when I got into my teens, and I actually met Pagans and some of them were like—because they were Wiccan, and it was all about "the Goddess" and the "faces of the Goddess"—and they were like, "Well that must have been the Crone, or something like that. I was like, well, okay. If that's what this is. So they were more pantheist and I sort of fit it into that, but I knew She was about Death by then. I could smell Her. I didn't get to see who she was until I was 30, but I knew She was about Death. I was very clear by that time that while I had run into other Gods and spirits and had relationships with Them, She was always there in the background. Then She was waiting, and She was still telling me to do things.

I rebelled a lot during my teens and early 20's and said I didn't want to do those things because some of those things were very hard. Like, have a baby. She was like, "I need you to breed," and I was like, I didn't want to breed. So She made sure that I got accidentally pregnant. Because She knew I would not refrain from having sex. The only way I could have done that was to have been celibate, and She knew I wasn't going to do that. All my attempts to get rid of the baby fell through in bizarre ways until it was too late and I had to have the baby.

There were other really hard things. The last hard thing was when She told me to get a sex change. Then, when I started hemorrhaging to death, and after I had my near-death experience, that's when I got so see who She was. And She showed me and then She was like, "Okay! Now we get to begin. All this has been lead-up. Now we get to begin...."

When asked about the rituals, ceremonies, or other observances he has to commune with his Holy Powers, Raven is quick to distinguish between his work as a shaman, and his personal devotional practices. As a shaman, much of what Raven does is "cultivating allies," or building productive, goal-driven relationships with different entities. In some ways, these relationships can be characterized as pragmatic and businesslike.

Because much of what I do is cultivating allies, you know. The problem is that the shaman stuff—I'm gonna answer that in a minute—but I want to say that the Shaman stuff does permeate 98% of everything in that the Gods are my allies for the most part, and I spend an inordinate amount of time on that. I mean, I spend a weekend at the beach every year just propitiating Aegir and Ran and the Nine and throwing things into the water. For me, while I love Them and They are wonderful, for me that's a business arrangement…In fact, I write it off on my taxes.

But—that's been very difficult because Hela does not ask me to do devotional activities. Or rather, the only devotional activity that She asks me to do for Her is work. Much of what She has pushed me for my whole life is just to become this tool and let that permeate everything. It's all part of the same thing. For Her, it really does feel like She does just keep chipping at me and chipping me into this perfect tool. Or at least as perfect as a flawed human being can come. Perhaps She would like it if that's all I was—the entirety of my life and every single thing I did from the moment I got up to the moment I went to sleep revolved around that. But I'm not up to that yet. That's why concessions are made. That's why I have partners that I need in order to not go crazy. I would say that I didn't have a…for the longest time, I didn't have a devotional relationship. Which seems strange, as I've worked with thousands of Gods and Goddesses and spirits. Thousands, I dunno. It feels like thousands but it's probably more like a few hundred. There's 200 of plant spirits, just plants alone.

Despite the fulfillment of his work as a shaman, Raven felt the need to have at least a handful of purely devotional relationships. It was difficult, he says, because Hela had decided that such devotional activity was unnecessary.

But I didn't have a devotional relationship for a long time with anyone. I would periodically ask about that and She would say, "That's not necessary. You're already doing work. You're already doing what's necessary." She's all about the absolute necessity. I did feel that I needed that, and the Deities that I have personal work ended up being Frey, Angrboda, Fenrir and Baphomet. They are not in my life as allies. They are in my life … Baphomet and Fenrir are in my life as teachers…I assumed, "You're here because of work," and They're like, "We're here because of work you need to do on yourself." That's different. So

They are my teachers. And let me tell you: Dojo of Hard Knocks. (Laughs) They're not the only Gods who call me on my shit. But They are the ones who call me on my worst shit. My relationship with Them is intensely personal because it's all about me and my problems, and me and my flaws.

Raven's relationship with the God Frey does not focus on working on the darker and more flawed aspects of his deeper self. For Raven, Frey is a God of beauty and light whose generosity and graciousness are a much-needed counterbalance to the other parts of his life.

My relationship with Frey came about because I ran into Him in Vanaheim while journeying and just got a big, fat, mad, schoolgirl crush. Took one look and was like, "Aaaah." Sometimes a Deity will just hit you that way, you'll just look at Them and go, "Aaah. (smitten sigh and laughter) Will you sleep with me? Please?" And you get that whole groupie vibe. He was very kind about that. He was very clear that I was not, in any way shape or form, one of His. In fact, when He came, He'd come for Josh, my partner. Which kind of surprised Josh. But He graciously accepted me having a devotional relationship with Him. He did teach me a few things. He was kind about that. I do sometimes feel like this little dark, twisted thing. I'll go to His altar and it's all full of light and I'll go, "But I'm this dark little twisted thing." My relationship with Him, there is no work involved at all. I can just sort of sit there and love Him and He sort of sits there and—Sort of pats me on the head and gives me a cookie. Gives me a little bit of that light. Lets me bask in His light. Rarely asks anything of me. Occasionally He asks me to pass a message to Josh‡ or carry Him§ for a particular purpose for the community, but that's strictly, that's a very traditional worship relationship in that way.

One of the things that Raven felt the need for was nurturing and encouragement. Yet because he is dispositionally opposed to gushy, indulgent, maternal love, it was difficult to find a Deity to work through these needs with. He found an unexpectedly perfect fit with the fierce Jotun Goddess Angrboda.

My relationship with Angrboda is that I really felt like I needed

---

‡ Raven's partner, Josh, is a henotheistic devotee of the God Frey.

§ In saying "carry Him," Raven is referring to the act of Deity possession, wherein he would "carry" the God so that Frey might interact with His devotees. The process is identical to the phenomenon of lwa possession in Vodou and orisha possession in Lukumi and Candomble. Raven learned this technique by studying for six months working in a house dedicated to the Orixa and African Diasporic Religion.

some nurturing, but I really hated the whole concept of gushy nurturing. I am really not into gushy mother Goddesses and that sort of thing. But Hela is really not—my relationship with Her is not with that part of Her. She is much more boss-employee in that sense. So I don't get that from Her. So She sent me to Her mother, who is not gushy. Who is very much the wolf mother, and the coach, and the "You can do this!" Angrboda, I think She's the only one with whom I have a relationship that's on the little end. The personal, more human end. The other Gods I don't really. She looked at me and said, "You think that no God loves you? Well, I will love you. I'm the mother of monsters. You think that you're a monster and you can't be loved, well, that's my job." So I have a very personal relationship with Her in the sense that She will show up sometimes and She will buck me up. And that's pretty much all She does with me. People think She's scary, and She can do a lot of scary things, but I got plenty of scary Gods in my life. She leaves that to Her daughter and everybody else. So She just comes and says, "You can do this! You can keep going. C'mon, you're strong. You can do it." And that's the sort of mothering I need. More the coach than "oh-you-poor-thing."

Raven has relationships with many Deities whose mythology is very vague. Very often, it is difficult to find mythological material on Them to help guide one toward an understanding of Them. Other times, the mythology is so dense, labyrinthine, and seemingly contradictory that it is difficult to sort out deeper spiritual truths that could lead to greater understanding. The need to rely heavily on personal experience in these instances has led Raven to deemphasize mythology in general, if it clashes too harshly with his personal understanding, or "personal gnosis" of a particular Deity.

I find myself in the difficult position of not being able to take myths too seriously if they clash with my personal gnosis. Which sounds so incredibly arrogant, but you just cannot look at the Deity who is facing you and say, "But what you're doing isn't fitting with the myth!" That just doesn't go over well. I have to make decisions about what I write about. At first I was very conservative about that. I would only write about things that weren't covered by the myths—they just weren't in there so it didn't really matter. I could say "That's just my personal gnosis." There's nothing arguing against them. Or they worked with them. Eventually, I would say that the Gods—I've not run across things that are glaringly different with the exception of human ideas about that—when I run across something that's glaringly different it's because the humans who have thought about this are stuck in some human paradigm of good and evil. Or good and bad in a sense of "what's convenient to me or not convenient to me; this could hurt me, or did hurt me, therefore it is evil." So, in those cases it's often "wrong." It's very often the myths, the slant that they put, is often wrong.

Aside from that, it's mostly a matter of details. You wouldn't think that God X would have five different myths about Them and they would contradict each other. Of course, I like things neat and tidy and that was HARD. I accept that sometimes different Gods will show different sides of themselves. It's not just that They show different sides, it's that different sides of Them could have done different things in different linear times, so to speak. They can live multiple realities. That's so hard to fit into my head, or to get my head around as sort of an abstract concept. Sometimes I have to grit my teeth and say, "Okay. This is one of those multiple-reality God things. Maybe there's a reason that They're showing me this." I think that Gods sometimes sort of have a main reality that is like a tree, and then there's little branches off of it that might be what could have happened, and They'll show you what could have happened for Them, or what maybe did happen in this other alternate reality sort of thing as sort of a lesson, like, "You need to see this." Even though it's kind of like an abstract. Maybe it's not even as concrete as saying, "You need to see what could have happened to me," because maybe it did. It's not that. But I'll never see that branch because it's not relevant to me. And similarly there will be branches that I'm given to see that are not relevant to other people. The reason I write about those is because there is somebody out there that they'll be relevant to. There is someone I will show those to and they will be like, "OH!"

In the animistic cultures that still have shamanic traditions, shamans aren't necessarily tasked in dealing only with Deity; they are concerned primarily with interceding between the community and the ancestors, nature spirits, and Deities in order to maintain the spiritual health of the land and the community. Although Raven is a hard polytheist working from a northern European viewpoint, his shamanic practice very much involves work with the ancestors and the spirits of the land. The spirit that resides on the land of Cauldron Farm is integral to Raven's health and work.

The land spirit of this land that I'm on right now is incredibly important to my practice. When I first moved to this land and realized that it had been arranged for me to come here, it was like, "Bing! Here you go, here's this little farm with a big, private field in the back that's perfect. There you go. You're going to live here. It's got everything that you need and you can actually afford it on the chunk of money that's given to you." So at that point, I said, "If I'm going to be here forever, I need to talk to the land wight." My wife and I both gave the land wight our blood and It—It doesn't really have a gender but It definitely does have a personality—runs all my wards for me…So, I'm not worried about people throwing anything at me, it's like "Bounce."

Besides which, me and my land spirit have a relationship with the spirit of Mount Wachusett which is tied into that. I've left things there and brought things here from there…That was brokered by the Birch Tree spirit, because these things happen. And also it helps to power the labyrinth in the back, which is off right now but when I turn it on, it's like WHOOSH! It's a door to Helheim, or other places. But in exchange, I can't leave here. I think about a month is all I can do and that would be pushing it. And in fact, I do take a little sack of dirt from my land with me to put under my pillow, to sort of maintain a thread of that, because the land wight also feeds me energy. It's one of the many pillars that prop up my life. I have medication-resistant Lupus. I'm supposed to be dead. I'm not dead through many different props, and the land spirit is definitely one of them. I get spoons from that. I get fed from that. Or I wouldn't [be alive], and especially since it's not just about me staying alive. It's about me doing an energy-heavy gas-guzzling job and staying alive. So in exchange for all that feeding, when travelling I take that little bag of dirt.

And yes, there have been jokes about "native earth" and so forth—me sleeping on my native earth. But there's really something to that. I really think that myth has got … there's something going on with that myth that is a tie-in or a leftover from other myths. Yes, really, if you are for some reason dependent—if part of your power is dependent—upon a piece of land for whatever reason, if that piece of land is sustaining you, yeah, you take the little box of native earth with you. I will be buried here. I will live here the rest of my life and I will be buried here. And that is the deal. That means I can't move. I can't sell this place and move somewhere else. I'm here forever, so I have to do my damndest to pay the property taxes.

As a shaman whose patroness is a death Goddess, Raven is accustomed to working in some way of other with the dead. Yet he says that he has had significant difficulty in connecting with his own ancestral line. According to Raven, generations of madness and spiritual disconnectedness have posed significant challenges to his attempts at engaging with them.

Now, let's see, the Ancestors. I have less of a tie with...well. Okay. My ancestors are all cursed. I come of two different family lines. My parents actually have similar genetic backgrounds. I come of two different strains of families that produce shamans. And they had made a deal with the spirits—I dunno, thousands of years ago? Over a thousand years ago at least — that when such a child is born that it will be taken to the proper old man or woman in the hut and given to the spirits. Only, nobody remembers that anymore. And there's no old man or woman in the hut. But the spirits don't care. It's still breaking a promise, so for a thousand years my family has been riddled with disease, madness, and violence. It just goes back further and further and further and that's the result of—I don't know if I want to call it a curse—but the spirits' displeasure.

It is sad that They will do that even when there's no way that my parents could have known, or my family could have known. There is no way they could have known. But the spirits don't care. And so because of that, most of my ancestors are fairly neutralized, fairly powerless. I don't call on them. I would like to call on them, but it's like, they really don't have much to offer me. They're all sort of...I can't even get ahold of most of them.

The big exception is this 1,300-year dead man that Hela sent to me who was the last big shaman in the line, I guess. 1,300 years dead and he is a better shaman than I will ever be...I don't even know his name, it's something in Sami and I can't really translate it or pronounce it. The dialect of Sami that he speaks is gone. There were 16 dialects as of the turn of the century and now there's only 11 left. None of those are his. So I just call him "Uncle Noaide". If you go downstairs and you'll pass a little dresser covered in stuff and there's a little birch bark Santa. That's his altar and his spirit-house. And yeah, eventually I'm going to have a big altar for him.**

**"Sami" is the term which indigenous Scandinavians prefer to use to identify themselves. Formerly known as Lapps and Laplanders, the Sami can be found stretching from Sweden through Finland and across Russia. The Sami have retained indigenous language, customs, and religious practices. Barbara Helen Miller, <u>Connecting and Correcting: A Case Study of Sami Healers in Porsanger</u> (Leiden; Leiden University Press, 2013), 1-16. The name "Noaide" is the Sami word for "shaman."

He's a teacher. He's not so much a devotional ancestral figure as he just sort of shows up and kicks my ass and tells me, "You need to be doing this." He taught me how to use my healing drum. I let him borrow my body once in a great while, just to sort of walk around out there and have some food and smell the moss and sit by a fire and experience that. He doesn't think much of my body, but it's flesh and it moves and that's sort of a way in which I pay him.

I still have some stuff from my grandmother that I put up as well. I have my grandmother and I have my Uncle Noaide. With my grandmother it's really more of a respect thing. She doesn't really do anything.

Raven admits that accepting the role of shaman has required tremendous personal sacrifice on his part. Yet he also believes that by agreeing to make these personal sacrifices, it might keep his descendants from suffering the misery of his ancestors.

But aside from my own blood kin—by becoming a shaman I saved my daughter. I told her this. And she told her first boyfriend this. I said that, "If you have a kid"—she's not a shaman; she's just a carrier of the genes, that's why I had to have her—I said, "If you have a kid, this is what needs to happen. If the kid has these particular traits and talents and it shows up really early, you need to bring the kid to me if I'm still alive. If not, here are other people who are doing this." In fact, her first boyfriend, she told him this, and he said, "I don't know about that," and she said, "No. I saw what happened to my grandparents. I am not going there." But I couldn't save the rest of my line. I don't know what it would take.

The belief that tremendous spiritual power comes from having strong and powerful ancestors is not uncommon among cultures that have retained practices such as those found in shamanism. Not having a healthy ancestral line posed significant challenges to Raven's work. Yet during the process of sorting through his ancestral issues, Raven discovered that the members of your family tree are not the only spiritually powerful ancestors you have.

So the other thing is, basically, Hela said She was going to give me ancestors that weren't of my blood. I had to basically replace the power of my entire ancestral line. Because they are cursed and no matter what I did, I could not—my own sacrifice wouldn't remove that. One of the things that [Hela] did was She made me Speaker for the Transgendered Dead. I have them.

They are now my ancestors. They are…But for the trans* *dead—I don't have an altar for them because I don't have any* *space in this house, but I go every year; I do priestly duties at the* *Trans* Day of Remembrance. I speak for them whenever it is* *appropriate to speak about them. I teach other people about* *them. I'm one of two people that I know of who have this job* *as Speaker for the Trans* Dead and have a votive relationship.* *The other one is an intersex woman who—they saved her life.* *She's blind and was attacked in an alley, and they came and* *saved her life, and now she belongs to Them.*

They give me a good deal of power. The fact that I am the ergi[††] *shaman. I have to be publicly the ergi shaman. That's one of the* *ways in which I pay; I don't get to be closeted, I don't get to be* *normal. I have to be out about everything I do. Everything I do,* *there are no closets. No matter what it does to me. In exchange,* *I get an enormous amount of power from them.*

Raven's concept of being an "ergi shaman" comes in part from his research about ancient Norse spiritual traditions. The ancient Norse shamanic practice of seiðhr was based on the principle of physical ecstasy as a gateway for the soul's transcendence into other spiritual realms. It was almost exclusively the province of women. Any man who engaged in seiðhr would be referred to as "ergi." In fact, Odin was referred to as ergi for having undertaken, through study with the Goddess Freyja, mastery of seiðhr. "Ergi,"[‡‡] roughly translated, means "unmanliness," and is associated with softness and was often used to depict sexual subjugation. In the context of Raven's practice, "ergi" has less to do with the transcendental power of physical ecstasy and more to do with the practice of gender transgression to gain spiritual power. In Raven's view, anyone who transgresses the culturally-drawn gender lines to hunt for spiritual power, whether it involves a sexually ecstatic practice such as seiðhr or not, is practicing ergi.[§§] There are many cultures that associate some form of ergi practice with shamanism.

People have different opinions on what ⌊ergi⌋ means. For me, it's

[††]Solli, Brit. Seid, Myths, Shamanism and Gender in the Viking Era. Oslo: Kilden Press, 2004.

[‡‡] Sørenson, Preben M.; Turville-Petre, Joan (transl.) The Unmanly Man: Concepts of Sexual Defamation in Early Northern Society. Studies in Northern Civilization 1. (Odense: Odense University Press, 1983).

[§§]The principle of attaining power through sexual ecstasy achieved in the context of gender transgression is a significant feature of many modern Western occult traditions. Foremost among proponents of this technique was the great Aleister Crowley who developed his philosophy through working with the Hermetic Order of the Golden Dawn, Ordo Templi Orientis. These "ergi" philosophies play a significant role in Crowley's magico-religious system of Thelema. Hugh B. Urban, Magia Sexualis: Sex, Magic, and Liberation in Modern Western Esotericism (Berkley: University of California Press, 2006), 223.

less about, well, I have decided what it means or the concept I think it is tied to. That is, I think it is the Nordic word for the same taboo stellium. Okay. There are taboos that are like one thing, "You may not cut your hair," or whatever, and then there are taboos that are a whole constellation of "You can't do any of these things and you must do these," you have many taboos that you must do and can't do. If it's not mandated, it's forbidden and vice versa. This taboo stellium, if you go over to the Siberian tribes a little ways over from Scandinavia, they are very clear on that. They have their owns words for that. To me, what I've gleaned, those are Norse words referring to that stellium originally, and later got other meanings slapped onto it. The meaning is, open gender transgression in a spiritworker, and being that open third gender and third gender sexually, too, there is a sexual component to it and an outsider component to it. Doing that all for power. Doing that as a way to gain power. You find that all over the world, and not in every shamanic culture absolutely, but in plenty of them. So this [ergi practice] is what I do for power, and partly because I can't do anything else.

Amongst some native American tribes*** the spirits show up when someone's like, 40 years old and say, "Okay, put on a skirt and embody this right now and we'll give you power." In Asia\†\†\†, there's still a lot of traditions about that. So for me, that is what those are about. People disagree, especially about the fact that I think those things are related to the spirit work constellation, not just to average gender expression. Although I think anyone can tap that power, I think they have to be out, to be public, in order to tap the power because that's part of the power.

When asked if there was anything he wished people understood about polytheism, Raven says that he wishes people would understand that it isn't a "superstition that one grows out of." When viewed objectively, polytheism doesn't make less sense than monotheistic religions. In fact, Raven attributes much of the negative views of polytheism to cultural assumptions that have been made in accord with underlying monotheist ideas about Divinity and religion.

***Sabine Lang discusses this at length in her book on Native American cultures and gender transgression. Sabine Lang, "Women-Men as Shamans, Medicine Persons, and Healers," in Men as Women, Women as Men: Changing Gender in Native American Cultures (Austin: University of Texas Press, 1998), 151-168.

\†\†\†Vicky Noble, The Double Goddess: Women Sharing Power (Rochester, VT: Bear & Company, 2003).

Most people see it as superstitious, and I think this is a holdover from monotheism. Certainly I run into this even among polytheists. That they want to conflate Deities and stack Them on top of each other because what they really want, is [that] they only want to have a "decent number" of Gods. If you go to your average tribal society with their indigenous beliefs and you say, "How many spirits do you have?" they'll say, "Hundreds." Maybe the average Joe cannot name Them all, but the local spirit worker sure as hell can. Even if they don't work with all of Them, they know who the spirits are. For them it's no big deal to have hundreds. And yet we try to smoosh Them together to get it down to an even dozen or something like that. And that's because we are affected by the monotheistic idea of the real, "decent" number of Gods, which is one. And the closer you get to one, the more rational you are, the less superstitious you are. That's one of the things I want people to know.

There are those of us who are doing this, but not in an unthinking way. We're not doing it because it sounds cool and we aren't thinking about it too much, and it doesn't make sense if you actually think about it too much. We're doing this because this is the way we experience the world. Also, it does give us immense comfort and immense spiritual attainment and we don't have to "not think" in order to do that. We can think about these concepts deeply. Sometimes we come up against the mystery of what "God" is and everybody struggles with that. No matter how many Gods you've got, you still come up against the "This is my mortal brain trying to comprehend," but we can think deeply about it, and we can find it. It's not being practiced by people who don't think about it deeply. It is practiced by people who do think about it, who do talk to the Gods and ask Them these deep questions, so it's not an unquestioned superstition. It can have just as much theological depth as religions with a "more decent" number of Gods.

Raven has the dubious honor of receiving death threats and hate mail on a regular basis. Some of it comes from people who resent his transgender approaches. Some of it comes from adherents to Heathen religions such as Asatru who are outraged that Raven worships the Gods from the Norse pantheon in the manner in which he does. Some of it comes from people who are angry and uncomfortable about his work in reviving traditions of ordeal spirituality. This sort of hostility might break most people down. Raven has learned to persevere.

Yes, I get hate mail and death threats from the Heathens. Actually, the Neo-Pagans like me for the most part. They certainly keep having me at events to speak and buy books in droves, so I'm not worried about that. So yes, I have to be out and open about a whole lot of things, and my connection to sacred BDSM, sacred ordeal path has really upset a lot of people because it's scary…

My spiritual sister, who is another Hela's person over in Europe, calls me "Hela's lightning rod." I gotta say, lightning rods transmit a whole lot of power. A whole lot of power runs through this lightning rod. One of the things I love about Hela—besides the fact that She doesn't lie, I think that's #1—is that She has this really long view of things. She keeps saying, when I experience conflicts with people in the Northern Tradition, "This will pass. This will pass and your work will be there. This will pass and what you're doing will stay. The things I'm having you do are not the things that are blowing away. They are the things that are going to stay, so don't worry about it." I am blessed with an ability to not really give a shit about what most people really think of me. Which is why you don't find me arguing on email lists or anything like that. I have better things to do.

Caryn

Caryn has been active in Paganism for 36 years. Although she started out in a non-Wicca Craft tradition, Caryn eventually segued into the contemporary Druid fellowship Ár nDraíocht Féin. It was at that point that she first began working with individual Gods and Goddesses. In 1991 she helped found the Cedar Light Grove. In 1996, the grove moved into its own building, which Caryn works hard to maintain. Although Caryn recognizes that her beliefs and practices are hard polytheist, she definitely identifies as Pagan and enjoys participating in the larger pagan community. While her primary work is with Indo-European Gods, she also has personal relationships with the Orisha of African Ifa.

Caryn's understanding of the concept of "polytheism" centers on practice. "Polytheism," she says, "is a spiritual practice that involves multiple Gods and Goddesses and any number of other things—spirits, ancestors—vs. one—monotheism, or two—God and Goddess duotheism." Her understanding of "faith" goes well beyond mere "belief." According to Caryn, "you can believe there are Gods and Goddesses but never have had some kind of experience that makes that belief concrete. Faith is when you know, with or without concrete evidence. There's just no doubt in your mind anymore." When asked what role faith has played in her life, Caryn is very clear that her faith, her certainty beyond mere belief, has been a powerful force. She says that "it has kept me with my Grove and providing public rituals through all manner of blow ups, inter-group firestorms, disappointments, personal failings, personal loss, depression, raising teenagers, and just about every manner explosion that could have happened," then adding, "but as long as I have kept going, the ways have been opened for me."

Caryn began studying Craft-based Pagan traditions in the seventies. Even though she began as a practicing "duotheist," or a believer in one great God and one Great Goddess, Caryn had always suspected that the Gods and Goddesses of the world's myriad pantheons were more than simply facets or archetypes. But it wasn't until years later that she began to practice as a polytheist.

Back in the seventies, I began exploring magic, simply because I was having experiences in my life that no other spiritual path could explain. I began to find explanations, and my first leaning toward polytheism was more duotheistic God and Goddess, but I never practiced what they call Wicca now. Back then, it was just "the Craft." So I never considered myself Wiccan. My practice was mostly solitary for a long time, mostly because I have always been a little too individualistic for most covens anyway. I joined the Coast Guard in 1985 and I met my first husband who was also Pagan and his mother who practiced Native American spirituality in 1990. It was in 1999 that we discovered ADF (Ár nDraíocht Féin) and began focusing more on the Gods and the Goddesses instead of two who represented all the rest. It's not that I didn't believe in other Gods and Goddesses before that, it was more that I didn't have personal relationships with any of Them. That changed in 1999 when I began to develop personal relationships with specific Deities.

While Caryn had known that the Gods and Goddesses were real for several years, it wasn't until her experience battling a life-threatening illness in 1999 that her belief was confirmed. Her experience of being healed through the blessings of the Goddesses Kali Ma and Brigid led Caryn to pursue learning those skills so that she could pass that healing on to others.

We had invited Isaac Bonewits down for a weekend intensive on Druidry. In the end of it, he'd teach and perform a ritual for us, and he called on Brigid, and I saw Her very clearly in my mind's eye. When we passed the waters of life (a chalice of mead), in my mind I saw a light come down and hit me directly in the chest. I'd ask to be healed as I had recently had surgery. I was hurting pretty bad from this scar. That was the first instance, and it felt like "wow She was really here. I asked for a blessing and She gave it to me."

A few weeks later, I found out that I had cancer. I was in the Coast Guard at the time and about to receive my commission to Chief Warrant Officer. Unfortunately you can't be commissioned if you are not fit for full duty, so on the working day before, I was told that I would not receive the commission. I thanked them and walked out, I refused to cry in front of them. My life had just hit a huge brick wall. I stopped at a stop light, and I heard very clearly "it is time you acknowledged Me." I thought, who's "Me"? In my next thought, I knew who it was, and it scared me, because She has always scared me. But I knew that I was in no position to turn down help from anybody at that point, and so at the top of my lungs, with my windows down, at a stoplight, with a car on one side of me, and a car on the other, I yelled at the top of my lungs, "KALI MA, I ACKNOWLEDGE YOU. PLEASE HELP ME." And the light turned green.

It took me about 10 minutes to get home. I didn't notice any change. But when I got home, I opened the door, the door hit the wall and put a hole in the wall, I walked into the house. My ex-husband said later it was like Hurricane Caryn just walked in. The barometric pressure dropped about 30 points. My family was all sitting around, and I walked into the room, and I shouted, "I'M NOT TAKING THIS! WE'RE DOING MAGIC!" They sat wide-eyed and nodded. It was as if [Kali Ma] just took my fear away. We started working on a ritual. It was the most powerful ritual I have ever experienced. For an offering to the Gods, I cut off all my hair and gave it to the fire. This happened about forty-eight hours before the staging operation for my cancer. At this point, the doctors were not saying anything that gave me any hope at all. It was clear cell carcinoma, a very deadly kind of ovarian cancer. Later, I came away from a five hour surgery and they found absolutely nothing. So…I'm a believer. This is how the Gods came into my life.

Unfortunately, Caryn's healing process was disrupted by the departure of her husband, who subsequently divorced her and married someone else. Caryn doesn't dwell on the negative details of the situation, however. She knew her Deities were looking out for her best interests.

A new woman came into my ex-husband's life, and he took off…During this process, I began to hear Them talking to me. They kept saying, "it's going to be okay. Don't worry about it. He's a supposed to leave. This is supposed to happen." It was so weird. I'm sure if I talked to a psychiatrist about this, they would probably not have thought of it in the same light I was thinking of it in. (Laughs). But, it was all supportive, it was all encouraging.

It was then that I had begun to do a lot of meditation. I had a couple of visions. Some of Them were of African Deities. I didn't know anything about the African Deities at this time—I mean, nothing other than: well yeah, They exist. I didn't know any of Their stories, any of Their names, what They looked like, nothing. I had a friend who was raised in Santeria…I called her up…and I began to describe the spirits I was seeing, and the messages They were giving me and what was going on in these visions. Basically, it was the healer Babalu Aye, He is the wounded healer. He takes you through the healing journey. He took me through a re-birthing vision of Oshun as the Mother. It was very intense. And They have been around—not as prevalent sometimes as the Celtic Deities, but They seem to come as needed. There is much more to this story, but in the end, I dedicated my life to service. I have become a reiki master, a priest, and an herbalist. I give back because of what They gave to me.

Caryn's healing skills are an important part of her work as the priest of her Grove and as a servant of Brigid. There are a number of Deities who have helped her with her healing work. While much of her work is with the living, there are times that Caryn's task is to heal places, or to assist those who have died.

There are those [Gods] that work with you very closely, and then there [are] those that will come in and teach you stuff and wonder off, just like people come into your life that need to be there at a particular time and then wander off. That's the way it has been for me. Brigid has been there, Kali has been there very steadily. Manannan has just come into my life here recently to teach me things about walking between the worlds, I'm assuming, because that's what He does.

Kali taught me not to be afraid and She taught me things about slaying "demons"—and I use that word carefully because it's not specifically what I mean—but as a reiki master and a reiki teacher, there are many times that I pull things out of people and had no idea what to do with them. I just followed my intuition and gave them to Kali because She is the demon eater. She transforms negativity. It just made sense to me. She's worked with me very heavily and I've worked with Her very heavily.

If I find things in doing healing, and this might not necessarily be a person, it could be me working on a house—finding things there that are like, "ew, you're yucky, get out!" My guides told me, "there are things that don't need to be in this world." So, I give them to Kali. That's how I've worked with Her. The Morrighan came into my life, and we go around collecting stuff after people die. I do this through a lot of journey work.

I lead reiki shares at my Grove and we all work with the Gods, our guides and our intuition to do energy healings on people. People get a lot of 'stuff' and 'things' attached to them and we help them get rid of it. [They're] hard to describe. I mean, I get impressions in my mind, but I don't have any scientific word for it. I went to a workshop by Ivo Dominguez from the Assembly of the Sacred Wheel once and he had some theories about what happens once the spirit leaves the body. He proposed that the spirit leaves and the body decays. But there is the etheric body (part of the aura) around the physical body, that doesn't decay as rapidly. It has enough of a sense of being alive that it doesn't want to die, but it doesn't have a way to create or self-generate its own energy, so it tends to go around looking for sustenance from other people. Now, I don't know if this is true or not. It's a theory. All I can tell you is that I see things in people and the only impression I'm getting is that they are some kind of energy suckers—like parasites. They need to be removed. Whether my impression is what they truly are or not, I don't know. I do know, however, that there are places where very bad things have happened and there are energies there, living or not, that need to be cleaned up. It's that kind of stuff/things. So, that's what some of the Deities I work with teach me.

As a priest of the ADF, Caryn makes a point to research and interact with the Gods the Grove will be honoring for a given ritual. She leads the grove members to do the same thing.

As a Druid, I call on so many different Deities in ritual because within ADF we're Indo-European. We might do a Norse rite, we might do a Celtic rite, we might do a Greek rite, and if I'm going to call any of these Deities, I am going to know who I'm calling, and I'm going to do my research. And the whole grove feels this way, so before we embark and doing a ritual to Deities we're not close to as a grove, we sit out to do research on Them and know we're talking to. Particularly you want to know how not to make Them angry, how not to insult Them or go in a completely opposite direction. One time, some people in the grove wanted to do a Sumerian rite. Well, Sumerian was not Indo-European…We were like, "we can do this," but we had to do our homework. The cosmology was foreign to us, the gates between the worlds were totally different, the myths were different. We had to understand that to put it into the same context as our ritual. It was a very interesting and enlightening process. It was fun to do.

I kind of feel like I have a personal relationship with a lot of Deities, and a professional relationship with a lot more. I wouldn't feel uncomfortable calling Them in a ritual, They know who I am, even though I'm not dedicated to Them, per se. It's kind of like when I was in the Coast Guard, I had a professional relationship with a lot of people, I wasn't afraid to talk to Them, I knew who They were.

Ritual practice is the backbone of Caryn's polytheism. Ritual is perhaps the major part of her duties with the grove. Even in her personal practice, ritual is key.

We do our eight high days at the grove, and that is certainly communing with our Gods. We have a short and ritual every Sunday at the grove that we do, which is more of a Druid ritual lite. It gives the folks a place for personal prayers and offerings. In my home practice I have a daily morning ritual during which I speak to the Gods and ancestors and nature spirits who are closest to me. I do journey work to talk to Deities and ancestors, distance reiki healing work for people and for the land and greater Earth.

One thing we started doing at the grove, that has been very successful is, a few days to a week before a high rite, we do a guided journey to meet the Deities of the high rite. It's hard to explain that to someone who has never experienced it, what it means to have a personal experience with "Other." For many years, I was looking for ways to help people have an experience like that and experimented with a lot of different things, but they mostly weren't all that successful. Then we tried the journey working prior to the high rite and that has been very successful. A number of people have gained insight into who their patrons or close Deities might be, or Who is watching out for them. A number of them have gotten homework. There are a lot of us who need to do more work.

Caryn's devotion to the Gods takes many forms, and one of those forms is the making of offerings to the Gods. Offerings can range from food and drink to acts of service. According to Caryn, the most important thing about the offerings is that they are given with love and deference.

The best ones, in my opinion, come from the heart. Like, going out and doing something. Like, I have worked in a soup kitchen and volunteered for the past six weeks. Or, I have done this or that for my community. Other options might be a beautifully written prayer, going out and learning a song or a poem by heart and presenting it in the ritual. Making the effort to learn how to make an offering in the language that a Deity particularly came from is also very potent. It requires a lot of effort.

The origin of the word sacrifice means "to make sacred." In my life and experience, my greatest sacrifice is offering my heart and my hands in the service of the Gods. This is what I meant when I became a priest. Having said that, I also light incense, give offerings of food and drink, write songs and poems, and I do healing work for Them.

In the old days, they did offer animals. But what you don't hear so much about is that they didn't have refrigerators or grocery stores or butchers. If you wanted to eat a meal, you had to kill an animal. Why not offer the life of the animal that you are killing to the Gods, and then you share the meat? In any small community, they didn't just have animals that they could throw away. So in that context it makes that much more sense. You are making the animal sacred before you eat it.

There are many myths about the Celtic Gods, and Brigid in particular. While the myths can be informative and a good place to begin to get to know a Deity, personal experience is usually more useful in the end.

The myths are a good place to start. Let's take Brigid of Ireland for example. In the myths, She is spoken of in both singular and in trinic form. She is Brigid, and She is Brigid plus Her two sisters all of which have the name Brigid. In some stories She is one, and in some She is three. In modern Pagan circles, I've noticed that whether people experience Her as one of three generally they experience Her as very kind, and loving, and motherly. This is not the Brigid I know. The Brigid I know is tough. She will not put up with me slacking or whining or crying about things. She's just like, "get up and do it." To me She is like the Celtic mother who teaches Her children how to fight and gives them their first weapons. There were women warriors in both the Celtic and the Norse cultures. The other forms of Brigid, the healer and the bard also work with me at different times. So, mostly They are similar to the myths but that doesn't mean the individual is not going to develop a personal relationship that goes well beyond what is in the myths.

Some of the Deities I have experienced, when I first saw Them in journey-work and/or meditation—I didn't have any preconceived notions, because I didn't know who They were. However when I figured it out, They matched and meshed with Their stories. I've always thought it was kind of interesting how that happens. There are also people who experience Deities in a number of different ways and I think They show up to you in a way that you need Them to at that time. It's rather like, if I was coming into your life to be a teacher, I might take a different approach to you than if I was coming into your life to be a comforting friend.

Ancestors and nature spirits are very important to the ADF theology, and they are very important to Caryn personally. She endeavors to honor them both in her practice.

Well, in ADF, the ancestors and the nature spirits are part of our core ritual practice. I have developed one further because I don't only use Druid spirituality. I draw from a number of different traditions. I heard a comment years ago that, "if it works, it's real" and I like that. Some traditions incorporate an ancestor altar in their worship. This is familiar to us in the table full of pictures that perhaps an older relative had of those who had crossed over. I have a small corner with pictures on the wall and every Monday I have a ritual where I make a big pot of coffee and I have all these little coffee cups and I go around and I give coffee to everybody. All the altars get coffee and I take one to the ancestors. I recite the names of everybody in the pictures and I tell them they're not forgotten. In the African tradition, you only put people from your own bloodline and family in there, but I have friends and pets on my altar too.

At our grove, we have an ancestor altar outside and we used to leave a small plate of food out for them. Unfortunately in my grove, which is up in northeast Baltimore, that's a really bad practice because in Baltimore there are rats. We attracted rats into our yard. Now we just offer coffee or alcohol and make offerings to the nature spirits by hanging birdfeeders up from trees. Both at the grove and at my home, there are special places dedicated to the ancestors and the nature spirits both inside and outside for giving them food and water. I make special offerings to the spirits of the house that work with me and help me. What are they? Some people would tell you they are fairies. Some people will tell you they're this or that or the other, in different mythologies who's called them what names. I don't really worry about it. I just acknowledge they are there and thank them. They help me when I lose things. They like whiskey. They will help me find things real quick if I give them a shot of something they like.

Caryn is not unfamiliar with the experience of conflict due to differing religious views, specifically as regards her personal emphasis on polytheism. She has experienced conflict with both Pagans and non-Pagans on account of her polytheist practice.

When I first became a Druid and we started creating a proto-grove in the Glen Burnie/Pasadena area just south of Baltimore, there was a small Wiccan group that seemed to think we were invading their territory or something, and went way out of their way, particularly their High Priestess, to go around telling people, "well, they don't cast a circle and therefore you're in danger if you go to their rituals. You are opening yourself up to all kinds of things." She even went so far as to say, "I went to one of their rituals and my breast cancer came back, and it was because of them"...I was just flabbergasted by it. I know that there was a proto-grove up in Salem and she had a very tough time of it because there are some very deep-rooted Wiccan groups up there that are quite set in their ways. But in the past ten years, with that one exception, we kind of do our own thing. We own our own property; we're not trying to compete with other groups for a particular space, so there's no competition going on. We don't go out and do recruiting. Our information is on the web, we put up fliers in the shops and all, but that's about it. If you want to find us, you will find us. We tried recruiting one time and we found we are much better off waiting for the people who really want to find us, because there are a whole lot of people out there, Pagan and otherwise, who are just looking for a place to hang out. You really want people who are interested in the mission and vision of your particular group. I teach leadership concepts in my grove, mission/vision statements, business plans, group dynamics. Being Pagan and hanging out only requires a coffee shop or a person's living room. If you really are serious about forming a group, buying property and keeping this group going, then it requires work—a lot of it.

One thing Caryn wishes everyone understood about polytheism is that the Divine is so much more immense and powerful that humans can honestly imagine. Whether it takes a singular form or many individual forms, Caryn recognizes that it is still so far beyond human comprehension that it is unreasonable to assume that any one theology is the correct one. Each person has the right to believe and practice as they see fit, but it's important to know that it is possible for everyone's belief to be correct.

I wish they could understand that whether your concept of the

Divine is one or many, that whatever it is, it is so much greater than anything we can conceive of. Why does it not have the power to manifest in singular or multiple forms? As I wrote your questionnaire, one of the analogies I give to people, usually the ones who show up on your doorstep and want to proselytize to me about "the lord," is that if you can imagine a father having thirty different children, of thirty different ages, speaking thirty different languages, would you speak to them all in one voice, in one language, in one way, and say that is the only way? Even if they didn't understand you, would you continue speaking in that way, or would you change your approach so that different people in different places and different times would be able to understand the communication? You know, and I'm not saying that the message is all the same, because I don't know that it is. I have had people insinuate that what I'm hearing is not the Divine, it's something demonic. You know, it's kind of weird. I have run across a lot of things in 53 years, and the only real evil I have ever felt—and I'm very empathic—was in the hearts of humans. I can go to places and I feel things, sometimes those things are very angry, but they aren't evil. That's a sad statement, I know. But evil is not in the natural world. It's humans who manifest it. I wish they could understand that instead of looking at the drastic differences. I don't know why certain religions came up with, "if you don't believe our way, then you're wrong. If you don't believe what I believe, then either I'm right, and you're wrong or you're right and I'm wrong." Why can't we both be right for us?

Joel

Joel has been a polytheist for over 13 years. At one time, Joel was fairly strict in his identity as member of the Kemetic Orthodox religion, a group that is dedicated to recreating the traditions of ancient Egypt. He kept this tradition separate from his participation in a local Wiccan coven. Through his growing and evolving relationships with his Deities, Joel eventually came to identify primarily as a Wiccan. Today, his strongest relationships are with Yinepu and the God and Goddess of Wicca. Joel maintains a regular devotional practice to Them, as well as to his Ancestors and the elements.

When asked to define the concept of "polytheism," Joel becomes somewhat circumspect. He recognizes that there are many working definitions out there, and says that he is as yet undecided on which one he agrees with philosophically, but his practice tends to emphasize approaching the Gods as powerful, individual, discrete Divinities.

In my experience, modern Pagans kind of define polytheism in two different ways. I haven't really decided on which way I view it. There is a type of polytheism called soft polytheism, where the idea is that there is a Divine God who is so massive, so immense, and so unknowable to us as finite beings that it interacts with us through more relatable forms, masking as the Gods. These are the Gods of the many different pantheons. Some of the soft polytheists would adhere to the belief that if you are serving one God, you are also serving all Gods because all Gods are part of one God. Whereas hard polytheists more so perceive the individual Gods as being entities unto Themselves and personalities unto Themselves without any kind of relationship between the different pantheons. Whereas soft polytheists may see Bast of Egypt as a form of Artemis from Greece, and they would relate to Her by saying, "You who are Artemis, who is also known as Bast." A hard polytheist would see those two beings as pretty distinct entities. I fall somewhere in between. I definitely do feel that the whole truth about a God, any God—we can only get a fraction of what that is. So, I kind of feel like it's up to the perceiver to determine whether or not the Gods are related to each other. When you start realizing that it isn't easy to determine how much the Gods are defined by human perception, you start to get into the real thick of soft polytheism…

It's just a really different experience that one gets when approaching different Gods. You can try to use the same formula, and in my experience, it will come out with varying results if you get any results at all. I kind of feel like the Gods, whichever God you want to have a relationship with, has at some point had a following and has related to people in a particular fashion. To try to use another culture's—let me take a step back a little bit. The rituals that we use to communicate with the Gods, to me I think, are more focusing tools for us than for Them. It is a symbolic language that we use to communicate with Them and to call upon Them. To use one culture's language to call upon certain Gods from a different culture may not make much sense. It's like dialing the wrong area code.

According to Joel, faith doesn't seem to play a role in modern Paganism. In his view, Pagans rely on personal experience rather than belief to inform their spiritual practice.

Faith, in my opinion, is about believing even despite lack of evidence and experience, or in face of contrary evidence and experience. I do not think many Pagans are "have faith" in this sense because many Pagans base their beliefs on experience and personal gnosis. So, I suppose I have faith that my experiences of my Gods and of religion in general are genuine but I do not think blind faith—that is, believing despite evidence to the contrary or lack of experience—is a common feature in Paganism.

Joel was raised in a Catholic family, but felt increasingly alienated from that religion as he came to terms with his sexuality. Ancient mythology had always interested him, and as he began to delve into history, the religion of ancient peoples began to make more sense to him than Catholicism ever had.

I was raised Roman Catholic. It was at the age of 12 or 13 that I actually kind of turned a critical eye towards my birth religion and through my own personal study of the Bible and the Catholic faith and the Catholic religion. I just kind of felt there was something missing and felt no spiritual connection with Catholicism. Especially as a gay youth, I felt both alienated and condemned. So I began to feel that I couldn't practice or believe in a religion that thought of me—my very existence—as an aberration and as sinful. I knew from a very young age that I was born gay and I flat-out refused to believe in a God who would create me this way and be so hateful of me.

Ancient mythology always interested me. Having taken a critical eye toward my birth religion, I started to think about, "well, you know just because the Bible says that this God is the only God, is that really the case? People were worshipping Gods long before Christianity came along, so I started to study what these other people believed and why they believed it. A lot of it just seemed to make a lot more sense to me and it resonated with me more so than anything that was Christian.

Joel has had many experiences which have convinced him that the Gods are there and welcome people who want to interact with them. These experiences weren't necessarily gigantic and fantastic, but they were powerful and meaningful. His first important Deity relationship was with Yinepu, whom the Greeks called Anubis.

Though it continues today, it started early on, when I was a teenager, when I first started on this path ten years ago. When I had no other place to turn to, when I really felt like my back was up against the wall, there was nothing—and not only on an emotional level—more comforting than praying to my patron God. Not only that, but I felt there was much more feedback than there had ever been when I was praying to Jesus or the Christian God. There was also, I certainly believe—and this is the part where faith somewhat comes in because I can't prove to anybody else—but in my experience, it is a fact of my experience that there was a physical manifestation when it comes to interaction with my patron God. For example, we were really, really dirt poor. I would just be so upset because I did not have any money for my lunch or my younger sister's lunch and yet I would find $5, $10, $20 every week for months straight, just laying on the ground somewhere. I mean, how often do you come across money—I mean honestly—laying in the street? I was in the suburbs, so it wasn't like, you know, a big city with a lot of traffic. There were also certain people who were dangerous elements in my life at the time and they were, after one prayer, removed as obstacles in my life. Those are just two small examples of in the past how, at the time that I needed intervention the most, it was the most profound intervention that I have ever experienced…You don't have to be standing on a mountaintop waiting for lighting to carve words into tablets. You just need a response. Something to acknowledge that you're not *alone. I think that's one of the most impactful parts of Paganism.*

Even thought he attended ritual with a local British traditional coven, for many years Joel identified primarily as Kemetic Orthodox. He was brought to the Kemetic path through his relationship with Yinepu. Through Kemeticism, Joel came to know the God Ra.

When I was studying ancient religions, I really studied different religions. I studied up on the Greek pantheon, the Roman pantheon, the Norse pantheon, the Celtic pantheon, I even went to the pantheons of the Far East and Africa. Praying. Praying and trying to interact with these Gods. I didn't really get very much of any kind of response. I didn't feel like anybody "up there" was paying attention to me. So I kind of got desperate. For a long time I disregarded the Egyptian pantheon as a primitive pantheon because I thought they worshipped animals and wanted human-looking Gods, because that's what Gods look like. So, from years before I had gone to a museum and bought a statue of Anubis and it was sitting there. I finally just said, "what the hell?" I learned what would be the good way to approach this God, what this God was about, and I just started with a real simple ritual. Lighting a candle, saying a prayer, offering an apple. The response I got was profound.

When you first come into Kemetic Orthodoxy and decide that you want to be a part of the temple, there is a divination that they do. Part of the divination is to determine who created you, as they say in the African tradition, "who owns your head." Who your parent is, who is responsible for you, in a cosmic sense. A part of that that comes up is your parent Deity, who Yinepu is for me. But they also have a beloved Deity who is like your uncle or your aunt or would be like your godparent—somebody who's also involved in your life in this current incarnation and also has a predominate influence in your life as well…Ra is more backseat, but He's always there. He's like a very quiet in the background, not as hands on or directly involved.

I had been working with and worshipping Yinepu long before my divination, like 3 years prior. I was very concerned that He would wind up not being my parent. But that was not the case. My brothers and sisters in the faith, even the one who was working the divination said that they would "be very surprised if you are not the son of Yinepu because you just have His influence written all over you." It was a relief.

Eventually, Joel sensed that Yinepu was "stepping back," because there were other Deities who wanted to work with Joel. In time he discovered that They were the God and Goddess of Wicca. In the past few years, Joel has come to embrace his Wiccan identity. Ra has stepped back altogether, and although Yinepu is still important, Joel's has established a powerful relationship with the Wiccan deities.

Yinepu sort of stepped back for a minute, kind of clearing the floor for somebody else to speak. I just kind of felt like my mind was being lured to think about topics that in the past I never had any interest in... Like, I never really had any interest in the Greek Goddesses but I had been told to check Them out, or the Greek Gods like Dionysus. Then I'd been interested in reading about Cernnunos or the Horned God...I just felt like there was something...it's sort of a similar feeling I had when I first started exploring Paganism, like, "there's something out there," tapping its foot waiting for me to find it.

I also had a strong interest in Witchcraft, as both a practice and a religion. So I began studying European Witchcraft, specifically, British Traditional Wicca with a traditional coven here in Pennsylvania and that's how I met the God and Goddess of Wicca...I have been working with the Wiccan God and Goddess for the last few years. It's an interesting dynamic having three Gods from two different traditions in my life.

Joel describes his relationships with his Deities as very parental. It is amazing to Joel that such powerful and mysterious beings would show any interest in him, much less have such willingness to engage with him and be in his life.

Yinepu is very much a father figure and patient. Very, very patient. It's more than something that solidifies my belief that my God, as opposed to, say, the Christian God who is supposed to be this kind of figure but is very impersonal whereas Yinepu is how I imagine the perfect father to be. He guides you, He's not gonna smack you down with a 2X4...The fact that this huge, immense Deity has taken His time and interest to bother Himself to care about me, you know. That something incomprehensible and powerful has taken it upon Himself to make an effort to make my life better. Then you realize, you ponder your own individual God. That you may have a God, like for example Yinepu is a God of embalming, He's a cthonlic Deity of the underworld. Westerners tend to compartmentalize the Gods with these words, but They never really are just that thing—They are so much more. Like, when you think about how vast They actually are, it's just amazing…The God and Goddess and God of Wicca, too, are like parents. I'm still developing my relationship with Them, so I haven't entirely sussed Them out. But paternal is also a very good word for Them.

Joel is understandably reticent to discuss the intricacies of his relationships with the God and Goddess of Wicca because those relationships are still very new and very open. His years of experience with Yinepu, however, encourage Joel to share some of the important things he has learned from this God.

Patience and balance. Balance is very important personally in the personality, in the life, and in the thinking. I was very, well—of the thinking that, you know, "things are this way," and I will argue with you until I'm blue in the face to make you understand why things should be "this way." Or, if somebody did "that" wrong. Or if some people are just "wrong" in their thinking, in their personal behaviors, it would just be enough to make me completely blow them off or make judgments on them. But He has tempered me to a point where I'm not so easily stuck in one way or the other. Which is interesting because He is also, in the underworld, the God who deals with the scales of the underworld: when you die, whether or not you are a just soul deserving of a good afterlife…He's the balancer of the scales.

Joel observes a devotional practice to Yinepu and to the God and Goddess of Wicca. He used to keep the two practices completely separate, but over time he began to combine the two into a dynamic devotional framework.

The Kemetic Orthodoxy is an international religion at this point…I have never participated in a group ritual with them. But we do have a standard ritual that is provided that all of us are encouraged to do on a daily basis. It's a standard ritual Kemetic Orthodoxy. And while I still have a relationship with Yinepu, the Kemetic God, it's become more informal and I don't really identify as Kemetic Orthodox anymore. I've been Wiccan for the last two years and I do celebrate Sabbats with a coven, and it is a completely different experience. They are more European-based. They celebrate the God and the Goddess, they are duotheistic. They celebrate the Esbats monthly. I have a shrine set up for both the Gods of Wicca and Yinepu and I light a votive candle for Them each night…I have a shrine that I tend for my Ancestors. The only nature spirits I work with are the Four Elements.

Joel studied mythology heavily prior to becoming a polytheist, but he never felt that the myths should be taken as literal truths. For him, mythology provides an opportunity to gain insight into the Gods and his relationship with Them.

> *I feel a healthy and rational approach to spirituality (if there is such a thing as a rational spirituality) is one that is grounded in personal experience but also tempered by the experiences of others, particularly the historical experiences of others as codified in myth. It's a balance and a way to ensure you're personal gnosis isn't just imagination or personal delusion. So, for the most part, the myths corroborate my personal experiences and the instances in which they do not, lead to a lot of spiritual insight—figuring out if it's a genuine experience of the Divine or imagination, what the significance of the experience is, and how or why it differs from mythos and why that's important.*

Joel has experienced a degree of friction with non-Pagans as regards his emphasis on polytheism, but he has experienced no conflict with other Pagans about the matter. Pagans, in his experience, tend to be curious and respectful about different religious practices. Joel explains that the only conflicts he has seen within Paganism tend to revolve around orthodoxy.

> *In my experience, you get two types of people…You get the Christians, who are the most ubiquitous. But then you also get the atheists, who are almost as bad. On the one hand, you have those who think either you are just playing Xena* or you're being misled by dark evil forces. No matter what you say to them, they're going to—they already decided what your deal is, so you're kind of talking to a brick wall. So it either becomes vitriolic or it becomes patronizing.*
>
> *I think Pagans tend to be very interested in each other's spiritual practices, so the Wiccan coven was very interested in what I [was doing] as Kemetic Orthodox, what the Kemetic Orthodox is, how it started, what they believe, and how they practice. A lot of people in the Kemetic Orthodoxy actually come from other Pagan traditions like Wicca, so it's got the same kind of feedback that way.*
>
> *In general, I think the only conflict you really find within the Pagan community is when you get into specifics or the orthodoxy of a particular tradition. The most prevalent one in the Pagan community is who really should be considered Wiccan. Somebody who has been initiated through a lineage tradition, or the people*

who "self-initiate"—air quotes—themselves. Should they be considered Wiccans? Getting into specifics is where a lot of the friction comes from...I think both sides have a valid point. On the one hand, using a word like "Wicca" I think kind of requires a group consensus. It requires a group identity. I think some people have used it as a personal identity. I think it's understandable on both sides, but that is probably one of the biggest things I have seen. It's a sort of conflict that occurs due to an over-arching tension between the traditionalists in Paganism—and it's not just specific to Wicca—and people who feel that religion is what you make it and feel it's best to draw from and incorporate from many different sources without adopting the system as a whole.

Joel doesn't have anything in particular he wishes that people understood about polytheism. He is interested in theology from a non-Western standpoint and does not expect that others would or should have any interest in the matter simply because it is important to him.

I look at my theology as kind of "my thing." I have circles that I hang around with and talk theology with. I'm not really that concerned with what people think about what I do unless I'm involved with them in a relationship or it's a family member and then I'm borderline. But I'm not...what I do is what I do, What they do is what they do. I am not concerned unless you are interested in learning. I'm not concerned about whether or not they understand it. As long as they respect my right to freedom of religion, I'm entirely unconcerned about what people think about my religion.

---

* Joel here refers to the mid-90's television show, "Xena, Warrior Princess" which centered on a quasi-mythic warrior queen who quested through the ancient Greco-Roman world. Often the storylines relied significantly on the interaction between humans and the Greek Gods, who were portrayed as physically manifest in human form.

Jax

Fiction writer and piano teacher Jax has been a polytheist for over a decade. She a Heathen who honors the Norse Gods of her ancestors. One thing that really bothers Jax is the stereotypes of Pagans as being counter-cultural, esoteric, and "into woo-woo stuff." She very much considers herself to be a material "girly girl," a fact reflected by the name of her blog: Pagan Princesses. Yet she is steadfast in her conviction that Paganism is "a force for positive change in the world" and considers herself a Pagan advocate dedicated to showing that Paganism is as normal and acceptable of a religion as Christianity. Jax maintains devotional relationships with Forseti, Frau Holde, Frigga and Bragi, but the most important part of her religious practice is tending to her ancestors and house wights.

Jax recognizes that different members of the Pagan community have different definitions of polytheism. While Jax thinks both are valid, she identifies as a hard polytheist.

> To me polytheism is, to me it actually has two slightly different definitions. There's hard polytheism which is, "I believe in separate Gods. There is Zeus and there is Athena, and there is Mercury. Or there is Freya and there is Odin and there is Thor and they are actual entities...Each is a fully separate entity or God you can interact with. Another definition of polytheism to me is, soft polytheism, [where] there are separate entities of Gods which are actually a part of a divine source. That would be more like the Hindu, version of polytheism or some version of Hinduism which sees the different Gods as spokes of a wheel, parts of a whole...but that they have enough independence that they can be appealed to as separate aspects. Those are my two definitions of polytheism and I would actually call somebody who ascribes to either one of those a polytheist.

Jax's understanding of faith is fairly straightforward. For her, faith is "is belief without scientific basis." However, she doesn't think that faith is necessarily a function of religion, and she sees atheism as a sort of faith as well.

> When we take one step beyond what we know and go "OK, this is what I have seen in my life, and so based on the evidence I will believe." Or "this is what I've been taught and combined with

what I have seen I will believe this." To me, . . .atheism is actually a faith because they are going on faith that whatever hasn't been scientifically proved or can't be experienced with the five senses is not real. That's the belief that they have. . .based on what they see and what they have been taught. For me, based on what I have [seen] in my past and what I see in my present and what I have read, I believe They are real. I also "believe" in ancestor worship, but that's not something I can necessarily "prove."

Jax' journey into Heathenry began, like many others, by stepping away from Christianity and towards Pagansim. The trouble that Jax encountered with Paganism was that she could not divide her worldview into two gendered compartments, and thus found it difficult to connect with the Goddess and the God.

I was raised Christian like many Pagans...I always...Inside I have never had any doubt there is something out there. Of course logically I think most of us question if there's something out there or not...but inside there's always some sort of core faith that there is something divine...I had problems with some of the doctrines of Christianity, some of the dogma, and so after college I started looking for a faith and something about Paganism really appealed to me. I don't think I was a Polytheist when I first called myself a Pagan, I think I was more interested in the whole concept; but the longer I sat with it the more I realized what a valid concept it was that there actually could be multiple Gods. I'd always been taught there was only one and it didn't make sense to believe in multiple Gods and I think that prejudice I was taught as a child took me a while to get over...

I will tell this story because this is actually full of Paganism and Polytheism at the same time. This was when I went to the very first circle I ever had. I went out to a creek near my house. I set up my deck of Tarot cards and my grandmother's Bible. . .I cast my first circle and prayed to multiple Gods as opposed to Jehovah. And lightening did not strike and I did not feel strange and I did not feel suddenly evil and I did not think I suddenly was a bad person. It amazed me how much nothing happened. And, I left there with a sense of peace. This idea that I wasn't evil, this is actually OK, that I didn't have a negative experience so I can actually continue on with this. This first time released so much of my fear. And that was really a big deal...

I live in a pretty liberal community so there are a lot of people who are Wiccan, and they have less of a polytheism and more of a duo-theism, but was still different from what I'd experienced before. But that never really resonated with me at all; I never understood why they divided the world up into male and female. I just think that is a strange division and I don't think the world is either male or female. And all of "this all female and can be summed up in one Goddess"—I don't know, but that's what I'd mostly encountered and so I think that was one of my early signs to me that this was not for me because I tried. I cannot divide my world view into two so neatly.

She realized that she wasn't Christian, but that she also wasn't really Pagan, either. It was when she began to research her Teutonic and Celtic ancestry that she started to feel a connection to the Gods. These Gods felt real and immediate to Jax, because she saw them as fully fleshed out beings with personalities.

Researching more into individual Gods and, and at first I was a little more cautious in looking here and looking there. Some of them from the Greek pantheon never appealed to me. I don't feel very connected to that. And…Polytheism started hitting more home and I started researching more of where my ancestral heritage should be, "ah: Celtic and Norse." And I guess I felt a very tight connection when I started researching Norse Heathenry, and I started writing characters that had practiced this…the connection was just so strong and these Gods, I loved, loved…Norse Heathenry, one of the things I loved right off the bat was that it just isn't, they don't divide it like the God of love, the God of war…I don't think all reconstructionist polytheists actually do this. We're kinda taught it that way in school, you know Athena the Goddess of war and wisdom; that takes Gods and makes them abstractions as opposed to fully developed characters. My early experiences with the Norse Gods weren't categorical like that. They were beings who had these different experiences and did these different things and they had personalities. But they weren't an aspect, or a category or an archetype. They were more, actually they were characters—that sounds fictional and I don't mean the word that way, but as well-rounded individuals, they had personality, not just adjectives. I'd never thought of mythological Pagan Gods that way, I'd always associated them with an archetype and actually viewed them as full-fledged entities. Revolutionary for me. I really liked that and I think that helped develop me into a more hard-polytheist. Gods are people, too.

So, yeah, I think that I was starting to connect with different Gods. . .and I think at first I did connect with certain aspects, like there is a divine something out there. So when I started researching Heathenry, which I did because I'm of northern-European ancestry, I'd check out what my ancestors actually observed. . .the first God I actually reached out to, and I'm not really sure if I was reaching out to Him as an individual or reaching out to Him as an abstract something, was Forseti the God of communication and the intermediary of the Gods. And it was clear to me in a way that it never really had [been] before.

When asked whether she has had experiences that confirm for her that the Gods exist, Jax explains that she has always believed that the Gods exist, and has always felt that they were "there" and heard her prayers. She also admits her dislike of the term "proof" when used in relation to religious convictions.

I have had experiences since childhood that tell me something is out there. I used to pray all the time to the Christian God, and I felt like I was answered. Now that I venerate the Northern Gods, I feel like they listen, too. I don't like talking about "proof" as I feel like that's just asking somebody to tell you how you misinterpreted and it's coincidence or all in my head or whatever. Faith is all about taking that extra step, and there is no story that will convince somebody who believes differently than you do that your beliefs are justified. But I have proof enough that works for me, and that's all I need. I don't feel the need to convince anyone else.

What originally drew Jax to Forseti was her need to solve a pressing problem. Serving as the leader of her writing organization was very difficult because of conflict and strife among the members. Her research led her to conclude that Forseti could really help with the issues she faced. According to Jax, that is exactly what He did.

Actually I was having a problem. I'm president of a writing organization in town and we were having internal conflict with some members and I was just really frustrated and didn't know what to do about it. I was like wow, you know, ok. I've been studying the Norse canon, I've been thinking about things from more of a Heathen perspective: "What would happen if,. . .who would I talk to," you know. And Forseti was the one that seemed to match up more closely with my problems, so I prayed to Him and it went, the conference went incredibly smoothly and everything worked out way better than I could ever have anticipated and…I was incredibly thankful.

Although some see Her as strictly a folk heroine, Jax recognizes Frau Holde as a Deity, one she feels quite close to. Jax prays often to Frau Holde for help with those parts of day-to-day life that are difficult to manage. She also appeals regularly to Frigga, Queen of Asgard, for help with wisdom and perspective, especially regarding household matters.

> *Oh, I love Frau Holda. Frau Holda is interesting because really She doesn't come so much in the original myths, like when you're reading the Eddas, and so there are a lot of research that sort of has Her as a version of Freya, or "this is what Freya really is." I don't know. I love Frau Holda and I totally pray to Her more than anybody, because I am a terrible housekeeper. This is some part of my life that I'm really trying to get better at, and to become a better person at. I love Her stories, this person who is so happy with things running smoothly and it actually reminds me--more than Freya it reminds me of Sunna, the Norse Goddess of the sun, because the sun in female in Norse mythology.*

> *I think it's a lot like the idea that…my mother was, at least, the "sun" in our household and we revolved around her. She kept everything going. She really did. I don't think it has to be the woman that does that, but in my family, it was. And she loved that and she loved being that sun that we all grew around, that rock we could all hang onto when things were not going right. And Frau Holda has that aspect of: I can make peace and I can make things smooth here, I can make my home that I live in and that my husband returns to be a place of peace. My husband works outside out home, and I don't, so it's my favorite term. Again I'm not saying I think women should stay home and cook and clean and men should go out. But in my house that's the way it happens to be. So there we are…I find Her very inspiring and I find Her industriousness—which I lack—to be something I would like to emulate more, and I think I [am] a better person for having Her in my life.*

> *Frigga again, I care about Frigga cause She is more on the same as with Frau Holda, in that She is the key to something that I am not particularly good at. I would like to be better. I have always been a wanderer, a traveler and Frigga is so calm and is so wise and grounded. She can be more circumspect, I guess. And so Frigga again is someone I'm trying to understand better and I want some of Her wisdom because that is something I*

lack.

As one who aspires to be a successful professional writer, Jax has found that the God Bragi plays an important role in her life. Jax definitely feels that He has been helpful in establishing her writing career.

> *Bragi Is the God of poetry and he's someone I'm trying to get to know better because I'm a writer and would love to have some of His energy. So whenever I do a piece, I always say His name sometimes before I start writing—especially if I'm having a difficult time forging ahead—to help me have better inspiration or a better word so I can tell the story...*

> *I'm a fiction writer. I only recently started taking it seriously, but I've been writing my entire life. And I have found I tend to deal with reality through fiction. I can always tell: "hey look at this story I've just written, it's very clearly about something I just went through," an allegory or I don't know, I don't mean to it's just very clearly things I'm going through just come out in my writing. . .and I have for the past many years now been working on my relationship with Bragi, which has been the time I've been taking my writing much more seriously. Yes my writing has become very Pagan, with Pagan characters. The first book I ever wrote was actually before I was a Heathen, but the main guy was a Viking and he dealt with Odin. The main guy had lost his faith because he didn't understand why things happened the way they did and he's angry about it. And at the end of the story he finds it again and is able to accomplish more than he could have before. He's successful because he found his faith again. So I have a lot of that in my stories about finding faith or reconnecting with faith or being lost and trying to figure out where to go on basis of hope. That's sort of a major theme for my fiction.*

While Jax is happy to honor the Gods and is sure to express gratitude for Their blessings, she doesn't think the Gods actually need humans to worship Them. In her view, the Gods would rather be honestly and sincerely honored than worshipped out of fear.

> *To me, growing up the way I did, a God that requires worship is that "you will be punished if you do not worship me whether in this life or in the next life. This is your requirement for being a good person" sort of God. I don't think that the Gods feel that way though. I think if you choose to worship Gods or if you choose to worship some and not others, the ones that are not*

getting worshiped by you won't be mean or planning revenge…I do worship on high holy days, but it's not because I am under duress, or required to, or because I am afraid something bad will happen to me…It brings joy to me.

I want a relationship with the divine and it has always been important in my life even when I was a young child. I think for some people having a connection to the divine—however they define it—is important, and I think for some people it really isn't. I'm one of those people that having that connection is important. And so of course I pour a measure out for the different Gods and welcome Them into my life— because I want Them to be in it…

Veneration of the Gods is a reconnection to something larger than myself, a reconnection to something outside of mortal trappings, but still vital in mundane life. Knowing I have someone or something that will listen when I need it because I have asked for Their presence in my life. Not that I think the Gods are at my beck and call—it's not like I ask for something all the time. But we have a connection and a relationship, and I have that extra well to draw from when I need it.

While the Gods are important to Jax, she says that the majority of her daily religious practice revolves around honoring her ancestors and the wights, or spirits of place. For Jax, keeping the ancestors and wights happy is very important to keeping peace in her home.

I feel like worshiping and interacting with Gods is more of something that is a major holiday affair or for when you are having a big trouble kind of thing. My ancestors are really on my side. I talk to them on almost a daily basis. I honestly think that is one of the things I love about Heathenry is that it is a reminder that we are, how connected we are to other people, to our ancestors, to future generations of our families, to the land we live on, and finding our peace. And to me, the land wights and the ancestors are that connection…so much of who I am is because of what came before me, and my whole life I've been so thankful for my family because I look at a few generations ago what were we doing. And I think of the work that my parents and grandparents and my great-grandparents did to put me in the fortunate position that I am in. And I thank them for that and I want to be a part of that so that my children can look back on me and say "I'm thankful that my mother and grandmother did so much to make life better for me. And ancestors are just that connection to the past and concerned with future and a reminder that we are one link on a chain.

At least once a week I thank my Tomte, the house spirit, as well, to help me remember that households are, in a way, living things. They affect us so much because our house is where we come back to everyday. So taking care of that and being responsible for that, with the land, working in harmony with the space that we live in and trying to be environmentally conscious about that. I have an enormous pecan tree in my back yard but I never even paid attention to it until after I started honoring the wights, and I realized what a miracle it is that a tree of this height has been around for maybe a hundred years growing in my back yard in a small space between my house and an apartment complex; being cognizant that tree has been here for longer than I have and might be here when I'm gone. This tree has a permanence that I have not. How I interact with it—I need to be cognizant of that. To me, Heathenry is working with ancestors—our connection through time—and the spirits of the house and land—our connection to place. With these we make our place in the continuity of lives on the planet...

The lore, or recorded mythology and history of the Scandinavian peoples, is a major part of Heathen culture. Because she is a Heathen, Jax has had a lot of experience with reading the mythology and comparing it to her own personal experiences. Even so, Jax tends to think that the reconstruction of Germanic religion is less about quoting the history, and more about recapturing the worldview and cultural understandings.

I'm probably a middle-of-the-line reconstructionist. I'm definitely not one of these people that's like "Wow! Look on page blah blah blah it's in the Lore, people!" I think it's important that we read and we are cognizant because really reconstructionism is about what people were doing before Christianity took over. There was something real and something good going on. It wasn't perfect, just like no people in their time and no religion in any time is perfect, but it had something solid that got lost, got destroyed by a group that was determined to destroy anything that wasn't it. So for me reconstructionism is not about exactly replicating what we had...It's about trying to capture a spirit and a way of looking at things that was lost in favor of a monotheistic system that believes in forgiveness of sin, and heaven and hell. And I don't find that system valid for me, I don't think that's right. I'm trying to get back to the essence of what was. Now with the lore, I recognize that a lot of it was written by

Christians. I don't believe in strictly sticking with every single line you see because you never know time and place—and sometimes we know who—but trying to capture that essence of what was and bring it to the now. That's what reconstructionism is about to me.

While Jax enjoys being Pagan, she doesn't always feel like she fits in with other Pagans. She is less interested in the esoteric, magic, and counter-cultural aspects of Paganism than many other she meets. She also has less of a problem with Christianity.

I haven't had so much of a problem with other Pagans, more just, I'm not very "woo woo." I think it's more concrete. That's more what I've had a problem with because...I like having discussions with...I don't think everything is OK. I don't actually agree with the idea that if it feels right, do it and I feel like I've run into a lot of that. And a lot of anger towards Christianity. I didn't feel it was right for me. I don't think Christians are bad people, and I kind of got tired defending my family who's all Christian but me. [Even] so it actually, I haven't had a lot of negative interactions with other Pagans, mostly it has been very positive my interactions with other Pagans. I don't want sound negative about other Pagans at all, because most of the time I really do get along with other people without heartache. I've had enough every now and then where it gets really negative about Christianity and I'm like "whoa, my mother is not a bad person." Or I have words with them and very much, "it's OK," and I'm like, "you know, I don't know, I'm not OK with everything you've ever said; I'm OK with you making your own decisions about things and thinking about them carefully before you make them."

Despite Jax's occasionally uneasy relationship with Paganism, she has experienced more friction with her non-Pagan family and friends than with Pagans. Especially difficult have been her interactions with atheists.

My family is very not happy with the fact that I am Pagan. My sister she doesn't care. My parents are not OK with this. But they love me and I think they are hoping I don't go to hell...Actually what has cracked me up the most is the reaction I've gotten from my friends who are atheists. The monotheists, I kinda get that, I kind of was expecting that. But my atheist friend thinks like I'm worse than being Christian or something because I don't believe in one God, I believe in a bunch of them. So clearly I'm a superstitious wing nut or something. I think a lot of the reasons they left Christianity for atheism are the exact reasons why I left Christianity for Paganism. My atheist friends don't seem to see the similarities. They only see that one glaring difference that I believe in something they don't and I'm a complete crazy person. I believe in multiple Gods. And I'm like, "you do realize that Hinduism is polytheistic and they are the fourth largest religious group on the planet earth and one of the oldest?" No, I'm more of a wing nut than my Christian family because I believe in multiple Gods, so OK. I've had more conflict with actual atheists, it's surprising [how] much more [is] the amount of disdain I've gotten from atheists.

Yeah. I was out with one of my friends one time and it was just hysterical, he was like, "well you know you're telling everybody that they have to believe exactly like you do." And I'm like, "I have never said that." No part of my faith applied to any argument he gave me. It does not apply to polytheism. I tried to tell him, "You're arguing with somebody else because I don't think any of the things you've just accused me of thinking."

When asked what she wished people understood about polytheism, Jax made two related observations. She would like for people to take it seriously and not automatically dismiss her as a lunatic. She also wants them to respect it as a valid religious perspective instead of demonizing it or pretending it doesn't exist.

I wish that people understood that we do think about them and, well I guess it depends on who it is. If I'm talking to an atheist, I wish they understood that I really am serious, that I really do believe this. And you should respect my belief system. If I'm talking to other Christians, or monotheists, that believing in multiple Gods should not be considered stranger than believing in one just because it is less common. And I think that it creates a balance that can't happen when there is only one. It allows for diversity and any religion can be used for good or ill, but polytheism is a religion that allows for diversity and understanding.

P. Sufenas Virius Lupus

❊❊❊❊❊❊❊❊❊

P. Sufenas Virius Lupus is a 37-year old college professor who lives in the Pacific Northwest. When e was 15 years old, Lupus began eir journey into polytheism. E* says that it wasn't a conversion so much as it was a discovery "that I was something that I hadn't realized previously." For 21 years, e has worked both with groups and on eir own, but what remains constant is that Lupus is committed to a project of remembering and syncretism. Many of the Gods with whom e works are barely remembered and rarely venerated by those who have not sought Them out. Eir story reminds us that even when humans forget about the Gods, They never forget about us, and They are just as interested in working with us now as They were in centuries past. Among the many Deities Lupus works with are Antinous, Hadrian, Sabina, Hermes, Silvanus, Antenociticus, Cocidius, Polydeukion, Serapis, Cú Chulainn, the Trí Dee Dána, Hanuman, Iao Sabaoth, Thoth, Anubis, Hathor, Hekate, Artemis, Sarutahiko-no-Okami, Glykon, and Sterculinus.

Like many polytheists, Lupus is very syncretic in the traditions that e follows. The tradition with which e is most active is Ekklesía Antínoou, which e describes as "a queer Greco-Roman-Egyptian reconstructionist polytheist groups that's dedicated to Antinous," who was the deified lover of the Roman Emperor Hadrian, "as well as other Divine figures associated with Him and with Them." In this tradition, Lupus serves as the Mystagogos, or leader, of the group. However, Lupus has also reconstructed the Celtic practices of filidecht and gentlidecht and made them an important part of eir practice. "Filidecht," Lupus explains, "is poetry, but you can't do poetry in Irish without the otherworld and its Beings getting involved." The term "Gentlidecht" is a medieval Irish term that was "likely invented by Christians which refers pre-Christian practices." It is described as "taking auspices and making offerings and believing in otherworld beings and seeking Them out and so forth." Lupus uses the term "to indicate that many of my practices are drawn from medieval sources as we have them. I am assuming that they are

---

*At the respondents' request, the gender-neutral Spivak pronouns of e, em, and eir are replacing the gendered pronouns of she/he, her/him, and hers/his, respectively, in instances where the text refers to Lupus.

reflecting some version of reality," e explains rather than some "made-up propaganda about what 'nasty Pagans' used to do."

Lupus defines polytheism as "any set of religious principles that assumes there is more than one Deity that is an independent Being, that isn't synonymous with other beings. There could be as few as two." Eir idea of faith is informed largely from eir background in religious studies. "Faith," Lupus explains, "is one's experience of Divine realities...if I say I have faith in something it means that I have experienced it, or that I have, to my own satisfaction, verified the existence of a particular reality or Being or what-have-you that has to do with a religious matter." When asked whether or not faith plays a role in eir polytheism, Lupus insists that faith is "essential, because without experiences of the Deities, there is no use for or need to 'believe in' Them, and They would consequently have no impact in one's life," and further adds that it is "only because I have experienced all of these Deities in a variety of ways that I do acknowledge Them on a regular basis."

When asked to recount eir journey into polytheism, Lupus identifies three important factors that influenced em choosing the polytheist path. Like many polytheists, Lupus's doubts helped prompt em away from the Christian traditions e had been shown by eir family. Eir interest in mythology, especially books about ancient Celtic religion and culture grew stronger as e got older, and e found eirself exploring Paganism. Yet the hetero-normativity of conventional Paganism, which tends to divide itself according to strongly pronounced masculine and feminine lines, drove Lupus to explore a more gender-fluid and queer religious sensibility.

> I started out when I was a teenager, starting at age 15 or so, maybe toward the end of when I was 14, having serious doubts about the various Christian traditions that my family raised me in. As I explored mythology and what I was interested in, I started coming across lots of Celtic stuff. Being that there is a lot of misinformation out there, I was picking up books on Celtic Paganism as much as I was picking up books on actual Celtic mythology, not knowing there was a difference. But, luckily that got me into thinking about practical polytheism and, you know, getting into that. So I started to do that at about age 16 and then through various different periods, I was getting involved in different aspects of this and the Celtic side of things was always very interesting to me, and very appealing. But as I was studying it more academically, what I found eventually was happening was that what I was finding in terms of academic

study wasn't really matching up with the practical stuff that was written on Celtic Paganism. Eventually I did find reconstructionists who were doing Celtic stuff and I have been working within that broad framework for about five years. I mean, I was working in it previously, but I didn't have the name for it. The Ekklesia stuff, that really happened in the summer of 2002.

I was, for various reasons, dissatisfied with a lot of the Pagan things that I was finding. One of the large parts of my dissatisfaction came because, despite some degree of social acceptance, there was still a lot of hetero-normativity when it came to…Paganism, including even some things that were said to be queer Paganism. I mean, in some of the experiences that I had with it, even Radical Fairies practice in certain contexts was just regular old Wicca in drag. So I was finding that kind of upsetting and disappointing and annoying. What I eventually did was I sort of put out a prayer to the wider universe of "I'd like to find something that is based in ancient practice…" I wanted to find something that was based in ancient practice that could bring in elements of syncretism because I think I am a natural-born syncretist. And also that was not only queer-positive but in fact to some extent queer-based. So I had heard the name of Antinous on a couple occasions before that but the missing thing always was that He was deified. I heard He was like this famous love story and that Hadrian was depressed when He died and [Hadrian] put statues of Him up all over the empire. But the reason [Hadrian] put statues of Him up all over the empire is that He was deified, and there were temples to [Antinous] all over the empire. Once I kind of found that, that specific element, everything kind of fell into place. I shifted into high gear researching all of this stuff and was involved in co-founding one group in 2002, and then in 2007 we ended up having kind of a schism and so the Ekklesía Antínoou as it is called now began in 2007. Right about this time of year in 2007. So that's what I have done. Those have been my involvements with those particular paths.

A unique feature of Lupus' practice is that e venerates deified humans alongside established Gods. I asked em to explain more about eir understanding of the theology of human apotheosis. The first aspect Lupus identifies is the Hero cultus, which is "really just a special kind of ancestor cultus of specific people who were particularly important or exemplary or noteworthy who then get honored as individuals as opposed to in the collective the ancestors."

The second aspect of that theology, says Lupus, is "a quasi-gnostic type of belief or understanding, that we all have divinity within us." When certain people develop that inner divinity to very high level, Lupus explains, "it kind of shines through in Their life," and the community recognizes Them "as having brought into human form and into the human world of activity some increased amount of that divinity." And then, there are those cases like Antinous, whose manner of death had as much to do with Their subsequent deification as any heroic qualities and inner divinity.

I—my experiences I suppose are kind of odd in that the visual and the audio don't always line up well for me. They—I usually get one or the other but very rarely both. As of—let's see, Sunday night and the very early hours of Monday morning as in, yesterday, I finally had an experience where the two did line up. (laughs) It involved Antinous, Him coming in a dream I had. He's appeared before, but if He appears visually He doesn't speak, or sometimes His voice is there but you can't see Him. So this was, you know, it was certainly different. Things like this have accompanied Him from the earliest period for me. Once I found out that Antinous was a God in the ancient world, [as I found out] back in 2002, I was certainly on board with it theoretically. But what fixed my devotion to it was that I started having visions and experiences that confirmed for me that this particular entity did exist and does exist and interacts with us. As I was doing research, especially in that first year, there were lots of little coincidental things that occurred that told me this is more than coincidence. I would go into a library and there would be 6 volumes of books or an 8-volume set of books and I knew that something I was looking for was there. I would pick one of them randomly and open it up and it was on the page that I opened to. Things like that happened a number of times. Or I was in the right place at the right time to hear about something or see something in passing that led to finding out more about the ancient cult of Antinous.

It's funny because there are echoes of this down to the present time. Where there was some sort of UPG notion hunch or whatever, that has been, on further research, as something that has actually happed. We've been considering the date of summer solstice as important to Antinous and Apollo because Antinous was syncretized to Apollo. That was just a total kind of UPG thing. There was no evidence we knew of for celebrations of that type actually happening, or anything like that. It just turns out that about 5 days ago there was an article published that there are some archaeologists in Italy who are working on publishing their findings [about] the random placement of buildings at Hadrian's villa, [which] actually line up to sunrises on the summer solstice. So, all of a sudden here is this thing that is confirmed by actual research in the field that yes, in fact, the summer solstice was an important day for Hadrian, and because Hadrian gave the shape of the cultus of Antinous it may not have been directly connected to Him, but it was part of the larger picture context. So, yeah, lots of things like this where a nudge, or a hint, or a bit of UPG ends up leading in directions that do both give us information about the original cultus but also leads the various people who have been working on this into a deeper knowledge of Antinous Himself and sometimes to further experiences with Him in dreams and so forth...

Now, a lot of people say for the Emperors, that was just kind of a random thing or it was a political thing and it doesn't necessarily mean anything about [the people being deified]. Emperors had temples all over the Empire that seem to have been going strong for centuries. Hadrian is certainly one of those. He was so universally liked. Antinous, a lot of people say, "He just got to be a God because He was the emperor's boyfriend. How lucky for Him." But it was really the specific manner of His death. Whether it was a heroic sacrifice on behalf of the emperor, the thing was He drowned in the Nile and if you drowned in the Nile you got Divine cultus no matter what. The very substance of the Nile divinizes anything it comes into contact with. That's a belief that goes way, way back in Egyptian culture...If He had to drown, it was lucky He drowned in that river and not the Thames or something like that. But at the same time, it's always been our sense that there's been something about Him in His life that was noteworthy and exemplary. Maybe He wasn't the smartest person ever. Maybe He wasn't the most athletic or accomplished in feats of arms or whatever, maybe He wasn't the most spiritually-minded, and even though He was extremely beautiful, I think it's kind of hubris to say He was the most beautiful person who ever lived as some people do say. But He had enough of a combination of all of those things first of all, to have appealed to someone as picky and as multi-faceted as Hadrian... I don't think [just] a pretty face would have gotten that reaction out of Hadrian, based on what we know about Him.

Contrary to what might be expected, given the assertions that historians have made about the Emperor Hadrian's marriage to Sabina, Lupus confirms that Ekklesía Antínoou has a powerful relationship with Her as well.

Unfortunately so much of our historical information about the reign of Hadrian is written by the gutter press of the day. And not even of the day. I mean, the Historia Augusta that is very commonly used was written in the fourth century, you now, it's 200 years removed from when the actual events happened. It was written by Christians, for Christians. They were not exactly portraying everything in an unbiased fashion.

Various of us in the group had had the notion that Hadrian could at any point have divorced Sabina, and She was of an important enough family that She probably could have initiated divorce proceedings, but She never did. When She died, even though we don't know the exact date, or even the exact year, [Hadrian] did not have to deify Her, but He did…Then earlier this year, one of the mystaí‡ of our group tranced Hadrian for a particular ritual, and He had nothing but good things to say about Sabina…He said She was a good woman and He loved Her and respected Her to the utmost and He would never say a bad thing against Her. Even if it was a relationship that was kind of based on traditional values and respect and fidelity and even if there wasn't a lot of romance there, which there doesn't appear to have been, that doesn't necessarily mean that They weren't civil human beings to one another. I suspect that, like everyone, They probably had Their problems.

Something that has kind of disturbed me with this entire question in a queer context is that a lot of people just want to say "Well, Hadrian was gay. He didn't like women. His marriage was a sham and He really thought women were disgusting," and all of this. All evidence indicates that this was not the case. He was known to have been a ladies' man as well. I mean, they say He maybe had an affair with the Empress Plotina, and possibly with Sabina's mother. So He clearly wasn't adverse to women, it's just that maybe there wasn't a love-match as far as Sabina was involved. Nonetheless, He did at least respect Her and came to Her defense when other people were making accusations and things.

We instituted a holiday for Her on March 21st, so we always honor that as the Apotheosis of Sabina. For me at least, it's always been one of the most energetic holidays that we have. It

‡ "Mystaí" is a Greek term meaning "initiates."

always really feels good, and I don't think that's just because it's the beginning of spring. There seems to be, from my point of view, an appreciative presence that is there, even though She hasn't spoken directly yet. Although some people do have—have written some good poetry and things like that, relating to Her. She could very well be coming through in that. We have a lot of people in the group who are poets who, you know are for lack of a better term, mystical poets, and they look for their inspiration directly in the entities involved. So I'm sure we will get there eventually.

Another relatively unknown God Lupus honors is Polydeukion. According to Lupus, Polydeukion is "a very interesting figure in many ways" who bears some resemblance to the Roman Antinous.

There was a famous Sophist in the second century who was a friend of Hadrian's and a conscious imitator of Hadrian. He was probably the richest man at the time. He was sort of like the Bill Gates of his era. And his name was Herodes Attikos. The Odeon amphitheater on the acropolis in Athens that seats 40,000 or something like that—He built that for the Athenians just because He could. He had several foster sons, and all of them died fairly early, probably in their teens. Herodes was a devotee of the cultus of Antinous. Probably on that template, when Polydeukion died—He was the one [Herodes] seems to have liked the best of the three--Herodes founded a hero-cult to Him. What ended up happening is that it wasn't just Herodes and his family honoring [Polydeukion] it was other communities who started to, as well. There are actually more images of Polydeukion that survived from the ancient world than of any other non-royal Greek person ever. There's around 25 or so.

I started to get interested in Him as a result of various tangents on the stuff relating to Antinous, and He became really, really, really important to me last year. I ended up with a job in Michigan, kind of by chance and something always struck me as it's really odd that I got this job; I don't really know why I'm here, there has to be some reason for it. Through oracular means and so forth, Antinous pretty much said "I'm the one responsible for you being here." I thought: okay, why? What is it here that I need to do or see? Because it was only a four-month job. Then I was doing research while I was there and found out that of the 25 statues of Polydeukion that exist, only one of

*them is outside Europe, and it was in the very town that I was
working in. So I would go to the museum where it was and read
hymns to Him and make offerings to Him and things that
weren't visible to the people in the museum and just spend as
much time as I could there, so He's become very, very, important
to me. He has started to come through more strongly as far as
His appearances in dreams and in other contexts.*

When asked whether e had experienced conflict with other
polytheists for eir decision to honor Antinous, Sabina, and
Polydeukion, Lupus admitted that e had. E has endured accusations
of sacrilege and hubris lodged in response to eir honoring Gods who
are apotheosed humans. But, "these accusations absolutely floor me,"
Lupus says, "because the ancient people were doing that all the time."
Antinous is only one example, and there was no doubt in the ancient
Roman's minds "He started out as human. But He's never called
'divus,' like the Roman emperors are. He's called 'theos' like the Gods
are. Sometimes He's called a hero, but just as equally, He's called a
God." In contemplating this conflict, Lupus also makes the interesting
observation that "oftentimes people are taking ideas of what is Divine
from monotheism, which overinflates the entire question."

*[Antinous] wasn't perfect, and no, Hadrian wasn't perfect. A
lot of these people weren't perfect. At the same time, none of us
are. And even as far as the Gods are concerned, I think that in
a polytheistic system, Divine perfection is of necessity…People
want their Gods to be as big and a powerful and as omniscient
and omnipresent as possible, and it doesn't seem to me that it's
even a necessity or even that it's very desirable in many cases.
The fact that Antinous is not omniscient and therefore if I pray
to Him I have to pray to Him out loud because He can't get
into my head, I think is a really appealing thing about Him.
You know, I think the same is true of a lot of the bigger
Deities. People are just expecting Them to be able to read their
minds and that's not how it works. So, I think that whatever
possible limitations there are theologically with worshipping and
honoring humans who have been deified, really isn't a problem
when you look at polytheism in general. Whatever possible things
may make Them [seem] not quite "as good as" the Gods, aren't
really inhibitions when you get down to it.*

Syncretism has played a key role in the development of many
polytheist religions throughout history. Contemporary historians'
understanding of ancient polytheism has sometimes lead to a skeptical
view of syncretic Deities as being commercial or political

constructions. Two well-known and controversial syncretic Deities are
Glykon and Serapis. Lupus honors Them both, and assures us that
They are both very real.

> *Glykon is a Deity that a lot of people just think is a made-up
> Deity because He was first proclaimed by a prophet in the mid-
> second century. The oracle that the prophet set up to Him was
> basically a puppet show. There were various forms of trickery
> that were used to make it appear that this snake that they had,
> which the body of the snake that they had was a real snake, but
> the head was a puppet, and it would give these oracles…and
> He's probably most famous these days because Alan Moore
> talks about Him quite a lot. But connected to some of my
> experiences with Antenociticus was Glykon. The thing that I've
> come to think about Glykon, or to accept about Him, is that
> even though the original prophet of Him may have been trying
> to pull one over on everyone and was using it for his own
> personal gain, that doesn't necessarily mean that the God was
> fake. Just because the puppet show was fake, [does not mean
> that] the Gods is fake. So He has been a definite part of my
> life since 2003 and has taught me an awful lot about
> polytheistic theology, really. I've had a number of dream
> experiences having to do with Him and there is a kind of, I
> suppose for lack of a better term, this quasi-Kabbalistic system
> that I'm working with now in relation to Antinous and a
> number of these other Deities that Glykon is very involved
> with and has been a big part of.*

> *Serapis is kind of a weird one because He was sort of floating
> on the edge for me for well over a decade before I realized, "Oh
> geez—He's been here the whole time!" being that He is one of
> the super-syncretistic Deities like Antinous is, I think that the
> model of the cult of Serapis influenced Hadrian's innovation of
> the cultus of Antinous. Hadrian was also a Serapis cultist.
> Yeah, so [Serapis] was—it seems like everywhere I went, every
> museum I went to or every site I went to, I would find out on
> further investigation that Serapis was honored there, was or that
> there was an image of Him there. When I finally copped on to
> it, it was like, 'Oh yeah, He's kind of an avuncular Divine
> figure that I experience on certain occasions.'*

> *There's actually evidence at this point that the Egyptians
> syncretized their own Deities to each other on a regular basis.
> Before the time of Ptolemy, there are several attestations
> especially in Memphis of Osir-Apis. The basis of Serapis was*

there before   Ptolemy came in, but then during His reign, according to some of the sources we have on it, I don't think it was necessarily Him creating the cultus for political expediency so much as Serapis coming forward and making political expediency possible. The character of it, in the sources I've read, suggest to me that the Deity came before the cultus and I think the same is true of Glykon. That Alexander of Abonuteichos, a sensitive individual, ended up having a Divine insight that he and a couple of friends turned to his own profit...making it more about them than about the God. Ultimately, the mysteries they celebrated ended up focusing more on the prophet than on the God. I think that's always a difficulty when you're dealing with prophets. Sometimes they get a little too big of a head about things.

I tend to put some credence in the notion that there may be actual genuine Divinities behind these things when they come about. Then the way the cultus goes after that depends a great deal on history and various other factors. But even if there isn't at that initial stage, oftentimes there is eventually. I think in terms of the idea of egregores and things like that, that if you've got enough people thinking a particular thing and joining in particular practices at certain cult sites, even if there wasn't anything there initially, something will be there eventually...Certain things can come about but also be Divine Beings who inspire people to move in particular ways with what looks like the creation of new cults. This is the thing: that polytheism, being polytheism, the canon or the number of Deities is never closed. There [are] potentially billions of Them out there that have yet to be discovered or named. There's probably somewhere in the millions of those who used to be recognized that have been forgotten...I don't think...Discordians would say, "oh, a God being discovered and a God being invented is really the same thing." Possibly, but not always. I tend to put my benefit of the doubt on the action of the Gods in many cases.

In addition to worshipping syncretic Deities and Deities of human origin, Lupus is very involved with reviving the worship of less-known Roman, Romano-British, and Celtic Deities. The Roman God Silvanus, for example, is usually honored as the tutelary Deity of the woods. Lupus, however, tends to regard Him less as a hunter/forest God and more as a Deity of liminal spaces.

Of all the Deities I worship, He's the one I suppose is the closest to some kind of nature God, I supposed you could say. He's a "hunting in a forest" God. But He's also a God of boundaries. I experience Him most strongly when I've been out in the woods, or sometimes even a public park or something like that that is sort of a liminal area where there is wildlife and there is woodland, but it's not necessarily natural…because He—I mean, He is all about the liminal areas. Any place that is not quite one place or another is, as far as I'm concerned, a perfect place to encounter Him. I think that—it's not that He's not personal, but the feeling of Him is always a bit bigger. He's always larger than the mental box that He gets put in. There is more to Him than has been written about Him. But I mean, that's true of all of Them, but He's the one who, in many respects, least resembles His images and what's been said about Him. It's still definitely Him, but He is kind of both boundaries and beyond the boundaries, so it's only appropriate.

Many people haven't heard of the Romano-British God Antenociticus. He has only one remaining temple, which lies along Hadrian's wall. Lupus visited the temple in 2003 and conducted a ritual there to honor Antenociticus.

I went there in 2003 during July and did a little ritual at His temple, cleaned up the space around it and had an extremely powerful period leading up to that. I went up—I was in Newcastle for three full days. I looked at the whole thing as a pilgrimage and then went to the temple on the last day. The temple was only discovered in the late 1800s. We didn't even know that there was such a Deity until then. I've had a number of dreams that suggested to me that I was at least knowledgeable about the temple at an earlier period in history. In one of them in particular, I was in the role of Virius Lupus. Virius Lupus, that part of my name, is…several different individuals throughout history who had that name, but the one in particular was the governor of Britannia in the last couple of years in the second century. And I had this dream which, may have been a past life memory or something like that, or if not my own past life, then I'm at least viewing somebody else's, in which He had to account for the destruction of the temple of Antenociticus. It had been burned in a raid by a particular tribe of the Brigantes who lived up around Hadrian's Wall. So this all sounded interesting to me as a dream and I wrote down as much as I could about it. Later, I come to find out that Virius Lupus was the governor of Britannia at the time that the temple in question was destroyed by fire during this particular uprising in that year, all of these details ended up being confirmed. When I actually went to the temple it was actually a pretty powerful experience. There are certain constellations that are important to watch for, that there have been novas and things like that in them when particular experiences have occurred. On the day that I went to the temple, there were three novas in the constellation and on the days leading up to that there were three more. So, it was a strangely powerful time to be rediscovering that particular Deity.

Cocidius is another Romano-British Deity Lupus honors. Lupus identifies Cocidius as a male hunter-warrior Deity who was syncretized to Silvanus and possibly connected to Antenociticus.

Cocidius…is another Romano-British Deity, possibly connected to Antenociticus. In fact, He was syncretized to Silvanus. But He has come through to be a Deity in His own right. He has a fair number of attestations, but at the same time we don't know that much about Him. He is a young hunter-warrior type Deity. In many cases He's known—this isn't 100% comparable-for me, He has come through as sort of a Romano-British version of Cú Chulainn. I was sort of working with Him and ended up coming up with a poem that kind of told some of His deeds in brief and a lot of them seem similar to Cú Chulainn, but there's something that just felt right about that particular interpretation of Him. He's also kind of interesting in that it seems to those of us who have had some experiences with Him in the last few years, that I suppose probably like a lot of these Deities who have been mostly forgotten, He's a little lacking in confidence. There's something endearing about a Deity who doesn't think They're that great. That's not to say He's not great, it's just that someone who had a whole basically sacred area dedicated to Him along Hadrian's wall and had about 30-40 altars in Roman Britain that have survived dedicated to Him, but all of a sudden nobody knows about Him or can even pronounce His name or anything like that. Going from that to more or less nothing for several thousand years—well, you know, almost 2,000 years—where in the meantime everyone has heard of Mercury and Apollo and Diana and all of these. But nobody ever goes, "Oh yeah! Good old Cocidius!" So it's sort of interesting from that point of view that He's come across that way. But yeah, you know, He's someone I worked with a lot more when I was living over there. I still do from the U.S., but it's a little bit more difficult since He hasn't really taken root here as much.

As the God of manure-based fertilizer, Sterculinus played an important role in the agricultural aspect of ancient Roman culture. Given the contemporary disconnect with the agricultural realities, it isn't surprising that more contemporary people have yet to rediscover Him. Lupus recalls some initial bafflement at eir first being approached by Sterculinus, as well as the powerful confirmation of eir connection with this God.

> *Sterculinus is the Roman God of manure-based fertilizer. He was a tough one for me because He kind of started appearing in the corners of things for me about this time in 2008. I read up on Him what I could, but I just couldn't figure out what He was for or why He was there or what He was doing in my life, because I'm not a gardener, I'm not a farmer, I'm not any of those things. So what is manure-based fertilizer good for, for me? I don't know. So I kind of said, I don't quite know why you're here, but I'll keep my eyes open, and I'll try and figure out what is going on. Then in 2009, I was at PantheaCon and just kind of out of the blue one day, it finally hit me that being the God of manure-based fertilizer, Sterculinus is the God of doing useful things with shit....As soon as I figured that out, my personal confirmation was that for the rest of the day I had the worst diarrhea that I'd had in a long time. It was still a really good day even despite that.*

According to Lupus, the Trí Dee Dána, or Three Gods of Skill, are Brian, Iuchar, and Iucharaba. While some might consider Them to be somewhat minor Celtic Deities, these Gods play an significant role in Lupus' practice.

> *Their holy day is what most of the rest of the Pagan world knows as Lugnasad. They had a holy day called Iuchar, named after one of Them that takes place right at that same time. It's not a specific date of August 1, it's sort of the last days of July [and] the first couple days of August, which is the "dog days of summer." They are associated with dogs and with a number of different things. But Their relationship is actually antagonistic to Lug. So paying attention to Them is kind of paying attention to the minor, well, what a lot of people would consider the minor players, in the wider mythology. But also on the other side of things, They are the three sons of the Goddess Brigid. So there's this interesting relationship that we found. At Lugnasad, which is the opposite end of the year from Imbolc, these three sons of Brigid, if you're looking in the right place, are of major importance. And on Imbolc, which is supposed to be Brigid's*

day, Cú Chulainn the son of Lug also has some important associations. So for particular people, who I think are not the regular everyday householders and settled people, honoring these other Deities on particular occasions is important because in many respects They represent non-settled life. If you're not a householder and a regular member of society for whatever reason, it might be more appropriate to honor these Deities than to honor Brigid or to honor Lug, despite all the wonderful things They do and the important place They have. But if you aren't a settled member of society, these younger generation Deities who are also important have become a lot more of the focus for me on those occasions.

The tragic hero Cú Chulainn is widely honored among those who observe Celtic traditions. Immortalized in song and myth, Cú Chulainn has inspired the veneration and adoration of countless poets, Lupus included.

He's been around for me since 1994. He's probably the one I've had—yeah, He's definitely the one I've had the longest continuous relationship with. It was because of reading his myths that I ultimately got into Celtic Studies. He doesn't appear in His full glory very often, but when He does it's always been a very—what's the word I'm looking for?—"shocking" experience. Even though these experiences with Deities often lead to transformation and lots of things that we would consider good, all of them—in a way, at least for me, They're just so large and powerful that it's just too painful to see Them or to hear Them when you know it's actually Their voice. Yeah, so, He's the—there have been a couple of occasions where He has come through very strongly or very clearly and absolutely shattered everything. But He's also been the kind of small hint at the back of my consciousness on a lot of occasions that have just pushed me to continue doing certain types of work. And ultimately I kind of look at my relationship with Him as especially in the context of the Irish poetic tradition as He's the hero and I'm the poet who talks about the Hero. So we have that type of relationship. Yeah, that's been interesting.

While some of the Gods that Lupus honors are relatively unknown, many of Them are very familiar. Hermes, for example, is one of the more ubiquitous Deities whom Lupus venerates. Hermes' connection to writing and knowledge make Him an especially important Deity for Lupus, whose primary vocation is that of an academic.

Hermes, (laughs) I feel like we can't get away from Him. Not that you would want to. Just because so much of what I do is based in language and interpretation. Hermeneusis—that takes its name directly from Him. So, He's there a lot and He's specifically appeared in a number of dreams I have had, or kind of as a whisper in the back of the head on certain occasions. But because He's one of the major Deities that Antinous is syncretized with, it's primarily in that aspect that He's appeared for me in conjunction with Antinous.

Many Greco-Egyptian syncretists have discovered that whenever Hermes appears, Thoth is not far behind. This has certainly been true in Lupus' experience. Eir work as a writer has helped em forge a very intense bond with Thoth.

Thoth is another one of these who I think [that] even if I wanted to get away from, I couldn't because I am so involved in writing. He, yeah, I mean, the entire—it seems to me that perhaps even more than Hermes...If I think of Hermes as the one who influences me and who I interact with when I'm writing, Hermes is kind of the straight man and Thoth is the joker. Thoth seems to me to have this ridiculous sense of humor, and completely delights in every possible visual and auditory pun there is, and is very—yeah. Takes His job very seriously and takes the matter of communication and words and so forth very, very seriously, but is also like the funniest stand-up comedian that there ever was. Anything that involves linguistic play or so forth. If I'm not sure if a joke will work or not, I'll run it by Thoth, If He thinks it's funny, I'll go with it.

Through devoting time, offerings, and attention to the Gods, one builds stronger relationships to Them. Yet, devotion is not a thing that everyone is able to do easily, or even to understand well. Through the years, devotion has become a key element to Lupus' practice. Hanuman, Hindu exemplar of Divine devotion, has taught Lupus much about the art and craft of religious devotion.

Since abut 2007, I've been fairly involved with Him, although He was there on the sides for a few years before. His main focus in my life has been as an exemplar of devotion. I certainly honor Him and worship Him, but He has been the one who has taught me more than any other Deity or human for that matter, about what it is to be devoted to any of the Gods. Yeah, I mean, since I have become heavily involved with Him in the last four years, my devotional practices have taken on a whole different character and so it's been a very good thing, having that involvement. Being able to honor Him and have Him teach me how to honor other Deities.

Anubis, Egyptian God of death and embalming who leads souls through the underworld, is another Deity Lupus has a strong affinity for. Lupus' interest in Anubis began in childhood.

Anubis is, for me, obviously He's a psychopomp and all that, but even on a more specific level, He's the loyal guardian and the one that I always want near me when I'm going through something difficult. I've had a strong admiration for Anubis back to earliest childhood. We used to have a big book that had all kinds of stuff on Egypt and some of the stuff from the King Tut exhibit that I would just look at when I was a kid, and it was always the Jackal-headed figure or the big, black jackal on top of the sarcophagus. He's always had an appeal for me. So once I was able to become a polytheist, He was one of the first Deities after Cú Chulainn who just kind of came in strongly and has been there, in the background if nothing else, ever since.

Hator is another Egyptian Deity with whom Lupus has had a longstanding relationship. In many ways, Hathor has guided Lupus' ideas about romantic relationships.

She is probably the Goddess that I've honored the longest, specifically as an individual Goddess. I was a little skeptical of the monistic Goddess interpretations of a lot of the stuff I was reading in my early days, but since 1994, late 1994, She has very definitely been this very kind nurturing Goddess who is also completely tied up with, I suppose, my ideal experiences or thoughts around love. Whenever I have been in the position of being in love with someone or being in a relationship Hathor is almost always right there involved in it in some way.

Like many who honor Her, Lupus has found that Artemis is very much an independent, fierce, huntress. Yet, e has found Her to be friendlier and more open than She is typically given credit for being.

Artemis is probably the other Goddess that I'm closest to. Yeah, She's kind of on the more nature side of things, out in the wild and not too far on the heels of Silvanus in my experience. Definitely there is the edge to Her that is kind of scary, but on the other hand, I've found Her a lot more friendly than She is often portrayed as. As long as there's no indication of wanting to exploit Her or get something out of Her or whatever, She seems to me to be very amenable to people dealing with Her on any sort of non-exploitative basis. As long as you don't come at Her with your tongue hanging out of your mouth like Aktaion, you'll be fine.

In addition to the Indo-European Divinities, Lupus has developed a very distinct relationship with the one of the spirits whom the Japanese refer to as Kami. Sarutahiko-no-Okami is one of the six great kami, or Okami, of the Shinto religion, and the only one who resides in the earthly realm.

> *Sarutahiko-no-Okami is…the principal Kami of the Shinto shrine that's not too far from me and so since I've been involved with Shinto since late 2007, He's been the main Kami that I've dealt with. He's a very interesting one. He has a kind of paternal side, but He's about protection and He's also about guidance and leadership, as in leading people, and clearing obstacles and things like that. In fact, the practice that I do the most often in relation to Him—I go to the Shinto shrine at least once every two months or so—but I am an insulin-dependent diabetic, and I have an insulin pump. The insertion process for that is not always pleasant or easy, but something that I have been doing for the last couple of years and it seems to help a great deal, is to pray to Him right before I insert it. The Shinto belief on Him is that if you say His name three times He hears your prayer. So I say my prayer to Him beforehand. One of the things He does is He carries a great big spear. With the idea that I'm jabbing myself with a needle, He would be a good guy to clear out any of the obstructions that might be in front of that, and so I do that prayer to Him every time I inject and it has seemed to help.*

One of the virtues of polytheism is that there is always room for one more God, even one who has not been known to play well with others. Iao Sabaoth is the Greco-Egyptian name for the Hebrew God of Abraham, and Lupus has developed a relationship Him. Lupus has done some of this in an effort to honor eir ancestors.

> *Being a polytheist, I think that all the monotheistic Deities are all Deities, They're just not the same one and They're not the only ones. I never had much of a relationship with Jesus when I was growing up. Nor much of one with quote "God" unquote as the Christians defined Him. But at a certain point, Iao started coming through very clearly and there was no doubt that it was anyone but Him. In a larger context of polytheistic devotion He's a very big God and a very powerful God, but He is by no means the only or even the best one. Because I have Jewish ancestry it's been important for me to include Him when*

the occasion is appropriate especially in the last 3-4 years.

As is the case with many polytheists past and present, Lupus has also devoted a part of eir practice to honoring the land spirits and eir ancestors.

> *The local land spirit that I'm the closest to is probably the spirit of Mt. Erie, which is on the island I'm living on at the moment—it's the highest point on the island. I've been going there since the early 90s. If you're on top of Mt. Erie and you look in a particular direction, you can see the exact spot of where I was born. So that particular land spirit—and I think She's definitely female—has been involved in my life to some extent since I was born. I feel very connected to this particular place. Wherever I end up I at least try to make some connections. That one has been an enduring connection, even when I go to other places. As far as ancestors go, there are a number of dates throughout the year that we honor ancestors, generally, and then in the Ekklesía we have specific people that we honor as important ancestors who get their own holy day, in essence. But we also honor whole groups of them. We have a particular day of honoring our own personal ancestors, our genetic ancestors as well. Those types of things do happen amidst everything else for me, yes.*

While some prefer to improvise spontaneous devotional activities to honor the Gods, ancestors, and land spirits, Lupus has developed many rituals to meet those purposes. Some of eir rituals are conducted with Ekklesía Antínoou, or in another group setting, but others Lupus conducts on eir own, solitarily.

> *I don't have a "one-size-fits-all" ritual format or procedure, even for Antinous and some of the other Gods that I worship on a regular basis. But, we do have a lot of modular pieces that can be mixed and matched for many occasions, and then there are usually prayers or hymns that are particular to certain holy-days. I've written a huge number of poems, hymns, and prayers at this point that get used in ritual by me, and by a number of other people who have either read my blog or who have purchased the books which have those texts in them. Offerings of food and drink are usually, but not always, parts of my rituals. But offerings of song and poetry always are. And then, depending on the Deity and the occasion, there might be other activities specific to a given ritual. For example, on May 19th, we celebrate Bendideia, a festival in honor of the Thracian horse and hunting Goddess, Bendis. We know that the Athenians*

celebrated this festival with a torch-relay on horseback, according to Plato. Of course, horses aren't exactly easy to come by these days, and a relay race on horseback might require the fire department if it gets out of hand. So, instead, myself and my colleagues have gone up to Mt. Erie, and we do a procession to the various lookout points on the mountaintop with lit candles, and we try to keep them lit the entire time, which is not always easy. I have everything from a series of daily practices that I do in the morning and at night, all the way through full-blown dramatic rituals involving multi-part sacred dramas that take place in the midst of other ritual activities and which would last several hours, which I do for my Deities on a regular basis. The smaller and easier things get done on a daily basis, whereas the largest and most complex rituals that require lots of other people perhaps only get done once a year.

Sometimes it's difficult to know where the myths leave off and the Gods begin. Yet, if order to develop a personal relationship with the Gods, one must grow beyond myth in order to reach a greater understanding. Lupus is in the interesting position of having no mythic narrative for several of eir Gods, which has created a need to delve more deeply into historical sources and to strengthen the lines of reciprocal communication with those Gods.

Some of [the Gods], we have literally nothing to go on from mythic narrative, and so those ones can be relatively surprising in how They manifest. Bendis, for example, is very much a mother Goddess on the one hand, but She's a mother Goddess with a whip in Her hand, if you see what I mean—She doesn't take shit from anyone, and while She doesn't have a "bad attitude" about anyone and everyone, She is insistent on respectful conduct. The lack of confidence in Cocidius is something that I mentioned before, and [this] also applies, since there are no narratives relating to Him either. There was no way to know that apart from coming into contact with Him. Cú Chulainn, though, has quite a few myths recorded, and He has manifested for me in ways that are pretty close to how His character seems to emerge in those myths. He's every bit the overconfident teenager who is afraid of nothing and is eager to demonstrate at all times that such is the case. The only difference between Him and a modern teenaged skateboarder or snowboarder with no apparent fear of death is that He is a bit better spoken. Yet He is also even more quiet and aloof in general, but it is an aloofness that is full of sensitivity and perception and attention rather than the kind of blank and almost vacuous and even apathetic aloofness that one gets in many modern teenagers. It's the kind of aloofness that could at any moment strike like a cobra, you might say.

It is unfortunate that so many of the tangibly historical personages that I deal with on a Divine level have not had "character studies" done on Them by modern historians—They are far less interested in giving any indications of what the character of Antinous or Polydeukion might have been like (though more the latter than the former) than when and where a given statue of either of Them might have come from, etc. Lots has been said about Antinous being a "rather depressive" youth, but that is largely extrapolation from the fact that many of His statues—and not necessarily even the ones that have been proven to be originals from His cultus that were not reconstructed, or had His head put on some other body!—have a downward look, as if He never raised His head for His entire life or something, and was thus a typical sulking and sullen teenager. I've found Him personally to be anything but sulking and sullen, though He is certainly serious, and probably far more so than most teenagers would be then or now. I would never describe Him as depressed, though—I'm sure He's had His moments, both as a human and a God, but just as it is an error to take any such moment that anyone might have and assume it is trapped in amber and set in stone for life, so too with Antinous. A rather broody and moody-looking statue of Him, or even several such statues, need not define His character or His aspect once-and-for-all. And, sadly, because for academics He is an interesting side-note in history and not really any sort of God, they have no other way of trying to determine what His character was like, or what it actually still is. He is extremely gentle and affectionate, and sensitive in the best possible ways; but He also can have a temper, and a great deal of anger over things like social injustice or dishonesty. He prefers things to be as peaceful and as good for His devotees as they can possibly be, and He's angered and hurt by our own difficulties and trials.

In this, He contrasts a bit to Hadrian, who is very much still the Emperor who commands thirty Legions and feels they should be marched out for even the smallest offense. I had a situation in recent months in which Hadrian, on the one hand, wanted to launch an all-out attack, whereas Antinous was more circumspect. [He] was upset about the situation and offered His deepest compassion and sympathies and wishes for improvement, but also didn't feel that the strategy of overwhelming annihilation was the best one under the circumstances, in contrast to His lover. I personally was more of Hadrian's viewpoint initially, but came about to that of Antinous as time went on, and His strategy proved to be the better one in the end.

From time to time, Lupus has experienced conflict on account of eir emphasis on polytheism. Some of these conflicts have been with Christians, but others have been with Pagans who have a different view of Deity than Lupus.

I wouldn't say there have been a lot of those types of difficulties, but they do come up from time to time...I would say that the majority of my conflicts over any of this have been with other Pagans. There seems to be almost no one on earth who is more argumentative than other Pagans. That can be a good thing. A lot of times really useful stuff comes out of it, but a few too many people don't quite realize their own bias and their own exclusivity when it comes to these things...So I've had those kinds of conflicts with people who are culturally exclusive saying, "well, you're just one of these lousy eclectics" and it's like, "well, a lot of these forms of syncretism I do are historically attested forms of syncretism." It isn't as if I'm picking Deities at random and doing stuff with Them. I'm researching all of Them very, very, deeply and with a lot of mindfulness and attention and devotion as I do so, and always trying to engage Them on an individual level...I suppose the one that's been most prominent in my mind for the last number of months is Pagans who are insistent monists who will not allow that there is anything else even possible, who have said, "you'll figure it out one day, because there's no difference between you and me. So you'll figure it out. You'll get to be just like me one day." It's like, no, no, no. So, anyway, yeah, those. I didn't really realize how much of a problem some of those people are until the last couple of months. I had encountered them before but never as virulently and insistently as recently.

When asked if there was anything e wished others would understand about polytheism, Lupus said that e wished people would understand that the "recognition of many Deities, Divine Beings, and other numinous presences is not delusional, and is not "primitive." E also considers the pluralistic sentiment that all religions are simply slightly different paths up the same Divine mountain to be helpful in some ways, but harmful in others.

Something I often encountered back in the day...made me laugh because I knew that the people doing it weren't actually serious in what they were saying, they were just aping what they had heard. But when I was in Ireland, I met a number of very nice Irish people who like most people in Ireland went to a Catholic school for their education. The Catholics run about 95% of the primary and secondary schools in Ireland. You can't really get away from it. I would meet them and they would say they're not religious, and we would get on to talking about polytheism or Paganism and oftentimes there would be a time when they would say, "So, you worship the false Gods?" I would always laugh, and I would always say, "I know that you don't actually mean what you are saying there, but that's the vocabulary you've been given. They're not false, ya know!" I suppose this is one of the things that monotheists who are insistent monotheists are just never going to get, is that, you know, there are realities outside of the one they have been ingrained with. When you get ones that are kind of more monist-universalist, the they're "all paths up the same mountain" kind of thing, that's not quite as bad. [But] <u>*every one of them are attempts to make peace by erasing difference or erasing individuality, in a theological context but also more widely.*</u> *That kind of stuff absolutely drives me nuts…Because of the way the religion and religious studies has been taught, and the way that the discipline has been created in the U.S. and in other places around the world, polytheism is always less advanced, and less intellectual, and less sensible than monotheism. I wish that particular set of assumptions would go away…There are extremely reasonable polytheists and polytheist viewpoints that are out there. So that whole edifice of monotheism equals "more sensible, more intelligent, more civilized"…I really wish that would just go away.*

Confessions of a Formerly Reluctant Polytheist
An Epilogue

It would be unfair of me to ask 120 people to share their personal experiences of the Holy Powers with me yet remain silent about my own. Thus, I have chosen to share it in this epilogue. I, too, am a practicing polytheist. Like many of those in my study, I have had a few experiences which could most certainly prompt rationalists to call the mental asylum and monotheists to call an exorcist. In the interests of fairness to my study's respondents, and in appreciation of their generosity and courage, I offer the following account.

My path to this religious sensibility has been impacted by numerous powerful forces. Some from within my own psyche. Some from places that I believe to be well outside and beyond it. The oldest and most significant impact of these forces has been the growth and development of my own spirituality from Jung-zealous atheist to devotional polytheist. Having been born and raised in the Reorganized Church of Jesus Christ of Latter-day Saints, Christianity shaped me deeply—until I left for college. By my mid-twenties, I was thoroughly godless and wholeheartedly atheist. I didn't believe in any sort of Gods; I believed in exploring my Self. I spent most of that time as an archetype-wielding atheist firmly dedicated to search for Self which, as it turns out, more often than not amounted to spelunking the cavern of my own ego whilst believing I was plumbing the depths of Jung's "collective unconscious." I did not believe that any God was a real Being. I believed that the old Goddesses and Gods were simply archetypes, facets of my higher Self, and whenever I wanted a spiritual experience, I would go fish one out from Jung's great collective unconscious, and set to work.

Slowly, I built a wardrobe of these archetypes which I would try on whenever I needed help outwardly expressing certain aspects of my inner self. Even though I very much valued these archetypes, I was acutely aware that the archetypes were bound by the limits of my personal knowledge and experience. I knew that whatever advice or perspective the archetype could give, it would be illuminating and enlightening, but the actions and words of the archetypes would ultimately conform to the knowledge I already had. Eventually, I came to the realization that however mysterious the collective unconscious may seem, it is comprised of all that is already known, and the archetypes which are drawn from it primarily help individuals elucidate and articulate the known-yet-unconscious. Revelation of completely new insight and stunningly different ideas do not usually come from repurposing already-known material; it comes from experiencing the great mystery beyond the Self. At that point in my life, I refused to countenance the possibility that anything might lie beyond that Self.

This continued until about 2003, when I moved to New Orleans and discovered Paganism. The initiation, sabbats, esbats, and other group rituals were powerful, spurring spiritual growth of a sort I had never before experienced. Through those experiences, I gradually began to encounter a force that was much more powerful, immense, and substantial than anything I had ever experienced before. Even beyond the weight of this force, this energy, this presence, was the feeling of genuine revelation that I experienced during rituals where our priestess would aspect the Goddess. These seemingly Divine revelations were nothing like the earth-shattering dogmatic truths I'd been conditioned to believe in during my Christian childhood. Rather, they were brilliant flashes of perspective and insight that did not seem to be drawn from the knowledge and experience of the priestess or from the experiences of those convened for the ritual. It was insight the likes of which neither myself nor my circle-mates had experienced before. We all noted that the level of energy rituals generated was nearly overpowering, an observation made even by those with decades of experience leading rituals. When compared to my knowledge and the experience of my circle-mates, these insights did not seem to have emerged from any of our knowledge, individual or collective. In solitary work, I had still been using the old Goddesses and Gods as archetypes for the purpose of Self-exploration. But when we interacted with Them during rituals invoking the Goddess, those archetypes took on depth, nuance, and perspective that They did not have when I worked with Them on my own. There genuinely seemed to be something happening which was far greater than simply the sum total of all of the mental energy and subconscious expectations created by the ritual participants.

The difference between privately experiencing an archetype and collectively, ritually witnessing an archetype can perhaps be best explained through the metaphor of ballet. It is one thing to put on a beautiful swan costume, and set about imagining yourself as a graceful swan instead of a clumsy, graceless human. But it is quite another to see a world-class production of Tchaikovsky's Swan Lake, and become spellbound by the Swan Queen. Both are valid ways of exploring the idea of what a swan is, but the insights you gather are very different. Masquerading as a swan teaches you about the swan-like parts of yourself. Watching someone who is particularly gifted and specifically trained to dance the role of the swan will reveal heretofore unknown aspects of the swan, the ritual of dance, and humanity's relationship to both that you have had no previous understanding of.

Having just begun my academic study of folklore and ritual, of course, these experiences lead to a lot of thought and theorizing on my part. I turned these experiences over and over in my mind, subjecting them to the harshest intellectual critique I could. The more I thought about it and applied the proper theoretical filters, the more I concluded that these ritual experiences could perhaps be explained, but most certainly could not be understood, through the lens of psychological or anthropological criticism. No matter what Jungian loopholes I found, I always came back to the observation that what I had experienced with the archetypes on my own was radically different from the archetypes I experienced through group ritual. And they differed in a way that was not adequately accounted for by recourse to the Jungian ideas of archetype and the collective unconscious that I had used for years, or by the anthropology and psychology I had studied in college. It was the striking difference between the archetypes as I experienced them in personal practice, and the archetypes as there were revealed through ritual, that eventually convinced me there was a powerful force present during our rituals that was animating those archetypes. This force made those archetypes richer, broader, and more revelatory than a mere collection of human imaginations ever could. It became clear over time that this force exists independently of my own imagination and the collective unconscious from which the archetypes are drawn. I eventually came to feel that this force could rightly be recognized as Deity and referred to as "God" or "Goddess" (my preferred gender for Her).

At this point, I was faced with a conundrum of belief. I could continue believing in archetypes and denying the existence of any Deity whatsoever. My rational mind demanded this of me, but this could only come at the expense of my spiritual fulfillment. Or, I could reject rationality altogether, and begin to believe in a Deity. This option was as spiritually thrilling as it was intellectually distasteful. Eventually, I was forced to admit that the significant disparity between social science and spiritual experience could not be satisfactorily and meaningfully bridged through intellect and theory. The means by which to cross this abyss came as I was editing a friend's article on Gothic literature. In it, she referenced Coleridge's philosophy of the willing suspension of disbelief. It finally occurred to me that my problem had nothing to do with a perceived division between intellectual and spiritual realms. Rather, it had to do with the division between the thoughts and feelings I experienced during religious contemplation of the Divine, and the thoughts and feelings I experienced during every other mundane moment of my life. As it turns out, the conflict I felt was about how to fully embrace spiritual experiences in a sacred context, and still be able to live a rational, intellectual life in the profane world. The solution I discovered was that I didn't have to believe in anything new, I simply had to suspend my disbelief about things, and be completely open to the experiences. From that point on, whenever I set about seeking religious experience, I dismissed the internal censor who forced me to disbelieve everything that didn't meet the demands of rational materialism, and gleefully sought the mystery.

Finally, I leapt into the void, and gave myself absolute permission to experience everything as fully as possible without bending it to fit the contours which my intellect deemed reasonable and credible. I was at long last prepared to explore the mystery that lies beyond the Self, and that meant being open to the possibility that some spiritual entities exist beyond and independent of the human imagination. This willingness to suspend disbelief helped me to embrace, on my own, the energy that I had felt during group rituals. Whereas before I had been godless, my personal practice evolved to incorporate invocation of the Goddess along with the archetypes.

Gradually I began to understand that for me, belief was not terribly important for the purposes of religious experience, but practice is absolutely essential to it. It was the ritual engagement of the Divine on its own terms, without the cultural or psychological baggage of belief or disbelief, which finally brought me spiritual fulfillment. Then, something I had never expected began to happen. These direct experiences gradually convinced me that the Goddess exists on Her own terms well beyond the paltry limits of human unconsciousness and understanding, and that She is more real than the archetypes I'd been experimenting with. The more experience I gained through engaging the Goddess, the more convinced I became that She is real. Ironically, it was my dismissal of belief altogether that allowed me to become convinced that Deity, as such, exists.

This is how I tentatively stepped into working with Deity, and eventually developed a strong desire to connect with Her. I wanted to feel this presence without intermediaries, masques, or metaphors. I longed for a personal, immediate, visceral connection. Yet try as I might, it was very difficult for me to really connect to the Goddess without resorting to archetypes. The immensity of Her left me feeling a little lost and distant. Because I had discovered the vast realms that existed beyond and outside of my Self, I lost interest in the archetypal explorations of internal Self that had consumed my spiritual journey prior to my joining a Pagan group. The archetypes were still useful tools, but I was very well aware that their real power derived from how they were used and who was "wearing" them at any given time—myself or the Goddess. In and of themselves, they began to seem very hollow and insubstantial. It was with these feelings of frustration and desire that I decided to undertake a completely different sort of spiritual exploration: dream-work. Rather than explore my Divine Self through sacred masquerade, I decided to chart my internal spiritual landscape through exploring my dreams. I kept dream journals, and pondered my experiences.

I knew from Jung that encounters with others during my dreams were really just encounters with hidden facets of my Self, and that the dream world was a place to process these things in a safe and productive way. Normally I wouldn't remember my dreams, but the recall process became easier as I began to work on my dream journal. Most nights, my dreams felt flat, almost two-dimensional. Eventually I became lucid enough to exert conscious influence upon the events, environments, entities, and people/individuals in the flat-feeling dreams. It felt a bit like editing digital video footage, actually. I was able to work through some of my personal issues quite effectively through this fashion of dream-work. In fact, it was proving to be a more effective way of dealing with my deeper wounding than sacred archetypal masquerade because, rather than wearing the mask myself, archetypal old Gods and Goddesses would appear in my dreams, and I would actually have discussions with them. They still felt somewhat hollow, but I knew they were animated by my deeper, wiser Self, and those conversations did make the learning and healing processes easier. I never, however, encountered the Goddess in these dreams.

As I became more proficient in dealing with these flat, two-dimensional dreams, very strange things started to happen. Without warning, a dream would snap from two-dimensional to three-dimensional; it would become rich, vivid, immediate, and almost overwhelming—real, in every sense of the word. As the dreams intensified, the control I had wielded only moments before would evaporate. These three-dimensional dreams weren't like editing video, they were like being part of a live improvisational performance. Whereas the less-vivid dreams were peopled mostly with friends and family, these vivid, rich dreams were as likely to be peopled with strangers as with people I knew. And I didn't have as much control over things. In fact, the person I am in these dreams does not seem preoccupied with the problems and personal angst that sometimes plague my waking self, or to share the same mundane priorities, values, or motivations my waking self has. The biggest change was that I no longer controlled my interactions with others in these dreams.

The next level of strangeness I encountered while dreaming involved a phenomenon of continued conversations. That is, I would have a dream of having a conversation with somebody whom I knew in the waking world. Then the next time when I would see that person in waking life, the conversation would continue. They would ask me something about the conversation, thinking that it had actually happened during our waking hours but would be unable to pin down exactly when or where. It seemed as if I was actually meeting with others during these vivid, 3-D dreams. Still, I wasn't convinced anything in particular was special about them until I experimented with joke-telling. During the dreams I would tell a stupid joke. The next time I saw the person face-to-face in the waking world, I would deliver the same joke. Every single time that person would either beat me to the punchline, get slightly confused about why I was re-telling a joke they'd heard me tell, or ask why I had told them the same stupid joke AGAIN. On occasion, I have had friends who remembered a dream we had shared call me, seemingly out of the blue, to continue a conversation that we'd had or to discuss the particulars of an experience that we had shared while dreaming.

I gradually became convinced that I was, somehow, meeting up with actual people during my dreams which meant that not all of the people I'd meet in dreams were Jungian facets of myself. I do not pretend to have full understanding of the mechanisms or metaphysics of these vivid, three-dimensional, shared-dream experiences. There is always room for doubt no matter how vivid one's personal experiences are. But it became clear to me that they can and do happen, and that when they do, I'm not meeting with facets of my personality; I'm meeting with other living people. Over the years and fairly frequently, I have dream conversations with complete strangers who turn out to be people I meet soon thereafter. They are surprised at how familiar I seem and how much I know about them. When this happens, I usually don't say anything because the idea of shared dreaming is frightening and creepy on one hand, and totally against the bounds of science and reason on the other. The event gets filed away in my mind for further investigation at a later time, and dismissed from theirs altogether.

In time, it got to the point where I wasn't just encountering people I knew or strangers I'd soon meet. I began to encounter those Divine Beings whom I had always assumed were simply archetypes. Given that the human beings I met during these dreams always turned out to be real, actual people, it felt safe to assume that the Beings I was meeting in 3-D were also actually real—even if I didn't quite know what They were, where They came from, or why in the world They were popping up in my dreams. My real introduction to the Goddesses and Gods came through my dream work, and not through ritual celebration or experimenting with archetypes and sacred masquerade. In fact, I didn't always recognize Them because They were very different than the archetypes I had built up in my imagination.

The first time it happened back in 2005, I was having a nice, normal, two-dimensional dream conversation with my archetypal Loki, learning all about the trickster aspects of my Self that needed to be expressed. All of a sudden, a very hot, very strong hand clamped onto my left shoulder. Then, a male voice whispered in my ear so close I could feel His breath, "That's a lovely paper doll you've got there. Where'd ya get it?" I had no idea who this was, and was feeling alarmed and freaked out because the dream had shifted quite jarringly from feeling two-dimensional to feeling three-dimensional all of a sudden. Who ever this might be was probably a real person, but His presence was so overpowering and knee-shake-inducing that I almost couldn't think. Finally, I quietly stammered, "I'm working with my archetypal trickster: Loki," to which the voice scoffingly responded, "He doesn't look a thing like me." At this point my archetype burst into flames, curled up, and blew away much the way paper does when it is set on fire. "You wanna talk" the voice said, "then face me, and let's chat." Then that hot, strong hand pivoted me around, and I came face to face with the God Loki. "By the way," He added, "your problem is not the puniness of your inner trickster." I was stunned and absolutely terrified. Confused, too, because He truly looked nothing at all like I had imagined. I was utterly overwhelmed and engulfed by His presence…Thus began one of the longest and closest relationships I have ever had with any Deity. Loki was the first God to show me the difference between Himself and the archetype of Him that exists. He showed me the way in a manner powerful enough to dispel even the most stubborn doubts.

The large, distant, monotheistic Goddess who I came to know through Paganism remained just as immense and unreachable in the three-dimensional dreams as She had ever been in all other contexts. I am convinced from my experiences that She exists. But I am certain that Her existence does not preclude the existence of, or eliminate the desirability of relationships with, the actual Gods and Goddesses who

I had wrongly assumed to be nothing more than archetypes. The example of the ballet swan that I used earlier is also useful to explain myself here. The experience of using the archetypal masque of the swan to explore your Self is one thing. The experience of witnessing that same archetype as animated by the Goddess which reveals aspects of the swan, and of divinity, and of beauty, is quite another. But regardless of the quality of the swan mask or the individual wielding it, one fact remains: swans are real creatures who exist totally independently of your imagination or unconscious, who have individual personalities and habits, and whose Divine natures are individual to each of Them. The existence of a swan costume and a dancer to wear it does not preclude the existence of an actual swan, or negate the relative value of coming to know about and interact with an actual swan; nor does it eliminate the existence of several other uniquely individual swans.

In my experience, the archetype of a God or a Goddess exists, and you can work with it on your own, and there also exists an immense and unfathomable Deity who may don archetypal masques to interact with you. However, the existence of the archetype and of that massive Divinity do not preclude the existence of actual Gods and Goddesses with whom one can interact. They all exist, and They all offer unique and different opportunities for growth and learning. I have found that building relationships with the Gods and Goddesses has brought a very different kind of spiritual growth from my work with archetypes or my work with the Great Goddess. Further, it is the relationships that I have built with individual Gods and Goddesses that have given me the personal, immediate, familiar connection that I always longed to have with the Goddess but could not find.

By the time that Loki reached me, I had been living in New Orleans for two years, and was preparing to relocate to Lafayette, LA for yet more grad school. Throughout the previous two years I had felt very pulled to the Loa and Orisha of New Orleans Voodoo. I dreamed fleetingly of Them, but had resisted exploring Them out of a desire to respect other cultures and, to a lesser extent, because I was afraid. I had read heavily about Haitian Vodou—Maya Deren, Milo Rigaud, Zora Neale Hurston—and had attended a few fetes around town. I resisted becoming a student of any of the mambos or houguns there because I just didn't feel like it was my place, as a Caucasian woman, to be appropriating the religion of another culture, especially one that seemed so alien to the principles of Wicca I had been working with. Yet, one veve in particular had drawn me like moth to a flame: it looked like the wrought-iron gate of a cemetery, complete with curlicues and hearts. I thought it was one of the most beautiful things

I'd ever seen….until I realized it belonged to the female cemetery guardian and death Loa, Maman Brigitte. Then, it just weirded me out. It seems that I was open to all mysteries save one: death and decay. I pulled away from the Loa altogether, and sought other things.

During that time, I had also been making a very thorough study of the Norse Deities and poetic Eddas, and felt drawn to Them as well. Upon meeting the Heathens of a local kindred, I decided that Heathenry was my calling. Loki was my first Norse Deity connection, but I knew that there were just some things about my practice—Loki, primarily—that I would need to keep to myself so as to avoid being ostracized by my new chosen community. After I embraced the Norse path, I began to dream of Tyr, one-handed God of justice, and Freya, Goddess of magic and sex (I ignored the death part of Her mystery.) They became the two Deities I worked most closely with. I learned a lot about myself from these two generous Deities.

My path continued this way until halfway through my doctorate program. Out of the blue, the Goddess Frigga boldly appeared in my three-dimensional dreams, and within a month, She had taken over totally as my matron. It was because of this relationship that I accepted the possibility that sometimes you choose your Gods, but sometimes They choose you. I still had love and respect for other Deities, but my relationship with Frigga became, for all intents and purposes, a henotheistic one. She is an intellectual Goddess with powerful spiritual gifts and tremendous political acumen. Accordingly, our relationship seemed to focus primarily on my intellectual and spiritual development which unfolded across a backdrop of academia's Machiavellian politics.

Complicating matters was the occasional dream I would have about colleagues who had passed away or the relatives of colleagues who had passed away. In the spring of 2007, a professor I really liked was killed in a horrible accident, and I dreamed of him a few times after that. I spent time living in the group residence where a friend had lived prior to being killed by a drunk driver. Periodically, I'd dream of her as well. One man's younger brother, who'd committed suicide, plagued me for months until I explained that I had no intention of jeopardizing my tenuous social position in the department by sharing his messages with his miserable and callow older brother. The same thing later happened with another colleague's Japanese grandmother who turned out to be far more difficult to rid myself of.

Frigga was quite disinterested in me developing any sort of relationship with the dead, so I just shoved these experiences into a mental basement and forgot about them. In fact, She was disinterested in my developing any sort of relationships that did not serve Her goals for me or my career aspirations, and She was pretty strict in demanding that I focus on those. According to most of the accounts I've read, people who work with Frigga report feeing a maternal, supportive presence. I can honestly say that this was the absolute last thing I experienced with Her. Despite the intensity and sincerity of my devotion, She always seemed "just out of reach." No matter how far I stretched, I couldn't really connect with Her, although when I would give up and dejectedly back off, She would give small, subtle hints that She was around. As a result, the relationship was very difficult for me and fraught with tension. Even as my spirit and mind expanded, my heart ached, and I was physically ill a lot of the time. I didn't understand then that sometimes you need to draw boundaries if you want to have a healthy, balanced life, or that sometimes you need to directly ask for what you need and not just expect someone to know what it is and then give it to you. My career and my Goddess were the most important things. All other concerns fell by the wayside.

Things continued that way through graduation. I had moved home to Tulsa to write my dissertation and began adjunct teaching at a small community college in my hometown. I planned to live and work there while performing my job search. Things were going well. Then, on the morning of January 3, one week before Spring term started, I was told that all three of my classes were cancelled. I sat in front of my Frigga altar, tears rolling down my face, and said, "Fine. If you want my career on ice, could you at least put me somewhere that doesn't suck?" Thirty minutes later, the phone rang. It was a community college in the Bronx, New York that needed a visiting professor for the spring term. I had no other options, so I flew up to New York for the interview. Luckily, I got the job. Make no mistake, I was certainly on ice—the winter of 2010-2011 was rife with ice and record snowfall. A month after I got to New York, I met R. at that party. Work on the book began in April of 2011, well after the winter snows had finally melted.

Not long after meeting R., I attended my first ancestor veneration ritual. One of the women facilitating the ritual was a medium who had been raised in Santeria. It was the most powerful religious ritual I have ever experienced. More powerful, even, than my experiences in Louisiana. It was beautiful, heartbreaking, thrilling, and yet very solemn as well. I felt a much stronger connection to the ancestors than I had ever felt with the Gods. Afterwards the Santera said that she had messages to relay from my ancestors. I listened skeptically, if attentively. According to her, my ancestors were very proud of me. But they were very worried about how unbalanced my life was. One ancestress in particular wanted me to stop blaming myself for the lack of warmth and connection with my Deity, because it had nothing to do with me, and everything to do with that Goddess' method of working with me. It was further explained that, while there was nothing wrong with the Goddess or myself, to keep throwing everything I had into my career and what my Goddess seemed to want wasn't going bring me what I needed to be whole, balanced, and functional in my life. It also wouldn't help my work with the ancestors and the land. Then it was revealed that my work with the ancestors and the land was actually my main source of spiritual sustenance in this life, and that my relationships with the Gods were good and important, but they weren't the only, or the main, thing that I needed to focus on. I really didn't know that to say. When the Santera finished, I thanked her, and took my leave of the group shortly thereafter, confused and doubtful. It would take three years and a pilgrimage to the Caribbean before I came to terms with this radically reconfigured spirituality of ancestors and land spirits as my primary spiritual focus, with the Deities playing a significant but secondary role.

That night, my dreaming went into overdrive. It's as if attending the ancestor ritual opened a door that had previously been sealed shut, and from that moment on, my ancestors became a powerful, loving force in my life. My relationship with the land was more distant and has been slower to develop. But then, what I have learned about the land is that it tends to be slow and quite cautious when humanity attempts to engage it. Since that ritual, I have yet to experience a flat, two-dimensional dream where my ancestors, or the dead in general, are concerned. First came my mother's aunt Poodge, who was the one who spoke up after the ritual. I didn't know much about Poodge, or any of my mother's father's family, except that they were Catholic. Poodge introduced me to her sister, my mother's aunt Hazel, who had a message for my mother. I was pretty shocked that this was being asked of me, and really didn't quite believe it was happening.

The next day, I hesitantly called mom. I chit-chatted, then I awkwardly hemmed and hawed. Finally, she asked me what was wrong. I didn't tell her about the ancestor ritual, but I told her about the dreams. I asked who Aunt Hazel was, which surprised Mom who had never really mentioned Hazel growing up. They had always been on such lousy terms, and Mom always felt like her aunt Hazel hated her. Mom had no idea until I relayed Aunt Hazel's message what the matter was. As it turns out, Aunt Hazel had once had a baby girl. Shortly after the baby was born, Aunt Hazel went into the hospital with pneumonia for several weeks. During that time, they wouldn't bring Aunt Hazel her daughter, allegedly because they didn't want her to get pneumonia. It wasn't until Aunt Hazel was released from the hospital that her husband admitted to her that the baby had died and been buried while Aunt Hazel was recovering. Aunt Hazel never got to see her baby again or attend the funeral. She didn't have another daughter. Mom confirmed all of these facts for me before I continued to relay the message. Aunt Hazel explained that the sight of my mother always made her angry and heartsick, because her younger brother Robert's firstborn turned out to be a girl—my mother. Not only that, but my mother looked exactly like Aunt Hazel. Aunt Hazel had always wanted another daughter, but it just didn't happen. To even look at my mom was like a knife in Aunt Hazel's heart, and she just didn't handle it very well. The biggest part of Aunt Hazel's message to my mom was an apology. By the end of the phone call, Mom was in tears, and I was halfway in shock.

The night after that phone call, and many other nights thereafter, Aunt Poodge would introduce me to different ancestors, and they would introduce me to other ancestors. I dreamed much less of the Deities and much more of my ancestors. Always the dreams were three-dimensional, but I was still very skeptical about the whole thing because it was simply too fantastic not to be partly my imagination. Then, totally unexpectedly, my mother called me one day to announce she had joined Ancestry.com on a lark. She had located some ancestors, and started naming them off to me…the names she gave were the same names of the people I had been dreaming about which lead me to believe that I really was meeting my ancestors in my sleep. That was only the first step, however. Soon I was being introduced to other ancestors who would be very, very difficult to track down through ancestory.com. These ancestors are Creole, Haitian, Bajan, African, and Irish—slaves who were sold into the Caribbean and whose descendants worked up through the Caribbean into Louisiana. Of course they have no birth certificates logged into that database. The only way to track them is to travel, research, and locate bills of sale or plantation inventory lists (which I hope to do someday.) Meeting these ancestors in my dreams was key for what happened next: formally meeting the Loa.

My original objection to working with the Loa was based partly on fear of the religion that honored Them, and mostly on fear of wrongfully appropriating something that was not mine to take. The African Diaspora Religion-based rituals I had attended acclimated me to ancestor veneration and the honoring of spirits which are integral to Vodou. Having talked to people who practice spirit possession, the idea of it no longer bothered me. Living in New York and having to fight tooth and nail to survive there helped me respect the harsh material climate that Vodou comes from, and made the significant ethical differences between Wicca and Vodou inconsequential to me. Discovering that my pale skin hid some very black roots, roots that were nurtured by ancestor veneration many generations ago, made me more willing to embrace the Loa I had been drawn to almost a decade earlier. I realized that I wasn't appropriating the religion of an exotic "other" culture, I was reaching into my family tree to find what would sustain me, heal me. After these changes to my internal landscape had taken place, I was finally introduced to Maman Brigitte.

During this time, I was living and cat-sitting in a squalid urban Queens apartment. I was busy gathering interviews for this book, and planning the courses I would teach in the fall. It started as a series of 3-D dreams I would have just prior to waking up. A foul-mouthed and funny, yet overwhelmingly maternal woman in tattered, black, Victorian dress with pale skin and vermillion hair was speaking to me. I could barely remember what She said; but the last thing She always said to me was the same: Maman Brigitte. I woke up with that name on my lips for weeks, but never thought to look it up. I'd actually forgotten my previous brushes with Her in New Orleans.

Things took a very interesting turn when a colleague came to visit for the weekend. This colleague is a priestess and henotheistic devotee of Arianrhaod. She also has decades of experience with mediumship and spirit possession as expressed in the Celtic tradition. As we chatted about my project over coffee that morning, my friend all-of-a-sudden exhorted me to "explore the Loa." Given her total lack of experience with that Vodou, I thought it was odd. I explained that many Vodousaints just don't really consider themselves to be polytheist, and that they didn't want to talk to ethnographers such as myself anyhow. Later, during our walk to the diner to get lunch, she again exhorted me to "explore the Loa." I asked why she had said that, and she replied that she didn't know but that it simply popped into her head and out of her mouth.

On the trip back, we were chatting more about my project when she said, somewhat irritatedly, "but you really should explore the Loa." My gaze shifted over to her but stopped cold at the strangest sight imaginable: a gigantic, 3.5-foot tall, black rooster with an enormous red comb standing in the yard next to us. It squawked, and I felt a thump on my head. The sunglasses I wore fell off, and crashed onto the sidewalk. When I picked them up, the right lens had been knocked out and crushed by the fall. I realized that I had been standing too far out of reach for my friend to have bonked me on the head and that there was nobody else around who could have done it. So there I stood, contemplating my slightly aching head, my newly one-lensed sunglasses, and the sight of an enormous rooster that happened to materialize out of nowhere in my urban Queens neighborhood, when I felt an overwhelming urge to have some spicy hot rum. Tabasco-spicy hot rum, to be exact. I said nothing of it, but my friend was certainly surprised when I ducked into a bodega for rum and Tabasco on the way home. She was even more surprised when we got home and I downed a rum and Tabasco cocktail like it was water. As we sat enjoying the air-conditioning, completely out of the blue, she turned to me once more said, "explore the Loa." I assented, and began Googling with abandon. Then she suggested I should add "black roosters" and "spicy peppered rum" to my search terms. The very first Loa on the results page was Maman Brigitte. I sat there, shocked, as the dreams of the past few weeks began to roll through my mind like a banner unfurling. Things certainly made more sense after that.

During the last major dream of the summer, Frigga lovingly and ceremoniously handed me off to Maman Brigitte, who assumed Her role as my matron. Though Vodou recognizes Bondye as the one and only supreme God, and shies away from referring to the Loa as Deities, I feel it is perfectly acceptable to recognize Maman as a Goddess within the context of my personal polytheist practice. Given how fulfilling ancestor veneration had been for me, it really doesn't surprise me that Maman stepped forth to become my primary Goddess. Our relationship feels much more natural, and there is much more emotional intimacy. In New Orleans Vodou, Maman rules death, justice, education, the banda dance, the cemetery, and ancestral connections. She has been very good about helping me balance my spiritual striving with my mundane, daily material life and my relationships with other people. Through my work with Her, I was re-introduced to vodousaint I'd met years before the first time I lived in New Orleans. L has faithfully served the spirits for 35 years, and has been an invaluable guide to an otherwise perplexing religious practice. In no way do I consider myself to have any expertise or authority in the knowledge and practice of New Orleans Vodou or any other African Diasporic religion. Nor do I wish to portray myself as a having been formally initiated or trained in them. Rather, I take what I'm given and use it as the raw materials from which to build my relationship with Maman, the Loa, the Deities, and especially my ancestors and the land.

It's worth mentioning that not long thereafter I had a successful interview with a nearby college that happened to have on its grounds the oldest cemetery in Queens. I was invited to build my writing curriculum around that cemetery, which I gladly did. It was the first time in the school's history such a thing had been done. Despite everything else that happened in New York, that job turned out to be the most stable, enjoyable, and important gig I had. My willingness to build a cemetery-themed writing course began with that introduction to Maman Brigitte.

I honor Frigga, and remain thankful for Her blessings, especially the gift of understanding and manipulating socio-political power dynamics, the will to use that knowledge to my advantage, and the discernment of proper timing for it. Yet I am very grateful to be working with a matron who is a more natural fit for me as a whole person. Maman is important in my life, but there are several others Divinities with whom I have built relationships through love, service and devotion: Ashera, the tree-Goddess consort of El and Queen of the Canaanite Pantheon; Yinepu, the Egyptian Jackal-headed psychopomp and God of death and embalming; Dylan ail Don, the Welsh lord of the abyss; Simbi, the Loa of magic and wisdom; and so many others. These, in addition to my ancestors of the flesh and of the spirit, and the land spirit of my family's hometown, have made my life richer and more meaningful than I could have imagined possible even five years ago. They were instrumental to my departing from New York and being able to finally write this book.

In the two years I lived in New York City, I did a lot of interviews, and made a lot of research notes at the Schwarzman branch of the New York Public Library. I taught at several schools in five boroughs. I occasionally had a social life, and did arty things. But like many adjuncts in my position, I was never able to find stable, long-term, safe housing or long-term continuous full-time employment anywhere. If it hadn't been for the devotional relationships I had built and the blessings of guidance, luck, outrageous opportunity, and protection I was given from my Divinities, I don't think I would have even survived the two years I lived there. By December of 2012, I was exhausted of constantly moving around the city and not making much headway on my book, so I decided to leave. Despite my ancestors' wishes that I return home to my family immediately, I relocated to Baton Rouge, Louisiana to do freelance work and be near a major research library to work on my book. Two months later, my mother called with devastating health news, and by mid-April I was back in my hometown with my parents, helping to take care of them. As it turned out, this allowed me a much more open schedule for freelancing and completing this project.

The evolution from atheist disbelief to polytheist practice was helped considerably by my dream experiences, but it could not have happened if I had not given myself permission to have religious experiences in the first place. I had to allow myself to experience spiritual reality without diluting, diminishing, and demeaning it through rote rationalism and habitual intellectual critique. When I look back on my time of disbelief, I realize that my attitude had more to do with fear than with integrity. I wanted control. The best way to control reality is to alter your perception of it, and then act according to your perceptions. My perception of reality was that nothing existed beyond the material, rational world, so I set about reasoning my way through it and dismissing anything that didn't add up. I wanted certainty. The best way to guarantee that certainty was to deny the existence of anything that could not be scientifically observed and objectively verified as existing in nature. Belief that nothing exists which cannot be scientifically verified left me with an assumption that all which is naturally occurring can be known and understood, given sufficient time and study. It may not happen in my lifetime, but I could be certain that eventually it would because all things in the natural world are ultimately knowable and understandable. Improving my rational and intellectual capacities gave me a sense of control that was useful when I began exploring archetypes. I expected that I would find many powerful images within my mind, but I knew that I would never encounter something I could not control. I knew that everything I encountered was simply a manifestation created by the mind, and a disciplined mind could conquer anything that was set before it. Even the oldest archetypes I might find while fathoming the collective unconscious were simply powerful mental projections that had built up over time, and none of them could truly affect me unless I allowed such a thing to happen. Looking back, I realize that I was doing all of this because, underneath it all, I was certain that spirituality and religion were rife with foolishness. While I was interested in expanding my mental horizons through the psychological accoutrements or archetypes which were religious or mythic in origin, I wasn't about to be taken in by the foolishness that I believed was inherent to religious experience.

My convictions and assumptions served primarily to bolster my ego, to give me a sense that I was constantly improving, constantly evolving, and constantly developing greater control of my reality. Naturally, this egotism carried over into my spiritual exploration. Yet when I developed a powerful longing for spiritual connection, my campaign of Self-improvement hit a brick wall. In order to progress, I had to be willing to sacrifice my Self in order to connect with the Other that might possibly exist beyond that wall. I had to divest myself of many rationalist assumptions: the conviction that the source of all spiritual knowledge is the collective unconscious; the conviction that the human mind alone accounts for all spiritual phenomena; the certainty that given enough study, all things are knowable and should be treated as such; the assumption that the Gods and Goddesses are merely archetypes and are best approached as tools for inspiration and self-exploration; the assumption that any spiritual beings which might exist should be regarded as supernatural, superfluous entities rather than as intrinsic to and inherent in the planet's natural energetic ecosystem; the certainty that religious experience is an uncanny, undesirable side-effect of mental distress rather than a natural, positive manifestation of mental well-being; and the belief that a deep exploration of Self would bring me such empowerment and understanding that I could deeply and meaningfully connect to others and the world around me. All of these certainties that I had carefully engineered and grasped onto for dear life had to be released before I could have the sense of connection that I had so deeply craved.

Jumping off of that safe, carefully cultivated, rationalist foundation was terrifying. After that jump I learned, paradoxically, that the benefits of religious experience aren't related to any sort of prima facie belief, but rather to the willing suspension of disbelief, which is what allowed me to experience my Holy Powers. It wasn't until I jettisoned the requirements of belief altogether that I could viscerally connect with the raw, immediate, mystical experience religious practice can provide. In this way, the experience could enter on its own terms and forge its own connections in my psyche and soul, thus opening me up to the Deities, ancestors, and land spirits. Then, when those relationships started to evolve through ritual veneration that was reciprocated through my dreaming, belief became relatively unimportant. Experience negated the need for mere belief. All that really matters to me now is that my religious practice leaves me stable, connected, healthy, and whole.

If there was anything that I wish people understood about polytheism, it would be this: unless you are a practicing polytheist, whatever you think you know about polytheism is probably off the mark. However compassionate, tolerant, and respectful you may actually be, the monotheist perspective of the culture we live in has ensured that your knowledge about polytheism is in all likelihood tainted with bigotry, self-aggrandizement, misunderstanding, and lack of information. People who reify the Gods and Goddesses build devotional relationships with Them, and who endeavor to connect with Them, the land, and the ancestors are not mentally deficient, naïve, or foolish. Before you judge us according to your own religious or philosophical assumptions, pause for a moment. Allow yourself to countenance the myriad possibilities of a very different sort of spiritual engagement with the world. Suspend your carefully-honed disbelief just long enough to appreciate the mysterious differences between your own views and those of the polytheists you are judging. Understand that regardless of what religious view one holds—including polytheism—it is only a materially unsubstantiated opinion. The only fact we can all substantiate is that every single one of us is living together on this planet, and how we treat each other and our world today is the legacy of what we will leave our descendants tomorrow. Our beliefs are largely irrelevant because it is our behaviors, our habits, and our actions that impact our world. For polytheists, action is the foundation of connection with our Divinities, our ancestors, and the land we live on. If you open yourself to appreciating this perspective, you might just learn something wonderful.

Acknowledgements

This book would not have been possible without tremendous amounts of love, support, and inspiration. I would like to thank the following people:

Caer Jones: You are a brilliant theorist, a devoted priestess, a gifted healer, and a fierce protector. Without your hospitality to the Gods and to me, this book would not have been possible.

Ayn and Joe O'Leary: This project wouldn't have gotten off the ground if you had not so generously opened your home for me to work in. From the bottom of my heart, I thank you.

Geoff and Sonya Elliott: Of all the blessings I could have received living in New York, your love, friendship, support, respect, understanding, and super-comfy couch were the most crucial. You both work hard to live the teachings of Jesus. Your faith, and love, and respect are proof that religions of Jehovah and Jesus do not have to harden into the hatred, intolerance, and fear demonstrated by some. You also remind me of the good things that Christianity gave me when I was young, and that those good things are important to everyone, regardless of their particular religion.

Cordelia Nailong Smith: Your social conscience, academic awareness, and love of humanity inspired my efforts to strive for an ethnography that is inclusive, collaborative, and reciprocal. This work is immeasurably richer for your generous insight. Thank you.

Maureen Shockey: When I got too wrapped up in the Gods, you reminded me there are other important things in life; things like dark humor, good music, Hammer films, Radium-Age fiction, and candied ginger.

Eileen Murphy: Your ability to juggle your love of the Holy Powers and your spiritual commitments to the Gods, all while living a normal life, continues to inspire me.

Kelley Dickey: My Christo-Pagan friend, if you hadn't helped me sort through the themes of this project during the height of the "definition of polytheism" flame war in the blogosphere, I would have remained too heartbroken to finish this project.

Raven Kaldera: Thank you for inspiring this project and your generous example of showing us all how this independent publishing gig is done.

Diana J. Jones Wilkerson, Robert Larry Wilkerson: Mom & Dad, without your love and personal sacrifice I wouldn't be here today. I love you.

Grandma Jones, Grandpa Jones, Aunt Poodge, Uncle Gerald: you have never failed me, ever. Thank you for being my awesome go-to ancestors.

Jon Safran: Your "Jon Safran vs. God" miniseries was an inspiration to get through those difficult patches when it felt like this project would never come to fruition.

Jordan D. Paper and Vine Deloria, Jr.: My discovery of your groundbreaking works, <u>The Deities Are Many</u> and <u>God is Red</u> was a very important one to me, both personally and intellectually. They are passionate, circumspect, unflinching, and unapologetic arguments in favor of polytheistic worldviews offered to a jaded, conservative, and overwhelmingly monotheist theological establishment. You were both brave to write such works. Thank you.

Neil Gaiman: I imagine that you and I could not be coming at this subject from more different sets of convictions. You are an artist and a master storyteller. But as any folklorist like myself knows, stories are sacred things. Narrative truth has a power to move us which is far greater than the authority of mechanical facts. Your willingness to characterize the Gods so much more fully and intricately than your Victorian predecessors' romanticizing of the extant mythology had done helped pry open my own perceptions of Them. Thank you.

To the hard-working and deeply committed Open Source community: Thank You for your ingenuity, talent, and idealism. If not for GIMP, Inkscape, WordPress, Scribus, Calibre, Sigil, and LibreOffice, I'd still have a cache of interviews awaiting transcription, processing, typesetting and e-formatting. This project would never have happened and I am very grateful to have found this amazing software to work with.

www.ingramcontent.com/pod-product-compliance
Lightning Source LLC
Chambersburg PA
CBHW021213090426
42740CB00006B/199